Mommie
Dearest

Mommie Dearest

Christina Crawford

OPEN ROAD

INTEGRATED MEDIA

NEW YORK

This work is a memoir. It reflects the author's present recollections of her experiences over a period of years. Some names and identifying characteristics have been changed in order to protect the identity of certain individuals. Any resulting resemblance to persons living or dead is entirely coincidental and unintentional.

Cover design by Mauricio Díaz

ISBN: 978-1-5040-5771-4

This edition published in 2018 by Open Road Integrated Media, Inc.
180 Maiden Lane
New York, NY 10038
www.openroadmedia.com

CELEBRATING FORTY

November 2018 marks the fortieth anniversary of *Mommie Dearest*'s original publication. It was 1978 when *Mommie Dearest* was launched into the public arena, appearing almost instantly on the *New York Times* bestseller list, where it stayed for nearly one year. No one anticipated the firestorm that ensued. There was no internet, no personal computers, no cell phones, no social media. This was the first time anyone had raised the issue of child abuse and family violence to the level of widespread public discourse. We did not previously even have a language for it. And, furthermore, if it was recognized, it was a social service concern only relegated to the poor and disadvantaged. All of a sudden, here was a white family of privilege: children suffering abuse at the hands of a woman! Many could not accept that reality. They preferred to revere the public person they thought they knew and disregard the private one, just now revealed. It was difficult for all of us. As a country, as a society, we were a long way from understanding the psychology of abuse and addiction, or how sociopaths and narcissists can rise to power and harm others in the process.

And then there was SHAME. The myth was that "parents always want the best for their children." That may be true—hopefully for the majority—but when it comes to family violence and abuse, it is not. It is devastating for a child to see or feel that their parent does not love them! Why not? What has gone wrong? Is there something more the child could have done?

When *Mommie Dearest* was first published, statistics showed one million children abused. People were shocked.

Today, statistics show that there are seven million abused; although the increase is largely due to severe neglect, not physical violence, as in the past. The opium epidemic, changing labor market, and economic inequality may all be factors, but never excuses. Each person is accountable for their behavior. So when love is not love, when family is not family, when home is not safe . . . long-term consequences are sure to follow.

Finding the perpetrator guilty when the criminal acts involve women and children continues to be an ongoing issue. We have made progress because of the courageous women and men who demand justice, fairness, and protection for children and those in harms way. But that progress is far from complete.

Over these many, many years you have shared your personal stories, and I learned to marvel at your fortitude and how you overcame your past. Demands from all of you are the reason that laws change, that people get help, that neither the rich and powerful nor the inhumane and cruel control our communities. And, I have been saddened to learn of the tragedies that happened.

Next year I will celebrate turning eighty years old. My life has been an amazing journey! What I know is that there is more to be accomplished and it will be up to all of you to see it through. My gratitude to Open Road Media for making the ebook editions of *Mommie Dearest, Survivor*, and *Daughters of the Inquisition* available to new worldwide audiences.

With blessings on your journey,
Christina
2018

PREFACE

How amazing! When *Mommie Dearest* was first published in 1978, there was no such thing as ebooks, no internet sales, and no social media. What a privilege it is now to release this ebook edition, complete with photos from my personal collection and one hundred pages from the original manuscript that were never published until the 20th Anniversary edition in 1998.

Over all these years you have shared your personal stories with me and I have heard you. Thank you for trusting me to be your witness in a way that perhaps your own community could not. What you have taught me is profound.

So, to all of you who have suffered in silence, who have lived in despair of justice, who have turned to drugs and alcohol as pain relief, who have allowed anger to rule life, and whose stories may never be told except as cold statistics, this edition is dedicated to you.

Family violence is generational, learned behavior. And while new laws and better interventions can certainly help—and have done so—only the informed will of individuals can actually change behavior. That is the primary reason I have kept *Mommie Dearest* in constant publication over nearly forty years. It's important to me that the original autobiography is available to anyone who wishes to read it for themselves.

I believe that life is a journey, that life is about personal accountability—at some point there can be no more excuses and no more lies.

Therefore, I still have hope and deep gratitude for the journey itself.

Christina Crawford
North Idaho, USA, 2017

Mommie Dearest

Part One

CHAPTER 1

Dead. New York City, May 10, 1977, at 10 a.m. Eastern Daylight time. Official cause of death: coronary arrest.

As the wire services sped the news around the world we heard a brief obit on the radio all-news station on our way to the airport.

The only time so far that I had cried was when an old fan had called to tell me about the TV news station coming to film his collection of her clothes and photographs in his living room and to ask if he could have her dog . . . if no one else had asked for it. Would I bring the dog back with me? She's barely cold and someone wants the *dog*! It was the same story all over again—the old clothes and the anklestrap shoes and the 8×10 autographed glossies and the goddamned dog. The rage made me shake and tears spilled down my face . . . yet somehow my voice sounded ever polite. I hung up the phone.

Superstar is dead. Now the closet door will open and every weirdo in America will be on parade waving their faithful notes signed "God Bless . . . Joan." I cried. But it wasn't sorrow, it was anger . . . a flash of the old rage like one of those violent thunder and lightning storms that sweep across the eastern sky and are gone.

The rest was just phone calls and plane reservations.

I had a terrible headache and felt sort of shaky inside, but there were no tears. David held my hand and I felt his strength slowly calm me. Somehow if I could just hold onto his hand, I could make it through this.

Mercifully there was no food on this flight because I felt like I couldn't swallow anything. I tried to sleep and fell into a kind of suspended dream . . . I could hear everything but my eyes were closed. I was cold and uncomfortable and I'd already been in the same clothes for fifteen hours.

It was dawn when we landed in New York. Outside the baggage claim area a dark-haired man with a slight accent asked if we wanted a taxi. I said yes and he took our bags. There were no yellow cabs in sight. David and I followed him to a black limousine parked at the curb. I looked at David and smiled . . . well, why not? Twenty bucks was fair enough and it would be a nice change for us. An English woman going to the Village sat in front chatting away about how glad she was to be home again and how she loathed Los Angeles. As we drove through Queens, the dirty old buildings, the knee-deep potholes, the elevated subway trains rattling overhead and the people pushing their way through another day made me feel deeply relieved we didn't live in the city.

My brother Chris arrived at the hotel about 10:30. He looked older and much thinner. Hard times and troubles were so clearly evident that he may as well have been carrying a sign. We held each other in greeting and consolation and a kind of understanding that went back thirty years deep into childhood. "I'm really glad you're here, Chris" is all I said. It was very tough for him. Chris hadn't been included in any family event since he was fifteen years old. The four of us kids had always been in touch, but privately. Mother had rarely mentioned his name for the last nineteen years. Now that she was dead we were all together again. He'd gotten a 6 o'clock train in from Long Island. Actually, he only lived about a hundred miles from the city but it was like another world out there. His town . . . he belonged there . . . he knew almost everyone . . . married and owned a house . . . did his job . . . had been a volunteer fireman for a couple of years . . . found a place for himself after coming home from Viet Nam. I really love Chris.

We drank black coffee out of slightly soggy paper cups from the delicatessen around the corner and Chris took another Excedrin. David had changed into his blue Cardin suit and my heart overflowed with pride. What a terrific man, this husband of mine. I'm the luckiest woman in the whole world.

At noon the three of us took a taxi to the Drake Hotel. There, we were to meet the lawyer, the secretary and one sister with her husband.

The greetings were strained. Everyone was being polite and there was a lot going on underneath all that niceness. Words seemed hollow and as I looked from face to face . . . I sensed there was something strange. Chris sat across the room from the secretary. At one time years ago they had been arch enemies. She had gotten Chris in a lot of unnecessary trouble in her own struggle for a permanent place in the household. Chris had been a good target and she hadn't missed many opportunities. Chris smoked his cigarettes and watched. My sister's husband talked . . . and talked . . . Joan this and Joan that . . . I looked at David and then at Chris. My sister and the secretary had very defined ideas about what Mother's wishes were, or rather, would have been for funeral arrangements. Nothing had been written down before her death except that she wanted to be cremated. It was odd that someone so fanatically organized should leave all the details to anyone else, let alone to group decision . . . particularly considering the people in this group. But nevertheless . . . that was it . . . somehow we had to decide and soon . . . like right away. The lawyer mediated, which was all he could do anyway. And there we were . . . a disparate group to say the least . . . deciding how to arrange the formality of burying Mother when never in any of our other experiences with her had we decided anything in relation to her except how we would each live our own lives. As the hours dragged on it became painfully clear what some of those life decisions had been. A student of group dynamics would have had a field day with the shifting interaction, the assumptions of right and power.

Then, during one of the many phone calls to Campbell's, the lawyer got a really strange expression on his face as he listened to the voice on the other end. It was the only emotional expression I saw on his face during the entire time . . . it was surprise.

"Your mother has been embalmed. You may see her if you want to." He said it straight and without emphasis. It wasn't ordered because she was to be cremated. It wasn't exactly authorized either, whatever that means. I guess it means that it was just done. Maybe because of the time involved. She died on Tuesday, we didn't all arrive until Wednesday and she couldn't be cremated until Thursday because I guess everyone had to agree to the cremation. Well, whatever the reason . . . there she was . . . embalmed at Campbell's. Weird. In fact all of this was beginning to take on a spacey, weird feeling. I had to keep contact with David to hold onto my sense of reality . . . it was fading in and out. We were like a sequestered jury . . . decisions had to be made and no matter how much anyone would have liked to take over, some kind of ritualistic primitivism prevented autocratic rule. Nothing in anyone's relationship with Mother prepared them for making decisions for her . . . so they had to be made for us, by us. The secretary and my sister seemed to feel that they had an inside track to Mother's thinking. Chris, I think, had vowed to keep his mouth shut as long as possible. David had never met Mother and was being very diplomatic and rather quiet. My sister's husband jabbered on and on about their close relationship with Joan. I felt my anger again. I was the oldest and had assumed that some courtesy would be given to me, but not much was. The lawyer seemed to look to my younger sister and then to the secretary. It galled me but I put in my two cents worth whether I agreed or disagreed and somehow it worked out. Then it was off to Campbell's. My sister was to sign the papers and pick out the urn.

David and I went with the lawyer, my sister and her husband. The secretary and Chris stayed at the Drake. My other sister hadn't arrived from Iowa yet. Her plane must have been late. She'd taken the news very hard and we were all worried about her. Chris would bring her to Campbell's and the secretary didn't want to go.

The funeral home on 81st street was as you'd imagine it to be. It all seemed more like a movie every minute. The men were dressed exactly right and looked and sounded like undertakers. It was quiet and people spoke softly. I was beginning to feel very tired and a little sick to my stomach. I held onto David's hand whenever I could. He was my life and my reality. Cathy signed the papers and then she and I chose the simple brass urn without any grapes or goddesses. There would be no inscription on it.

When we returned to the room downstairs, Cindy and Chris had arrived. The little blue room with its love seats and simple chairs was full. The moment had come.

The man from Campbell's asked who would like to see Mother. For the first time a complete silence surrounded all of us. It was almost like no one could breathe. We looked at one another. What thoughts must have been careening around in each brain. Cathy said no. Cindy shook her head no. Chris swallowed hard and looked quite pale. He said no. The man from Campbell's looked directly at me, expressionless. Almost inaudibly I said, "I'd like to see her." He opened the door and led me to a small elevator. We entered and the door closed very softly. There was not much room in the elevator so we stood not more than two feet apart. He started telling me how beautiful she looked, and his own face was quite radiant as he described how hard he'd worked from some of his favorite photographs of her. I was completely caught up in his story . . . I got in a flash that, for a moment, he'd thought that no one would see what he'd done . . . that no one would appreciate it. He seemed almost grateful and his eyes sparkled. I stared at him in genuine fascination. I had never known anyone who did this. It seemed like a very long time that he and I were bound together in this special exchange. The lie was here, too, even in death. I was to be the final audience.

The little elevator stopped on the second floor.

He led the way again, down a short hallway past the room with the satin-lined coffins where Cathy and I had chosen the urn. At the end of the hall there was a large room, the door was open but the lights were off. He stepped aside to let me by and I walked slowly because I wasn't sure where we were going. The lights went on and startled me. I looked straight ahead of me and got a terrible fright. There she was . . . dead not ten feet away, laying on a table.

"May I be alone, please . . ." I whispered. My knees felt weak and my hands were shaking. I heard the man walk down the hallway. I stood there, alone, a lump filled my throat and tears covered my eyes. I looked and looked and looked. That's my mother and she's really dead. Some-how I had to know that. Somehow I had to take this terrifying alone time to make that real . . . to know for myself that death was real even if a lot of life hadn't been. To make sure that I gave myself this time alone with her at the very end so that I could go on. It was very fragile . . . I felt very scared. I mean really scared . . . scared beyond anything I'd ever known before. I didn't know what to do. I was still standing at the door-way to the room. I hadn't moved. There was no one here with me . . . this was my time. I didn't have to worry about keeping anyone waiting . . . or what anyone thought. It was just the two of us. Mother and me alone for the very last time. An incredible wave of sadness washed over me . . . my mouth was trembling and my eyes filled with tears that hadn't yet fallen free. I swallowed a couple times and heard myself say "Mommie . . . oh Mommie . . . I loved you so much . . ." . . . the tears inched down my face and I wiped a few away.

I walked up to the table and stood next to her. Her eyes were closed and they had done a good job with the makeup. It looked quite natural, surprisingly so. Her hair was short and brushed back from her face. It was gray. Her hands were resting on the cream-colored satin comforter which covered her and she had been dressed in a pale salmon-colored silk kimono wrap. Her nails were polished and she had lipstick on. As I looked carefully at her almost inch by inch, I noticed how terribly thin she was . . . in truth, she had wasted away to nothing, to skin and bones. It dawned on me in that moment that coronary arrest was not the whole story, not the whole story at all. It takes a long time to become that thin. There was hardly anything left to her at all. But her face was indeed her face and I looked at her a long time. I had never seen a dead person before. At any moment I expected her to open her eyes and say "Tina."

I reached out and touched her hand. It was cold. Mother had very strong hands and prided herself on a straight-forward handshake. Her hands were also very thin, her wrists little more than bones.

I don't know how long I'd been standing there thinking about her . . . about me . . . about the two of us locked into our turbulent relationship all these years. I was the first child . . . her precious, beautiful princess of a daughter, the golden child she wanted so much. Maybe it was only right that I alone should have had the courage to be the last . . . to be with her for a while in death.

"I know you're not really here with me anymore, Mother . . . I know your soul is gone already . . . I just want to tell you that I love you . . . that I forgive you . . . you know I forgave you long ago. We had so much pain together, you and I . . . but now Mother . . . God has set us both free. God has set you free to begin another journey. I pray the next one has less anguish. God has set us free, Mommie dearest. Go in peace." I could hear the sobs now, they were mine.

It was time for me to go. I leaned over and kissed her forehead gently. "Goodbye Mother . . . goodbye . . . and, I love you."

I wiped my face with the back of my hand and put on my dark glasses. Then I turned and left her.

As we walked down the stairs, I managed to tell the man from Campbell's that she looked beautiful. He had done a good job.

CHAPTER 2

Hollywood in the 1920s was almost like a lawless town of western folklore. The town of Hollywood had been developed by men like C. E. Toberman and Sid Grauman who decided how the streets should run and where the railroad would go through. They were the visionaries and knew that where orange trees, avocado groves and dusty unpaved country lanes ambled peacefully through the sprawling village there would one day soon sparkle, the jewel of the West, the luminary star in the fantasy of millions, the mecca of a new breed of hustler and dreamer: Hollywood. They helped decide where the studios should be built because they controlled a lot of land with the banking and insurance knowledge to back it up. Sid Grauman who built Hollywood's palace and architectural temple, Grauman's Chinese Theater on Hollywood Boulevard, was the entrepreneur, and C. E. Toberman was the man with the knowledge of finance and insurance. Together with men like Mullholland and Doheny they carved out the details of a large part of Los Angeles.

In those days the big silent screen stars built fantastic estates up in the hills that were usually copies of European castles or English manor houses. Mediterranean influence was very strong and artisans were imported to create hand-painted ceilings, intricate tile mosaics and hand-carved cornices, doors, banisters and all the other lavish decorations that adorned these modern-day royal abodes. There was no income tax then and the movies were beginning to pay their major stars fantastic sums. Mary Pickford and Charlie Chaplin both are reported to have earned in excess of a million dollars a year . . . tax free. Lesser luminaries, while not overnight millionaires, certainly had no thoughts of poverty and most spent their newfound and seemingly never-ending supply of wealth on gratifying whatever whim occurred. Since they were tied to Hollywood studios and often worked a six-day week turning out full-length features in a matter of weeks, their spending was attuned to local self-indulgence: palatial mansions, expensive cars, lavish parties and jewelry. Servants were no problem and most were imported from Europe where they had already been properly trained. In the midst of all this money and fame, most of the people had recently come from small towns and hard times. They really had no idea how to be the grand ladies and gentlemen of their own dreams so they copied what they read about the powerful Eastern families and European royalty. However, in order to do that and carry it off with any semblance of reality, someone in the local palaces had to know which fork went where and when to serve what wine. The simplest solution turned out to simply import the servants to run the houses as they had earlier imported the artisans to build them. And for the next thirty years the English butlers and nannies, the Scandinavian, German, French and Italian cooks, maids and chauffeurs, the Japanese gardeners and the Filipino houseboys streamed into Los Angeles.

Men like C. E. Toberman had realized nearly ten years earlier that the sleepy city of Los Angeles had to start moving west toward the ocean. There was as yet no real thought to developing the San Fernando Valley but by 1913, the water vital to expanding Los Angeles Basin was already being planned and the aqueduct which would snake its way hundreds of miles from Mono County to the north was underway. The movie industry which began in Brooklyn and Long Island was moving to Southern California with the alluring promise of cheap land, outdoor locations within easy reach and nearly 350 days a year of sunshine. The balmy climate and the cheap land advertised extensively throughout the East had been bringing people to the West for some time. They were a curious lot, these modern-day settlers. I think it was Frank Lloyd Wright who said that if you tipped a map of the United States, everything that wasn't nailed down would end up in Los Angeles. And that was just about it. Land swindlers and religious fanatics, health food advocates and aspiring actors all found a home in L.A.

However, no matter how much money they made, actors and Jews were rarely if ever allowed into the most fashionable residential district of the time. The old Wilshire district of Hancock Park frowned on these nouveau riche movie people and found ways to exclude them from their clubs and golf courses. It was quite natural then, that these latter-day gods and goddesses of the silent silver screen found their way into the vacant hillsides of Hollywood and a few years later moved even further west to build what is now Beverly Hills as a separate city of their very own.

For every Hollywood star I think it is safe to say that there were at least a thousand hopefuls of all ages living in the rooming houses, hotels and cottages that lined Franklin Avenue, Melrose and Santa Monica Boulevard. There were thousands more working in various studio office and crew jobs that formed the vast support systems needed to produce movies at the fantastic rate they were being turned out to meet the ever increasing box office demand.

From small towns all over America, the young hopefuls who had won a dance contest, a beauty pageant, anything even vaguely resembling show business, flocked to Hollywood. When they arrived they found themselves in fierce competition with the dancers from the Broadway chorus lines and the comics of vaudeville. Yet still they came with a suitcase full of dreams and a couple of dollars in their pocket.

Hollywood was a very small town in those days and if you could figure out how to get there you could figure out how to meet people and find a place to stay without too much trouble. That wasn't the problem. The problem was how to get into the movies.

It was customary to line up in front of the casting offices of the studios for two reasons. If there was a picture casting for bit parts and extras there was the possibility of work. But even if there wasn't any work, it was one of the best ways to find out what was going on at the other studios. Mother told me that actors got paid five dollars a day which included their wardrobe, unless it was a costume picture, and there was no such thing as an eight-hour day. In other words, there was no overtime and there were no unions. In fact, the Screen Actors Guild wasn't created until 1934, and when it was, Mother was among the first 200 charter members. But by that time she was a big star. She also told me that it was common practice for the actors who did get work to kick back two or three dollars out of the five they were paid to the person who hired you. If an actor or actress didn't kick back, they didn't work that studio the next time there was a picture casting. It was damn hard to support dreams on two or three dollars a day when you were really lucky to get a couple days work a month.

In between lining up at studio casting offices where the chances were one in a hundred of getting a job, everyone who wanted to get into movies and be a star worked diligently at the next most important part of creating a career . . . "being seen." Being seen meant getting invited to parties and then getting invited to the right parties. Being seen meant getting your name into the gossip columns which meant going somewhere with someone better known than yourself no matter who they were or what you thought of them. Being seen meant making sure that the way you looked attracted attention . . . any kind of attention . . . so that in addition to the beautiful people there was always an ample contingent of the outlandish and the freaky. Being seen meant spending hours dreaming up schemes of noticeable behavior patterns and idiosyncrasies of every conceivable kind. Entrances and exits were elaborately planned one-act plays all designed to "be seen" . . . to ensure heads turned and people inquired as to the identity of the player. If you didn't start out with any readily identifiable neurotic behavior you simply created some. If you couldn't afford glamour you became outrageous . . . anything to be noticed. This was a separate world altogether with it's own set of values that had nothing to do with the rest of the world. Here as nowhere else, make-believe was real and everybody wanted in. It didn't matter for an instant how you got where you were going because the studio publicity departments would make up their own stories for the public once you got there. Everyone was after the same thing . . . stardom . . . and they would claw and fight or fuck anything that walked to get there one step ahead of you. There was no protection from the kickbacks and the casting couches and no one felt bad if you didn't make it. If you failed that was just one less body in competition for the attention and the jobs. Fairness and morality were irrelevant and had been left behind in all the little towns across America.

The absolute mark of social acceptance could only be bestowed by one Hollywood invitation. Among the many luminaries that sparkled brilliantly none were more awesome than the unofficial royal family of Hollywood, the self-appointed king and queen of Tinseltown, Douglas Fairbanks and Mary Pickford. An invitation to Pickfair was universally acknowledged as the only legitimate indication that one had attained recognition in Hollywood.

Try as she might, the jazz baby ingenue with the big eyes, frizzy hair and the movie magazine contest name could not break the social barriers of Pickfair.

Lucille LeSueur arrived in Hollywood in January 1925 as one of the lucky newcomers. She already had a signed MGM contract. At the studio during the day she did the usual stand-in and bit parts while at night she danced in exhibitions and contests.

She became Joan Crawford a year later through a movie magazine "name the star" contest sponsored by MGM. Between 1925 and 1928 she appeared in twenty films, averaging four to five a year. But it wasn't until "Our Dancing Daughters" released in 1928 that she finally got close to stardom.

After an incredibly short four years, with twenty pictures to her credit and stardom virtually assured, there was still no hint of that invitation from Pickfair. However, Joan Crawford was not one to give up easily. In 1929 she married the prince of Pickfair, Douglas Fairbanks, Jr. The columnists acknowledged the union with mixed reviews. True, it seemed to be a love match but it was no secret in Hollywood that Joan Crawford never ceased trying to better herself. But Hollywood's royal family was evidently less than ecstatic about the entire affair and ironically for the new Mrs. Fairbanks there was still no invitation to Pickfair! For a while neither the prince nor his showgirl were particularly welcome. It was only at Douglas's firm insistence that nearly a year later, she was finally invited to lunch.

Years later Mother said that she didn't think they ever really liked her. They never made her feel comfortable or particularly welcome. But, regardless of in-law problems, her career continued to climb. During the next four years she made over a dozen more films. She acquired polish and glamour and Douglas helped her acquire some good manners and good taste.

The remake of *Rain*, released in 1932, was a dismal failure. The critics and the public responded with mixed feelings to this extreme departure in Joan Crawford's public image. Simultaneously the newspaper columns and movie magazines reported that the Fairbanks' marriage was saddened by miscarriage.

It may well have been that the young star in her late twenties had a miscarriage. But it is equally true that her mother-in-law, "America's Sweetheart" of less than a decade before, was horrified at the prospect of being called *grandmother*. In those days it was barely acknowledged by the major studios publicity departments that their stars were married, never mind having babies! If it was unglamorous to have a baby it was unthinkable to be called a grandmother. It simply wasn't done, it had never been done and it probably shouldn't start now. This was hardly the era of dowager queens.

Abortion or miscarriage, the results were the same. There were neither children nor grandchildren from this marriage and it ended in the spring of 1933.

Because Joan Crawford had become a full-fledged star by now, the number of pictures she did each year began to decrease to two or three. After her marriage to Fairbanks failed she devoted herself to her career and her love affair with Clark Gable. In Gable she found her match. He was a man big enough, charming enough and strong enough to deal with her spirit, her drive and her ambition. But he was also a married man and any permanent liaison was impossible.

It was during this time that she considered adopting her niece and namesake, Joan. Her brother Hal had divorced his wife of only a few years leaving her with a baby girl. Although the incident received a good deal of publicity, the adoption never went through.

Then in October of 1935 she remarried. This time it was to Franchot Tone.

Franchot was the epitome of the cultured, well-educated gentlemen. His family tree went all the way back to the American Revolution and he had ancestors who were master silversmiths rivaling Paul Revere. He was from the Eastern Establishment and had made substantial achievements on Broadway and through membership in the famous Group Theater. Not only did he have breeding, impeccable taste and a respected family, he was also an intellectual and an "actor's actor." They made several films together before and after they were married, but he never became a real Hollywood star.

Mother was fascinated by his stories of the Group Theater and the acting lessons patterned after the great Russians Boleslavski and Stanislavsky. Having never taken formal lessons in anything but singing and dancing, she badgered him to teach her what he'd learned. She told one hilarious story about the first time he agreed to give her one of the exercises. It had to do with something he called "sense memory" and it was intended to make the actor aware of possibilities beyond the obvious. It was to get you away from thinking just about the dialogue and the character and into the deeper meaning of relationships and motivation. In short, the exercises were designed to develop potential and untapped areas of emotion and physical sensations. She sat on the floor near him, enthralled by the way he explained what "real" actors went through to perfect their craft and what attention they paid to inner life and motivation. She waited with rapt attention while he gave her a short course on method acting, something she'd heard about but never known anyone to ask how it worked. Her big eyes followed his every move and noted each gesture. Finally, the lecture was over and he was ready to give her the very first exercise. The big moment had come. She hardly dared to breathe. As she listened attentively to the instructions, her heart sank.

Franchot had obviously decided to start at the very beginning. Since he was not normally given to practical jokes, that could be the only explanation for what was to follow. As the details unraveled it became clear that what Franchot had in mind for her was to be a carrot! She was to stand like a carrot, think like a carrot and feel like a carrot. For some several minutes she stared at him during the conclusion of his description. Then there was total silence while the full impact of what was expected of her crept through her consciousness. It was not what she had anticipated. However, this was the famous "method" of which she had heard so much and she was determined to give it a try. Slowly she rose to her feet and took her position as a carrot. No one will ever really know the extent of her performance as the ill-fated carrot because at this point in the story she burst into laughter. She said that she told Franchot that she thought this was ridiculous . . . she was never going to be cast as a carrot and she couldn't imagine how in the world this could possibly help her career or get her better parts. That was the end of the acting lessons.

She and Franchot lived in her house at 426 North Bristol. Together they finished the remodeling process and her friend William Haines had decorated it in a combination of modern and antique furniture. Franchot had a lot of beautiful family silver including a massive tea service. The formal dining room had shelves built into one whole wall to provide a permanent display for the exquisite pieces. When they were married she was a big star and he was just a leading man. Despite her box office setback during the next few years, she remained a star and he made little progress becoming one. It was a disappointment to her and a serious disadvantage to him. It became painfully clear that he missed New York, the theater and his own way of life. He constantly lived in the shadow of her stardom even though he was a well-known and highly respected actor.

It was during the years of this marriage that she became a wine connoisseur and learned about gourmet foods. Franchot taught her to appreciate fine art and literature, antiques and gracious living. Her dinner parties were impeccable. The long dining room table which could easily seat twenty was set in the most formal manner of Europe, the linen and silver and crystal all coordinated to create the perfect elegance. In the front basement there was a locked wine cellar stocked floor to ceiling with the finest wines money could buy. Three walls had wine racks built in and the temperature was controlled to age the precious liquids properly. The jazz baby turned slick sophisticate movie star was finally becoming a lady.

When Franchot's friends from the East would come to Hollywood they practically headquartered at 426 North Bristol. Some would actually stay there but others would just hang out around the pool. This entire atmosphere was totally foreign to them, something they'd only read about. They were the New York crowd, the Group Theater people. They all talked the same language and shared many of the same experiences. Franchot and his New York buddies would sit around for days on end drinking and talking about the good old days. She didn't relate to most of what they were saying and didn't really care about the majority of the people. She was too busy trying to salvage her sinking career. Nineteen-thirty-six was her last big box office year and she knew that the pictures MGM was giving her to do were getting progressively more shallow and less successful. On the other hand, when her MGM friends and the ever-present publicity folk gathered for a fun afternoon of gossip and "shop talk," Franchot seemed uncomfortable and out of place. Then there were Franchot's little flirtations which always threatened to turn into affairs. She was always busier working than he was and it irritated her enormously that he found time to be amorous with others and wasn't more ambitious. The gap between them professionally grew even though she had become aware that her career was not progressing well. This marriage had not produced any children either and when she actually caught him having an affair with another woman she threw him out of the house. The divorce was final in April of 1939.

If her marriage to Fairbanks can be said to have given her the mark of acceptance and respectability, the marriage to Franchot gave her culture and elegance. She kept the silver and the antiques and added periodically to the wine cellar. She planned superb dinner menus and artfully arranged the place cards which designated careful seating arrangements. The library shelves were adorned with beautiful collections of rare and esoteric leather-bound books, some of which she had taken the time to read. She still preferred to read the funny papers and liked cookies with butter on them, but she was at long last a lady.

But she was alone again after two unsuccessful marriages, numerous attempts to have children and fourteen years in pictures. And, she wasn't getting any younger. Publicly, her birth date was always reported as March 23, 1908, but Grandmother told me once that she was actually born in 1904. That made her closer to 35 years old in 1939 when I was delivered to her.

CHAPTER 3

My official papers simply say "Girl" born in the afternoon of June 11, 1939. My real mother was a student and my father a sailor and neither one of them wanted to take responsibility for me. So, from Hollywood Presbyterian Hospital to a private adoption broker to 426 North Bristol Avenue I traveled when I was only a few weeks old.[1]

In no time at all I was a chubby, smiling baby named Joan. My towels were monogrammed "Joan." The silver picture frame with birth statistics is monogrammed "Joan" and the small bible given to me as a baby says "To little Joan." Only a few weeks old and I was to be Joan Crawford, Jr. An awesome responsibility. There are pictures of me in my scrapbook with Mother holding me, feeding me from a bottle, bathing me. Baby Joan laughing and crying and doing nothing but just lying there in the satin lined bassinet. There are dozens of pictures of naked baby Joan and smiling baby Joan. There are candid snapshots and 8x10 professional photographs of Mother holding me. Beautiful, gossamer mother and child portraits which capture some of the eternity of that special relationship. At long last she had her baby and she never let go of that preciousness.

She took me with her wherever she went. I slept in dressing rooms and studio sound stages. I traveled in the car with her from the time I was only a few months old. She saved every bit of hair cut from my head, every tooth from my mouth. All were carefully sealed in envelopes and labeled in her generous handwriting. There were gifts for which she wrote little notes . . . "to my beautiful infant" . . . "I love you my darling, beautiful child" . . . notes I could not read and only she knew about.

---

[1] My biological mother was a nineteen-year-old student but my father was an engineer, as I was to discover. I was told my mother died giving birth to me, but the truth is she died at fifty-seven without bearing other children.

During the months of my infancy she showered me with the pent-up outpouring of love and affection that had been stifled in her for so many years. Better still, she didn't have to share me with anyone . . . I was hers alone. She was the wellspring from which all love and affection flowed and I was her longed for golden-haired girl. She named me after herself and through the lavish affection, attention and adornment she showered upon me, she tried to make up for the poverty of her own childhood. I was to be the best, the most beautiful, the smartest, quickest, most special child on the face of the earth. I wanted for nothing . . . toys, clothes and baby jewelry. She was constantly holding me and looking at me and trying to make my sparse hair grow into golden ringlets. Whenever she didn't take me to the studio, she would rush home in time to feed me and give me my bath. She would sing lullabies to me and rock me to sleep.

In truth, I was adorable. I also became quite spoiled under the constant tutelage of all this attention. I had everything . . . companionship which played endlessly with me and took care of me in the form of my nurse and an adoring, indulgent mother who couldn't resist anything I asked for from her. In return she had my total devotion. The sun rose and set on my beautiful goddess of a mother. Her laughter was the music of my life and the sound of her heart beating as she held me close to her made me feel safe and quiet. I sobbed whenever she left me even for a little while and I clung to her skirts if there were new people around. I learned very quickly to be adorable for company. I was very bright and seemed to know what pleased the big people. Everyone cooed over me and said what an absolutely beautiful child I was. I learned to walk and talk very rapidly.

The laws of the State of California did not permit a single woman to adopt children. So, when I was eleven months old, Mother took me to Las Vegas, Nevada, and legally adopted me in May, 1940. At some point before the final papers were signed, Mother had come to the conclusion that Joan Crawford, Jr. was not exactly fitting. She chose a new name for me and the adoption papers record the name as Christina Crawford.

In exchange for their more liberal adoption laws and a substantial fee, the state of Nevada attempted to provide some measure of future protection for the adopted children. Since Mother was a single woman and if anything should happen to her there would be no one to provide for me, it was decided that a trust fund should be set up in my name. The court felt assured that this compromise was in the best interests of all concerned and dispatched its duty accordingly. During my early childhood I heard numerous references to the trust fund and Mother said she periodically put the gifts of money her friends sent to me on special occasions in that trust.

For some reason I've never discovered, we went from Las Vegas to Miami, Florida. Curiously, Mother had never mentioned going to Miami. I discovered that we had been there for several weeks only when I went to Miami as an actress to do my first picture in 1960. There I was interviewed by a woman reporter who told me that she had interviewed Mother twenty years before and that she'd met me originally as a small baby. She didn't seem to have any explanation for our trip except that Mother had said at the time that she was on a much needed vacation. It wouldn't seen so peculiar except that we *drove* the entire way. In 1940 there was a war going on and gasoline was rationed. There were no freeways and it was most unusual for a woman alone with an eleven-month-old baby to drive nearly three thousand miles. But that is evidently what we did.[2]

From Miami we went to New York City where I celebrated my first birthday. The New York contingent of fans were there and a few of Mother's close friends. We stayed in the Sherry Netherlands hotel and then Mother took an apartment on East End Avenue which she kept for many years. I had a nurse named "Aunt Kitty" and every day she would

---

2   It was not until 1980 while I was having lunch with film producer Frank Yablans at the Beverly Hills Hotel Polo Lounge that the true reason for this mysterious journey emerged. Frank told me that in doing some of his own research for the film, he found out that Mother had underworld connections going back as far as her dance hall/nightclub performer days as a teenager in Detroit and Chicago. Through those connections she met Meyer Lansky, reputed head of the Jewish Mafia. In the 1940s he lived in Miami, Florida. It was Lansky who had arranged for my legal adoption in Las Vegas, Nevada, through mob connections there, since my birth state, California, had laws which did not permit single women to adopt children.

So, immediately following the adoption, Joan Crawford drove by herself with a one-year-old child, three thousand miles across the entire country to "pay tribute" to her benefactor in Miami.

However, only three years later she evidently felt no need to legally adopt brother Chris in Nevada or anyplace else because years later we were unable to locate any record of his adoption in the states surrounding California. And, since she bought all five of us on the black market, there wasn't any government agency to check.

take me in my big black English perambulator to Schurz Park on the East River. I was always dressed in organdy pinafores and by then had a full head of blonde ringlets. The fans were specifically forbidden to take pictures of me, but somehow they managed to hide the cameras and snap the contraband photos anyway.

During our stay in the East Mother took me to visit some Christian Science friends of hers who owned a beautiful dairy farm in Upstate New York. I was still very little and when Mother and I and the dachshund dog named "Pupschien" went for our walks through the fields surrounding her friends' house, she often had to carry me a good part of the way. One afternoon we had gone for one of these walks in the lovely countryside and I was toddling along beside Mommie as we watched the short-legged dog leaping through the long grass and disappearing momentarily in between each bound. All of a sudden Mother let out a scream of terror and already on the run swooped me up in her arms. Mommie was running for her life and I was hanging onto her body with my arms and legs like a little monkey. She ran at breakneck speed through the long grass, the dog doing his best to keep up with us. At some point, though I was bobbing up and down with the motion of Mother's running, I caught sight of an enormous black animal that was chasing us! I could hear the thundering sound of it's feet hitting the ground, sensing that the huge beast was gaining on us.

Ahead, about a hundred yards, was a long fence. Mother headed straight for it. Seemingly out of nowhere, Aunt Peggy appeared near the fence calling encouragement to Mommie. Aunt Peggy yelled: "Remember Joan, God is love." Through her accelerated breathing and never missing a beat in her stride, Mommie yelled back: "Damn it Peggy, *God is love on the other side of the fence!*" A moment or so later, Mommie clambered to safety through that fence dragging me with her. She fell exhausted on the soft grass crying and laughing at the same time. Aunt Peggy tried to comfort both of us and make sure we hadn't been hurt. The poor little dog collapsed in a heap, panting rapidly. We looked back toward the field and there behind the fence, weighing over two thousand pounds, was a champion breeding black bull with a ring through his nose, snorting and pawing the ground. Mother didn't say another word, but gathered me up and walked with Aunt Peggy back to the farmhouse. That was definitely the end of our walks in the country.

Before we left New York we went to visit Helen Hayes in Nyack on the Hudson River. She and her husband, Charles MacArthur, had two children. The oldest was a girl named Mary who later died of polio, and the younger a boy named James but whom we called Jamie. Jamie was just a couple of years older than I but the difference at that point was considerable, since I was still confined to a baby carriage. Jamie tried to entertain me while the grown-ups visited and he wheeled me in my carriage out into the garden. I was going through a stage when I was very big on kissing but Jamie wasn't too thrilled about that and set off to gather me flowers. I wasn't used to being left alone and after a short while began to cry. The sound of my crying brought the desired attention from my mother and also from Jamie. He rushed back with some flowers for me. In an attempt to please me and also hush me up, he presented me with a large rose which he stuck right in my face! The perverse humor of adults being what it is, they were delighted with this unexpected comedy and took several snapshots of the event. The more they laughed the louder I cried and the harder Jamie tried to shut me up. Not an auspicious romantic debut on my part, to say the least.

Mother and I departed for California soon after that visit. Aunt Helen always sent us lovely Christmas and birthday presents and we corresponded fairly regularly in later years. Helen Hayes was one of the people Mother truly respected and admired. They became friends when Mother was just starting out as a chorus girl and went to see everything Helen Hayes did on Broadway. Lynne Fontaine and Alfred Lunt were the other two Broadway stars that Mother loved and idolized. They all were to remain lifelong friends, a friendship built on mutual admiration.[3]

Mother and I returned to California and she went back to work. *Strange Cargo* and *Susan and God* were released in 1940 and in *Strange Cargo* she was again teamed with Clark Gable. Even though I was very little I remember Gable's visits to the house during the next two years. He seemed like a giant to me and had the most wonderful hearty laugh. Mother and he resumed their romance, I think, but again it was not destined to be any lasting romantic relationship. Mother once

---

3   As an adult I learned that Helen Hayes was my godmother. When I became an actress at seventeen and was on my own in New York, I went to her for advice about the Broadway theater, hoping she would help and guide me. She was pleasant toward me but never offered either mentoring or assistance.

said Gable was only interested in women who weren't available. Mother had her own problems with the relationship because as much as she yearned for and was attracted to strong men, deep down inside I think she only wanted men she could dominate. That definitely was *not* Clark Gable. He was known as a man's man, a sportsman and a lover. Gable had a spirit and a verve for living that set him apart. Although their love affair was relatively brief, Mother spoke of Gable with a special fondness and respect for the rest of her life. When asked by interviewers who her favorite leading man or male Hollywood star was she usually put Gable at the top of the list. Maybe it was because she never did manage to outshine him professionally nor dominate him personally that she retained her respect and love for him over a span of nearly thirty years.

During 1941 and 1942 she did two pictures a year under her Metro contract. But though she continued working she knew that her career was not going forward. The scripts were trite and the majority of her time was spent changing costumes. The reviews mentioned her clothes more than her acting and with a war in progress the reviews were often snide about the abundance of fabric available to dress her while the rest of the country scrimped and saved for the war effort. *Above Suspicion* was her last film for MGM. After seventeen years under contract to the same studio, the studio that had seen her develop from a brash flapper into a major star, the studio that had been her home, was now an adversary and she knew she was losing the battle.

Finally, she left and signed a contract with Warner Brothers for far less money than she'd been getting at MGM. Warner Brothers was to be an entirely new battle for her. She didn't have the ensconced niche that she'd gotten used to at Metro. She didn't know everyone and all the little stories of their past. She was not part of the family on this new lot and she still had to do battle with the senior producers and Jack Warner himself. The scripts they submitted were worse in her opinion that the ones she'd refused to do at Metro. What an irony that she had left one studio because of the poor quality material she was offered only to be given worse trash at Warner's. With the exception of *Hollywood Canteen*, a lavish propaganda movie featuring every star on the Warner's payroll, she didn't work at all for nearly three years.

I think when she married Phillip Terry in 1942, who at that time was a handsome but relatively unknown actor in his early thirties, she knew that her days at Metro were numbered. Mother had only been divorced for three years but I don't think she liked being alone so much. I think that for all the admirers and servants she was just downright lonely. By her own admission she never loved Phillip enough to have warranted marrying him and he certainly wasn't powerful enough to do anything for her career, so loneliness and a certain boredom were really the only answers left. Mother needed companionship and she needed an audience to reassure her that she was loved. She had an insatiable need for love and attention.

Phillip was the second husband who came to live with her in her house at 426 North Bristol where he had his own suite of a large bedroom and dressing room-bath. It always seemed that he was more of a guest than a part of the household and he never really had any say in how things were to be run. It must have been very demoralizing for him and I'm sure that had he known what he was getting himself involved in, he never would have married Mother.

In 1943, Joan and Phillip together, adopted a boy whom they named Phillip Terry, Jr. I do not remember the marriage day but I certainly remember the night my second baby brother arrived.

I was asleep in the big four-poster bed with the white organdy canopy. I heard voices and woke up slowly. There was a light on in the room and I could see the shadows of several people standing around the crib across from my bed. The people were whispering. I sat up. Everyone turned around. I scrambled out of bed and ran over to the crib to peer through the railing. I was about three and a half and not yet tall enough to see much in the semi-darkness. Someone picked me up so that I could see better. I looked down and there he was . . . a fat smiling baby brother. I wanted to touch him. He looked just like a big doll with his blue eyes and blonde curls.

I touched him and he started crying! It startled me and I nearly fell into the crib with him. Everyone seemed upset with me and back into my own bed I went. That baby cried for quite a long time. Everyone was fussing and cooing over him and saying how beautiful he was. They told me to go back to sleep and left.

The door to my room was always left open and the hall light burned all night because I was afraid of the dark. Sometimes the dolls on the shelves in my room would dance in the shadows and I would be scared of them. Sometimes there were wolves under my bed and I'd have to lie very still so they wouldn't know I was there. Sometimes I lay so still it was like I was frozen. I don't think I was so scared of the dark before I started sleeping in the big four-poster bed. At first I used to have nightmares and fall out of it. Mommie would come running from her room. I would be screaming. It was quite a distance to the floor . . . I had to use a step stool to get into bed.

I would have the same dream. I'd been kidnapped by a band of men on horses. Mommie was trying to find me. The men and horses would stop to rest. I could hear Mommie . . . she was just around the bend in the road . . . she was coming to rescue me. But, just as I could actually see her, the men would scoop me up and ride off. Then I would be crying and fall out of bed.

I had not made up the entire kidnap terror. Only a few years before I was born, the Lindbergh kidnapping was a national tragedy. Then before this baby brother arrived, there had been another one. His name was Christopher and he hadn't been with us very long when his real mother came and wanted him back. It was a terrible scene with screaming and shouting and a lot of running around. But she did get her son back and we were without a Christopher. From that time on, Mother changed the birth dates on the certificates. Not on mine but on brother Phillip's and later on the twins'. Evidently there had been some publicity on the first Christopher which had given the real birth date and through that story the real mother found him. So . . . Phillip's birthday was the 15th of October and the twins was on the 15th of January, but that wasn't the real day of their birth in either case. Mother and Phillip Terry adopted Phillip Jr. together, but I was still Mother's alone.[4]

---

4   Phillip told me in 1980 that they were married in Ventura, California, with little publicity. I never remember being told in advance nor meeting him beforehand. After they were married he was informed that a baby boy had been ordered from the same broker who found me. That child was named Christopher and lived with us for between six and nine months until his biological mother reclaimed him. She came to our house when Mother was working and Phillip was at home with us and the servants. She did manage to take the baby after a violent argument during which I hid in a closet, terrified by the screaming police sirens and scared I would be abducted also. Even with police and FBI assistance, that baby was long gone.

Immediately, Mother placed another order for a baby boy, requiring that he come from another state. This baby trade was completely private without any state or local social service/adoption agency involved. In effect, it was done outside the law, devoid of supervision.

Just before my fourth birthday, the second baby boy arrived at night and was called Phillip, Jr.

My stepfather Phillip told me that he tried to dissuade Mother from getting another baby so quickly but she insisted that they needed a "family." What she meant was that she

Baby brother and I didn't get along too well at first. He would cry and I'd want to get out of bed and punch him. But soon we began to work it out and I realized that I had a wonderful real life toy to play with. I dressed him up and wheeled him around in his buggy. I helped give him baths and feed him, just like with my dolls. When he got old enough to stand up in his playpen, he would put on a real show. He hated the playpen and would stamp his feet and hold onto the bars jumping up and down like a monkey. He broke three playpens beyond repair before the grown-ups finally gave up on them.

He and I were inseparable. We shared the same bedroom and the same bathroom until I was a teenager and used to lock him out. I got him to play all my games. I was teacher or chief or the boss and he was whatever else there was to be. He got mad at me for being so bossy, but I thought it was just great. As he got a little older he became a really great swimmer, a fish, and in the pool it was a very even match. Why one of us didn't drown is a miracle to me. Under water, where no one else could hear us or bother much with our game . . . we worked out all the brother-sister hostilities. He won more often than he lost. And in addition, we had vowed silence. No tattletales, even if you got hurt. That was our bargain and we kept it.

Stepfather Phillip was a kind man, but he and Mother didn't get along very well all the time. He got the unpleasant job of spanking me. We worked out a deal. We would go down to the building across from the pool where they showed movies and sometimes had parties and that's where I got my spankings from him . . . in the theater.

The deal was that I would get one additional spank each time I had to be punished. At first it was okay because I only got one spank and it was all over. Compared with Mother's spankings it was a real bargain.

She used the hairbrush or her hand. She'd succeeded in breaking three hairbrushes across my bottom after she said she'd worn out her hand. I was only about five.

It was actually a nice time with Phillip in the theater at the beginning of our deal. We would talk and he'd ask me what I thought I was being

---

needed a positive image for her fans and the publicity a new baby generated because she had been labeled "box office poison" by movie critics and the press. Her career was careening toward the toilet and Warner Bros. gave her no film roles except a cameo in *Hollywood Canteen*.

punished for and I'd tell him and he'd give me his ideas on the subject and I'd vow never to do it again. Then he'd pick me up and carry me back to the house. It was nice and I liked the feeling of being close to him. He had a kind face.

Then one day I got the shock of my life. He gave me a spanking that really hurt. I mean really hurt. His hands were bigger than Mother's and, of course, he had a lot more strength. I cried. But not all of the crying was for the pain of spanking . . . about half of it was for the betrayal. After that, all the spankings hurt . . . more and more. It had turned out to be a rotten deal. Now he didn't pick me up and carry me back to the big house. He just held my hand firmly as I walked beside him sniffling. We didn't even look at one another.

CHAPTER 4

In the early 1940s, our house at 426 North Bristol Avenue, in the area known as Brentwood, stood in the middle of a quiet but very fashionable neighborhood.

Our property covered nearly an acre which began on Bristol and ended on Cliffwood. It was one of the very few which went clear through from one street to the other. We had four next-door neighbors, two in the front with Bristol addresses and two in the back with Cliffwood addresses.

In front, Mr. and Mrs. Robert Preston occupied one house and the Feddersons owned the other. Their son, Mike, was a friend of my brother's and they played together frequently. In the back, a woman named Mrs. Hudson had two children: Martha and Tommy. We went back and forth to mutual birthday parties but mostly we played with Martha and Tommy through the fence. Our other Cliffwood neighbors were very private people whom I never knew and rarely even saw. For a while, Larry Olivier (later Sir Laurence) rented the Hudson's house and we became good friends with him and his son.

Across the street Frank Fay, who had been a big star in the early days of motion pictures, owned the entire block fronting on Bristol. We used to see him in the morning and evenings walking his big Saint Bernard, but other than that he kept pretty much to himself. When Mother had first moved into our house, Frank Fay was married to a young actress named Barbara Stanwyck with whom Mother became friends. They were about the same age and when Barbara decided to end the marriage and escaped by climbing over the high wall entirely surrounding the Fay estate, Mother took her in until Barbara could find another place to go. But now, Mr. Fay was an old man who lived quietly and walked his dog. He did, however, contribute generously to the Catholic church and on many Sundays donated his estate to church functions. Mother was always provoked by the usually empty street being filled with automobiles, but there wasn't much anyone could say about it officially. When Mr. Fay died, the estate was broken up and the Doheny's built a new house on a large lot taken from the far side of the property.

On the corner, Jennings Lang and his wife had a pretty house. I had been in elementary school with their son and we continued to be friends. Jennings was one of Mother's agents at MCA.

Behind the Fay estate, Cole Porter had a beautiful house where Mother often went for small dinner parties. I visited it once years later when Mike Nicols was living in it. A few houses down lived Mr. and Mrs. Hal Roach. I was very good friends with both of their daughters and we were always at one another's birthday parties. We played together frequently because I could easily walk to their house without Mother worrying about my safety. They had a lively household and always offered us something to eat. Mr. Roach, of course, owned Hal Roach Studios.

Too far away to walk, but still considered part of the neighborhood, lived Shirley Temple. She was a number of years older than I was, so we were never actually friends, but Mother took me to visit her once. Her parents greeted us at the door to a nice but not lavish house. The major thing I remember about that visit was taking a tour of Shirley Temple's closets! Her parents had saved all her clothes and all her movie costumes. They were hung very neatly in several rooms that were converted into closets. Those closets ran the entire length of the rooms on both sides. They had sliding doors and inside there were clothes racks on two levels. The clothes seemed to be arranged chronologically because on the beginning of the tour we saw tiny little dresses which seemed to grow larger as the tour progressed. I never saw so many clothes. Even Mommie didn't have so many clothes and she had lots of closets filled to the brim. I met Shirley Temple that day, but my most vivid memory is of those closets.

There, of course, were lots of other people who lived in the same neighborhood . . . Tyrone Power, the Henry Hathaways whose son Danny was a great favorite of mine, the Jaffes whose son Andy was my very first boyfriend in elementary school, the Wheelwrights and the McCauleys. Sharon and Linda McCauley were two of my closest friends, particularly Linda who was just about the same age as I was. In fact, Linda was probably my best friend throughout most of the early years I lived in the house on Bristol. We told each other all our secrets. She was just about the only person in the whole world that I totally trusted. She kept every confidence and all the little childhood secrets just as though she'd never heard them. I loved her dearly . . . she was a true best friend if there ever was one.

The legend of my birthday parties has already been established. In truth, there were several years when they were circus spectaculars.

We had a very large backyard. In it there was a rectangular pool of near Olympic size, a building on one side of the pool called the theater and another building opposite it called the bath house. Beyond the pool and these buildings there was a badminton court flanked by large flower beds and olive and magnolia trees. Past the court was a lattice-work pavilion that spanned the width of the garden.

When Mother bought the house and this property, there was only a dirt road out to it from Sunset Boulevard. Everyone, even her closest friends, told her she was crazy to move out so far into the country and that no one would come to visit her. The house was originally small and she added a second floor and two wings for a total of twenty-four rooms, including the baths. The day she moved into the house she saw deer, fox and rabbits. There were not even any street lights yet.

But ten years later the house had been completely remodeled, the pool and other buildings all constructed. This entire backyard was turned over to the birthday parties when I was little.

It was a private circus . . . a miniature Disneyland before one ever existed for the public. There were balloons everywhere and music. There were brightly colored clowns, an organ grinder and his monkey. There were ponies to ride and a magic show to watch. There were games . . . group games like "pin-the-tail-on-the-donkey" and tug-o-war. All the children were dressed up, even by Hollywood standards. The girls had fluffy dresses of pretty pastel fabrics and ribbons in their hair. The little boys had short pants and long socks and ties. Some even had velvet jackets. Everyone had a starched and polished look . . . clothes and faces as well.

If this was the progeny of the royalty of Hollywood . . . then I was the crown princess. My dresses were of the finest hand-embroidered organdy. My petticoats and fancy panties trimmed in lace and ribbons. My shoes and socks were so white they gleamed. My pale golden hair fell in cascades of soft curls that were held away from my face with more satin ribbons. As close as hours of devoted human effort could make me . . . I was perfectly beautiful. The perfect child in every respect, my clothes were certainly gorgeous, my manners impeccable, my curtsey smooth, my hair beautiful and golden . . . there was no doubt about it . . . I was the incarnation of the perfect child. Mother had created me in the image of perfection and then created these birthday parties to celebrate another successful year of happiness with that creation.

The luncheon feast was in our formal dining room which was nearly a separate wing in itself. The big dining table was removed (heaven only knows *where*, since it could easily seat 25 people) and a rented table that could be lowered to "kid size" was substituted. Little child-size chairs were placed around it. The table stretched nearly the length of the dining room and was always decorated with wonderful, fanciful figures and animals. All the children were given party favors at each place.

Not too long ago I saw photographs of one of these childhood extravaganzas and I was struck by the image of all these little children without any smiles on their faces sitting around this long low table with these pointed hats on their heads like so many little dunces. The mothers and servants hovered over us ministering to our wants and passing out the food. The uniformed servants in the background looked very stern in their white starched uniforms and sensible shoes.

The expression on my face in that photograph is beyond description. I am sitting at the head of the table presiding over a rather large group of four-, five-, and six-year-olds . . . but no one is paying attention to me and I look quite bewildered.

There was one thing I didn't like about those birthday parties. I didn't know most of the people there very well. I only saw them a couple times a year . . . at other birthday parties. Oh, there were always a couple of my friends from Bristol Avenue and a couple of other people I liked, but most of the children were practically strangers. However, many of them knew each other independently because their parents were close friends. And a strange thing happened at several of those parties . . . I got left out of most of the games and the playing. I rode the pony and talked to the clown . . . I slid down the slide with the rest, but I wasn't included in any of their games. Today I cannot tell you the names of most of the children in the picture of my birthday party luncheon table. I didn't know them then and I don't know them now.

It was during those parties where everyone seemed to be having such a good time and I felt so left out that I had my first memorable feeling of loneliness. There I was . . . it was my party and I was all dressed up in organdy with satin ribbons in my hair . . . feeling vaguely out of place.

One year, I think I was about six, I threw an absolute fit just as all the children were about to arrive. I was up in my room getting dressed with the nurse tying the bow of my pinafore and Mother putting the finishing touches to the ribbons in my hair. I asked if my friend Alma had arrived yet, she was supposed to come early. (Alma is not her real name.) Mother said she'd forgotten to tell me, but Alma could not come to the party. I looked directly into my mother's eyes and announced: "In that case, I'm not going to the party either." I should explain that Alma was my constant playmate. She lived a few houses away from us with her mother who was a housekeeper. Alma was black. "If my friend Alma can't come to my birthday party, then I'm not going to it at all." With that I sat down on the floor and refused to budge. There was much scurrying around and in just a few minutes Alma appeared in the doorway to my bathroom. She looked at me sitting in the middle of the floor and the two of us started to giggle. I got up and the two of us went hand in hand downstairs to the party.

To this day, when I look through that baby book, which is a large black scrapbook easily six inches thick, and I see the photographs of that party . . . Alma and me on the slide . . . Alma and me playing pin-the-tail-on-the-donkey . . . and see a smile on my face, I'm grateful to her all over again.[5]

Those legendary parties only lasted for about four years. From the time I was about three until I was about seven. Later on there was just a group of school friends over for a swim and after that a lot of teenage birthdays were spent at boarding school.

---

5   Her real name is Yvonne. She called into a Larry King show I did and we spoke for the first time as adults.

A lot of times I had to choose between Mommie and Phillip. I remember the last time. It was about which movie to show . . . his or hers. I didn't want to see either one, I just wanted to get out of there. I'd never seen one of Phillip's, so I really should have and wanted to choose his film. They were angry with one another and for some reason at that point Mother walked out of the room. "Call me when you've decided," she snapped at me as she left.

I waited a moment feeling very uncomfortable with Phillip staring at me and knowing that in all fairness we really should see his movie. We were standing in the kitchen and when I figured that Mother had time to get to her room upstairs, I called on the house phone.

That night we screened a movie of Mother's, I don't remember which one.

It wasn't long after that that Phillip left.

One day he just didn't come home. I don't think much was said about it, except that he wouldn't be back. I don't even think we had a chance to really say goodbye to him. He was just gone.

Then an amazing thing happened: within twenty-four hours of his departure there was not a trace of him left anywhere in the entire house. He'd had his own room and bath and every single personal item was gone. All the pictures of him in Mother's room and in the downstairs library were gone. And, in our baby books where all the photographs of my brother and me were neatly mounted on page after page, Phillip's image was ripped out of every picture in each of our books! Sometimes only his head was ripped off but other pictures were ripped down the middle to remove him completely. Except for those torn photographs, it was like he never existed at all. It was so scary that I couldn't think about it much. We never dared mention his name and it was years before we ever saw him again.

The lesson I really got from that was that Mother could make people disappear if she wanted to . . . grown people too, not just kids. If she got mad enough, maybe she'd make me disappear. I couldn't think about that very much either.

Phillip had been a nice man and we did miss him even if he and Mother did lock me up in the shower a couple of times and left me there until the nurse found me tied up. Even if he did let Mother make me stand in the linen closet with the door closed as another punishment . . .

when they knew I was scared of the dark and thought rats might come down from the attic and eat me alive in there. I had a vivid imagination.[6]

Shortly after Phillip left, my brother's name was changed from Phillip Terry, Jr. to Christopher Crawford. He was about three and a half then and can remember it very well. I was just six years old.

---

6   Phillip told me later that his mother and father were very upset that he left two helpless children with "Crawford" as he called Mother. He said that since he could not get custody of us, the best he could do was insist that my brother have a trust fund and guarantee of a college education. For that he agreed to give up all visitation rights. The divorce papers he signed had those clauses in them. But, when I found them on microfiche in the Los Angeles County Courthouse archives (purposely difficult to locate because she used "Lucille LeSueur" and Phillip, his legal name, also) when my brother and I were contesting Mother's will in 1977, the official record showed no mention of children at all and no provision for my brother.

When I told Phillip, he looked shocked. His face registered anger, sadness and finally resignation. All he said was: "I shouldn't be surprised, after all, that was the 'old days' and she was part of the system." His career as an actor never fully recovered after his divorce from "Crawford" because she sabotaged both friendships and progress behind his back.

CHAPTER 5

We used to spend part of each summer in Carmel. First with Mother and later at Douglas Camp.

It was a long drive up the coast in those days. We would pack up the car and leave home in the early afternoon. The first night we would spend in Santa Maria at a lovely old Spanish inn which was covered with bougainvillea and honeysuckle vines. There were no freeways, of course, so about an hour after we left home we were really out in the country.

Mother loved the country and we used to go for long walks picking wildflowers and watching the dog jumping through the long grass. We used to have a lot of picnics near home in Mandeville Canyon before there were any houses there.

The next day of our journey, we would get up early, pack up the bags and have breakfast. Then we would drive on to Carmel. We always stayed at the Pebble Beach Lodge in private cottages. They were just like little houses with the bedrooms upstairs and a living room downstairs. Because it was often cold and foggy, each cottage had a big stone fireplace which we all adored.

We would have lunch in the big dining room at the lodge which overlooked the lovely green lawns and the sea beyond. Mother was always happier here. She seemed to relax and enjoy us and her friends here more than in Los Angeles. It's hard to imagine now, but there were many years when Mother never left California. She lived and worked in Los Angeles and the furthest she traveled was Carmel. Even if she wasn't working she didn't take vacations as such. She'd create busy work at home . . . cleaning out the basements and endless correspondence. So Carmel was a super treat for her and for us.

During the days, Chris and I would go off swimming and sometimes horseback riding. I was always crazy about horses and went riding every

Saturday at home over in Will Rogers Park. I rode a beautiful palomino mare named Lady and I pretended she was really mine. Almost every night I would wish on the evening star . . . "Star light, star bright, bring me this wish I wish tonight." What I always wished for was a horse of my own like Lady. I even devised elaborate schemes for how we could keep a horse in our own backyard. I would lie awake at night imagining the day when I got my very own horse.

Mother would knit and read and take walks and sometimes play tennis. She would always have stacks of scripts and weeks of trade papers and the funnies. I don't know when she had time to read the rest of the newspaper, but she always read the comic strips.

After a few days, she'd be telling jokes and playing tricks on us. Little practical jokes that we never quite felt comfortable with, nor completely understood. Mother valued a sense of humor and insisted that we develop one . . . more often than not at our own expense. We learned to laugh at ourselves and to at least appreciate the irony, if not exactly the humor, in life's most unexpected situations.

Mother loved the walks and must have walked miles before we left Carmel each visit.

One night she was a little restless and asked me to go for a walk with her. It was dark and we didn't have a flashlight. But the sky was relatively clear and the moon was bright. I followed her across the lawns to the sea wall. We walked along the sea wall with only the sound of the waves pounding and the dampness of the sea spray for company. It was kind of a lonely place.

We sat down on some flat rocks and looked out toward the open sea. We sat there in silence a long time. She took my hand and held it firmly. Very softly she started talking to me. I had to lean toward her to hear above the sound of the surf against the rocks. She looked so beautiful in the moonlight that I had a hard time listening to what she was saying. The wind blew her hair gently away from her face and her profile was illuminated by the moon and reflections from the clouds. She was talking to me about life, about herself and what she wanted and how hard it was to get . . . how hard it was to be happy. She said that I made her happy, but all of life wasn't that easy. She told me how poor she'd been and how lonely as a child, how hard it had been for her. She said she just felt sometimes like she'd never catch up. She talked for a long time and

I tried with all my might to understand what she was saying to me. But, some things I couldn't understand. I was only about seven and I just didn't know what she was talking about. So I held onto her hand with all my strength and concentrated on her face. I never took my eyes off her for an instant. I was trying so hard to understand . . . to help her. She started to cry. She said she wasn't really sad, but that it was so beautiful here. I put my little arms around her neck, hugging and kissing her. I wished with all my heart that I could make it all right for her. "I love you Mommie dearest" is all I could say. She turned and looked at me through her tears. She smiled at me. Then she ran her finger across my forehead, rumpled up my hair and gave me a hug. "Let's go . . . it's getting cold."

She held my hand the whole way back. At one point she stopped and looked down at me. "You don't understand very much of what I said, do you?" In despair I shook my head no. She sighed as she said, "It's all right, Tina . . . you'll understand more when you're a little older."

When we got back to the cottage she made us both hot chocolate and we sat in front of the fire until I fell asleep with my head in her lap.

I've wondered sometimes if I hadn't been just seven years old and I'd really understood all the things she said to me that night . . . I've wondered many times if my life with her would have been any different.

Mother had finally started working again, doing a movie for Jerry Wald called *Mildred Pierce*. It was the first real picture she'd done for Warner's under her new contract and she was very nervous. She left for the studio about 5 a.m. while it was still dark and she wouldn't return until well after dinner. Sometimes she didn't get home until after we were asleep. She worked on the picture six days a week and on Sunday she slept until almost noon. The afternoons were taken up with the hairdresser, the manicurist and finally the masseuse who came to the house in succession to prepare Mother for the coming weeks work. We rarely saw her during those days, but since we had a nice nurse at the time, our life went fairly smoothly.

Mother was so glad to be working again in a good film with a really good part that she hardly had time to think about anything else. She hadn't worked in over two years and what with the war and rationing, most of our house had been closed up, the furniture covered and the doors closed to any rooms not necessary for everyday life. Those were the days of no extra servants and she did do a lot of the housework. For a while even our big kitchen was closed down and we cooked over sterno in the basement. We had to help in any way we could, but we were too young to be of much real use. Our entire front lawn was turned into a victory garden to grow vegetables and after our Japanese gardener was taken off to the relocation camp quite suddenly, we had to tend it ourselves.

But now, in 1945, even though the house seemed a lot emptier without Mr. Terry, life seemed to be going better for Mother.

Unfortunately, the picture couldn't last indefinitely and the day eventually came when it was totally finished. All the publicity pictures had been taken, all the dubbing and trailers finished and Mother's dressing room cleaned up. Since she had a permanent dressing room in a bungalow on the Warner's lot, she didn't have to bring everything home. But she did remove anything of real value to her and brought it home in several trips. Then there was nothing more to go back to the studio for and she had to face finding another picture to do even though she was under contract and still getting paid.

When Mother was home, our lives changed drastically. I was in second grade at Gretna Green public school and left every morning long before she got up. That year I took the bus to school and back so there wasn't much of a problem for me. Jenny, the cook, would get me up and I'd get dressed while my little brother still slept. Then it was downstairs to eat breakfast and off to school I went with my lunch box. When I came home, Mother was often gone and I'd go out to play with my brother. Mother came home in the afternoon and usually had friends over for dinner or went out with someone.

At first it was only the weekends that were difficult. Then we lived according to a rigid and unchanging schedule. We got up every day at the same time whether it was Monday or Saturday. We ate breakfast at the same time and did the dishes and made our beds at the same time every day. The older we got, the more inflexible the schedule became.

Since our lives were scheduled like the army, it will not be a surprise to know that we had a half-hour to eat each meal. We had another half-hour to wash the dishes. We were not allowed in the kitchen except to get things necessary to set the table. The cook was a crucial factor in my life. If we happened to have a cook who not only had some talent but also some compassion, I fared rather well. If not . . . my life was made miserable. There weren't many things I absolutely hated, thank God, but there was one: blood-rare meat. (The other was black bean soup.)

During the war, meat was scarce and Mother used to buy it on the black market and lose no time telling us how expensive it was and how lucky we were . . . to think of the "starving children in Europe" . . . and eat every single scrap of food on our plates. This was no idle threat either, nothing easy like no dessert if we failed to heed the warning.

The punishment for not eating was progressive, and I do not mean in the sense of being enlightened. I mean it had a number of phases to it. First, if I hadn't finished the quivering piece of reddish-blue steak in the allotted time, I indeed received no dessert. I didn't really care about that part very much. When it was evident that we were going to have beef of any kind for dinner, I would beg the cook for an end piece, if it was a roast, or to cook my piece of meat a little longer. All this was done in whispers, of course, so the nurse couldn't hear me. Mother usually wasn't there and we almost never ate meals with her during the week and only lunch on weekends, but everyone had orders to report any infringement of any of the rules to her. If there were no broken rules reported for more than a few days, Mother figured someone was holding out and the household inquisition began. Most of the time, I guess it was less hassle for the people who worked there to just follow the rules, even if they didn't agree with them.

Anyway, sometimes my pleading went for naught and I ended up with this blood-rare food. Mother had some idea that at those prices, raw was more nutritious for us.

At the beginning of the meal, I would try to eat the meat in teeny bites covered up with whatever else was on the plate, hidden under mashed potatoes or carrots or anything. I wasn't allowed to drink my milk with my food (another one of those stupid rules) so I couldn't just put a little piece in my mouth and wash it down. Well, try as I might, the food never came out even. I would have eaten all the edges of the meat which were slightly cooked and be left staring at the blood-rare center. I couldn't swallow those pieces because every time I tried to I gagged.

So . . . my dinner plate was removed to the refrigerator to await breakfast. In the morning, I got a glass of milk and this cold plate which by now was greasy and yucky. I also was not allowed to sit down at the table, but had to stand for the half-hour. I did drink my milk and that was all.

Very well . . . back to the refrigerator with my plate. Lunch progressed the same.

So far, since yesterday I'd had two glasses of milk and a lot of water. I could hear my stomach gurgle and I didn't feel very good. I didn't think it was funny or cute and I wasn't trying to be impossible. I wished I could have sent all of my portion of the meat to those starving children for the duration of the war. But the war was over and I absolutely could not understand *why*, if meat was still so expensive and I hated is so much, why did I have to eat it?

For dinner I had the same plate cold from the refrigerator but I was not allowed at the table. I had to stand and stare at this horrible grungy plate placed on top of the chest-type freezer on the back porch. I guess my plate was becoming an unpleasant sight for the rest of the table. I tried to eat a couple pieces of the wretched meat and ended up vomiting in the servants' toilet.

The next morning I didn't even want to get up. I knew that awful plate was down in the refrigerator waiting for me. And the worst of it was that now I was really getting hungry. Three glasses of milk were not enough to keep a nine-year-old going for very long. I was unhappy and had begun thinking of ways to hide pieces of the meat so that it would look like I was eating it. But there was no place to hide it and the dog was not allowed near us during meals.

Breakfast smelled delicious . . . bacon and eggs were cooking and the aroma reached up to my bedroom. My stomach was not gurgling now, it was growling. I went downstairs thinking that the ordeal just might be over . . . after all I was just a kid and it was two full days now. I set the table with a place for myself as usual. There were three of us at the table: the nurse, Chris and myself. The twins were in highchairs. When the nurse came downstairs, she told me I would not be allowed breakfast until I finished my plate at the freezer. I couldn't believe it.

I marched myself out to the freezer and there it was . . . the same plate from two days ago.

How I hated the sight of it. I felt so helpless . . . why did everybody hate me so much? It's so unfair. What did I do that was so bad? I hate bloody meat . . . so what? Everybody hates something. Even Mother . . . she told me so. When she was a little girl she took a big helping of mashed potatoes. Her mother told her if she took that much she'd have to eat it. Mother laughed and said she'd be happy to. It turned out to be mashed turnips! She hated mashed turnips, but her mother made her eat every mouthful.

I looked down at my plate and cried. I just stood there alone on the back porch looking at that disgusting plate with the congealed grease and the piece of meat that had started getting shriveled and icky . . . like moldy . . . and I cried.

I didn't eat another mouthful of it. I just stood there getting madder by the minute, smelling the bacon and eggs for everyone else. When my half-hour was up I marched in without a word, put the plate in the refrigerator and did the dishes. I'd been doing dishes since I was four years old and had to stand on a step stool to reach the sink. For some weird reason it pleased Mother to tell people that I'd been doing dishes since I was four.

Someone called Mother to tell her that I wouldn't eat and I had to talk to her at the studio that afternoon. She yelled at me for being a selfish, ungrateful child . . . how *could* I be so ungrateful with all the starving children in Europe. Didn't I realize how hard she worked to pay for all the things we had . . . how much better off we were than other children . . . I was to go to bed early without any dinner and she'd take care of the spanking tomorrow. She hung up without saying goodbye.

I lay in my bed crying. I wasn't even hungry anymore. I don't understand why she gets so mad at me . . . why everything I do seems to make her angry. I thought about the starving children in Europe. I thought about running away from home . . . but I had nowhere to go.

On Saturday mornings from the time we got up, through breakfast, all our regular chores and even when we went out into the backyard to play, we were never allowed to speak above a *whisper*. The nurse had to whisper and the rest of the servants had to whisper. The entire household had to whisper until Mother was ready to get up. Whispering inside the house was difficult at best, but whispering way out in the backyard past the pool was impossible. It was very hard to think up games that didn't require any communication. The easiest was "hide and seek" but a silent version of cowboys and Indians came in second. It must have been quite funny for the nurse to watch us "galloping" around the yard with our toy six-shooters, whispering "bang, bang" and the victim falling to the ground silently. Badminton was also easy to play without any noise but we didn't really have enough people. In the summertime we could go swimming, but we were forbidden to dive or splash or make any noise. So Chris and I became adept at underwater swimming and played all our games under the surface. We even learned to talk to each other under water which was hilarious.

If the weather was bad and we had to stay indoors, whispering was a torture because we weren't allowed to play the radio or any of our other records.

In addition to whispering inside the house, we also had to walk on tiptoes. It may sound ludicrous now, but it wasn't in the least bit funny then. The whole house whispered and walked on tiptoe until Mother decided to get up. More often than not she arose around 11:30 just before lunch. If we were out in the yard we could see the Venetian blinds on her bedroom windows open and that was the signal that she was up. Usually she would call out to us and say good morning. But even if she didn't, we would know that the open blinds meant that she was up. Then we would go into the house to check and make sure that the cook had received the call for her breakfast. If she had, it was safe to talk in a normal tone of voice. If she hadn't, it was still whispers. And if she didn't get up before our regular lunchtime, we had to continue to whisper through that meal as well. This was not a special occasion procedure, it was not connected in Mother's mind to any kind of punishment. It was standard operating procedure, one of the many house rules and it was fully enforced all the years I lived in that house. It was her house to be run entirely on her orders, for her personal convenience. No one else had a bit of say in what went on or how things were to be done. Since she paid all the bills, she pointed out to us that it was her privilege to have things done exactly as she wanted them and that was that. There was never any further discussion on that or any other subject once she'd given her opinion. And about the whispering, she was adamant. If, woe be unto us, we ever made a sound that should have the awful misfortune to be blamed for waking her before she was ready to arise, the entire house heard her wrath. If we were outside playing, those Venetian blinds would fly open, the window shoved up and her voice bellowed across the garden.

"Goddammit . . . how many times do I have to tell you to keep your voices down?!" At this point, all movement would come to a screeching halt in the yard. The nurse, Chris and I would literally freeze in our places. "Christina, you come in this house this instant." With that, the bedroom window would slam shut. Slowly I trod toward the house, knowing that one of those vile spankings that hurt for days was in store for me. Mommie was always in a terrible mood if anyone accidentally woke her up and the spankings for this infringement of the rules tended to convey the full force of her anger. She had already broken several hairbrushes across my bottom. It really was a wonder that I hadn't developed calluses on both cheeks by this time. But unfortunately I had no such luck and the spankings often left large painful blisters and always the long red welts would be visible for days.

In the fortuitous event that nothing prematurely roused our mother from her bed, one of us would usually take her breakfast tray upstairs to her dressing table. Many mornings when I arrived to set the tray carefully on the glass-top table, Mother was across the room at the sink washing her face in ice water and then taking her two Bufferin. It wasn't until a couple of years later that I understood the significance of the Bufferin. No one looks terrific when they first get up, but my mother looked about as far away from being a movie star at this time of day as anyone could possibly imagine. Even in the summertime she wore white pajamas that were tailored like men's pajamas. She had dozens of sets of them exactly alike except that they had different colored piping around the edges and matching monograms. Under the pajama top she wore a white tee-shirt and on her feet she wore white socks. Sometimes she even wore white gloves to keep the cream on her hands during the night. She had short red hair which she kept away from the cream on her face with an elasticized headband. When she first got up her hair somehow was always standing straight up looking rather like a firecracker explosion. To top off this outfit, she had her face tied up with something called a "chin strap." Before she had breakfast she unraveled all this paraphernalia and put on a robe. I would stay a minute or two and then scurry down to lunch.

On Sunday if she got up in time we had to go to church. We would
get all dressed up and drive to the Christian Science church in Beverly
Hills. Most of the time I went to Sunday School which I hated. Not the
school itself but the whole process. Because we didn't go often enough,
I had to constantly go to the office and be reassigned to a class. I almost
never knew either the teacher or any of the other children and was usually
behind in the lessons. I liked the singing and used to wish that the rest of
it would just be over quickly. I was always given quarters for the donation
and had them securely tucked inside my white gloves. We didn't always
have to wear a hat, but I always had to wear white gloves whenever we
went anywhere. Once in a while, I was allowed to go inside the big church
and sit with my mother. I always tried to sit very still and be a good girl.
Even though I liked the big church a lot better than Sunday School, it was
very hard to sit still that long, especially since I didn't really understand
most of the big words in Mary Baker Eddy's book. The singing was always
nice and I knew most of the words to the hymns, so I enjoyed that part
and looked out the window or daydreamed through the rest of it. The
problem came on the drive home when Mother asked me the inevitable
question of "What did you learn today in church?" Try as I might, I never
quite got the whole thing straight. I could remember some of the Bible
stories, but not much from Mrs. Eddy. Mother would sigh and explain the
parts I'd left out and I would sit in silence the rest of the way home.

If we didn't go to church on Sunday for whatever reasons, after lunch
Mother would call me into her sitting room while Chris took his nap.
She would sit on the couch and I would sit on the floor and together we
would do the lesson. Christian Science had each Sunday worked out
so that you could do it at home. I always thought that was very clever.
There was a little pamphlet that told you which chapters and verses of
the Bible to read followed by which pages from Science and Health by
Mary Baker Eddy. By this time I could read adequately and Mother
would always give me some of the Bible parts to read aloud. When we
had finished with that, she would read Mrs. Eddy's words because I
couldn't yet pronounce most of them. What I remember most is the
part about God is good and there is no evil, sickness or death. But again,
I'm afraid I daydreamed through most of it.

After the lesson was over which took about an hour and a half
and she'd given me a few moments to stretch, Mother would place the

regular call to Sorkie in New York. I met Sorkie only once when I was a very small child but until her death in 1959 she was probably the most influential person in Mother's life. Sorkie was a Christian Science practitioner who lived by herself in a small apartment in New York City. Mother had met her when she was quite young herself and was devoted to Sorkie. I understand that Sorkie was a plump if not rotund woman and to the best of my knowledge she is the only fat person Mother ever tolerated.

Mother called Sorkie almost every day for nearly 25 years. Sorkie knew everything there was to know about Mother and us and Mother's friends and every event of our lives. On Sunday we called Sorkie to tell her we loved her and had done our lessons. We always had to report to Sorkie after church as well. She had a kind voice and was always pleasant to talk to. After I told her I loved her, she would speak to Mother for a while when I was not allowed in the room.

Mother could call Sorkie any time of the day or night. Sorkie was somehow always home when Mother called and would talk to her for as long as she wanted. Mother trusted her absolutely and as I look back I think she was the only person in the whole world that Mother did trust. Year after year Mother poured out her heart, her troubles and her triumphs to Sorkie and Sorkie was always there, as close as the phone. In the years to come, whenever there was trouble in the house which was progressively more frequent, Mother would be on the phone to her for advice, solace and counsel. I think Sorkie was the only person in the world that Mother felt was really there for her under any conditions and all circumstances. It was a constant sustaining influence in a turbulent unpredictable existence. Sorkie was a combination surrogate mother, spiritual leader and emotional counselor. Although Mother categorically refused to even consider any form of psychological guidance in later years, I think in many ways Sorkie provided that kind of therapy and much more.

For us kids it was often infuriating to have a voice on the phone be so overwhelmingly influential in our lives. When we got in serious fights with Mother or some other equally disastrous event had taken place we either had to speak to Sorkie who usually made us apologize to Mother or Mother herself would call Sorkie and translate what advice she had supposedly given. One way or the other, the result was usually that Mother was right and we were wrong and nothing much had changed except that Mother felt vindicated and morally justified in meeting out the punishments that always followed. I don't know if Sorkie really ever knew the entire story or not and it really doesn't matter any more one way or the other. Among her friends no one had the influence over Mother that Sorkie did and in fact I don't think most of them even knew about their relationship except that she was a Christian Science practitioner and to most people that was not a particularly specific definition. But for me Sorkie's voice over the phone was often the court of last resort. Though she was a kind lady, I'm sure, the decision was rarely in my favor.

That Mother was a Christian Scientist did not preclude us being sent to doctors nor prevent her from either smoking or drinking. Those were ideals, she explained, goals toward which one worked. However, in the meantime, one had to do what was necessary. We had regular check-ups by old Dr. Fish and when we were sick he would come to see us on house calls. Mother also had her doctors upon whom she increasingly relied as the years went by. I think it might be an oversimplification to say that later on she became a hypochondriac, but it was something very close to that.

There were times, however, when her fetish for cleanliness became a mania and took possession of her. It was then that she took three and four showers a day and brushed her teeth every few hours. She never could stand to have her hands dirty and would wash them regularly. She had one closet with shelves full of cleanliness potions for every conceivable part of her body and used them all with religious fervor. She bathed and scrubbed and brushed and douched. It never seemed to be quite sufficient, but rather just managed to keep the worst of the scourges away from her.

This same preoccupation with cleanliness permeated the house we lived in. When she wasn't working she organized regular forays into every nook and cranny of the house and yard. No sergeant in charge of latrine duty could have done any better. It was at these times when frustration or anxiety or just sheer insanity overtook her that she mustered every able-bodied creature within shouting distance of the house and pressed them into service. We were always an unlikely crew and one that fell far short of Mother's expectations. We were never fast enough nor diligent enough or tenacious enough to please her. She fired commands faster than any number of us could facilitate and that sent her into a frenzy. She was surrounded by dolts and nincompoops, dunces and malingerers. Was no one besides herself even remotely competent in this world? Was it so much to ask that literate human beings comprehend a simple order? Why was she chosen out of the multitude to suffer the indignities of inferior servants and simple-minded children? Through these exhortations and the added threat of permanent and total banishment from her presence forever she prodded her troops ever onward. Under her command three female fans, a nurse, a secretary and two small children under the age of eight accomplished miracles. Together we moved tons of books, boxes, furniture and clothes. In teams we cleaned out closets, scrubbed down and repainted lawn furniture. We moved trunks from one storage basement to another; we hauled and swept and pushed and pulled and mopped and rearranged until she was satisfied or until her own craziness had subsided, whichever came first.

CHAPTER 6

The worst of these voyages into cleanomania were what later became known between my brother and myself as the terrifying night raids.

What was so frightening about the night raids was that they could never be predicted. They sprang full blown without warning. We were always asleep and it was always dark outside when they started. Months would go by without a night raid and then there it would be startling you out of a sound sleep, running full speed ahead and already out of control.

I never did figure out what mysterious combination of external and internal events led up to Mother's volcanic behavior. To this day I still do not know. What I know is that they were the most dreaded of all the journeys she took us through.

There are three night raids that are still vividly clear in my mind and they are fairly typical of the others.

Chris and I had already moved into Mr. Terry's old room which had been totally redecorated featuring twin beds, new wallpaper and new furniture. There were sliding-door closets built into one wall of the bathroom which Chris used. My closet was a large walk-in the size of a small room which was right across from my bed nearest the door. It had it's own light and clothes rods on three sides. Shoes went on the bottom neatly lined up on the built in racks and there were shelves above. When a night raid was in progress I was awakened out of a sound sleep by a crashing sound in my closet. When I opened my eyes, sitting bolt upright in bed, I saw that the light was on and various objects were flying out of my closet. Inside the closet Mother was in a rage. She was swearing a blue streak and muttering to herself. I dared not move out of my bed for fear of her wrath being taken out on me directly rather than the contents of my closet. After my closet was totally demolished and nearly everything in was spewed out unto my bed and the floor, Mother emerged breathless and triumphant. She had a wild look to her eyes and as she descended upon me I was terrified. She grabbed me by my hair and dragged me into the closet. There before me I saw total devastation. The closet was a total shambles. It looked like she'd taken her arms and pushed everything off the shelves. Then she'd ripped the clothes off their hangers and thrown both clothes and hangers out into the room where they lay strewn over half the floor. Last to go were the shoes which she'd taken up and thrown hard enough to hit the far wall of the bedroom clattering against the Venetian blinds as they fell.

Shaking me by the hair of my head she screamed in my ear, "No wire hangers! No wire hangers!" With one hand she pulled me by the hair and with the other she cuffed my ears until they rang and I could hardly hear her screaming. When she finished cuffing me she released my hair and dumped me on the floor. Then she would rip my bed apart down to the mattress cover, throwing the sheets and blankets across the room. When she had totally destroyed my entire part of the bedroom she stood in the doorway with her hands on her hips, "Clean up your mess," she growled turning on her heel. The only other sound I heard was the double doors to her room slamming shut.

Had I bothered to look at the clock I would have seen that it was well past midnight. I didn't make the effort anymore because it was a useless waste of my strength. I did look to see if Chris was still alive in the next bed. Once he was sure that she was gone and not going to come back he turned his body slowly to face me. It was probably the first time he'd dared to stir since the beginning of the night raid. He couldn't get up because he was tied down to the bed. Mother had a barbarian devise she called a sleep safe with which she made sure Chris could not get out of bed. It was like a harness which was made out of heavy canvas tapes and it fastened in the back. It was originally designed to keep babies from falling out of bed but Mother had the thing modified to accommodate a growing boy. The way it worked was that the person lay face down upon the sheet and the straps came around the middle and across the shoulders and all four pieces were fastened together with a huge steel safety pin like they use for horse blankets. From the time I can remember, we were forbidden to get out of bed at night to go to the bathroom or get a drink of water. However, there were times when Chris simply had to go to the bathroom and I would undo the wretched sleep safe and stand guard while he raced to the bathroom and jumped back into bed. We had it timed as well as an Indianapolis pit stop. Both of our lives depended on expert teamwork. I would have gotten in more trouble than Chris if we'd ever been discovered and we both knew it. He would have gotten beaten for getting out of bed, but I would have been nearly killed for letting him out of the sleep safe.

This particular night raid he had escaped scot-free and I didn't begrudge him that. He couldn't get up to comfort me and didn't even dare whisper for fear Mother somehow would hear us and return. He looked at me sadly and through my tears I stared back at him. My head hurt where she had grabbed my hair and as I gingerly rubbed it a few snatches of hair actually fell out. But the frightful ringing in my ears was beginning to subside and I was grateful for that at least. Slowly I pulled myself to my feet and surveyed the damage. All this, I thought, for a couple of lousy wire hangers. Evidently what had happened is that something had come back from the cleaners or the laundry downstairs on wire hangers. They were forbidden in our closets and although I knew that in advance, I hadn't changed them right away. I guess it hadn't seemed terribly important at the time which at the present moment I found very unfortunate.

It took me hours to redo the closet with everything neatly folded and put back on the shelves, all the clothes returned to their proper hangers. I then blearily mated up the shoes and lined them neatly on the rack. Just as I turned out the closet light I remembered that my bed still had to be remade and seriously thought about just sleeping on the floor. But there was still the possibility that Mother might return and I dared not chance a repeat performance. Chris had fallen asleep hours before. As I struggled to remake my bed in near exhaustion I realized that it was beginning to get light.

The day after one of the night raids, all was ominously silent. I don't know if the servants knew about them and simply kept their doors locked or if our room was far enough away that the sound didn't carry to the other side of the house. Generally Mother didn't speak a word to me for several days after a raid and in fact I rarely saw her. I was sort of silently banished for a period of time and then as mysteriously as it had materialized, the situation disappeared and life returned to near normal.

There was one night raid the whole house heard because it took place in Mother's dressing room with all the doors open and lasted for a long time.

As a punishment for some infringement of the rules now long forgotten, Mother had decreed that while she was out for the day I had to clean her dressing room. It was a large room with mirrored walls over the sink at one end of the room and the glass top dressing table built into the other. The floor was blue linoleum of some kind and there were two white throw rugs. So during the better part of the afternoon I had cleaned the large mirrors, polished the dressing table and scoured the sink. Then I had to scrub the floor with a mop and dry it on my hands and knees with an old torn bath towel so it wouldn't streak. Both the nurse and I were satisfied that I'd really done a good job even though I wasn't more than nine years old. It had been one of the hardest jobs I'd been given to do alone and I was glad it was over. I didn't get to play at all that day but at least the punishment was over.

However, I was not destined to get off so easy. In the middle of that night one of the most vicious night raids took place.

As usual I was sound asleep when Mother burst into the room. She was already yelling as she hauled me out of bed. Before I was fully awake she had dragged me by one arm down the hallway that connected her suite of rooms with ours. Through the open double doors I stumbled as she shoved me ahead of her. I had no idea what was wrong or where we were going but I was now wide awake. When we arrived in her dressing room it began to dawn on me what was happening. Something was wrong with the way I'd cleaned the room earlier in the day, even though the nurse had inspected all my work and told me it was perfectly satisfactory. The best I could gather from Mother's ranting and raving was that the floor had streaks in it. I couldn't see anything wrong with it, but then neither I nor anyone else seemed to have the same set of standards as she did. Then I made one of my classic mistakes and said that I didn't see anything wrong with the floor. That sent her into a renewed fit of anger. With lightning speed she backhanded me squarely across the face which caught me off balance and sent me to the floor. She then threw open the door under the sink and grabbed the large can of Bon Ami scouring powder. Just as I got to my feet she flew at me in a frenzy, wielding the can of Bon Ami like a baseball bat. She beat me over the head with the Bon Ami until the can burst open with a small explosion. A cloud of white scouring powder filled the entire room settling over every square inch of mirror and glass and linoleum. I had that powder in my hair and all over my nightgown. It was getting into my mouth and I sputtered and spit it out for fear it would poison me. She was still screaming and beating me with the mutilated can. But this time I know I was yelling back at her to stop and the noise must have awakened everyone. When finally she threw the useless container across the room in total disgust it looked like there had just been a snowstorm inside these four walls. "Clean it up" was all she said. "How?" I asked. "You figure it out," she stormed and left me. I sat down and puffs of the white powder billowed up around me.

I can't even begin to describe the terrible mess that faced me. I couldn't use a vacuum cleaner because in those days all we had was one of the old-fashioned uprights that were only good for carpets. All I had was a broom and a bucket, a couple of big towels and a mop. I had to go over everything in that room four or five times because the powder made a white film as soon as it got wet and there was an entire can of it scattered around the room. It was tedious and torturous work. Before I could even begin I had to wash my own face and neck. The powder stuck to my body and as I sweated with the work, little rivulets of perspiration coagulated with the powder in white patches that began to itch after a while. There was no time to go and take a shower so I just continued to try to clean up this unbelievable mess.

Throughout the whole night I worked and sobbed. I didn't even care if anyone heard me as I trudged through the process again and again trying to get the damnable white powder cleaned up. I prayed to God to punish my mother and told anyone who would listen how much I hated her.

Somewhere around 4:30 in the morning I decided I would work no longer. I didn't care if she punished me again, I just couldn't do any better. If it wasn't perfect, I couldn't help it. I was only nine years old and I couldn't do any more. I was only nine years old and I truly wished that the earth would open and just swallow me up and take me out of this eternal misery and punishment. I sobbed as I wrung out the mop for the hundredth time and I sobbed as I emptied the dirty water in the bucket. I sobbed as I walked to my room and I was still crying in the warm shower. It was nearly 5 o'clock in the morning when I wearily climbed back into bed and still the tears were streaming down. Finally I just gave up fighting and cried myself to sleep.

There was one kind of night raid, however, that was not directed at me personally and was not intended as a punishment for any of us. This particular night raid was Mother's alone although we all participated.

It was summertime and the evenings were cool in Brentwood. This night the moon was nearly full and shone brightly over the garden. Somewhere near midnight I was roused out of my bed by the nurse. She whispered for me to put on my robe and slippers immediately and come downstairs. I looked at her face to try and discern what was going on but she just looked tired and agitated. Quickly I followed her instructions and together we hurried down the stairs and she led me out into the yard. Once outside I heard some noise over by the rose garden and could see a couple of people scurrying around.

We had a most wonderful rose garden. It was one of those old-fashioned formal gardens with stepping stones through it and each plant labeled carefully. The roses it produced filled our house with lovely fragrant bouquets most of the year. It covered an area approximately fifteen-by-fifteen-feet and had dozens of different varieties. Since it was summer, the entire garden was in bloom and even in the dark the fragrance filled that part of the yard.

Nurse and I proceeded in the direction of the rose garden. As we came closer I saw Mother and the cook already in the middle of the rose garden. I didn't see particularly well in the dark and even with the extra light from the moon it wasn't until I was standing right at the hedge that separated the rose garden from the lawn that I fully realized what was going on.

Mother had a pair of large pruning sheers with which she was systematically cutting each and every rose bush to the ground! The garden was in full bloom and some of the bushes were over three feet tall. Most of them had great big flowers on them and as the branches fell to the ground the lovely roses were getting trampled underfoot. I was horrified. I started to say something but the nurse quickly clamped her hand over my mouth. Since Mother's back was to us, she didn't see what had happened. She was finishing with one of the bushes which was now not more than a stubby knob sticking a few inches out of the ground. As she straightened up in preparation for a fresh assault on a neighboring bush, she saw me. As the moonlight lit up part of her face I could see that look in her eyes again. It was a haunted, excited look and there was no use trying to talk to her or stop her from completing her current course of destruction. "I want all these branches cleared out of here," she commanded with a sweeping gesture.

I was grateful that my thin summer robe, at least, had long sleeves because there were large thorns on most of the bushes and we had no gloves and no wheelbarrow or tools with which to work. I don't know how long the poor cook had been out here with Mother but the woman looked to be on the verge of tears. She was a plump middle-aged lady who kept to herself and usually got along with Mother. The only trouble she'd had with Mother is when Mother threw out everything in the entire refrigerator during the cook's day off. When the cook returned, Mother informed her that the refrigerator had been a mess and she didn't want to find it that way again. Cook later told me that Mother had thrown out half a roast beef, a new ham and all the fruit and vegetables as well as the leftovers which cook usually saved for the laundress and the cleaning ladies' lunches. Cook was furious at the waste and what she considered an invasion into her domain. She was a fine cook and she took great pride in running an efficient kitchen. But it was Mother's house and she could do whatever she wanted.

So plump little cook trudged back and forth with armloads of stickery rose branches along with the nurse and myself. We worked in absolute silence punctuated only by Mother's muttering to herself and an occasional order to speed things up.

After about an hour of this thorny work, we were all scratched and bleeding. Mother wouldn't let us stop until we were finished so I licked the wounds on my arms and wiped my hands on my robe. We were all a bloody mess in a very short period of time, but the job wasn't finished.

When Mother had finally succeeded in cutting every last rose bush right down to the ground and the last branch had been hauled away, I thought we would be able to go back to bed. So did the cook and the nurse, I'm sure. But there was one last surprise in store for us. Mother told me to go down into the gardener's tool room by the incinerator and get the big saw. Totally mystified, I simply did what I was told and returned in a few minutes with the largest saw I could find down there. I handed it to Mother without saying a word. Talking to her when she was in these moods was equivalent to asking for a beating and I had learned to keep my mouth shut and just try to get through the ordeals as quietly and unobtrusively as humanly possible.

Mother walked over to the orange tree which stood at one end of the now mutilated rose garden. It was a mature tree standing maybe eight feet tall, producing lots of oranges.

The nurse, the cook and I stood at a kind of incredulous attention watching Mother as she proceeded to saw the trunk of the orange tree. We must have stood motionless like that for a half an hour as Mother huffed and puffed and sawed away at the poor tree. Finally we heard a cracking, splintering sound and the orange tree toppled over into the stubby remains of the rose garden.

Mother stood back to survey her night's destruction. Apparently satisfied, she ordered us all back to bed.

Without a word we dispersed like shadows in the night. I climbed back into my bed without bothering to even wash. The blood had coagulated by now and wouldn't get my sheets dirty, so I could wait for the clean up until morning.

The next day after breakfast I took Chris and we went to look at what had happened the night before. In the bright sunlight it really looked hideous. The beautiful rose garden that our Japanese gardener had planted years ago and Les, our gardener had labored over so lovingly, was totally destroyed. I didn't know enough about plants to know if it would ever grow back but it looked ugly and sad right now. The fallen orange tree was not completely severed and sort of dangled by its partially sawed off trunk. Chris couldn't believe his eyes, but we all had the scratches to prove the story. The cook and the nurse were particularly quiet that day.

When the gardener, Les, showed up for work that day he went past the kitchen window as usual with his cheery "Good Morning." It was only a moment later that the devastated rose garden came into his view. We waited with bated breath for his reaction since no one had the heart to tell him in advance, no one knew exactly what to say. Mother was still asleep and the whispering rule, as usual, was in effect. But Les didn't whisper when he saw the rose garden. He let out a graphic string of swear words that rang out loud and clear in the early morning air. As he stomped past the kitchen window again on his way out to his truck, he shouted so the entire neighborhood could hear "You can tell that crazy woman I quit!" That, unfortunately, was the last we ever saw of Les, the gardener.

CHAPTER 7

I don't have any pictures of Grandmother, but I can remember her vividly. Her name was Anna and she was a small woman with brown hair, sparkly eyes and a soft voice. She spoke with only a hint of a Southwest accent. She wore simple dark cotton dresses and black shoes. Mother didn't like the way she dressed. She said it was depressing to see those dark dresses with the little flowers or polka dots.

Grandmother could do everything. She made wonderful pickles and relish, jams and jellies. She also crocheted and made wonderful simply delicious pies and cakes. Whenever she would come to visit us she always brought our favorites: chocolate pie for my brother and banana cake for me. To this day I can remember how that banana cake tasted. In between the layers of cake there were layers of thin sliced bananas and some kind of filling but never any frosting. No one else much cared about the banana cake so I had it to myself. For Chris she would always have the most scrumptious chocolate pie. He would have eaten the whole thing by himself, but he always had to offer some to everyone else. Those were our particular special treats, something just for us from Grandmama. She always seemed so pleased with our squeals of delight each time the shower of our hugs and kisses fell upon her.

Twice Mother took us to visit her. She lived in a small house in a quiet street and had a beautiful garden. It was like pictures of English gardens with things very close together and flowers tumbling over everywhere. There were little paths through the flower beds and the vegetable garden where she grew the pickle cucumbers and tomatoes for the relishes she brought to us so faithfully.

I liked Grandmother's little house. It was warm and old-fashioned and looked like a grandmother's house. She seemed happy there too and I always wished I could stay with her overnight.

One time Mother got Grandmother a new car. It was delivered to her house and she was very surprised. When she came to visit us on Sunday, we all went out to the driveway to look at it. It was a regular two-door sedan with the big running boards and it was shiny black. Grandmother thanked Mommie (she called her Lucille) as we ran around examining the new car. I think Grandmother must have said something about it being so black because Mommie got one of those storm cloud looks on her face. We all went inside and Grandmother left soon after.

Curiously enough, I don't remember having any meals with Grandmother. She would come over in the afternoon and stay about an hour and then leave. I don't think she was ever asked to stay any longer. Most of the time she was just with Chris and me. We would sit in the big kitchen and tell her our jokes and stories and she would ask us about school. The big craze then was riddles and poor Grandmother must have heard each of them a hundred times . . . first from me and then from Chris.

For Christmas and birthdays Grandmother would make us things. One of her specialties was crocheting covers for wooden hangers. When we were little, she cut the hangers to fit the size of our clothes. Do you know that during the entire time we were growing up, we *never* had even one plain wooden or wire hanger in any clothes closet in the entire house? Grandmother must have made literally thousands of those hangers since they were for all our clothes as well as Mother's.

I realized not too long ago that I didn't have any pictures of us with Grandmother. I was really sad about that. But when we were little I didn't think about it even though we were constantly being photographed for different magazines and publicity stories.

I don't even think there was a picture of Grandmother in the house. I can't remember Mother having one either. Grandmother's visits were usually confined to the kitchen when no one else was there. She was never at any of our birthday parties, nor Thanksgiving nor Christmas. She was never invited to have dinner with us that I can remember nor did she ever spend a whole day with us kids in the backyard. I know that in all the time that I was at home she never once swam in the pool.

I really don't know what happened between them, but the time came when Grandmother was not allowed in the house at all, not even in the kitchen. She didn't come to visit for a while and we asked if she was sick. Mother didn't want to talk about it but she said Grandmother was ungrateful for everything Mother did for her . . . after all, she supported her and gave her a car . . . what more did she want . . . there was no pleasing Grandmother . . . all she knew how to do was take and take.

Chris and I were very sad. We loved Grandmother and always looked forward to seeing her . . . not just for the cakes and pies either. She was fun for us. She was always loving and would give us big hugs. She was little and not much taller than we were and she used to tease us about how fast we were growing.

The last couple of times I saw Grandmother, it was through the back screen door. She was not allowed into the house and we had to talk to her through the door. She handed the chocolate pie and the banana cake to us and we tried to be cheerful always, but we three had tears in our eyes. She didn't stay very long but we did sneak the screen door open quietly so it wouldn't squeak and we each hugged her. Both of us gave her a big kiss and whispered "Goodbye Grandmama." We closed the screen door very carefully without making a sound. Grandmother didn't come to visit us any more.

Over the years that followed, I tried to keep in touch with her. I wrote her little cards and called her from my different boarding schools. When I went to New York I would write her and she'd send me little notes and some hangers with the crocheted covers and little handmade sachets. I had a friend in Los Angeles who would go to see her at least once a month and make sure she was all right. She was the one who sent me the telegram that Grandmother had died.

When Anna B. LeSueur (or Crawford, as she later called herself) was dying, her doctors called Mother in New York to tell her that Grandmother was very ill and was calling for her daughter. The doctors put Grandmother in the hospital in Los Angeles and a few days later called Mother again to tell her that they did not expect Grandmother to live very much longer and that she kept calling for "Lucille."

Grandmother died in August 1958 without ever seeing her Lucille again. Mother had been too busy to leave New York, but she and Daddy (Al Steele) did fly to Los Angeles to make the funeral arrangements at Forest Lawn.

My cousin Joan and I spoke to one another on the phone. We were not terribly close but we both lived in New York at that time and we saw one another occasionally. Neither of us had the money to go to the funeral and we were both heartsick. Joan's father, Uncle Hal, was Anna LeSueur's son and so she was Joan's grandmother, too. My friend in Los Angeles told me where Grandmother was being buried. It was she who had told me about the doctors calling. She had visited with Grandmother until she had been taken to the hospital.

I don't think my mother ever forgave Grandmother for the early days of poverty and for not providing a father. I don't think she ever forgave Grandmother for hoping that Uncle Hal, the eldest and the son, would fulfill the promise of the family and get them out of their dismal circumstances. Mother told me only one story about Grandmother and Hal. The story was that when they were very poor and living in the back of a laundry when Mother was a little girl, Grandmother thought the sun rose and set on Hal. Indeed, from the one picture I've even seen of them as children, he was a handsome boy and later he grew to be a handsome man, tall with large expressive eyes and the same strong bone structure as Mother had. According to the story, Grandmother used to divide up the bread between son and daughter: the inside portion went to Hal and the crusts to Mother. Mother said that Hal always got the best and she got the leftovers. That's what Mother told me.

Curiously enough, in all the years of my growing up I never saw Mother eat anything but the crusts of the bread. At breakfast she would cut them off and wrap a piece of bacon around them. It always looked delicious the way she did it. She always laughed and said it was one way she stayed on her diet. She never ate a sandwich. She would put the meat on a lettuce leaf with some mayonnaise and eat it that way.

Uncle Hal came to Hollywood before Mother did. He was good looking and people say he was a charmer. He started getting bit parts in movies and was beginning to work fairly regularly by the time Mother arrived. Most people don't remember that anymore and she never mentioned it at all. Uncle Hal's career never really went anywhere, but Mother became a star. I've heard rumors that she wouldn't help him later on even though he had introduced her around when she was a newcomer. Uncle Hal became an alcoholic.

There was a terrible scene in the dining room one night when Mother was having a small dinner party and Uncle Hal arrived in what appeared to be a rather desperate frame of mind. Mother said he was drunk and for him to leave immediately or she'd call the police. She said she'd given him all the help she was going to and that all he ever wanted was more money. Uncle Hal was crying and pleading with her . . . he called her Lucille, too. She ordered me out of the room and I skittered around the table and through one of the dining room doors, scared by all the name calling and the sight of Uncle Hal crying. I don't know if he was really drunk but I remember that he looked terribly upset and kept saying she'd ruined his career.

I never saw Uncle Hal again after that night. I heard Mother say to someone on the phone once that Hal was in a sanatorium. She often called him a drunk, said he was weak and couldn't manage his own life. Then he was just gone . . . no mention of him ever again.

Not that he'd ever been a regular visitor or that we had any close relationship with him at all, but I used to wonder what happened to him.[7]

A number of years later when I was finishing high school I heard that he had gotten a job in a sporting goods store and that he'd been sober for some time. He liked to go fishing and the job seemed to be good for him. I think he was living with Grandmother then. I think Mother was furious with Grandmother for helping Hal.

One of the last letters I got from Grandmother included regards from Uncle Hal. Although I had spoken with Grandmother recently, she and I did not talk about him. She didn't bring the subject up and neither did I. But my friend in Los Angeles saw them both and told me they were doing fine.

It was after I'd moved back to California in the early sixties that I heard Uncle Hal had died. He was all alone then, living in a downtown hotel and working as a night clerk.

---

7   Later I learned the truth. Hal needed to borrow money. Mother told him to come to the house at an appointed hour one evening and she would lend to him one last time, making him promise never to ask her again. He promised and the time was set.

When Hal arrived that night, so did the police and attendants from a mental hospital. Mother accused Hal of threatening her and being drunk. The police arrested him and the hospital attendants took him away in a straight jacket.

I was there that night and heard it all. Mother had her brother, Hal, committed for three years without his consent just to get rid of him bothering her or being around.

Uncle Hal and Grandmother . . . I've often thought they were made to pay a terrible price for the early years of poverty they shared in common with Mother. I think they represented only pain for her and I think she was ashamed of them. Sometimes I used to think she must have hated them.

CHAPTER 8

During the years I was growing up at 426 North Bristol, I came to depend rather heavily on the servants for some sense of continuity and for most of my everyday learning. The central person in my life on a daily basis was my nurse. A good deal of my happiness revolved around whomever that happened to be. When I was just a baby I had my Aunt Kitty. Several days before my fourth birthday a Scottish lady named Anne Howe came to take care of my infant brother and myself. Mrs. Howe was married and didn't live with us but would leave in the evening after we were put to bed. It was Mrs. Howe who taught me to skip rope and how to ride my bicycle. She played "tea party" with me which was one of my favorite games. I would make dreadful concoctions out of sand and seeds and olive pits I found out in the yard and set a little table with my play tea set. Then she would be Mrs. Smith and I'd pretend to be Mrs. Jones and we'd sit around and gossip. I loved pretend games and could play them for hours, sometimes alternating between two and three characters at a time. Mrs. Howe had a hard time teaching me any patience because I usually wanted to have the game go my way. She also had a devil of a time teaching me to ride my bike because when I fell off time after time, I'd get mad and cry and vow I'd never touch it again. But her persistence eventually paid off and I learned most of the normal child's skills. I was stubborn but Mrs. Howe was wonderfully tenacious and we had a good time together even though she made me mind her and stick to all the rules. She may have been firm with me but she always was honest and fair. It was Mrs. Howe who helped me through one of the first really serious punishments of my young life.

I had to take a nap every afternoon and sometimes I just wasn't very sleepy. Often I would lie awake in my bed and tell myself stories I made up that had elaborate plots and lots of running characters constructed from books that had been read to me and records I'd listened to. On this particular day I wasn't falling asleep and I was bored. I was about five and sharing my room with my brother who was only two and still pretty much of a baby. My bed was up against the wall on one side and as I daydreamed I ran my finger over a seam in the wallpaper tracing the design.

Without much real thought on my part I picked at the loose seam as I followed my daydreams on their private journey. Before I knew it, several little pieces of the wallpaper had fallen away leaving a rather obvious blank spot in the wall. All of a sudden I realized what I had done and tried to retrieve the little pieces of paper and patch up the spot with the paper attempting to stick them back on the wall with some spit. Needless to say, it didn't work. Worse still, where the wallpaper had gotten wet there were smudge marks so the whole thing looked even more obvious than if I'd left it alone.

At about this time Mrs. Howe came in to get me up. When she saw what I'd done she slapped my hands and scolded me. She said she'd have to tell my mother about it. I cried briefly and then went out to play promptly forgetting all about it.

When my mother came home, Mrs. Howe did tell her and Mother went straight to my room to see the damage for herself. Right then and there she put me over her knee and spanked the daylights out of me. I really cried now. Mommie's spankings hurt.

But that was not to be the end of it. She was determined to teach me a lesson that no amount of spankings could accomplish.

She marched herself into my dressing room and slid open the closet door. She reached inside the closet and withdrew my most favorite dress. It wasn't the fanciest dress in my wardrobe nor the most expensive, but it was far and away my favorite and she knew it. It was a little yellow dress with white eyelet embroidery and it looked like a spring daffodil.

Mommie held it up ominously. She took it off the hanger and went to a drawer where the scissors were kept. I looked at Mrs. Howe who was in the room with me, but she appeared to be as mystified as I was.

When my eyes returned to my mother who was standing way across the room, I was horrified. Mommie had taken the scissors and completely shredded my favorite yellow dress! It was hanging in tatters with just barely enough left to indicate it had been a dress and not an old rag. Tears sprang to my eyes and I started to cry.

Then as she marched toward me holding the tattered dress in front of her, the sound of her voice stopped my tears. She told me that I was going to have to *wear* that shredded thing for *one week*. If anyone asked me why I was wearing a torn dress, I was to reply, "I don't know how to take care of pretty things." With that pronouncement, she dropped the dress at my feet and left.

Mrs. Howe and I were both stunned. Finally it was Mrs. Howe who made the first move. She helped me change into what was left of my poor yellow dress.

That week seemed interminable. I cried most of the time and kept to myself. I was mortified and tried to become invisible. Mercifully none of the servants ever mentioned the dress and in fact tried to behave as though there was absolutely nothing amiss.

The one humiliating time I had to go downstairs and see company they were just a few old friends that I'd seen a lot and I simply stared at the floor and tried to get through it as fast as possible. My mother's brief explanation regarding my rather shocking appearance was that she was teaching me a lesson. When I was dismissed, I scampered away and returned to the safety of my room. Within a few days the dress started to get soiled. I thought maybe then it would be washed and I wouldn't have to wear it for a while. But that did not happen. I wore that dress every day . . . all day . . . for one solid week. As the days went by it got dirtier and dirtier until it was nothing but a filthy rag. The material had raveled and there wasn't much left to cover me. You could hardly tell that it had been yellow. As I lived through the disintegration of my most favorite dress and the humiliation of looking like a street urchin, I wondered if I wouldn't have been better off in the orphanage. Mother seemed totally oblivious to my pain and humiliation. In fact, no one seemed to recognize what I was going through. No one comforted me and indeed no one seemed to want to even talk to me. I felt like a total outcast, my sins and transgressions too serious to be mentioned. By the end of the week what I'd originally done was totally overshadowed by this hideous, lingering, living punishment. At the end of the seventh day, after I had taken my bath and gotten into my nightclothes, I marched myself down to the incinerator and threw the filthy ragged remains of what had been my favorite yellow dress into the coals and watched as it disintegrated into the soft gray ashes.

I didn't find out until years later that Mrs. Howe had told the rest of the help what had happened. They'd all agreed not to ask me about the dress so I wouldn't ever have to give the answer Mrs. Howe heard my mother prepare for me.

CHAPTER 9

The first real steady boyfriend Mother had after Mr. Terry left was Uncle Greg. He was a boisterous, fun loving man that I thought was the most handsome and dashing man alive. He was very good to us and always took the time to be attentive. At Christmas and birthdays his presents were perfect, showing thought and taste. When he and Mother had been going together for some time I asked him privately once if he was going to be our next daddy. Though somewhat taken aback, he leaned down to me and said he didn't know about that but he was evidently touched that I had asked. I noticed that he had tears in his eyes but didn't understand exactly why. I grew to love Uncle Greg and used to look forward to the days when he came to take Mother out.

There was only one part of their relationship that scared the daylights out of me. They used to have terrible fights late at night. My bedroom door was always left open and the light in the hallway was always left on. More than once I woke up with the sound of very loud voices downstairs. Then Mother would come running up the stairs and into her room, locking the door behind her. Uncle Greg pounded on the door swearing at her. She yelled back but I couldn't hear what she said very clearly. He continued to kick and yell until finally she opened the door and the fight continued in her room. While Uncle Greg was pounding and kicking at the door, I would lie totally still, afraid to move a muscle. I didn't know exactly what was going on, but it went on regularly. I was scared because I hated screaming and yelling and kicking and pounding. I wasn't scared for Mother because she never seemed to look like she'd been hurt the next day and she kept on seeing Uncle Greg. A couple of times I thought about hiding under my bed but then I remembered how much trouble I'd be in if Mother ever found out, so I just pulled the covers over my head and waited out the battle, hoping no one would think about me.

One fight they had was a corker. After all the shouting and pounding at the bedroom door and the fight in her bedroom, which was the usual routine, I heard Mother climb into the outdoor balcony that connected her suite of rooms with a door to my room. She was yelling something about calling the police and he was calling her dirty names. The whole neighborhood must have been informed about this lovers' quarrel at this point. I don't remember the details at this point but they used every four letter word ever invented. Uncle Greg followed her out the balcony whereupon she climbed up to the roof! At this point Uncle Greg must have thought better about the entire affair because he called her a few choice names and then left—through *my* bedroom door. The next thing I heard was the sound of his Cadillac peeling out of the driveway and down the street. Mother eventually managed to get down off the roof but I heard a lot of clattering and swearing in the process. Uncle Greg didn't come back for days during which I heard Mother telling her friends some very unkind things about this eligible bachelor and well-known man about town. She even said she was damn sorry she'd bought him all those presents and mentioned some suits and jewelry. But eventually Uncle Greg returned and in front of me they acted just as though nothing had ever happened. I never dared mention to Mother that I heard all these fights and she never acted as though I knew, which I always thought was positively weird. I mean, how could I help hear them when they took place right outside my open door? It didn't really matter though, because I still adored Uncle Greg. Years later when I heard he was going with another movie star I knew that Mother's blood must be boiling.

Mother had other dates as well. No matter what time they were supposed to pick her up she was never ready. She would be up in her dressing room with just her underwear and makeup on when the doorbell rang. It was my job to go downstairs and greet the date, fix him a drink and depending on my instructions, either bring him upstairs or sit in the bar and talk to him. Even though I was not yet ten years old I'd had a good deal of practice being a bartender and could make most of the ordinary mixed drinks. In fact I took a sort of secret delight in making drinks just a little too strong at parties just to see what would happen to the adults within a short time. Usually they got drunk.

So when I asked the date of the evening what he'd like to drink, if he was new he seemed surprised but if he was one of the regulars he told me not to make it as strong as the last time. I never paid any attention to his instructions even though I smiled charmingly and vowed to follow his wishes.

One night the doorbell rang and Mother told me to go down and answer the door. The man's name sounded like Brenner and I'd never met him before.

I skipped down the stairs, knowing the entire routine by heart. I opened the door and gasped. Some bald-headed gypsy man wearing yellow satin pantaloons, sandals and nothing else was standing at our front door. Except for a necklace, he was naked from the waist up. I slammed the door in his face, locked it and dashed upstairs to tell Mother to call the police immediately! Instead of being upset she asked me to calm down and tried to explain that the man at the door was Yul Brynner and he was making a picture called the *King and I* and he must have come from the studio in his costume. I stared at her and thought: the fights with Uncle Greg are one thing but a half naked, bald-headed gypsy man at the front door that I'm supposed to fix a drink for and be nice to is something else altogether.

Against all my protestations, I found myself headed downstairs for the front door again. I tried to be polite to Mr. Brynner but it was very embarrassing for me. I fixed him a whopper of a drink and left the room immediately.

I didn't mind so much that Mother wasn't ready when it was friends like Uncle Willie and Uncle Jimmy (William Haines and Jimmy Shields). They were wonderful good sports and always filled with jokes. Uncle Willie had been a big movie star in the silent film days and he'd done a couple of pictures with Mother when she was first starting out at Metro. The studio had given Uncle Willie an ultimatum, however, and Uncle Willie had to choose between his career and his relationship with Uncle Jimmy. Uncle Willie left pictures and became an enormously successful interior decorator. (It would be years before I understood the meaning of homosexual.) He and Mother were great buddies. He called her "Cranberry" and she would laugh. It was some old joke about how much she hated the name MGM won for her in the magazine contest. Uncle Willie had a very cutting sense of humor and I always enjoyed sitting with the three of them and listening to the gossip.

My Uncle Butch (Caesar Romero) was the same. He would take Mother to parties and they'd go dancing together. Uncle Butch was a tall, dark-haired, handsome man that Mother had met originally in New York when they were all in a Broadway musical chorus together. We all adored Uncle Butch. He was like a brother to my mother and like a member of the family to us.

Somehow it was okay for these men to see my mother getting dressed because they were such old friends and really like members of the family. But the others, the dates we didn't know very well, that was uncomfortable. Mother would have her underwear on and a light robe wrapped around her. Then as she and her date sat and talked over a drink she'd put on her stockings. I always tried to find other things to do about that time.

After a while I began to tire of this constant parade of "uncles." It got to be that everywhere we went, there we'd find another "uncle" appear out of nowhere. When we went on a vacation to Camel or to Alisal Ranch . . . Surprise! There was an "uncle" waiting for us. Supposedly this always came as an unexpected bonus but I couldn't believe in *that* much coincidence after a while.

Once on what was called a family vacation, Mother left my two sisters and myself to fend off reporters in a San Jose motel while she drove to San Francisco to see someone, and she left no instructions except not to let anyone into the rooms. I didn't know how to contact her in case of emergency. The girls were about three years old and I was eleven. I didn't know what the hell to say to the reporters who showed up rather mysteriously so I just said that we were on our way to Portland to meet some friends (which was true). That particular trip was really a zoo because we met one "uncle" (lover) in Carmel and a different "uncle" in San Jose and yet another different "uncle" in San Francisco. I don't think any of them knew about the others. I felt that the twins and I were merely a camouflage for all the other activity in which she engaged. I was treated like the maid or a secretary as I took messages, washed clothes and packed endless suitcases every time we moved.

Finally I put my foot down. I refused to call any more of these latter-day Don Juan's "uncle." It would be "Mr." from here on in unless I particularly like them or they lasted more than a couple of months. There was something about looking into the eyes of a perfect stranger who couldn't care less about me and having to smile and say "uncle" that I couldn't bear any longer. It was all so shoddy and such a sham. The caliber of dates and escorts seemed to me to have declined steadily and it appeared that Mother was getting desperate when I noticed that some of the men were from the East Coast or the Midwest and couldn't even speak proper English. Mother had always been such a stickler for good grammar and proper pronunciation that I was a little shocked with the "deese, dems and dosser's" that had started hanging around of late. I didn't like them and I certainly didn't want to call them uncle. They were not my uncles and I was no longer going to call them that. Mother was furious with me, but nothing she did made me change my mind and finally she gave up. As long as I was polite to each and every one of them, she never said another word about the uncle business. I don't think she really liked these men very much either because she said dreadful things about them after they left, even though she always kept the jewelry they gave her.

After the dark-haired Eastern types vanished from the scene, Mother seemed to stick with her directors as dates and lovers for the next few years.

Years after the event itself, Mother said that receiving the Academy Award for her performance in *Mildred Pierce* marked the end of her Hollywood. I thought that was a curious statement particularly in retrospect. But the more I thought about it, some of what she may have meant began to take shape. The seventeen years she spent at Metro were not only the Golden Age of Hollywood but the golden years of her own career. She climbed the ladder to stardom rapidly and rode the crest of fame with a joy and a dedication unmatched by most other stars. She loved being "the Star" and she devoted all of her considerable energies to the perpetuation and nurturance of her career. She had to battle every inch of the way, but for the majority of her career she had won more of these battles than she lost. Then with the departure of her mentor, Louis B. Mayer, and the beginning of world war, major changes began to take place over which she had no control. I think she felt that her studio family had deserted her and a lonely bitterness began to seep through the entire fabric of her life. Willingly and happily she had traded Lucille LeSueur for Joan Crawford and become the creation of the publicity department. Now they had abandoned their publicly-spawned offspring for the younger stars. Joan Crawford was on her own for the first time in her adult life. This feeling of abandonment must have signaled a return of all the old fears and a lot of the old pain of her childhood.

Signing a contract with Warner Brothers, she not only took less money, she knew she was taking second best. Metro was "the" studio and everyone knew it. Warner's roster of stars couldn't compare with MGM's nor did the caliber of the films they turned out. It was a come-down, the beginning of the long descent she battled for the rest of her life. She was already beginning to feel old and cast-off, though she was only in her mid-thirties at the time. By all rights she should have just begun to come into her own as an actress, but instead she found herself out of work, cruelly labeled "box office poison" and in the position of having to make a "come-back." In those days as now, come-back really implied having already failed. For her, failure was the worst indictment of all. Hadn't she devoted her entire being to the pursuit of stardom? Hadn't she sacrificed her personal life and three marriages to her career? Hadn't she made every major decision and most minor ones in favor of her work over everything else? And this was what she got in return . . . "box office poison." Her big house was mortgaged to the hilt and practically shut down to four rooms. Yet she had still held out for something worthwhile, a picture that would be worthy of her stardom again.

She won that battle in the eyes of the world, the press and the studios by capturing the Academy Award but privately she knew it was a victory of enormous irony.

Years before when she had been on the board of the Academy, she'd had a fight with them over their policy of allocating the awards. She told me that the awards were more of a dole and a reward to the studios rather than a fair vote of the members on the basis of merit. The policy was to rotate the awards from year to year so that no studio would win in the same category two years in succession. She strongly objected to that procedure particularly on behalf of the actors. It meant that no matter how brilliant someone's performance was, if a star at the same studio had won the award the year before, no one at the same studio had a chance the next year. She lost her fight with the Academy and walked out, vowing that if she was ever nominated and won the Oscar she wouldn't be there to accept it.

The irony was that in 1946 when she was nominated for *Mildred Pierce*, the first picture (except a walk-through in *Hollywood Canteen*) she'd done in three years, she was at home in bed with pneumonia. Whether it was perversity or anxiety or genuine illness, the result was the same: she was not present at the Academy Awards to accept her Oscar in person.

I remember the night vividly. Mother had been in bed most of the day and friends had called periodically to see if she was going to be well enough to attend. When it became apparent that she was going to remain in bed, the phone stopped ringing for several hours. Then the all important call came through . . . she had won the Oscar for best actress of 1945. Her health seemed to improve dramatically. She bounded out of bed and took a shower. Then she put on some make-up and got into her prettiest negligee and satin bed jacket. She brushed her hair and waited for the photographer to arrive. Her director, Michael Curtis brought Oscar to her and the photographer snapped pictures of the three of them together from all angles. They shared some champagne and congratulations.

After everyone had left, I sat with her for a while. Even though I was just about six and a half years old, I knew this was a big moment. She sat in bed holding Oscar and turning him around to view him from every angle. She let me hold him for a few minutes and he was surprisingly heavy. Then we walked down the stairs and placed him all alone in a niche at the bottom of the staircase. Mother stepped back to admire him. Turning to me she said with a note of sarcasm, "I said I wouldn't be there, but I never thought it would turn out like this!"

Though she received two additional nominations in 1947 and 1952, she viewed the rest of her career a constant uphill battle. Some of the joy had gone out of it for her. She had reached the peak too soon, and too young. She felt like she was backsliding, a slow and painful descent brought on by forces she couldn't see and circumstances she couldn't control. So she dug in deeper and became more hopelessly entrenched in her preconceived notions and all the while clinging desperately to the maintenance of her previous image as a real star. It was the image alone that she nurtured and with it she tried to turn back the clock. It was then that she became a fanatic about her public appearances and began to drink more than before.

It was then too that the fan mail began to take on more importance. It at least was a measure of her old glory and she devoted herself to answering every last piece of it and autographing every single photograph with the name of the recipient and a personal message in her own handwriting. The fans became the source of her last vestiges of hope and the wellspring of her claim to stardom. As her pictures steadily declined she had to have something to hold onto, something to sustain her and the fan mail was like an infusion of her life's blood.

Our house became a veritable production line geared to servicing the prodigious amount of letters and requests for photos. She spent thousand and thousands of dollars on updating the 8x10 photographs and providing the mailing envelopes. She had two secretaries, one who worked at the house and one who did only fan mail. However, Mother signed every single letter and each photograph.

Half the downstairs was turned over to this production line for days on end. Several fans would be asked to volunteer and Chris and I worked for hours on Saturday and Sunday. The photomailers had to be addressed and then a picture attached. Mother would sign the photo and then it had to be stuffed into the mailer and sealed. Hundreds of pounds of those photomailers left our house on Sunday evenings.

Part of her personal publicity campaign was the secretary's job of noting on the calendar every birthday and anniversary she'd ever heard anyone mention or read in the trades. There were spouses' birthdays and children's birthdays. When I was still a child, the top of each page on the calendar was filled with these notations. At the end of the year, the secretary dutifully typed them onto the new calendar, omitting the divorced and the deceased. The secretary sent appropriate wires and Mother was notified in advance each week so she could dictate special notes if she wanted. That practice went on until she died. What started out as a little more than a memory jogger, turned into part of the stardom hype and finally became a trademark that gave her something to do long after the work and the public life had ended. It was the last vestige of the image and the career and in later years answering the mail was just about all she had left to remind her of the glory and sustain her sense of purpose.

But in the years after her Academy Award she was just doing battle with the world. She was fighting for her life and it took a heavy toll on all of us.

CHAPTER 10

Chris and I spent the winter of 1946-47 back east in New York but I don't know why. Mommie still had her apartment on East End Avenue, but we didn't stay there with her more than a few days at the most. She'd rented a big house for us in Bedford Village, Upstate New York, and that's where Chris and I lived with three servants: Miss Brown, who was our nurse and the older couple who ran the house.

Before we left for the house in the country, Mommie took us to lunch at the "21" Club, after which we were going to see a matinee performance of the Broadway musical called *Annie Get Your Gun* starring Ethel Merman.

Mommie had just won the Academy Award for *Mildred Pierce* that year and she was a big star again in New York. We'd heard rumors that there was a lot of unrest in New York that winter, but Mommie didn't pay much attention to it, even though in Los Angeles she had a bodyguard named Lou Bennett. However, just as we were finishing lunch and getting ready to leave "21", Uncle Bob Kriendler, the owner, came to the table to talk with her. It seemed that there was a sizeable crowd gathered outside the restaurant waiting to see Mommie. They were not just the usual small, faithful band of fans who followed Mommie wherever she went. We knew all of those women by first name. I had known Bernice, May and Bea since I was just a year old. They and the others in the regular group were lovely, sweet women who just became friends over the years. But this was different. This was a crowd who was getting tired of waiting to see a famous movie star. Uncle Bob looked very concerned and told Mommie that he was going to have the waiters line the short walk up the couple of stairs between the restaurant and the street where our limousine was parked.

Mommie hurried us into our little coats and hats. I was seven and Chris just four. Our nurse, Miss Brown was with us and Mommie told us to hold onto her hand tightly when we left the restaurant and head straight for the limousine, no matter what happened. I looked at her, wondering what all this was about. Outside I could see a big crowd pressing against the iron grillwork at the top of the stars. I could begin to hear what sounded like angry voices filtering through the restaurant's heavy glass and iron front doors. Uncle Bob was on the phone . . . calling the police. He wanted Mommie to stay inside the restaurant until the police arrived.

Mommie said that she'd never had any trouble with fans before and that they were probably just cold and tired of waiting. As soon as she went out to see them, she thought they'd calm down. Uncle Bob emphatically disagreed with her and pleaded with her *not* to try and leave just yet. Mommie said we'd be late for the matinee she'd promised us if we waited any longer and decided to take matters into her own hands. Uncle Bob made all the waiters form a living wall around Mommie, Miss Brown, little Christopher and myself.

The moment the restaurant doors opened, I could feel a rush of cold air and hear the angry shouts of the huge crowd. The strange, angry people were everywhere! They were down the stairs in a flash surrounding our little family and knocking down some of the waiters. They were hanging from the roof that covered the stairway to the street. It couldn't have been more than thirty feet from the front door of the restaurant to the door of our limousine, but we couldn't get there. Literally hundreds of people were shoving pens, pencils and autograph books at Mother. She was separated from us by this hoard of shouting fans who pushed and shoved and jabbed at her. Miss Brown had been knocked down and nearly trampled by the mob. I was absolutely terrified. I clung to my little brother and tried to protect him from the mob with my own body. But I was too little and the big people pushing and shoving and falling all over us simply swept the two of us up in their own momentum. We were clinging together crying, terrified by the chaos.

Mommie realized that she'd lost us somewhere in the crowd and she began screaming for her babies. I heard her voice over the others begging the crowd not to hurt her babies! Everybody was yelling . . . the people in the mob were yelling . . . Mommie was screaming . . . the waiters from "21" were shouting for the crowd to calm down and finally the police arrived with their nightsticks. Mommie was nearly hysterical with terror. Chris and I were sobbing and clinging together. I couldn't see anything but dark coats and flying autograph books, but I did manage to keep my brother and myself from being trampled underfoot. A policeman grabbed us and carried the two of us, still clinging to one another, to the merciful safety of the awaiting limousine. The police pulled Mommie from the mob and once she was inside the car, the police slammed the door. The driver couldn't move the big limousine an inch. There were crazy people rioting all around us, beating on the car and climbing on top of it, peering upside down into all the windows. It was a nightmare.

More police arrived and forced the crowd off the car and onto the sidewalk. Then the policemen and their cars made a path for us and the chauffeur slowly began moving the long black car away from the crowd.

Miss Brown was not with us. She'd been stabbed in the head with a ball point pen and had to be taken to the doctors.

Mommie calmed us down and wiped our tears. She looked us over carefully to see if we'd been hurt. Since we appeared only to be shaken up, she decided that the best thing for us was to go to the matinee . . . it would take our minds off what had just happened.

We got to the theater just as the orchestra had started the overture. In the darkness, an usherette led us to our aisle seats in about the tenth row. Mommie sat with us until the play started and then left. Poor Mommie spent the entire show in the bathroom, throwing up. She finally had to go back to the apartment and go to bed.

Chris and I had a wonderful time. Miss Brown was back from the doctors by the second act. For *years* after seeing that musical, I wanted to be just like *Annie Get Your Gun*. But I must admit, after that incident I didn't care for either fans or large crowds.

The next day we drove up to the country. Mommie spent the weekend with us and then left for the city.

I had schoolwork to do every day, since I'd been taken out of regular school in California to come on this trip. Chris was luckier . . . he wasn't in school yet, so he got off easy.

In the afternoons, the two of us would build snow men, igloos and play other winter games. There was a wonderful little hill not far away and Miss Brown would often walk us over there with our sleds. After dinner Miss Brown would read to us for a while and then we'd listen to radio shows until time to go to sleep! Our favorite, of course, was Jack Benny. After a few weeks with no other kids to play with, it got sort of lonely. Sometimes Mommie came up on the weekends and sometimes she didn't.

Once Uncle Charles McCabe came to visit us and brought some beautiful pheasants he'd shot. Years before, Uncle Charlie took Mommie into the Poconos where they went walking in the woods and Uncle Charlie taught Mommie how to shoot again. I remember the stories because she still had a beautiful rifle with a hand-carved stock. I had come across it once when we were cleaning out the basement at our house in California. She said she didn't want to shoot it any more but she couldn't bear to give it away. She loved Uncle Charlie. I knew that by the way she looked when she told me the stories about the Pocono Mountains and walking in the woods with Uncle Charlie. But, she said, Uncle Charlie was married and would not divorce his wife. She had tears in her eyes when she got to that part of the story. Poor Mommie, the two men she'd really, really loved were both married when she loved them. One was Uncle Charlie and the other was Clark Gable.

When Mommie arrived for Christmas, she had Uncle Greg Bantzer with her. It was a total surprise to see him and we were delighted. Chris and I put on a little play for them which Miss Brown had made us rehearse over and over again. Mommie and Uncle Greg applauded and we gave our ceremonious little bows.

CHAPTER 11

When I was a very little girl, Christmas was like a department store delivered under our tree. Santa Claus came down the chimney in the living room and filled the house with toys and clothes and music.

We always had a huge tree. It touched the ceiling and filled half the room. I used to sit for hours looking at the lights dancing their way merrily across the shiny red, blue, green and silver balls. The radio would be playing hours of Christmas carols and Cook would make wonderful special holiday goodie treats. It was a glorious, exciting time.

Friends would come to visit bringing armloads of presents and the mailman made two deliveries a day to unload cards and packages by the dozens. People I never met would send beautiful gifts, many of them handmade. Each year there would be another little pearl for my add-a-pearl necklace and savings bonds which Mother put away in the bank for me.

Christmas Eve was when Mother opened her presents. When I was very young, she would open them after I had put out the cookies and milk for Santa Claus and had been tucked into bed. As I grew older she allowed me to stay up and have Christmas Eve with her.

Her presents were always in the formal blue and white living room. They were beautiful packages and so many that even wrapped, they filled the couches and chairs. We were hardly ever allowed in the living room because it had a white carpet which got dirty very easily and there were a lot of little antiques on the shelves which we were not allowed to touch.

I used to stand in front of those shelves with my hands tightly clasped behind my back and be fascinated by the miniature furniture on display. There were also little porcelain boxes with old-fashioned pictures painted on them. I used to look at the pastoral paintings of ladies in long full skirts and gentlemen with short pants and lace cuffs and wonder what story they were telling.

It wasn't until years later that I had the courage to sneak into the living room by myself and actually pick up one of those little boxes. I could hear my heart beating and kept a wary ear tuned to catch the sound of approaching footsteps. I almost felt like a criminal and my hands were shaking. Very carefully I picked up my favorite little porcelain box, noting exactly where it had been placed on the shelf. I wanted to put it back precisely so that no one would ever know. Slowly I turned it around to look at all sides of it, then upside down to look at the bottom. There was painting on all sides and some French words I couldn't understand.

Then I opened it. I must have done it wrong because I got a terrible fright; the top seemed to come apart and I was sure I'd somehow broken it. But, to my enormous relief, it was just a double top with sort of a secret compartment. This secret place was painted too, only at first I couldn't figure out what the picture was about. As I looked closer, it began to dawn on me that it was like some kind of dirty book! The lovely lady and gentleman painted on the outside top of the little box were naked from the waist down and her legs were spread apart. I couldn't believe my eyes! Then I started to laugh. Quickly I closed the box and replaced it exactly. Then I went through the entire collection. Almost every one had a secret top and a different scene inside. One that was particularly memorable showed a marketplace. One stall was hung with an array of male sexual organs . . . sets of cocks and balls in all sizes. A lady in a long ruffled dress was making her selection and she had a large basket with her. She also had a sly smile on her face. I was horrified and laughing at the same time. In fact, I was laughing so hard that tears were rolling down my face.

When each box had been thoroughly examined and replaced, I left the living room. I had to go upstairs and wash my face. *And*, I couldn't wait to tell Chris! This was the best thing that had ever happened. The funniest secret in the whole house.

Chris and I tiptoed down the stairs when we were supposed to be taking our nap and the nurse was safely on the other side of the house. I showed him the inside hidden compartment in each of the little boxes and he was just as shocked and giggled as much as I had earlier. He couldn't believe it either. He told me he thought I was making it up. We laughed ourselves stupid over the years of not being allowed to touch these things. So that was what grown-ups do . . . we thought the whole thing was embarrassing but hilarious! This was really a super-secret. Some kids' parents had dirty books, but we had the all time prize: antique French dirty boxes!

From that time on, whenever we had a friend that could prove they could keep a secret, we led the expedition down to the living room. If anyone had ever caught us . . . tiptoeing down the stairs single file and sneaking into the living room like a miniature commando raid . . . they would have thought we were totally nuts. We even posted a lookout and then took turns. It was a super colossal venture which gave us particular standing within our group of trusted friends. To the best of my knowledge, no adult in the house ever found us out. We never got caught, that's for sure.

Anyway, on Christmas Eve after dinner, Mother would begin to open all her presents. There was always perfume and lots of lace things. There was usually jewelry and silver pieces for the table. If she had a steady date, they often had given her their present already and she would be wearing it. It was usually jewelry.

Mother liked matching sets of things and monogrammed things, so almost everything was monogrammed and matched.

When I was old enough to write legibly, she would hand me the card from the present and I would write a brief description of the gift on the back, including color. She would write thank-you notes later but there were so many presents that she'd never be able to remember exactly what was from whom.

When she was about half through opening her gifts, she'd stop and we'd go into the library where the tree was and we'd put out all the special gifts that weren't wrapped. That was, of course, long after she was sure that I didn't believe in Santa Claus anymore.

Then I would go to bed and she'd finish opening her presents by herself in the living room. Sometimes she'd be there till after midnight.

One Christmas Eve when I was about six, I lay in my big four-poster bed and listened with all my might to hear Santa Claus. The next morning I announced that I had indeed heard Santa Claus arrive and that I had even heard his sleigh and the reindeer on our roof!

Christmas morning was the same for many years. Chris and I would wake up and run downstairs. The library door would be closed. Behind the library door would be Christmas . . . waiting for us. We would try to peek through the keyhole but we couldn't see much. Anyway, we had to have breakfast first. I never knew exactly why, but the regular schedule had to be followed on Christmas morning as well as any other day. So, we ate breakfast and did the dishes and went up and made our beds and got dressed. By that time Mother was usually up and Christmas could begin.

Like wild Indians, we dashed into the room the minute she opened the door. The Christmas tree lights were always on and gifts piled high everywhere. It was truly like magic and it looked unbelievably beautiful. The special presents from Santa Claus were placed under the tree . . . the first ones to be gotten. They were things like bicycles, big stuffed animals or outfits of clothing.

Then we had to take turns opening presents. Each one had to have a thank-you note written for it, so we had to write on the back of each card just like Mother did. There were a number of Christmas mornings that lasted until it was time for lunch. The opened presents were replaced under the tree neatly in their boxes and the papers and ribbon taken to the incinerator. Some of the satin ribbon was saved and we rolled that up neatly and put it in a separate box.

We usually had brunch with Mother. Then in the afternoon we would go out and play with our new toys just like millions of other children all over the world.

As the years progressed, Christmas became less of a family holiday and more of a public spectacle. Christmas presents were on display for the many guests that came over on Christmas day to have a few drinks and exchange gifts with Mother. Many times we weren't allowed to open all the presents until there were other people to watch. Then we could each take one package and open it in front of whatever audience happened to be in attendance.

The process of Christmas also changed from one of excitement and surprises to just a lot of hard work. I was enlisted for the last week or so before Christmas to help wrap packages, which in those days was a veritable production line. Not only the presents for the family and friends but dozens that had to be sent to other cities and wrapped for mailing.

There was something defeating about all those gifts and all that paper, ribbon, rolls of brown paper and balls of twine. The whole thing turned into just a lot of hard work for people I didn't know, would probably never meet and couldn't care less about.

If our family Christmas had continued to be a happy occasion, I probably would have felt differently. But by the time I was about nine years old, Christmas had changed. Chris was about six and the girls were only a year old.

There were still a lot of presents under the tree but they turned out to be mostly for show. Some were from Mother and her close friends, some were from fans. Most of them we never saw again after Christmas was over. They were put in their boxes and given away to other people. At first we were allowed to choose which ones we'd like to keep and if Mother agreed, we kept them. But that didn't last very many years. One or two at the most. What really happened from about the time I was ten until we didn't have Christmas anymore was that Mother chose about a dozen gifts for us . . . mostly inexpensive remembrances from various fans. Things like T-shirts and handkerchiefs and a couple of sweaters, pajamas, slippers, play clothes, and the inevitable boxes of stationery were separated out from the other presents. These combined with whatever Mother had given us we were allowed to keep. The rest was stored in closets and we had to take them, rewrapped, to birthday parties during the remainder of the year. Of course, it was usually the best of the presents that we couldn't have, because Mother wouldn't want to be embarrassed by giving children of other Hollywood celebrities in show business cheap presents for their birthdays. Toward fall of each year, Mother would figure out how many more presents were needed adding a couple more for insurance and the rest would be given to a hospital or children's home. None of us kids were given a second chance to choose anything more to keep. That way the closet shelves were cleaned out for the next holiday.

As if it weren't enough to open all those presents knowing full well that we'd never see them again until we gave them away, we were required to smile dutifully when visitors and guests expressed awe and admiration, even envy, over the beautiful gifts and asked us if we knew what lucky children we were! There were several times when I just wanted to scream at them that it was all a fake . . . there really was no Christmas and this was all a scene from another movie starring Joan Crawford and her four lovely children . . . the epitome of the glamorous movie star in the make-believe world of beauty and happiness forever. But I didn't scream, I didn't say anything, I didn't even try to tell them the truth because nobody would have believed me anyway. What they saw on the surface was what everyone wanted to believe, like a real life "Land of Oz." I'm sure it all looked perfect. Oh sure, a few people saw through it, but though they may have registered a sense of discomfort when they saw me paraded out to smile and shake hands and curtsey while Chris bowed like an English gentlemen at the age of six, they never said anything. Our manners were both impossible and archaic, well executed and mechanical. We had to bow and curtsey, we had to smile and say nothing, we lived by "do not speak unless spoken to."

I often drifted off into some daydream while smiling politely and appearing to pay attention to what was going on. I knew by then that if I didn't hear it the first time all that was required was an "I beg your pardon" and it would be repeated. I guess I started tuning out about nine or ten. Not so much because I was bored but because it was less embarrassing that way. Mother seemed to take great delight in finding ways to make us look foolish or to accuse us of doing something wrong in front of everyone. She was really at her best with an audience.

But categorically the worse thing about the entire Christmas holiday was thank-you notes. I would take the boxes of stationery and the gift cards up to the desk in my room and the ordeal would begin. Each gift had to have a note and I was not allowed to simply compose one standard reply and copy it. Of course at nine, ten and eleven years old I didn't exactly have a huge repertoire of phrases, but I did the best I could. At first I used to have to line the paper faintly in pencil. Later on I was able to write fairly straight without the lines. There could be no mistakes on any note, so that if I made a serious error, I had to start all over again. I started in the morning after breakfast and my chores were done and would work until time to set the table for lunch. After the lunch dishes were done and we'd taken our rest, I sat back down at the desk and had to fight with myself to get started. I stared out the window past the giant oak tree and down into the garden below. I longed to go out and play but I wasn't allowed to do anything except my housework until those thank-you notes were finished. So I plodded on, hour after hour trying to write pleasant notes without any mistakes for presents I was never going to get to enjoy or play with from people who, for the most part, I didn't know. It was tedious beyond words. My hand would get stiff and my back would begin to ache. I wasn't allowed to listen to the radio or play any record. The silence was broken only by the sounds of my own paper and pen. Every once in a while I would have to get up and stretch but it would be furtive and done quickly in case someone would catch me not doing the notes. The worst part was being all alone all day. I could hear people talking in other parts of the house and in the yard. I could see my sisters and the nurse out in the garden. Chris didn't have to start on this dismal chore until a couple years later because he was only six or seven and couldn't really write yet. But even he had to print a lot of notes that were written out for him to copy. When after a couple days of this solitary confinement, the task was nearly finished, I would take the stacks of notes to Mother and she would look over them. To my absolute horror she started making marks through them. She said with a tone of contempt that my writing wasn't clear enough or this line was slightly crooked and she became angry as she said that she didn't think I'd said nearly enough about how wonderful the present was or I hadn't described it fully. With a sinking heart and a hatred of her I could barely conceal, I took the majority of the notes she'd thrown at me back upstairs. It became a never-ending process. No matter how hard I tried to make them perfect the first time, she always found something wrong with most of the notes and I had to write them over two and three times. As Christmas vacation dragged on, my other privileges were gradually taken away because I hadn't finished the thank-you notes. If I were so foolish as to complain, I had more work given to me as a punishment. Mother bawled me out for being the most ungrateful child she'd ever known and then I got into more trouble for my sour face and bad attitude.

In truth, I was grim. I hated those notes so much that some days I had to force myself to pick up the pen. I ruined several of them with my own tears which fell all over the stationery making big splotches that partially erased the ink. I ached all over from the hours of sitting at the desk and I hated Christmas. I started daydreaming about the day when I'd be free to leave home. In near silence I did my work and wrote those hateful notes until school mercifully started again.

When the time came to take down the tree, I was ordered to put each present I wasn't going to be allowed to have, back in its box and replace the lid. These boxes were labeled in pencil as to their contents and then I took them upstairs and neatly stacked them on the closet shelf. There they would lie in untouched repose until someone else's birthday party months later.

It was with some astonishment, years later, that I heard a radio recording made in 1949 about our family Christmas. (NOTE: The following is a direct transcript of that recording.)

GEORGE FISHER (Announcer)

I know this report wouldn't be complete without a thorough description of exactly how one Hollywood family spends Christmas Eve and Christmas Day. So a few hours ago I took my tape recorder out to the Brentwood home of Joan Crawford. Miss Crawford and her four children have graciously consented to tell all of us exactly the way in which they'll spend this holiday weekend. The broadcast marks the radio debut for Miss Crawford's eldest children. They are as excited about it as any youngsters would be. So now, let's hop into an imaginary sleigh and whisk out to the home of one of the foremost actresses in America today, Miss Joan Crawford.

Now we are settled in the living room of Miss Joan Crawford's tastefully decorated home. A colorful Christmas tree at one edge of the room is almost snowed under with packages. Across the white carpet on the other wall is a stately colonial fireplace as prepared for the flames that will be warming the room before long and the mantel is waiting for the Christmas stocking. Miss Crawford and her children are seated on one davenport facing me.

Miss Crawford, my listeners and I are so pleased that you have invited us in to share a few moments of this Christmas Eve with you.

JOAN CRAWFORD

We are very happy to have you with us, George.

GEORGE

Suppose you start, Miss Crawford, by introducing your children to our radio audience.

JOAN CRAWFORD

This is my eldest daughter, Christina.

CHRISTINA

Hello everyone.

JOAN CRAWFORD

And my son, Christopher.

CHRISTOPHER

Hi everybody.

JOAN CRAWFORD

My twins, Cynthia and Cathy, who will content themselves with smiling for your listeners since they are not quite three.

GEORGE

Hello Cynthia and Cathy, and how old are you Christina?

CHRISTINA

I'm ten, Mr. Fisher.

GEORGE

Christopher, you're certainly growing up fast. How old are you?

CHRISTOPHER

I'm just seven, Mr. Fisher.

GEORGE

Will there be four stockings, one for each child, or does your Mother have to hang up a stocking too?

CHRISTINA

Oh, we insist that Mother hang up her stocking right beside ours.

GEORGE

Christopher, are the stockings always full when you wake up?

CHRISTOPHER

Sure, Santa Claus fills them up while we're asleep.

GEORGE

Have you ever tried to sneak downstairs and catch St. Nick at work?

CHRISTOPHER

No. He won't come to our house if we're awake.

GEORGE

That's a fancy tree here in the corner of the room. Who decorated it?

CHRISTOPHER AND CHRISTINA

We all did!

CHRISTINA

Except Mommie had to put the decorations on the top where we couldn't reach.

GEORGE

Miss Crawford, here is a question that will interest every parent in America. At what hour do you suppose the youngsters will awaken tomorrow morning?

JOAN CRAWFORD

I am afraid they are likely to be awake and up by six-thirty at the latest.

GEORGE

Will they come straight into your room and awaken you?

JOAN CRAWFORD

I'd be disappointed if they didn't. Christmas morning is the favorite day of the year for all of us.

GEORGE

Well, do you try to get your children to eat breakfast before they start opening their presents?

JOAN CRAWFORD

Yes. I've always insisted they eat before coming into the Christmas tree. Every other morning of the year they dawdle over their food, but Christmas morning, awh, breakfast is the quickest meal on record.

GEORGE

Christina, do you and your brother and sisters send presents to lots of people at Christmastime?

CHRISTINA

Yes we do. But besides giving to your friends, we like to send presents every year to boys and girls from other countries across the ocean.

GEORGE

And I suppose you receive all sorts of gifts from people you don't even know.

CHRISTINA

Oh yes! People who see Mommie in the movies send us lots of lovely things.

JOAN CRAWFORD

It's so nice, George, remembering the children every year.

GEORGE

It's easy to see looking over the gigantic group of packages under the tree now that the youngsters will have enough presents to keep them busy for months.

JOAN CRAWFORD

Yes. *You see, I don't let them have all their presents at one time. They'll get to play with them all, you know all day tomorrow, and then we put a large group of them aside. From tomorrow on they earn their gifts.*

GEORGE

How do you mean they earn them?

JOAN CRAWFORD

Well, if they stay on their good behavior, they are given their choice of what present they want next. Christopher had his birthday in October and he still hasn't received all of his presents.

GEORGE

I suppose you give away a good many things.

JOAN CRAWFORD

We don't give away any of the Christmas presents. I don't think that would be fair to the people who send them. What we do is to have a complete housecleaning three times a year, every plaything, every article of clothing, is carefully gone over and large bundles go to the children's homes and hospitals.

GEORGE

Do the children help you with this?

JOAN CRAWFORD

Oh, yes. I think its excellent training for them. I always see to it that they give up something they really love; otherwise, they don't really learn the value of giving.

GEORGE

Christopher. What one thing do you want more than anything else to be in one of your packages tomorrow?

CHRISTOPHER

A pair of Hopalong Cassidy guns.

GEORGE

And Christina, what do you hope St. Nick leaves for you?

CHRISTINA

More than anything else in the world, I'd like a Collie dog like Lassie.

GEORGE

Miss Crawford. Could you tell us what you would call your most exciting Christmas?

JOAN CRAWFORD

I think the happiest moment of my life was the Christmas the children came into our home. I don't see how any home can be complete without children or how any Christmas can be really enjoyed without youngsters around.

GEORGE

Now, suppose you tell us what's going to happen for the rest of the evening after I leave you?

JOAN CRAWFORD

Well, Cynthia and Cathy will be off to bed pretty quickly, but I've discovered that there's no point in trying to get Christina and Christopher to bed for hours. So they'll help me with the last minute things and we'll talk about tomorrow and watch the Christmas tree lights. Then in a little while we'll welcome some of the children's friends who'll be in to help us sing Christmas carols. I imagine we'll sing Jingle Bells even before Cynthia and Cathy go to sleep.

GEORGE

Christina, what's your favorite Christmastime song, dear?

CHRISTINA

My favorite Christmas song is "The Little Town of Bethlehem."

GEORGE

And Christopher, what's yours?

CHRISTOPHER

"Away in a Manger."

GEORGE

And we'll want to know your favorite too, Miss Crawford.

JOAN CRAWFORD

I think I've always loved "Silent Night" best, George.

GEORGE

Then when your friends leave, Christopher, what happens?

CHRISTOPHER

Mother reads to us.

CHRISTINA

Yes, we're reading the Christmas Carol this year.

JOAN CRAWFORD

Helen Hayes sent us about four years ago a beautiful illustrated copy of Dickens' Christmas Carols and it is one of our most prized possessions. I started to read it to them last year but Christopher couldn't take it, it was too scary for him. He's a bigger boy this year, though, so we started it several weeks ago and we'll finish it tonight.

GEORGE

And then surely you finish up by reading "'Twas the Night Before Christmas"?

JOAN CRAWFORD

Oh, no Christmas Eve would be complete without that.

GEORGE

Do you remember the last two lines?

CHRISTINA

I do.

CHRISTOPHER

So do I.

GEORGE

Well, then, as a Christmas present to all of us, do you suppose you could say those lines for us?

ALL TOGETHER

"And I heard him playing as he drove out of sight, Merry Christmas to all, and to all a good night."

GEORGE

And a Merry Christmas to you, Cathy, Cynthia, Christopher and Christina, and, of course, to you, Miss Joan Crawford. Thanks again for allowing all of us to share a part of your Christmas Eve.

JOAN CRAWFORD

Thank you so much, George. Merry Christmas to you and to all of your listeners.

And so the millions of fans across America were given a capsule glimpse into the glamorous world of Hollywood with the nearly perfect picture of one happy, lucky family. We had everything, so the story went. We had the gifts and the money and a beautiful famous movie star mother and the world should have been at our feet. I remember being dressed up and paraded in front of interviewers and photographers with my little rehearsed responses and photo-perfect smile. Our manners were those of model ladies and gentlemen that no longer existed in 1949. We were like little echoes of Mother's constant drive for perfection and gentility. Out of the cauldrons of Hollywood's melting pot she had clawed her way to the top and now we were the final stars in the crown proving her not only successful but morally superior. Her generosity in taking not one, not two, but *four* orphaned children (we were never referred to as illegitimate) into her home was extolled in numerous movie magazine stories.

When the reporters and photographers left, we returned to our room and changed our clothes. It was a case of extremes: one minute being treated like privileged royalty with reporters paying careful attention to your every word and a few minutes later all that attention was gone.

CHAPTER 12

At times when there was no man around, Mother often wanted to go out anyway. On those evenings she told me that I was going to be her "date" and we were going out to dinner. The two of us would get dressed up and get into her big black Cadillac.

In no time at all we'd pull in front of one her favorite restaurants. Sometimes it would be the old LaRue's on Sunset Boulevard, other times it would be Romanoff's where her friend and erstwhile prince, Mike Romanoff, would greet her warmly and show us to one of the best tables. For lunch we often went to the Cock 'N Bull, but my favorite place for dinner was Don the Beachcombers in Hollywood. I loved the Polynesian food, the waterfalls and the booth we always sat in that looked like a little grass hut. Wherever we went, the owners always fawned over us and Mother would smile happily. She always told them she was taking her big girl out to dinner and they would beam with pleasure and tell me what a pretty young lady I was. No matter what restaurant it was, people would always come by the table and sit to talk with us. Mostly Mother would talk business with them while I sat quietly and ate my food. She always told her friends that I'd wanted to come to this restaurant and I'd been such a good girl that she couldn't refuse me. I was used to the routine and I'd just smile politely. I already knew that unless Mother and I were alone, I was not supposed to join into the conversation and by now I didn't really mind.

One night at Don the Beachcombers a tall, strange looking man came over to our table. Mother greeted him warmly and introduced him as Howard Hughes. He sat down and ordered drinks. He stayed with us through most of the meal and was obviously trying to get Mother to be more than just cordial toward him. When he finally realized that he wasn't getting anywhere, he kissed her on the cheek and left.

"He's weird!" I whispered to her, not entirely sure he was out of ear-shot. Mother laughed.

"He's Howard Hughes, Tina, and he's *very* rich." It was while we were waiting for the check that she told me that years before Howard Hughes was starting in the films and had wanted to put her under contract. She had refused him a number of times, even though he was offering her a tremendous amount of money, because she didn't want to ruin her reputation. She said that Howard wanted to buy people and own them. Many times he'd put some unsuspecting young actress under contract and she'd never do one movie. The others, like Jane Russell, were just used for exploitation and Mother didn't want any part of it.

When Howard failed to entice her into a contract, he tried to get her to go out with him. She finally accepted and they went out a couple of times, but all he wanted to talk about was machinery and she wasn't interested. He was also quite deaf and wore a hearing aid which he was vain about and didn't like to have anyone mention.

I thought about him for a while as Mother was paying the check and felt sort of sorry for him. He was a strange, tall, rumpled man who hadn't seemed very much at ease with us or himself.

We usually had a very good time on our dates. Mother would chatter away about the people that came to the table for one reason or another. It was funny that she hated to have dates that were what she called "table hoppers" but if it hadn't been for all the men that did table hop, we would have been left talking to ourselves! I guess she just didn't like being out with a man who did that. She never got up and went to anyone else's table, she said it was bad manners. So . . . everyone else got up and came to ours.

When we got home, having discussed the entire evening during the drive, Mother would often ask if I wanted to sleep in with her. I always felt badly about saying no for fear it would hurt her feelings. She had two giant beds in her room, one at either end of what we called the sleeping porch. Sometimes I would sleep in the other big bed but often she would want me to sleep with her.

She divided her bed into two parts down the middle with great big pillows so we wouldn't bump into one another during the night. Then she got into her half and I crawled into my half and she went to sleep.

There were two things I didn't like about sleeping with Mother. One was that her blankets were so heavy I felt like I was being buried alive. The other was that I couldn't move all night long. She claimed that I wiggled incessantly and it woke her up. So I would try to remember not to wiggle, which meant not to move and it would keep me wide awake half the night.

I was a very good student even in the elementary grades and enjoyed Gretna Green Public School. Because the work became increasingly easy for me my teachers decided to skip me ahead one half grade. So, over a weekend in February I went from the top of third grade to the top of the fourth grade.

The transition wasn't particularly difficult except for one subject: math. Somehow I had missed a significant part in the process and I had to have Mrs. Howe tutor me after school for the rest of the year.

There were new friends to be made as well and I was now a little younger than most of my classmates. But we were all near enough in age that making friends wasn't impossibly difficult and indeed the relationships developed.

I had been walking the two or three miles to school, but now I was allowed to ride my bike which made me feel quite grown up and was a lot easier. I had been absolutely forbidden to accept rides from strangers and walking to school many mornings I was sorely tempted to ignore the stern warning. I took a shortcut through several alleys and there were always dogs that seemed to lie in wait to scare me half to death. The bike was a definite improvement.

I joined the Brownies and had to wear my uniform one day a week to school. The only reason I joined was to be with some of my friends because I didn't really like Brownies that much. We did one fun thing though and that was a play, which Mother directed. The play was *Hansel and Gretel* and I had to be the mother. We rehearsed on the small stage in our own theater and Mother managed her little troupers very patiently. I was furious at having to be the ugly old mother, but she explained that because I was taller than the other girls, it would look ridiculous for me to play one the children. Since we were only girls in the Brownie troop, there were no boys in the play and being the mother was better than having to be Hansel! We were all very excited the day of the performance as we put on our costumes and Mother helped everyone with their makeup. Unfortunately, I got a classic case of stage fright during my unauspicious acting debut and forgot half of my lines which shortened the entire play by about ten minutes.

Mother was quite strict about where she let me go, so most of my friends had to come to my house to play. My two best friends were Judy and Cynthia. Their families had nothing to do with the picture business and they were as different as any two people could be.

Judy was tall, had carrot-red hair and was a terrific athlete. Cynthia was a petite blonde and much more socially conscious. Cynthia had wonderful slumber parties which were great fun because her mother was not so strict and let us make noise and be silly.

Judy and I started out as rivals. She was the tetherball champ and no matter how I tried I couldn't beat her. We battled it out on the school playground and then after school we would actually meet behind the fence and have a fist fight just like the boys. She had long red hair and I had long blonde hair and there was more hair pulling than punches. I didn't have any more success winning our fist fights than I had at tetherball and after she finally landed a solid punch that gave me a whopping black eye, we called a truce. I lied about the black eye at home with some story about getting accidentally hit with the tetherball during recess and after that Judy and I were great friends.

Mother had a very peculiar habit that I grew to find downright embarrassing. With my close friends she insisted that they call her something other than Miss Crawford. At first she suggested they call her Aunt Joan, but that didn't work very well because most of them didn't feel comfortable with our aunt and uncle convention. It was then, to my horror, that Mother suggested the nickname "Stinky." The girls were as taken aback as I was hearing the name, but that's what it was to be . . . "Stinky." It was absolutely humiliating for me to have my friends call her "Stinky" to her face and then laughingly tell the other kids at school behind her back. When other kids would tease me about it, I just told them to go to hell.

That wasn't nearly as bad as some of the other things that the kids said. There was the whole business about not having a father. I tried to explain that I was adopted and Mother said that made me specially wanted, more than even people who had their own kids. But what I got in return was snickers and pointed remarks about being a bastard without a father. It was so unusual for someone to admit being adopted that I didn't meet any other children who had been adopted until many years later. The more common practice was for parents not to tell children they were adopted until the child was nearly grown up, if indeed they told them at all.

But Mother had told us even before we were fully able to understand all the details. She said that she chose us from a pink cloud. When I was very young I used to look up in the sky and think that the different colored clouds were the explanation for the different colored people.

There was, in addition, the business about being a movie star's daughter.

This was a public school and although it was in west Los Angeles, not all the families were wealthy. Most were sort of middle class and some were downright poor. In fact it was a shock for me when I was invited to some of the birthday parties of my classmates that year. I was eight years old then and for the first time allowed to go to some of the parties given by people other than the members of the movie community. Mother was extremely cautious because of the kidnapping business and always felt uncomfortable when I was with people she didn't know very well. Unfortunately, this overprotectiveness was taken as an insult by some of my friends' parents and I actually lost some friendships because I was never allowed to go to their houses, they always had to come to mine.

The first such birthday party I was allowed to go to was difficult for me. This time I knew everyone there because we were all classmates. But I was horribly overdressed compared to the other girls and it was quite embarrassing. What I wanted to do was to fit in and to be accepted but my expensive party dress set me entirely apart. Then too, I had to be so careful of my clothes and not scuff my shoes so that I wouldn't get into trouble when I returned home that I couldn't participate in most of the games they played. I had taken off my white gloves the minute I got into the house and I knew Mother couldn't see me, but it wasn't quick enough to escape the eyes of my friends who had never seen anyone their own age wearing gloves. Nobody said anything but I could see them exchange glances. My present was one of last year's Christmas gifts I wasn't allowed to have and it was a lot bigger than the other packages. It was wrapped in beautiful paper with an elaborate satin bow and stood out like a spotlight in the midst of the more ordinary presents. If I felt uncomfortable, the girl's mother was nearly beside herself. She tried her best to be normal but she kind of lost it in the excitement of introducing me to all the neighbor friends who "just happened" to drop by to wish her daughter happy birthday. She introduced me as Joan Crawford's daughter, which seemed to be the important part, and several times forgot my name or didn't think it necessary to add. I shook hands, smiled and curtseyed as I'd been taught to do when meeting anyone for the first time and had the sense that everyone was staring at me. After the first few introductions I just said "Hello" and left it at that.

When we went out into the small backyard no bigger than the space we used to hang out the laundry at home, I felt sorry for my friend. Her family must be very poor, I thought, and tried harder to be polite about this sort of sad situation.

It wasn't until after a couple more of these birthday parties that a monumental truth began to dawn on me. The houses of most of my public school friends were quite a bit better than the site of the first birthday party, but they weren't at all like our house nor any of the homes of Mother's friends. And it wasn't even the houses that surprised me so much as the yards. I was well into the eighth year of my life before I realized that not everyone in the world had swimming pools! Little by little it dawned on me that most people didn't live like the way we did. They didn't have swimming pools but they didn't have to wear white gloves and their parents weren't nearly as strict as my mother was. It was a different world entirely.

At first I didn't realize exactly what was going on with some of the kids I met during that fourth grade year. It was a confusing time because they teased me about dressing funny and then would be very nice to me. It was a bit of a paradox that I was overdressed at the birthday parties and had to wear overalls to school. What Mother's thinking was, I don't know, but it was unusual for little girls to wear pants to school in those days. I guess she thought it was most practical, but it made me feel funny not to be dressed like the other kids. After a while I begged and pleaded and she got me some cotton dresses for school. Not enough to wear one every day, but at least part of the time I didn't stick out like a sore thumb.

The same kids that teased me about my funny clothes and high-topped shoes, the same kids that snickered about my not having a father were the very kids that for no reason I could figure out suddenly did a complete turnaround and became super nice to me.

Sadly enough I guess I was so pleased to have the teasing subside that I naively interpreted their change of behavior as an indication of friendship. Since it was well known that I was hardly ever allowed to go anywhere on the weekends or during the summer, the only way to pursue the friendship was for me to invite them over to my house. Usually after a couple of hints on their part about having heard that we had a pool, I would ask my mother if I could invite a couple of school friends over for a swim that Saturday and she would usually say yes.

On Saturday afternoon the children would arrive and we'd all go swimming. Afterwards Mother would let us have some Good Humor ice cream bars as a treat. Somewhere during that span of time, one or another of the kids would bring up the subject of Mother being a movie star. Then someone else would ask if they could maybe have a photograph. If Mother was home, I would go into the house and ask her if she'd give my friends an autographed picture. She was always quite happy to oblige and would come down to the pool with the latest 8x10 glamour portraits and sign each individually with the child's name on it.

In a short while, the kids left with their movie star pictures tucked under their arms.

I'd only seen one of Mother's movies. It was called *Humoresque* with Johnny Garfield. I was in love with John Garfield. I adored him. He was my hero. I was about eight when I saw that movie. At the end of the picture Mother walked into the sea and died. I had been sitting next to her during the film, but she'd gotten a phone call and left before the end. I was so engrossed in the movie that I didn't realize she was gone. The movie was very sad and then at the end she walked into the ocean and died. I was crying. When the lights went on I turned to hug her . . . she wasn't there! Before I could sort things out, I thought the movie was real and that she was really dead. I screamed and ran out of the theater like a little crazy person. I ran everywhere looking for her screaming "Mommie . . . Mommie" until I finally found her in the house, still on the phone. I threw myself across her lap sobbing with relief.

Monday at school when I'd bounce up to the same kids who were at my house on Saturday, the reception was entirely different. It was just one step short of the cold shoulder. I was very hurt and didn't understand what could have happened.

One day I was nearly in tears. After school, my friend Judy and I sat down to talk about it. It was Judy who finally told me: the only thing those kids wanted was to see a movie star's house and get the autograph to prove it.

I got so mad at her we nearly had one of our old fights. I called her a liar and rode off on my bike in a total fury. By the time I got home the exercise had calmed me down somewhat and I began to try and sort out what she'd said. I didn't talk much to anyone at home that evening, just ate dinner did my usual chores and homework. When it was time to go to sleep, I lay awake in my bed going over and over the last few months. I realized that what Judy had told me was true. After I'd invited those kids over for a swim and they'd gotten Mother's autograph they weren't my friends any more. I didn't know anything yet about what I later called the big lie, but I'd already felt the full impact of it's force and it's cruelty. It was inescapably clear to me that those kids didn't care a bit about me and that all they'd wanted was to get to see some Hollywood star in person. Some of the kids hadn't even tried to get an invitation, they just asked me point blank for an autographed picture and would continue to bug me about it until I either had to tell them to forget it or go though the whole embarrassing process of asking Mother and then taking the picture with me to school. I felt like a pawn constantly being used.

I already knew that Mother used us for all those publicity stories in the movie magazines. Even at eight years old it wasn't hard to tell the difference between our regular routine and the make-believe situations the photographers always wanted. Everything changed when the publicity people were coming. I had to get dressed in one of the many "mother and daughter" outfits we were always photographed in and my hair was specially curled. Then Mother and I would go through the whole day doing things for the camera and changing from one matching outfit to another. The publicity people would have all these scenes they wanted us to act out like it was part of our normal day and there was always somebody asking silly, set up questions and writing down all the pre-rehearsed answers.

Mother told me what she thought the writer was going to ask me and also told me what to answer in reply. We would practice that a few times until she was satisfied I had it right. She made me pronounce my words carefully and stand properly. She said that if they asked any other questions, I was to let her answer. You couldn't be too careful with the press, she said, and it was better to say nothing than to risk being misquoted. So I was to smile and look pretty and be polite and speak only when spoken to and do as I was told like a good girl.

My young world was getting to be full of contradictions. When the publicity people and the photographers were around I was still treated like the little golden princess. But at school the kids were mean to me because I wore coveralls and didn't have a father. Worse yet, they pretended to be my friend in order to get a lousy picture and see a movie star. It was the beginning of the confusion as to who I really was and none of the images rang exactly true.

Once I decided to run away from home. It was one of those frequent times I'd found myself eating on the freezer in the back porch for some minor infraction of the rules. I was going to school anyway and decided just to leave early. Out the back door I went and headed for Cynthia Shaw's house. It wasn't a very major attempt at running away because before I got very far down Sunset Boulevard I heard the sound of screeching brakes and looked behind me to see Mother's black Cadillac coming to a dusty halt. She jumped out of the car and hauled me off the street. She was furious with me and demanded to know just what in the world I thought I was doing and where I thought I was going. Scared to death, I mumbled something about going to Cynthia's house. Despite all my protestations, she took me to the Shaw residence where the entire household was told about my "runaway" plans. Of course the entire incident was a complete surprise to Mr. and Mrs. Shaw and although they seemed to be sympathetic, they clearly didn't want any part of the mess. Driving home in the car, Mother seemed to be pleased that the family had disavowed any pleasure in my choosing their home. She asked me how come I always seemed to like everybody else's house better than my own. She said, "Every time you go over to someone else's house they always have such glowing reports about how helpful you are, which is odd because you never want to lift a god-damned finger in your own house. You constantly complain about having to help."

As I sat there listening to her I wanted to run away all over again. Somehow she'd turned the reports of my good behavior into a condemnation of me. I didn't know how she did it but I couldn't win. No matter whether I was good or bad it somehow got me into trouble. If I tried to be a good girl, she said I was only being good to show off to others, or worse still that I was only being good because I wanted something.

For some reason Cynthia and I weren't as close friends after that. Mother was always suggesting that she come over and they were good friends. At Mother's own request, Cynthia called her "Stinky" and they seemed to have fun together. I don't know why but I never quite trusted Cynthia to be my friend from then on. It seemed that it was getting harder to trust anyone to be my friend. And if it looked as though Mother was paying a lot of attention to any of them, I would decide never to tell them anything important or any of my little secrets anymore. They could still come over and play from time to time, but they wouldn't have any more real information about how I felt or thought about anything in particular.

I think if it hadn't been for my really good friend Judy Clayton I would have died of boredom and loneliness.[8]

---

8   After the book was published, people who personally witnessed the abuse toward my brother and me came forward to tell of their remorse never saying or doing anything to stop it. Everyone was a studio employee and afraid of losing their job if they interfered. One of these eye-witness accounts involves Chris. It was a Sunday afternoon in summer. Several guests were sunning themselves around our pool when they heard a commotion. My brother had been caught playing with matches and accidentally set papers in a wastebasket on fire.

As a punishment, Mother dragged him by the arm to stand in front of the guests and then she proceeded to forcibly hold his hand over lighted matches until his skin burned and he howled in pain. He was then spanked and sent to his room.

The second eyewitness was about me. Mother's studio publicity had acquired a "Mother of the Year" award for her from a children's charity. One evening, publicists from the studio and the charity were gathered in our formal dining room with samples of the advertising campaign strewn across the long table.

Evidently my brother and I were playing "hide and seek" in another room when a shriek followed by crying was heard by everyone in the dining room.

Mother sent for us and moments later the governess brought me into the room saying quietly that "the children" had been playing and Chris got his fingers caught in the door when I ran through it and closed it behind. She made clear that it was an accident.

Without a word, Mother grabbed me by the arm and in front of everyone gathered for the meeting, shoved my hand in the doorframe, slammed the door shut with considerable force while I screamed.

The nurse ran to me, opening the door. Mother ordered us out. She then turned back to the stunned group, resumed work on the publicity campaign for "Mother of the Year" behaving as though nothing had ever happened!

Anyway, I continued at the Gretna Green school for another year. With the exception of math which still posed problems, my schoolwork was straight A's. Again the teachers suggested that I be double promoted and again over a weekend I went from the top of the fifth grade to the top of the sixth grade. This time the transition wasn't so easy. Now the other children in the class were a full year older than I and it made a difference. It happened so fast that I had no time to catch up on what I'd missed in the first half of the sixth grade and Mrs. Howe had her hands full with the twins who were still pretty little, leaving no time to tutor me. I picked up most of the subjects all right but math was beginning to be quite confusing. As hard as I worked at it, I couldn't seem to fit all the missing parts together. Mother had always been very demanding about my grades and I got into a lot of trouble if I didn't get all A's on my report cards. If my grades slipped, my privileges at home were taken away and I had extra work to do, so there was more than enough incentive to study. Fortunately for me, I always liked school. It seemed to come fairly easily for me and I never had to work too hard to accomplish good grades. Ironically that's why the school kept promoting me, because they could see that I didn't have to struggle. I guess the point was that if you didn't have to struggle, something was wrong.

It didn't matter too much though, because my scholastic vacation was about to come to an end.

RECOLLECTIONS FROM JUDY

"Christina will spend the rest of the afternoon in her room, Judy. Please phone your Mother to come drive you home." Another visit with my friend ended much before planned. I was bewildered and embarrassed. Over the years, detailed plans would be made through our mothers for me to spend overnight or the weekend, to accompany Christina to a specific event or for us to spend the afternoon playing in her room, swimming in the pool or watching a movie in the theater at her house. But it was not uncommon for the plans to be abandoned without warning. Some disciplinary action taken by Christina's Mother to punish her usually for not cleaning or scrubbing or straightening some personal item or household space to Joan's satisfaction, would be announced violently. It was confusing and embarrassing to me, but something to which I adjusted, as it was the price paid to visit with my longtime friend.

Christina and I had met on our first day at Brentwood Elementary School. When my mother drove me to school that day, she recognized the driver of the large wooden-sided bronze-colored station wagon next to our car as Joan Crawford, one of her most admired movie stars! And the little girl standing up in the back seat with long, white-blond curls I would later meet as Christina, one of my kindergarten classmates. In my years at Brentwood School, we would to be in many classes together and, even if not in the same class, we enjoyed playing together at recess. We shared the experience of being in Brownies together. One year, my mother was the troop leader, which gave her an additional opportunity to interface with Miss Crawford (as I always addressed her).

I realized that Christina had less freedom than I and my other friends as a security measure. For in those years, the fear of kidnapping the child of a famous star was realistic. As she and I became friends such that I was invited to her house to play or sleep over, I felt privileged. I was always coached on displaying good manners by my mother, not that I had a separate set of behavior mannerisms for Really Special People. Even so, my excursions into this privileged life brought me into contact with people and situations with which I had no prior experience. Despite coaching and manners, I alone established and practiced my own personal policy of nondisclosure with regard to Christina's life. I do not remember discussing with other friends any of our excursions or activities or the extraordinarily severe punishment pattern that was a dependable feature of her life. In retrospect, I believe I accepted her friendship and the awareness of both the typical and the unique aspects of her life without breaking the confidence of her privacy.

On at least one special occasion, Christina was allowed to come visit me at my house. It may not have been unusual for her to be allowed to visit friends' homes, but my house was quite different from any she would have visited, I felt sure. It was a small, meticulously clean stucco house about one-twentieth the size of the mansion at 426 N. Bristol. I think our house covered about as much square footage as the Crawford swimming pool. We had a garden in the backyard that produced a few vegetable varieties which we happily consumed at the time of their appearance. We also had a well kept inner yard of chickens that provided a continuous supply of fresh eggs. The day that Christina came to visit, my initial embarrassment at the comparative humbleness of my home was quickly replaced by my recognition that she was experiencing a place different from those she had visited before. Most of all, we felt free of those unannounced guerrilla raids that invariably preceded severe punishment. FREEDOM for the day.

For ten or so years our friendship allowed me to visit what appeared from the outside to be a fairytale world. I came to see the unreality of that illusion. Despite the elegance of furnishings in a mansion set on beautiful grounds with exceptional recreational facilities, and a household staffed by functionaries who performed with militaristic precision, this was an empty castle. The people were not real people. Most of all, there was not a real family in any sense with which I was familiar. I do not remember ever seeing Joan, "Miss Crawford," as I carefully addressed her, display any affection, not even the smallest gesture, except when adult visitors, especially movie industry dignitaries or photographers, were present. At such times, most elaborate preparations were made to create the impression that what the eye saw or the story told was everyday life. In actual fact, the illusion of maternal involvement in the small details of Christina's life, like my own mother's or that of any child's mother among my own friends, was pure, concocted fiction. Christina was brought up by governesses, cooks, secretaries and a corps of temporary contract characters in the charade-life through which she was led.

How did this dynamic change after the arrival of Cindy and Cathy, "The Twins," as they were usually called? To me, the outsider, it seemed not at all. When The Twins joined the household, they were infants. They were of a different time and, as it turned out, were treated to quite different lives. Their activities and care kept them almost completely separate from Christina's and mine, although we sometimes had Christopher "around" when we played. I noticed that Christopher also seemed to be punished often and probably just as severely. Most people would think that these had to be a couple of very bad kids to be punished so often and so severely. But they were not. Christina knew the rules. She maintained her room and bathroom exceptionally well. Her regular chores included cleaning floors and sinks elsewhere in the mansion. More than once during my visits, she was required to scrub the bathhouse floor again. (It already seemed quite clean to me.) My sincere requests to assist her would be rejected by Miss Crawford.

After Christina was transferred to the Chadwick School, we were able to visit only occasionally. I would be invited to stay one or both weekend days or sometimes during a school vacation. But not often. And then there were no more calls. No more contact from Christina. No word. I would phone to ask about her. She was unavailable. No word. It hurt. After several years, the pain of never hearing from my friend subsided and was forgotten.

When *Mommie Dearest* was published, I did not rush out to buy it. In fact, I have never read any more than couple of pages that were marked in a copy that my mother sent me. They were the pages where Christina recalled some of the events of our friendship in the Brentwood School days. She referred to me simply as "Judy."

With the benefit of forty years that have passed, during which I also have become a parent, I think back in amazement, sadness and even horror that my dear friend, almost lost to me forever, did not ever have the assurance so basic to most children as to be taken for granted: that their parents were there for them. Christina was used. She was a prop that served a particular role that her "Mother" played at one time. When the play was canceled or the movie was over, there was no further need for the role. And the prop was discarded.

Judy Clayton Hopkins Yoho, Ph.D.

Part Two

CHAPTER 13

About four months after I started in the middle of sixth grade, leaving all my friends behind one-half grade and, before I'd really had a chance to make any new friends among my classmates, Mother transferred me to Chadwick School in Palos Verdes.

Again, in keeping with all the other major changes of my school life, this transfer took place over the weekend. There wasn't any long discussion about it either. On Friday Mother asked me what I'd think of going away to boarding school and two days later on Sunday she packed me up and drove me there.

I didn't have much chance to think about whether or not I'd like boarding school and I didn't have any chance to say goodbye to my teachers and friends or to Judy. The whole thing just sprang out of thin air. It wasn't a punishment because things had been going unusually well for me at home. I had no idea that I'd never live at home again on a regular basis. I was ten years old.

I hadn't the vaguest idea where we were going but we seemed to drive for a long time, at first along the ocean and then out into the country. After about an hour Mother started looking for the school sign along the pepper tree–lined country road. Finally the blue and white sign appeared and we drove up a long hill with fields on either side of the road. When we stopped it was in front of a small house known as The Cottage. The housemother came out to greet us with a friendly smile. The Cottage was really a dormitory for elementary school girls. The housemother showed us to the room I was to share with three other girls and introduced me to my future roommates. This was such a totally new experience for me that I became very shy and hardly said a word. With all the changes happening so rapidly, I was beginning to be unsure of myself. I didn't seem to have time to adjust to one change before another was upon me. As I looked around the room at the strange girls who were staring curiously at me and then at the two sets of bunk beds we were all to share, I wasn't very sure that I was going to like boarding school. It was no surprise to me that I had been assigned one of the top bunks, since I was the newest arrival. Everyone was quite polite to Mother and to me and the housemother seemed like a nice lady.

Then it was time for Mother to leave. I was overcome with a sense of panic. I burst into tears and clung to her as though to prevent her from leaving. She held me for a moment and then very firmly made me let go of her. She tried to reassure me that I'd make new friends here and that I'd like the school. Nothing seemed to stop the waterfall of tears. I couldn't believe that she was really going to make me stay in this strange place where everybody else already knew one another. I wanted to go home with her and forget about boarding school. She said no. That was impossible. All the arrangements have been made and I was to stay and try to make the best of it. I'd be coming home in two weeks . . . my mind sort of wandered away from her at this point. *Two weeks!* That sounded like an eternity to me. The school policy was to let the students go home every other weekend. Two weeks. I wondered if I'd make it. I was still crying when she drove away.

The housemother came out to the driveway and put her arm around me. She gently guided me back into the cottage and helped me get my things unpacked. She took me around and introduced me to some of the other girls. By then it was time for dinner. We all walked up to the dining room together and that was the first time I saw some of the rest of the school. Chadwick School sat perched on top of a hill like it's own little community. The buildings were mostly white structures that fit neatly into their country surroundings. The dining room was a large separate building divided into the main dining room, the "porch" where the elementary students ate and the big kitchen presided over by John, the cook.

Everyone had assigned tables and one of the girls from my cottage showed me to mine. Food was served family style and there was a faculty member assigned to each table. The food wasn't bad, though all the kids joked about it and dinner went rapidly. I just couldn't quite believe that this was where I was going to live now and every time I started to think about it tears welled up in my eyes. I didn't say much during dinner.

The next day I walked with one of the girls up to the elementary school classrooms in a separate area of their own called the Village. There I met my teacher, Miss Collins, and the rest of my class. The first thing that surprised me was that there were only about a dozen of us in the whole class. Coming from public school I was used to more people in the room. The other thing that surprised me was that Miss Collins taught everything but French. Even though we stayed mostly in the same homeroom in public school, different people came in to teach different subjects. But here at boarding school, we spent the whole day with Miss Collins who was also the principal of the elementary school. During the very first day it became obvious that something was sadly lacking in my math background. This class was doing fractions and I'd never heard of them. I couldn't follow what was going on and when it came my turn to go to the blackboard, I had to tell her that I'd never had fractions in my other school. Except for giving my name to the class earlier, that was about the first thing I'd said. Miss Collins said she'd work with me after school that day and not to worry about it. The rest of the class looked at me like I was a dunce.

Even though I was quite a way behind these students, Miss Collins did work with me enough so that in a relatively short time I was getting good grades again. Math was a continual struggle but somehow I managed to get through it.

I didn't particularly like boarding school and was continually homesick. On the weekends when I went home I would cry all the way back to school. I began to notice that my brother and sisters had developed a way of life that didn't really include me anymore because I wasn't there most of the time. Sometimes when I went home there were new servants I didn't know and often Mother had a new boyfriend. Often on the weekends there were parties and I had to help with the preparations. Sometimes Mother got in extra help and when she didn't I would play bartender.

By and large, the end of my sixth grade went smoothly and even though I ended up with decent grades, I didn't particularly want to return to boarding school the next year.

That summer I turned eleven. In many ways I was still just a little girl, but because I was big for my age and already stood at just over five feet tall, Mother took some precautions and tried to tell me about the physical changes my body would soon be going through. She recognized that my breasts were beginning to develop but refused to let me wear a bra like the other girls. She said it wasn't good for you to wrap your body up so tightly when you were young, that it would weaken the muscles and hinder the natural development. Then she tried to explain about menstruation. I listened attentively and nodded my head but although I understood the words I didn't really comprehend the full impact of our conversation.

The majority of the summer was peaceful because Mother wasn't home at all. She went to Lake Louise in Canada with Uncle Vincent, one of her directors. I liked Uncle Vincent even though we'd had one awful run-in with each other.

One night months ago I was sitting downstairs watching television by myself when I heard a noise coming from the office which was two rooms away. At first it was just some loud voices and I didn't think anything particularly unusual about that. I think I was watching an old Hopalong Cassidy movie and the sound of the TV drowned out most of the argument. But in a few minutes, I heard what sounded like screaming and my heart leaped into my throat. It sounded like my mother screaming.

I dashed through the door and toward the office. When I ran into the room all I saw was Uncle Vincent hitting Mother. She was sort of sprawled across an armchair and looked like she was trying to defend herself.

Without stopping to think about much of anything, I flew at Uncle Vincent and started pounding on him with my fists trying to kick him and screaming at him to let go of my mother. She was crying by this time and I was crying too, but out of shock more than anything else. I'd heard other fights she'd had with men but I'd never actually seen one of them. Until Uncle Vincent could manage to get a grip on both of my arms and hold me away from him I continued to beat at him while Mother cowered in the chair. We were all yelling at once and it's a wonder we didn't have the entire household as an audience.

In a matter of minutes it was all over. Mother was still crying but told Uncle Vincent that he'd better leave. I walked to the door and rather imperiously told him to get out immediately. After he'd left and the door was securely locked I went to Mother and tried to find out if she'd been hurt. I wanted to call the doctor, but she refused. She didn't seem to be bruised and I helped her upstairs.

As coincidence would have it, a few days later was my piano recital. I didn't like piano that much but this year the recital was to be at our house and Mother had prepared a lovely party. The real reason I didn't like piano was that I knew I didn't play very well. I had no real instinct for music and each step was a struggle. Years before when I was just beginning and Mother was very much the proud parent, she invited Helen Hayes to listen to one of my little pieces. Dutifully, I went to the grand piano and played. Aunt Helen said something like "Very nice, dear," to me but to my mother she shook her head and said, "Joan, I'm afraid she plays like an iron butterfly." Mother was not daunted by the evaluation, however, and insisted that I continue to take lessons and practice for many more years.

So, by the time of this recital, I was competent but not talented. However, since I was to be the hostess, the timing was unfortunate. Mother informed me the morning of the recital that she had invited Uncle Vincent and it would be rude to not let him come because of the minor incident a few days earlier.

I stared at her totally appalled. It was unthinkable to me that she should ever want to see such a person again, let alone invite him to *my* recital. I also thought it showed very little concern for my feelings, but I didn't say so. Then she landed the final blow. She said that no matter how I felt I had to be polite to him and that she'd appreciate it if I would also apologize.

Apologize? I said no . . . flat out . . . I wouldn't apologize because I hadn't done anything wrong. She replied that no matter what I thought it would be necessary for me to say I was sorry.

I was sorry, all right, but evidently for the wrong things. I was sorry that she'd invited him, I was sorry I had to have this stupid piano recital, I was sorry that I had to play hostess and I was very sorry that I didn't just let him beat her up or do whatever it was that happened during these fights she'd been having with men since I was about seven years old. Then I wouldn't have to be humiliated by apologizing for something I didn't do. Then and there I decided that it was the last time I'd try to intervene even if it sounded to me like someone was trying to murder her. There was something I just didn't understand about these situations and it was better for me if I just left it that way.

But all that had happened some time before. After I apologized, the subject was never mentioned again. It seemed ironic to me that twenty years later when I was an actress myself, Uncle Vincent was one of the few people from my childhood who actually helped me and hired me to do a part on one of the television shows he was then directing.

Near the end of August, that summer I turned eleven, I was in my bathroom changing clothes and getting ready to take a shower. I notice a spot on my pants and when I took them off I saw blood all over me. I stood staring at myself transfixed for a moment. Then I let out a shriek like a wounded animal and ran half naked down the hall into the nursery where Mrs. Howe was supervising my sisters' bath.

By the time I found Mrs. Howe I was screaming and crying, "I'm bleeding . . . I'm bleeding . . . what's the matter with me?!" Mrs. Howe tried to calm me down and explain to me but I was sobbing inconsolably. I was sure something dreadful had mysteriously happened to me and I was going to bleed to death while everybody sat around talking. No one but me seemed in the least bit upset and that made me furious. How could Mrs. Howe take my disastrous condition so calmly? I was *bleeding*. Bleeding meant you had been hurt. Bleeding meant you needed care and attention but all I was getting was a lot of words I still couldn't completely understand.

Mrs. Howe took me back to my room saying something about not wanting to upset my sisters and found me some Kotex and one of those ugly elastic belts. She told me I was to put all that paraphernalia on after I'd taken my shower. I was still in a state of shock.

After she left me alone, I burst into a renewed fit of despair and threw myself on the floor where I kicked my feet and pounded my fists and had a good old-fashioned temper tantrum all by myself.

I couldn't understand why my mother smiled when she found out. I couldn't see anything so wonderful about "becoming a woman." I tried everything to make my feelings understood. I fainted and took to my bed; I got terrible cramps and took to my bed; I got headaches and took to my bed. I hated not being allowed to go swimming, not being allowed to play kickball or climb trees. I hated the bleeding and all the messy stuff that went with trying to cope with it. I was convinced that the doctor could have done something about it but no matter how much I pleaded no one would do anything except get that weird smile on their face.

And so I stomped my feet and pounded my fists and sobbed my heart out to no avail because puberty and my "period" were inevitably upon me.

The most embarrassing part of all was that my mother insisted on telling anybody that would listen. It was like she thought of it as some kind of accomplishment. I would blush crimson whenever the story about becoming a "lady" started.

So I was doubly mortified when she took me back to boarding school in September and told practically the entire dorm about my period. I didn't even have it any more and still she told the housemother and my new roommate, Dolores. I tried not to notice while she was telling everybody and started unpacking. They all got those same funny smiles on their faces and I failed to see the humor.

During these next few months at Chadwick I began to appreciate that I was in a different and rather special school. My seventh grade class was a bit larger than it had been the previous year and I was no longer the "new" person. I had made some friends and liked my classes. But those were not the major differences I came to realize.

The first thing that dawned on me after I moved into the main girls' dorm was that the rules were not nearly as strict as the ones under which I lived at home. We all were given weekly chore assignments like sorting laundry or cleaning the bathrooms and hallways on Saturday and working one of the three meals in the dining room. But these assignments rotated every week and we worked in teams. Compared with the work I had to do at home, this seemed easy to me even though some of the girls complained. None of the duties took more than an hour and most of them much less. There was a merit system as well and for certain serious infractions of the rules a faculty member could give you demerits. But there was even some leeway on that if you hadn't been in trouble and had earned enough merits to counteract the report. The only real penalty was extra work if you got over a certain number of demerits within a time period or at worst you couldn't go home for the weekend.

To me the system seemed fair, logical and not very difficult to live with. I already knew how to do most of the work and never had much of a problem with it.

The second difference that set Chadwick apart from the world I'd known in public school was the other students. Most of them, I soon discovered, were from backgrounds similar to mine. By that I mean that a good number of them were from families who were involved in the motion picture business in one way or another. Many of them were also from what used to be called "broken homes." In some cases, keeping the family tree straight was something of a full-time job. We used to have a terrible joke that circulated among us that went something like:

Kid #1: "How do you like your new father?"

Kid #2: "I like him a lot."

Kid #1: "Yeah, I liked him too. We had him last year."

The nice thing about being at Chadwick was that you didn't have to start at ground zero with the inevitable "What's it like to be a movie star's daughter" routine. I felt a sense of companionship and understanding here that I hadn't expected.

Most of the teachers lived on campus and we all got to know one another like a family. There were only about 150 students in the school and the classes were still small.

Commander and Mrs. Chadwick who ran the school were already in their early sixties when I met them but they were of pioneer stock and two more energetic people you could not have imagined.

Commander had been in the Navy and was only referred to by his rank, as though it was his first name and last name all in one. Margaret Lee Chadwick was the daughter of a Utah minister and had been the first woman to go to Stanford on a scholarship. They were both remarkable people and ran their school with love, dedication and hard work.

Besides being co-educational, which was a radical departure, Chadwick also prided itself on being one of the finest preparatory schools in the Western United States. All of its graduates went on to college and many of them were admitted to the hallowed universities of the Eastern Establishment.

Commander took charge of the financial and disciplinary aspects of the school. Mrs. Chadwick supervised the curriculum and believed that anyone could achieve anything if they worked hard enough. She had great faith.

In 1950 Chadwick was a country school. There was not only lots of space but also a working farm on the school property. The fields grew hay and some wheat and the farm raised chickens, pigs and rabbits for the dining room. There were also stables, corrals and a pasture for the horses. Not much of Palos Verdes had been developed yet and there were wonderful wide-open places to ride. As the months went by my life seemed continually better. Of course there were rules and minor differences with classmates and the fact that Mother still wouldn't let me have any bras even though I was now more developed than most of the girls wearing them, but I liked the school and the people very much.

I had only gotten in any real trouble once and even that wasn't too bad.

Somehow a group of us had gotten the idea that it would be funny to spike the punch at our class Christmas party. One of the girls on our committee was not a boarding student and we managed to sneak some whiskey into all the Coke bottles and carefully reseal them so it didn't look as though anything had happened. We studiously figured a way to mark several "clean" bottles for our teacher, but during the excitement of the party, someone screwed up and we were caught.

It was a terrible moment when we were all called into Mrs. Chadwick's office. She had a way of looking at you that made you feel worse than whatever the actual punishment was going to be. Somehow you felt as though you'd betrayed the ultimate trust she put in each child under her care and it would have been a lot better to just have someone yell at you rather than have to look at the disappointment on Mrs. Chadwick's face.

After we'd all told our version of the story and vowed we'd never even think of participating in such a travesty again, we were given demerits and a sound lecture on the responsible behavior expected of each student in the Chadwick School. We were all very ashamed of ourselves for bringing such a disgrace on the school and in truth, I don't think anyone in the room ever forgot the lesson.

However, in the early spring of 1951 when I was eleven and a half years old, an event occurred that would change my life forever. It was one of those definitive experiences that binds everything together and yet rips the fabric of your emotional life into shreds so small you wonder if you'll ever be able to piece it all together again. It's one of those times that afterwards become a reference point in your life and you think of things in terms of before and afterwards. For me and my young years, it was like a dying and fighting your way back out of the grave.

It's hard to go back all those years and look clearly at something that took place such a long time ago. The only memories are of pain and the only landmarks are events still so crystal clear that they almost stand alone like Dali figures on an otherwise empty canvas.

I had been listening to the stories of some of the older girls at night in the dorm. In between the whispers and the giggles and the long silences I had begun to put together the excitingly romantic story of one girl's adventures with the guy who was in charge of running the stables. He was a student on a scholarship and spent most of his time outside of classes up at the stables taking care of the horses. I vaguely knew who he was but it didn't matter because the stories were better I'm sure than the boy himself. As the weeks wore on I became totally captivated by veiled references to what went on at the stables and the flushed, happy look on the face of the girl who told the stories.

I secretly decided to see for myself what all the excitement was about. The only place I had a chance to see the boy in question was during art class. The boys took shop in the room right next to the art class and I managed to slip him a note without anyone else seeing me. After an exchange of several notes, it was decided that we would meet Friday night while the basketball game was going on. I would sign out of the dorm to watch the game and since the basketball court was right next to the stables, it wouldn't be too hard to slip away unnoticed for a little while and still get back to the dorm by sign-in time.

There were several days to go until Friday and I thought about meeting him a lot. It was sort of like my own adventure, my own secret. I'd never really even talked to this boy because he was about sixteen and much too old for me, but he was good looking and tall and kind of looked like a cowboy. Ever since I had been a little girl, cowboys were my heroes. After I saw the play *Annie Get Your Gun* in New York, I'd wanted to be a cowboy. Then I discovered that little girls weren't supposed to want to be cowboys and so now, even though I knew I wanted to be an actress when I grew up, cowboys were still my heroes. I loved cowboy movies and I loved riding horses. For me, then, it was all a perfect combination even though I didn't know the specific boy at all. I'd never even spoken to him face to face. We had only exchanged looks and notes before Friday night.

Before the basketball game I took particular care with my shower and washed my hair until it squeaked clean. Even though I had to be cautious not to look like I was getting dressed specially, I did my best to look pretty without the help of makeup. My jeans weren't wrinkled and my shirt was pressed. I borrowed a bra from one of the other girls so that I wouldn't seem like the kid I was if he touched me and with my heart beating a mile a minute, I signed out after dinner for the basketball game. I could hardly act natural during the first half of the game. I tried to cheer for the boys I knew and it sounded hollow and false. I thought that at any minute someone would ask me what was the matter with me and the whole adventure would come to a screeching halt, but nothing of the sort happened and in fact no one paid particular attention to the cleanly scrubbed eleven and a half year old sitting on one of the back benches. At half time, when everyone else went to the bathroom, I left the court and disappeared into the darkness at one turn in the path. From there it was just a matter of making my way carefully through the bushes around to the back of the stables. Since no one rode at night, there was only one light on in the tack room at the far end of the row of stalls. The rest of the stable area was in darkness.

There was only a small sliver of a moon and I could barely see where I was going. Finally, after what seemed like an hour but was in reality probably only five minutes, I found my way along the back of the stalls to the corner of the tack room. The night sounds were all around me and crickets interspersed with the sound of horses moving in their stalls.

Carefully I crept around the protective edge of the board walls and past the big stack of hay bales. I stood in silence for a moment looking at the tall dark-haired boy I had planned to meet here.

Though I didn't say anything, he must have sensed me standing there in the half light that spilled past the door of the back room because he turned to face me. I could still hear the sound of my own heart beating, half in anticipation and half in fear. I thought that he was better looking than I'd remembered him in the woodworking shop and also seemed taller, nearly six feet. He walked toward me and smiled. I didn't move.

When he was standing next to me in the semi-darkness, he took my hand. He wasn't exactly handsome but I liked the looks of him and sort of quivered when he touched me. "Let's go over here," he said, and led me quietly to one of the empty stalls.

Inside the stall it was even darker than in the pale moonlight. There was the smell of fresh hay and old wood, of leather and horses. These were all happy smells for me, familiar smells of days spent riding with my braids flapping behind me and a sense of freedom as the horses galloped through the countryside.

He kneeled down on the hay and drew me to him. I was glad it was so dark because I felt very awkward and embarrassed. He was gentle and easy and I started to relax when he kissed me. I lay back on the soft crinkly hay and heard it rustle beneath me as we moved.

He was so warm and the sensation of his hand on my body so comforting that I didn't even realize that he's unbuttoned my shirt and unfastened my borrowed bra until it was already done. I struggled a little bit but as he continued to kiss me I sort of felt like I was melting. He had slipped his jacket underneath me and I never felt the hay as my jeans slipped down below my knees. I wasn't really thinking about anything just sort of floating around the feeling of him touching me and talking to me very softly.

The stab of pain that shot through me like a rocket nearly made me scream. My whole body contracted with that pain and involuntarily I started crying. He slapped his hand over my mouth so that no sound actually escaped and the pain disappeared as quickly as it had occurred. He lay on top of me now and held me very tightly.

I was scared and felt like I'd been hurt but I didn't quite know how. He dried my few tears with his hands and continued to kiss me gently. "You've never done this before, have you?" he asked. I shook my head, no. "How old are you?" he whispered. "Almost twelve," I replied. He let out a low whistle between his teeth and said, "I thought you were closer to fourteen." I didn't know exactly what he meant by that, but I did have a strange sense that somehow I was a disappointment, though he was being very kind about it. Then he said, "Let me tell you something and try to remember this as you're growing up. Don't let just anybody do it . . . you choose who you want and be careful." I nodded my head in agreement and then he helped me get dressed.

He kissed me once more when we were standing in the doorway to the stall. Without saying any more I walked away into the darkness.

That would have been the end of it I guess except that I told one of the girls and he must have told a couple of this friends and by Sunday afternoon I was summoned into Mrs. Chadwick's office. Later that same day they had a doctor examine me and his verdict was that I was still a virgin despite any rumors contrary.

However, those rumors had spread so fast that the school was faced with a potential scandal. Finally, my mother had been called and she of course was horrified. After a tear-stained meeting between the three of us during which Mother called me a common whore, Mrs. Chadwick told me to go back to the dorm and take a long hot bath. They would decide what was to be done and she would call me back to her office after the decision had been made.

Walking despondently back to the dorm my head was filled with a dozen thoughts at once and they tended to collide with one another so that it was impossible to sort them out. First of all I was scared to death. Secondly I was extremely embarrassed by all the personal questions I found difficult to answer. And, third I kept wondering . . . if nothing has really happened to me then what is all the upset about? The doctor said nothing happened, which I kind of already knew, so why was everyone so angry?

My mother's reaction had hurt me very much. Somehow I thought she'd understand a little better. Mrs. Chadwick had her school to think about. She'd always been very nice to me and I was sorry to see her upset. Up until now everyone had thought of me as just a little girl and I think that's what really shocked them the most about the whole situation.

But nobody seemed to really care about me and how I felt or if I was scared and confused, which I certainly was. I hadn't really started out to do anything so terrible. I don't know how to explain it but it was like I was looking for something. Something special that I'd seen on the faces of the older girls when they were confiding their secrets with one another. A look, and an excitement, a belonging . . . love . . . I don't really know. One thing is certain: never in a million years would I have done any of it had I known that this was going to be the result.

But what I couldn't figure out was why I was getting in so much trouble for something they knew hadn't even happened. Those older girls never had anything happen to them.

I took a bath as Mrs. Chadwick had instructed me to do and tried not to think about it too much.

However, the next afternoon, I was back in the office. This time there was just Mrs. Chadwick and myself. I got scared all over again sitting there waiting for her to begin speaking. I tried not to start crying and it took all my will power to hold back the tears. I sat with my hands clenched in my lap and a stinging lump in my throat.

Finally, Mrs. Chadwick started speaking to me and her voice sounded shaky and strained. She told me that she was very sorry that this incident had happened . . . that it was very serious . . . and that I was going to face a very difficult time in the days ahead because of it. They had decided to let me stay in school because I was so young and could not be blamed for the entire thing. However, the boy was going to be expelled and I was not to see or speak to him again. In addition, I was going to have to be punished. I was not going to be allowed to go home for some time, nor was I allowed to go on the school's mid-semester ski trip. The final punishment was one hundred hours of hard work. This work was going to be assigned at a rate of one hour per school day, six hours on Saturday and six hours on each day of the two-week mid-semester vacation until such time as the entire one hundred hours had been completed. During the time that I was working off my punishment, I was allowed no privileges. That meant I was not allowed off the school premises to go shopping or riding, that during normal on-campus weekends I was not allowed to go to the school movies or dances.

As the litany of my punishment droned on, I sat dully staring at Mrs. Chadwick. I couldn't believe my ears. Until that moment I don't think I fully realized that what I'd done, or tried to do, or not done according to the doctor, was so terrible. I honestly didn't think I was capable of doing anything that bad.

I left the office and walked like a ghost back to the dorm. The bleakness of my future had been graphically spelled out for me and my shoulders could almost feel the physical burden of it.

So that was it: no privileges and one hundred hours of hard work. I fleetingly wondered if it wouldn't have been a lot easier just to be expelled and get the agony over with, but then I forgot about that when the image of my mother's wrath appeared before me. She hadn't even asked me if I was all right. I probably couldn't have answered anyway. I had a miserable habit of not being able to say a word when I was put on the spot. All my thoughts became a hopeless jumble at those times and I couldn't seem to get them sorted out into words. My standard answer was "I don't know" and in part that was the truth. So it probably wouldn't have mattered if she'd asked me.

Somehow I got through the next week. I knew that a lot of people knew because I saw them staring at me and if I'd look at them they'd quickly turn away. But mostly everybody just left me alone . . . I felt badly for the boy too. He left school very quickly and I only saw him once by accident. We didn't say anything even though I wanted to tell him I was really sorry. He didn't look like he hated me, just bewildered by the circumstances.

During the vacation I worked six hours a day, every day but Sunday. I pulled weeds and washed windows. I cleaned out classrooms and washed cars. I dusted every book in the library and scrubbed down all the tables and chairs in the dining room. I had mopped and polished half the school it seemed and still at the end of the vacation I had over 25 hours of work left to do.

At first I hated the work but gradually I got used to it. No one bothered me much and I was left alone most of the time. I ate my meals just outside the kitchen in one little corner of the porch. John, the cook, was a kindly, gruff man who was always very good to me. He'd think up little goodies to give me which brightened my day a lot and I'd look forward to his brusque greeting and twinkling eyes.

When school started again it was a different story. By then the rumor had turned into a full-fledged story and it seemed that everyone had heard it. Some of the girls decided not to be friends with me when there was anyone else around and some of the guys made snide remarks and rude jokes at my expense.

For the next few weeks it seemed that I was constantly on the verge of tears. At night I would cry silently into my pillow so my roommate wouldn't be able to add to the rumors. During the day I did my best to get through classes and keep my studies in order. In fact it was during this time that I really began to pour my energy into my schoolwork. It was the one avenue left open to me and the only source of my rewards. Getting "A" meant that everything was not a total loss and I could still be good at something. So my grades were astonishingly good through an otherwise miserable time.

Not all my friends turned their backs on me. Classmates who had known me better were still at least polite to me. But there were two friends in particular with whom I became a lot closer. One was Jane Davis who turned out to be a sort of buoyant free spirit with a wonderful sense of the absurd and the other was Hoagy Carmichael. Hoagy was a true character. Because he was always overweight he had years of experience dealing with unkind jokes and constant needling. It was Hoagy who began to teach me to let most of it roll off me and not pay any attention to it . . . even to act as though I hadn't heard it. It was also Hoagy who, through a series of verbal sparing matches, taught me to be quicker with a sharp reply. Even though Hoagy was always the class clown and the life of any party, everyone knew that if they were going to start in on Hoagy they'd better be prepared to get some of it back in lightning quick zingers that Hoagy became sort of famous for. Hoagy had come from a very difficult home and he understood without too many stories exchanged between us what I had gone through. It was a relief not to have to explain everything and still have someone else understand. I think that was the basis of our friendship starting in seventh grade and lasting for many years. Hoagy sort of let me hang around with him and I could be in a group of kids with him and not be the center of attention, because he usually was. In return, I would help him with his schoolwork. Hoagy was smart but he got bored with the routine of homework and since it was easy for me, I was more than delighted to help in any way I could. In fact, because I was so good in school a lot of the kids would ask me to help them and I found that it was one way to get friends. It was a purely selfish exchange, I guess, but it was better than being alone.

At the end of the school year, I went home. It was nice to see my brother and sisters again, but it didn't take me long to discover that we had a horrible nurse. Mrs. Howe had decided not to work full time for one family and was just working relief days. The woman we had was a young Swedish task master who had her own ideas about how to treat us. It wasn't that she was stricter than Mrs. Howe had been but that she was meaner. Her spankings were often with a hanger or a belt strap and not always confined to our bottoms. She had a miserable habit of twisting your ear to get you to do something and we all hated her.

One night Mother was going out on a date and left instructions that I could watch television until Spade Cooley was over. My brother and I loved to watch that show because of the old guy that did the car commercials. In those days the commercials were live and this guy called "Leatherbritches" would come on and bang his hand down on the hood of the car while he was telling you what a great deal it was and the whole car would rattle and shake. He slammed doors and pounded away while my brother and I would roll on the floor with laughter. That was our favorite part of the whole variety show.

This particular night the Swedish nurse came in while Chris and I were in our usual state of hysteria over "Leatherbritches'" antics and without saying a word she turned off the TV.

"Mother said we could watch to the end of Spade Cooley," I told her.

"This show is nothing but silly trash," she replied with a note of disgust in her voice.

"It doesn't matter what *you* think. Mother said we could watch it!" I snapped back. With rather amazing speed she slapped me across the face. I hated being slapped in the face. I absolutely hated it. It wasn't the hurt so much as the insult. I raised my hand to hit her back and she grabbed me by the hair. She was considerably stronger than I was and she managed to pull me by the hair all the way upstairs and into my room.

Once inside the room she released me by throwing me down on the bed. It looked to me as though she was coming after me again. I pulled my knees up to my chest and just as she was leaning over to hit me I kicked her in the stomach with both my feet as hard as I could. To my astonishment she went flying across the room and landed in a heap under the window. I had effectively knocked the wind out of her but she was not unconscious. I sat on the bed staring at her and wondering what would happen next. After a minute or so she muttered something to me in what I supposed was Swedish and sort of staggered out of the room holding onto her stomach.

The next morning I didn't say one word to the nurse and when Mother asked me what had happened I told her exactly. She asked me where I had gotten the idea to kick the nurse in the stomach. With a look of total innocence I replied, "That's the way they do it in cowboy movies!"

The nurse was fired on the spot and I didn't get to watch cowboy movies for a week. In retrospect, I thought it was a fair price to pay if it got rid of the nurse whom we all hated.

However, we were generally having a lot of trouble keeping any servants. Cooks, nurses, secretaries and the rest came and went with astonishing regularity. Many of the nurses couldn't stomach what one referred to as the "reform school discipline." If they were ever caught trying to bend the rules even a little bit they were fired. After a while it was hard to keep their names straight as one blended into another. At one point, we hadn't been able to keep anyone longer than a couple of months. Just as we got used to them, they packed up and left, and we never saw them again. It seemed to us that the nicer they were, the faster they left. We also had a couple of old battle axes, but mercifully they were fired too.

We had one terrific nurse at this time named Ishy. I think she was English, but I'm not really sure. She was neither young nor old and she knew wonderful games which she taught all of us. She was strict enough to satisfy Mother and kind enough to be tolerable to us. Unfortunately there was another situation in the house at the time that proved to be too much for Ishy.

It was during this time that Mother did one of her last pictures for Warner Brothers. It was not very good and she knew it. She also probably knew that her days under contract were about over.

Since she didn't share most of her problems with anyone in the house, we were only aware that she seemed angry and edgy much of the time. Mother had a "wounded animal" attitude toward adversity in that she tended to go off by herself and suffer alone rather than let anyone share or discuss the trouble with her. That attitude may have spared her ego to some extent but it kept things bottled up and left little room for negotiation in her relationships. She thought other people should behave in the same stalwart, solitary manner and saw it as a mark of weakness if they didn't. What it really did was confine her behind a mask of strength and kept people, including her children, at a distance. It contributed to a great measure of her loneliness and her feelings of having to fight every inch of the way alone. She really had a terrible time trusting anyone and letting anyone see that she was human with the failings and frailties that implies. She had set her course. Any deviation or relaxation from that proscribed routine was interpreted as failure, lack of will power. She put great store in personal will power and attributed most of her own success to it. That will power guided her through the rough waters of each day. It was translated into rules governing all facets of household management, the children's discipline and her own career. Nothing was left to chance or experiment or negotiation.

She set the rules without consultation and enforced them without deviation. By virtue of having been created, the rules carried with them the weight of moral rightness. They absolutely were right and everything, everyone else was simply wrong. Her way was *the* way and she would not listen to contrary opinion. It was as though she believed that enough rules, rigidly enforced, would keep the world in order. It was a way of trying to hold back chaos and with it any spontaneous, chance infringement on her territory.

CHAPTER 14

I suppose there is no creature more perverse than the human being. If there is chaos in a life, no amount of regulation and will power will hold it in total abeyance forever. The inner turbulence will seek an outlet and find the weakest link in the armor of the personality.

For Mother the weak link was alcohol.

One summer night I had been watching television until my usual bedtime. When I went upstairs I noticed that one of the sliding doors to Mother's suite of rooms was open. I knew she was home but I didn't hear any sounds of movement or talking on the phone. I went into my room and got ready for bed. By then it was maybe 9:30 and I knocked on Mother's door intending to say goodnight. There was no answer to either my knocking or calling which I thought was strange. I went downstairs to check and see if she was anywhere else in the house but she wasn't.

When I went back to her doorway I thought I heard a small noise like a moan but I wasn't sure. I walked into the upstairs sitting room and through the main door into her dressing room. There were a few lights on but I didn't see her. I made a circular tour of the dressing room and bath area and started down the narrow hallway on the opposite side of the room and when I went through the first door I nearly stumbled over her body lying on the floor! Seeing her lying there startled and shocked me at the same time. I kneeled beside her and tried to rouse her, thinking maybe she'd fainted. I couldn't seem to get any response, though it was apparent that she was still breathing and alive. Since I was unable to move her by myself, I rushed to get help and the first person I found was the nurse, Ishy. Sort of half talking and half babbling my story, I pulled Ishy back to where Mother was lying unconscious. I was scared that she was sick. I had to fight to remain even relatively calm. Ishy leaned over and turned Mother face up.

"Should I call the doctor?" I whispered to Ishy. She only shook her head negatively. "What's wrong with her?" I whispered again.

Ishy looked me straight in the eyes and said, "She's drunk."

"Drunk? Are you sure?" I asked her.

She just nodded her head again. "It's not the first time," and indicated that I should help her carry Mother to her bed. I was surprised how difficult it was for the two of us to maneuver the limp body safely across one room and into her bed. Once there, Ishy covered her and I arranged the pillows under her head.

We turned out the lights and closed the sliding door behind us. I said goodnight to Ishy and she went back to her room on the other side of the house.

I lay in bed thinking about what had happened, trying to piece it all together. I was still shocked but it didn't seem to surprise Ishy. I thought about how sometimes Mother seemed to be different but I never knew why. Then I realized that it was usually in the evening after she'd started drinking around five or six o'clock. Then I thought about the aspirin in the morning and knew enough to begin putting that together with what was called a hangover. I realized that the aspirin in the morning had been going on for several years but I had never known why. That was probably why she was so grumpy in the morning even if she'd slept until nearly noon and we'd had to whisper all morning. I'd heard other kids talk about their parents drinking and I knew that some of them had parents who had a real problem with booze. I tried to think back over some of those conversations and sort this out for myself, since I was quite sure there wouldn't be anyone I could trust to talk about it.

Needless to say, nothing was ever mentioned about the incident. I don't know if Mother ever even wondered about how she got to bed, but I never said a word about it.

Before I left for camp that summer there were several more times that Ishy and I carried Mother to bed. It didn't scare me now, I just listened for the significant noises and then went to get the nurse. There was sort of a dreamlike quality about the whole thing, since in the light of day, no one mentioned either the event or the problem, as though it never happened. But at summer's end when I came home from camp, Ishy had quit.

The rest of the help, particularly the cooks we were now getting from the employment agencies, were next to useless. They were downright incompetent. One woman was so nervous she actually burned a pot of green beans so badly that the entire mess including the pot had to be thrown out. She only lasted one day.

But the replacements were no better. They turned out frizzled, rubbery fried eggs, burnt toast, soggy vegetables and watery sauces. They couldn't be trusted to do the shopping properly, broke things and generally lived in a state of chronic nervous collapse. They were incompetent but Mother screaming at them certainly didn't improve matters. She had a way of giving people a string of orders all at once and expecting them not only to remember all the instructions but also to do them in the order she'd given them. For all of these people, that was an impossible feat. They couldn't even seem to do the job they were hired for, let alone anything creative.

Mother was in a constant state of rage that never let up between the firing of one unfortunate and the hiring of the next. The atmosphere of extreme agitation permeated the entire household. After a while, the most qualified person in the world could have come into that kitchen and never had a chance to succeed. The only good thing from my point of view was that I didn't have to eat any more rare meat. By some minor miracle, these cooks couldn't seem to get it that rare.

I am not surprised that word of Mother's rampages got back to the employment agencies. The turnover at our house became common knowledge and the agencies simply wouldn't send us any more applicants because there was no one left to send.

But fortunately I spent six weeks at Douglas Camp in the Carmel River Valley. Unfortunately, most of the six weeks was spent in the infirmary with a miserable combination of boils and acute poison oak. I was the original calamine kid that summer.

When I returned from camp looking much improved but still dreadful, Mother said that Mrs. Chadwick wanted to speak to me. There was some question about whether or not I would return to school. My heart was in my throat as I dialed the phone. In the last year and a half I'd grown to really like the school and was sure I'd made some friends. Because of the haste with which I'd been transferred out of public school, I'd lost touch with most of my friends there and really didn't know many kids in my own neighborhood either. I had sort of assumed that I would be going back in the fall and now I didn't know what to expect.

Mrs. Chadwick told me she realized that I still had a struggle on my hands in terms of full acceptance at the school and she wanted to give me the opportunity to decide whether I wanted to stay or if I thought it would be easier for me to start over fresh somewhere else. I hadn't anticipated that I'd have anything to do with this kind of decision about my own life and I had to think for a moment. The considerable difficulties of the previous school year paraded across my memory. I thought about what little progress I'd been able to make and knew that she was right about still having to struggle. But I also thought about Hoagy and Jane and some of the others. If I left now it would be an admission of defeat. If I left, I wouldn't even be around to defend myself. I told her I'd like to stay at Chadwick School. She accepted my decision and said she was glad to see I had the courage to see it through.

What I had no way of knowing at that time was that eighth grade was going to be the worse year yet.

Even at home I had been living under a permanent "second chance" status ever since that fateful Friday night many months before. There was no leeway for minor infractions of the rules under "second chance." I had the feeling that whatever I did was suspect and it began to make me very nervous. I was never quite sure whether this would be the day when I did something that would wipe out even the tenuous second chance status of my existence and I'd find myself in serious trouble again! I lived those days certain that I was standing on the brink of an unseen disaster.

There were only four eighth grade girls who were boarding students that year and it was decided that instead of living at the dorm, we would all live at Chadwick House. Besides myself there was Nancy, Marianna and Racquel who was from El Salvador. Nancy and I had our own rooms while Marianna and Racquel shared the larger room at the end of the hallway. Chadwick House was a large three-story hillside Spanish house with magnificent gardens and a spectacular view of the ocean. Commander and Mrs. Chadwick were used to having children living with them and taking us into their home was not the disruption for them that it might at first seem. In return, we helped with the cleaning and the dishes. We went to school with them in the morning and stayed there through dinner and until study hall was over in the evening. On the weekends we helped to clean the house and then were free to do as we wished.

There was nothing initially to indicate that this was going to be such a difficult year for me except perhaps the second chance business at home.

So many of the students lived in the West Los Angeles and Beverly Hills area that a private bus service was arranged to take us to and from school twice a month. At first I went home every other weekend just like everyone else. But these weekends were not going very well and I knew it. Because we were chronically short of help there seemed to be an unending list of things I was supposed to do when I got home. Many times I spent most of Saturday doing the laundry and hanging it out on the lines and then folding it and taking the different piles to their proper destination. There was always my room to be cleaned from top to bottom even though it had hardly been used. If Mother was having company, there was silver to be polished and extra housework. The only thing I really enjoyed doing was setting the table with the beautiful silverware and crystal and china. It looked so lovely afterwards that I often wished I had a picture of it. In the evening when the guests came I would tend bar and sometimes help serve dinner.

I would be fine on Friday when I first got home. By Saturday I would be tired and on Sunday I'd be nervous all over again. It was not unusual for me to lose weight during those weekends because Mother was after me all the time. Either I hadn't done something properly or I moved too slowly. She literally kept us running from the time we got up until long after dinner. Chris was about eight now and beginning to feel the brunt of the work too. More than once she kept him up until after midnight scrubbing the floor of the dining room in which we ate. She made him do that floor over time after time as she found one flaw or another first in his work and then in his attitude.

The worst part of it was that I couldn't do anything to help him. If I opened my mouth, both of us got in trouble. Mother's strategy was one of divide-and-conquer. One of us kids had to be in trouble all the time. Now it was Chris's turn to be the family scapegoat. I was at school most of the time and the girls were still too young. Mother also whipped Chris at the slightest provocation. In just a few brief years Chris had gone from being the fair-haired son to taking the brunt of Mother's wrath impatience.

He was just at the stage when he wanted to ride bikes and play ball and go swimming all day and here he was held captive in a house full of nothing but women. There was no father to play with, no man to understand from his own childhood what a young boy goes through growing up. I got the impression that Mother never really tried to understand either.

Despite the insistence and urging of several of her male friends, she refused to hear any compromise. She never changed any of the rules to accommodate a boy and Chris was forced into playing catch with the nurse and riding his bike around the pool. When he had a friend over they had to be careful about the flower beds and making too much noise. But rarely was he allowed to go to other boys' homes and almost never to ride his bike on the wide empty streets around our house. Most of the whippings and the trouble he got into would have seemed cruel indeed in any other circumstance.

It was during these years that Chris began to change from a happy-go-lucky little prankster with a mischievous twinkle in his eyes and a charm about him that was undeniable to a rather high-strung, fairly excitable young boy. If you had looked only at the way Mother treated Chris you would have thought that she really must have hated him and men in general. And I think some of that is true, I think she did hate most men.

But if my brother Chris was having his problems, mine seemed double. By the end of these weekends I was worn out. Not so much by the work which was always considerable but by the constant strain. I was on the verge of tears half of the time and the other half I was sullen and quiet, withdrawing into myself as the only means of self protection.

Mother had several long talks with Mrs. Chadwick after which it was decided that because I was a "bad influence" on my brother and sisters, it would be better if I didn't come home for awhile. How all the turmoil she created home turned into my being a bad influence I couldn't figure out. The only thing I did realize is that Mother knew that I took my brother's side, if silently, and that infuriated her. My sisters were still at the stage of trying to win her love and affection and totally innocent of anything more than being occasional tattletales.

I didn't particularly want to stay at school every weekend of my life, but in a way it was a relief. At least I knew what to expect both at Chadwick House and at school and, therefore, things went fairly smoothly.

What I didn't anticipate was that since I was no longer going home, Mother would call Mrs. Chadwick at least once a week in the evening to check up on me. I always dreaded those phone calls. No matter how calmly the week at school had gone, there would always be something that Mother found to magnify out of proportion. Then I'd have to sit there and take a verbal beating while she bawled me out for whatever trumped-up charge it happened to be this week.

After the phone calls, I'd usually be in tears and go upstairs to talk to Mrs. Chadwick. To her great credit, she spent hours and hours talking to me about whatever the problem happened to be. It took me months to figure out that Mother was usually drinking when she'd call. She'd badger Mrs. Chadwick to relate every minor detail of my behavior until she'd find something to get angry with me about.

What I couldn't ever seem to explain adequately to anyone was the change that came over Mother when she was drinking. It was very deceptive. She didn't sound drunk. By that I mean she didn't slur her words or wander off in her train of thought. If anything she seemed to become sharper and quicker than normal. But the two consistent clues were her anger and that she was totally irrational. She made up stories that had never happened and she became fanatic about rules and regulations. She made her charges with such authority and conviction that no one would dream of challenging the truth of them. It would be her word against mine as to what the truth was, and you can well imagine who won. Even Mrs. Chadwick, who believed in the intrinsic good of every human being, began to sense that I couldn't always be lying, particularly when she lived with me day after day and I didn't lie about anything else. The truth was that I was doing well in my classes, getting good grades, and managing to struggle through the difficulties of making friends. The truth was that I was working very hard to regain the faith and trust of the faculty and the friendship of my peers. But the truth was not good enough for Mother.

She insisted on perpetuating the image of me as a bad girl who lied and was not to be trusted for an instant. She insisted on finding ways to punish me even if she had to make up things I'd done to deserve punishment.

At first I did get punished and had normal privileges at the school denied, in addition to not being allowed to go home. Because I was always under fire, I was sort of set apart from the other kids. The faculty had been told to watch me carefully and I felt it. It was uncomfortable being under constant surveillance and there were times when I was tempted to do something wrong just to warrant the suspicion.

Christmas vacation at home was a total disaster. I spent the most time in my room either being punished or writing those never ending thank-you notes. The little time remaining I spent with the fans on the assembly line turning out stacks of photomailers because Mother was short one secretary and the photos to the fans all over the world had gotten backlogged for months.

I was so glad to get back to school I couldn't believe it. Of course Mother told Mrs. Chadwick that I didn't deserve to go home because of my insolent attitude and that I made the entire household unhappy. Mrs. Chadwick sighed and shook her head. I had the awful feeling I'd disappointed her after our long talk just before vacation when I'd promised to be good and try to get along with Mother.

I was always having to promise to be good. It never quite worked out though because when I got home Mother would start screaming and then there'd be a fight or a spanking and the result would be blamed on me. I rarely talked back to Mother. It was the look on my face that got me into most of the trouble. When she was drinking I'd try to stay out of her way but I was never completely successful.

When I was at school I had already learned not to call her after five o'clock in the afternoon. Right around five was all right, but any later than that and some unpleasantness was ensured.

However, I had no control over what time she called Mrs. Chadwick and it was always later on in the evening around nine o'clock. One night in February just such a call occurred. Mrs. Chadwick was on the phone with her for some time and then came downstairs to my room to tell me to get on the extension, that Mother wanted to talk to both of us. She looked more tired than usual and I knew instantly that something had gone wrong. I picked up the phone with trepidation, but though my mind was racing through the past few days, I could find nothing in them that might have caused the trouble.

Mother's voice had that icy edge to it and I knew that whatever it was going to be, she was already off and running with it. She asked me why I insisted on wearing my coat to classes.

I couldn't believe that this was the issue. One day during the past week, I'd kept my coat on during one class because it was colder than usual. Mrs. Chadwick had told me to bring a sweater that morning but I didn't think I'd really need it and hadn't brought one. That evening she told me not to be so shortsighted again and as far as everyone was concerned that was the end of it. At the most it was a miscalculation on my part and no one had considered it particularly important in the overall scheme of our mutual existence.

But here it was, blown all out of proportion and into an issue. I really couldn't believe it. As I listened to Mother spew her anger over the phone I wondered what in the world had possessed Mrs. Chadwick to tell her this infinitesimal incident in the first place. It didn't matter what the reason was initially, because now it was just an excuse for another of Mother's rampages against me. She was screaming on the other end of the phone and I had to hold the receiver away from my ear. She was going on about why the hell I always had to disobey everybody and who the hell I thought I was to know it all. I never had a chance to explain that it hadn't really been anything serious, I just shook my head and kept my mouth closed hoping that if I didn't add anything to the discussion she'd calm down after a while. I didn't have any such luck. Instead, my silence just infuriated her more. I couldn't win in these situations. If I said anything she said I was being insolent. If I didn't say anything she became enraged. I knew from experience that this particular conversation was getting progressively worse. I hadn't done anything wrong. Things at school had been going smoothly ever since Christmas. She had gotten herself into such a state that she believed I was bad and if she didn't get bad reports about me then it could only mean that someone was covering up for me, that somehow I'd conned them into thinking that I was someone *she* knew I wasn't. It was as though she considered herself the only real keeper of the truth. Again and again she glued herself to her own imaginings and refused to hear any opinion to the contrary, even if it was obviously the truth.

Then she said that if I was so determined to wear my goddamned coat to class I could wear it and nothing else! She would have all my clothes picked up the next day. "Mother," I interrupted, "the coat only has one button. I can't wear just that to school!" "You should have thought of that *before* you disobeyed," she snapped and without another word she slammed the phone down, hanging up on us.

I couldn't move. I heard Mrs. Chadwick coming down the stairs and I couldn't move a muscle. Now it was my turn to be in a rage. What the hell was going on around here that no one seemed to have the guts or the nerve to tell that insane bitch to knock it off? Everyone turned to jello the minute she started raising her voice, which was also her favorite tactic. She bullied everybody into subservience.

Mrs. Chadwick was ashen. She put her arms around me and I burst into tears.

"Mrs. Chadwick . . . what am I going to do? That coat only has *one* button."

Mrs. Chadwick sat me down and we started to talk. She thought that maybe in the light of day Mother would reconsider. I told her she was wrong, that Mother *would* send someone to pick up all the clothes. Mrs. Chadwick looked ill and every bit of her sixty-some years.

"Mrs. Chadwick . . . *why* did you tell Mother that?"

Mrs. Chadwick looked down at the floor and then straight at me. "She simply wouldn't accept the fact that you were doing well. She insisted that I go over each day until I came to the business about the coat . . .," her voice trailed off and the two of us sat in silence.

"Mrs. Chadwick . . . I am *not* going to school in my underwear and a coat! I don't care what Mother said or didn't say, I am not going out of this house in my underwear and a coat. Someone will have to forcibly drag me out and I'll fight every inch of the way. *I will not do it.*" I was surprised at the forcefulness with which I'd told Mrs. Chadwick how I felt. It was the first time I'd ever done that. I now sat and waited for her reaction.

To my relief, she was in complete agreement with me. It was absolutely unthinkable to send me to school like that . . . she might as well be considering sending me naked.

The next day, sure enough, Mother sent someone to get all my clothes while I was at school. They cleaned me out. Took my shoes, sweaters, jeans, shorts, blouses, skirts, jackets . . . everything but one short-sleeved cotton dress.

Since it was only February, that left me with two dresses to wear for the next *four* months! I was so mad, I couldn't talk. I was mad at Mrs. Chadwick for telling Mother anything. By now she knew when Mother was drinking that she became totally irrational. I'd told Mrs. Chadwick about Mother's drinking, but I really don't think she believed me. I guess, some things you have to learn firsthand no matter how smart you are.

Some of the girls offered to lend me clothes because they felt so badly about what had happened. Unfortunately, Mrs. Chadwick wouldn't let me wear anything except those two dresses to school. She was afraid Mother would find out that her orders weren't being followed and the situation would get worse.

That made me madder still. *How* was Mother going to find out if Mrs. Chadwick didn't tell her? Was everyone in the whole world afraid of Mother? Wouldn't anyone tell her she was full of shit?

My anger sank slowly into depression as the days turned into weeks of having to wear just those two dresses. Chadwick was a country school and the kids didn't get dressed up to go to class, but since most of them were from wealthy families their clothes were more than adequate. Some kids, of course, were very clothes conscious and a number of my girlfriends even had special clothing allowances. Then there was me . . . looking like a goddammed orphan. After a month of this idiocy, my one pair of shoes that had been new in September wore out. At first it was just the stitching around the top and a hole in the sole. Then the entire sole of the right shoe began flapping. I'd told Mrs. Chadwick to tell Mother I needed another pair of shoes weeks before, but nothing happened. Finally, one morning I was so mad I threw the shoes in the trash and appeared barefoot. That did it. Mrs. Chadwick took me down-town that afternoon and bought me another pair of shoes with her own money.

I didn't go to most of the school dances because I was too embar-rassed to go in either one of the two dresses when all the other girls would have planned special outfits. Anyway, none of the boys asked me because they didn't want to be embarrassed either.

As the months until the end of school progressed my punishment had some unexpected side effects.

Everyone in the school knew what had happened to me. Some people felt sorry for me and would look at me with pity which I didn't like at all. Some of the students avoided me and others couldn't resist an occasional snide remark. But having to wear my punishment week after week in full view like that began to make other people mad too. I began to sense an invisible turning of the tide of public opinion in my favor. I was too proud to ever complain about my dresses and continued to do good work in my classes. The faculty members began going out of their way to give me something extra in the area of encouragement, extra credit, little additional privileges. Whatever was within their direct responsibility and didn't break any of the rules, was stretched a little in my case. My friend Hoagy was great. He always dressed in something funny and then made jokes at his own expense which made me laugh. He was already emotionally tougher and wiser than I was. He had a heart of gold for his friends. We'd sit and talk for hours and he'd always tell me things about his own family. Afterwards I'd feel better, knowing that someone understood and also that I wasn't the only one with troubles.

When the heat of summer began, I cut the sleeves off one of the two dresses for variety. The trouble was the two dresses were exactly alike, only one blue plaid and the other was green. I was so sick of looking at those two dresses! They'd been washed and ironed twice a week for nearly four months now and they'd begun to fade. The only change of clothes I had were my bathing suit and gym shorts. Four months seems like an eternity when you're twelve and indeed it seemed like I'd been wearing those two dresses half my life at this point.

When school was finally over I went home for a few weeks. It was the first time I'd been home in a while and it felt odd leaving the Chadwicks' house which had become much more like a real home to me. I no longer knew exactly where things were kept in my own house. I'd go to look for something to set the table properly and it wouldn't be there. I was constantly having to ask someone questions and it seemed ridiculous.

I was more aware of the rules now that I'd been away from them for a while and learned to live quite differently. Not that Commander and Mrs. Chadwick weren't strict, because they certainly were. It was just that you could talk to them and the rules they set were more reasonable, more workable and a lot easier to live with, even if you didn't like them.

At home it appeared to me that a lot of the rules existed for their own sake and the timetables set primarily to keep everyone under control.

I tried to get to know my two sisters again. They were about five and cute little girls. Cindy was an outdoor girl and loved to play ball with Chris. Cathy was more sedate and we'd play "make-believe" games together, dressing up the dolls or the dog and taking them for strolls in the baby carriage. Cindy and Cathy were learning to be good swimmers and we all played water games together in the pool. I realized that they were growing up without knowing me very well because I'd been away at school a lot of the time during the past couple of years.

Mother took us to Alisal Ranch in the Santa Ynez Valley for a week. We all liked Alisal because it was a casual atmosphere and we were free to go riding and swimming all day. When we arrived I had to laugh. There, by total coincidence of course, was one of the current "uncles." I thought to myself that I should have known this would be the case, just like all the other trips we'd taken. The "uncles" did have an uncanny habit of turning up in the most unlikely places, but I was kind of used to it by now. It didn't really matter this time because Uncle David was very nice and I genuinely liked him. He was married and had brought his kids with him while his wife visited relatives, or some such story. Well, Mother had a right to companionship and we were away most of the day anyway. In the dining room we all ate at the same table just like one big happy family.

There was not one word about the dresses or my coat or the months of humiliation I'd just been through. It was just like it had never happened at all. I was just as glad to have it forgotten forever, but it was weird how quickly Mother changed. I suppose it was a case of out of sight, out of mind because *she* certainly hadn't had to look at me for four months in the same two dresses. The only thing I could figure was that she'd just forgotten about the whole thing. The dresses were totally unusable by the time I'd come home and they'd been thrown away, much to my relief.

After Alisal I was only home a couple of weeks before summer school started and it was back to Chadwick for Chris and me.

There was a new student in my summer school class that I soon realized was going to be my first real challenge in the race for top marks. His name was Jim Fadiman and he was undeniably brilliant. At first I didn't like him because he was a "know it all." Then I found out that he really did know most of it and decided that if we didn't become friends we were going to be enemies. That was the beginning of one of the best friendships I ever had. It was because of my fierce competition with Jim that I began to really zero in on my school work. I knew he was smarter than I was but I made up the majority of the difference with hard work. He questioned every answer I gave, every reason I could think up. He got straight "A's" but I was always right behind forcing him to stay on his toes. We had a great time with our fledgling intellectual rivalry and enjoyed the game immensely. He was the first really brilliant person my age I'd met and I admired him enormously even though I also teased him and badgered him constantly. He helped me set standards for myself that were way beyond what was required even by an excellent school like Chadwick. I couldn't touch him in math, but in every other subject I used his criteria and not the teacher's as my goal. It was exciting to compete with him and I used to hold my breath as papers were returned. He usually got an A and I'd get an A- but once in a while the tables turned and inside I'd be jumping up and down with sheer happiness. He knew all of this of course and we became friends on the basis of mutual admiration.

After summer school was over, I didn't go home. This time it had nothing to do with a punishment either. Mother was going to be in Texas or someplace and Mrs. Howe could only take care of the twins, so Chris and I had to stay at school. At first it wasn't so bad because there were some faculty members who stayed to finish up paperwork and grades and a few of the scholarship students remained to close up the buildings. Then, in a week or so, there was no one but Chris and myself and one or two teachers who lived on campus. Day after day we tried to amuse ourselves by ourselves. We walked the quarter mile down to the swimming pool but the walk back up soon got to be a drag. I went up and rode one of the school horses a couple times a week, but riding by myself wasn't very much fun after a while and Chris didn't like riding. We'd hang out around the kitchen and talk to John, the cook, but that couldn't last forever either. Eventually, I just sat in my room and listened to the radio and day dreamed about growing up and getting free. Mother didn't write or call us. At least it was peaceful but it was *very* boring. I was just thirteen and longed to be out at the beach with the other kids.

About five weeks went by like that and then I got an unexpected reprise. My old roommate, Dolores, lived in Long Beach and she'd asked me to spend a week with her. It sounded like absolute heaven and I was sure I wouldn't be allowed to go. But I did ask Mrs. Chadwick and a few days later she told me it would be all right. I couldn't believe my good fortune. Dolores and her mother came up to get me and off we went. In fact, I was astonished because Mother didn't even know these people. All I could figure was that Mrs. Chadwick must have vouched for them and caught Mother in a good mood.

That week was the most fun I'd ever had. It was like a dream come true. Dolores lived within walking distance of the beach and that's where we went every morning around eleven. Her mother wasn't strict at all and we were pretty much free to do as we wished as long as we told her where we were going and when we'd be back. Dolores was a year or so older than I and she didn't have to be home until midnight. I thought I was in paradise!

The first day we went to the beach I was so shy around her friends that I was sure she was going to take me back to school immediately. For me it was like something out of a movie and I couldn't quite adjust. The girls were cute and very friendly. We all congregated in exactly the same spot each morning to wait for the inevitable parade of guys. I'd never done anything like this so I watched the other girls and caught on quickly. Several of the girls had steady boyfriends which meant they automatically had dates each night. The rest of us had to catch what we could during the day at the beach or be left out of the fun at night. It was okay to be with a group of girls on the beach, but since only a couple of the girls were old enough to drive and had cars, it was impossible to do much without a date at night. Therefore . . . you had to work fast. It wasn't that there weren't enough guys, there were, but some of them you wouldn't want to be stuck with unless everything else failed. The competition looked casual but it was invisibly fierce.

I soon discovered that I was the youngest in the group by about two years. I also discovered that most of the guys were older than me by about three or four years.

I didn't do too badly the first day and managed to get a date with a guy that wasn't a total geek. Dolores and I double dated and the guys took us to the local drive-in. I tried to be cool and not let on that I'd never done this before. The drive-in was *the* place in town for kids. Getting a place at the drive-in was a matter of status. There were "best" places and "out of it" places and then there were the guys without dates that cruised in their modified cars with the illegal mufflers that made a deafening roar when they gunned the engine. My eyes were like saucers but fortunately it was darker in the back seat and I managed not to make a total fool out of myself. Dolores liked her date. I had a hard time remembering my date's name. After the drive-in we drove somewhere to park. Now I was really in a panic. I didn't want to neck with this total stranger but I also didn't want word to get around that I was a terrible date. So after a few half-hearted mushy kisses I whispered that I didn't feel very well and asked if we could go for a walk on the beach. I don't think he wanted to sit in the back seat and neck either because he was very quick to agree. We held hands and walked along the beach having quite a nice time. He was a pleasant sort but nothing that set your heart pounding. I think he felt the same about me. It was kind of dumb to have to sit there in the back seat if you didn't want to be there and we both laughed about that. We talked about schools and about the summer and the time passed easily. Finally we figured it was about time to go back and we were right; it was about ten minutes to twelve and we just barely had time to get home.

The second day on the beach I was more relaxed and had a really good time. That afternoon Dolores said that a guy she really liked and had been out with a couple times was going to stop by the beach. He worked and didn't get off till four, so that's why I hadn't met him yet. I didn't think any more about it until he showed up. I'd heard a car drive by and Dolores perked up. I looked in the direction she was watching and saw a guy get out of the car. He was quite tall and looked a little older than the rest. Someone was talking to me and I turned to finish the conversation. A moment or so later, Dolores said, "Hi Don" and I turned to see the new guy close up.

~

It was a good thing I was already sitting down because otherwise my knees would have buckled under. There, no more than three feet away from me was undoubtedly *the best looking* guy I'd ever seen. Dolores introduced me and I simply stared at him. When I managed a smile I thought it must look like the most foolish grin anyone ever saw. I tried to keep from blushing but I couldn't manage to say anything more profound than "Hi." The two of them chatted intimately and I wondered what I was going to do with myself now. What if they suggest a double date tonight? What'll I do then?

That's exactly what happened. Don and Dolores were going to a beach party and he had a friend and we'd all four double date. "Oh, that'll be nice," I said very weakly. After those arrangements were settled, Don left. Dolores went on about how neat he was and what a good time we were going to have.

I'd never been to a beach party either. I was beginning to feel like Rip Van Winkle waking up in an unfamiliar world. These were all contemporaries, but I'd never been allowed to be a part of the teenage world they all took for granted.

At eight Don and his friend came to the house to pick us up. Dolores wasn't quite ready when the doorbell rang so I had to get the door. As I opened the door and saw him standing there I nearly fainted. He was about six foot four, had blond hair and a deep tan. He dressed very casually and his shirt was open nearly to the waist. He was the absolute dream of every girl my age who ever went near a beach. "Hi," I said, and held the door wide open.

You dunce, I thought to myself. For someone with such a big mouth, so far you've managed two simpering "hi's" and that's all. I was determined to get a hold of myself. Not that I thought he'd ever be interested in me, but I didn't want to look like a total fool. He and Dolores's mother got along very well and mercifully he talked to her for a while.

The beach party was absolutely terrific. There were lots of kids there and a big bonfire. There were plenty of hot dogs and beer and radios, so there was music for dancing. I didn't like the taste of beer very much but I took a can just to join the rest.

At some point when Dolores left for a few minutes, Don asked me to dance. We were all barefoot and the sand was fairly soft so it was impossible to really dance. It was more holding and swaying than dancing. I was thrilled. We walked away from the fire into the semi-darkness. He put his arm around me drawing me close. Then there was just the music, the sound of the ocean and the feeling of his body swaying next to mine. I thought I was going to faint.

We only danced for a few minutes before Dolores came back. I had already made up my mind that I was going to find a way to go out with him. I didn't know how I was going to arrange it, particularly since I was staying with Dolores, but I was going to find a way.

Fortunately, I didn't have to do anything. He and Dolores had a fight going home that night and broke up.

The next day Dolores didn't want to go to the beach, so I went by myself. She wasn't in a very good mood and I couldn't blame her. Sure enough, about four o'clock Don arrived. My heart was in my throat as he ambled toward me with a grin on his face. "I wondered if you'd be here," he said. I could see that a couple of the girls were sort of shocked, but I really didn't care a bit.

Don and I talked for a few minutes and then he wanted to take a walk. I walked beside him, having to skip along just to keep up. He asked me if I had a date for tonight. I said no. He grinned again and said, "Now you do!" He had also devised a rather ingenious plan so that he wouldn't have to show up at the house to pick me up. I should go back now and change my clothes. His friend from last night would pick me up about six. That way we wouldn't have to upset anyone and it would look okay. Off I went, happy as could be. First of all, I couldn't believe that all this was really happening. I had never had particularly good luck with getting boyfriends. It always seemed that the ones I liked never liked me. I had never been one of the "popular" girls at school, always waiting till the last minute for someone to ask me to a dance.

Now I had the chance of my life and even though I knew it might hurt Dolores, I had no intention of doing any differently.

I saw Don every day and every night for the rest of that week. He was surprised to learn that I was only thirteen. I was very surprised to find out that he was nineteen and going into the Air Force that fall, but we had a wonderful time. He was sweet and gentle with me. He made me feel like a little princess. He never took advantage of me. We never went to bed together.

He also had a great car. He'd done all the work on it himself. It was lowered and modified and had a big racing engine. It had a custom paint job and "skirts" . . . he'd changed the gear shift on the steering column from the right-hand side to the left-hand side so he could steer and shift with one hand while keeping his right arm around a girl. I'd heard about cars like that but never seen one; I was impressed.

When I had to go back to school he came to see me a couple times a week and called me every day until Mrs. Chadwick found out. She put a stop to the visits, but we continued to write for months when he went into the Air Force. After a while we lost contact but I never forgot him. Ever.

Ninth grade had many of the privileges of high school but was more of a transition grade at Chadwick. I was back in the regular school dormitory after my year's stay at Chadwick house.

CHAPTER 15

After the trauma of being without a studio contract for the first time in her entire Hollywood career, Mother had made her first entirely independent movie called *Sudden Fear*.

Hollywood was in a state of enormous change during those few years. The major studios were losing their monopolistic control over the film industry and over their stable of stars, producers, directors, and writers. While it is true that very few independent films ever found their way into national release or prominence, some of the most courageous and diligent filmmakers were beginning to find a measure of success.

It was no small feat that *Sudden Fear* was a good film and that Mother received a third Academy Award nomination for her performance. An enormous amount of credit also has to go to David Miller, the director. He had a volatile and difficult cast to work with on a project that was risky to say the least. He also knew that he was not the first choice as a director. David became one of the "uncles", which was not an unusual occurrence these days, but I always had a special affection for him. He had a pleasant sense of humor, maintained his own self-respect and dealt with people in a very direct way.

After the picture finished filming, Mother was again in the position of having to find another job. There were now no guarantees, no automatic paychecks, no studio to back her up.

In addition to reading mountains of scripts, the production lines were set up in the office and small dining room of our house. On weekends that I did come home from school there was plenty of work to be done. There were always a couple of the loyal fans who volunteered and five or six women would work all afternoon and into the evening addressing photomailers and stuffing envelopes. By Sunday night the stacks would be bundled and ready to be taken to the post office.

I started reading some of the scripts and short treatments that were sent to her. She would choose the most likely candidates to read by herself but in order to read everything, she enlisted my aid as well. After I'd finished a script or treatment, I'd tell her the plot, outline the characters in some detail and give my own personal opinion on whether or not it was a movie I'd like to see. Most of the scripts were pretty bad but I learned a great deal from analyzing them for her. Often when the trade papers had stacked up beyond her ability to pour through, I'd read the columns to her while she was having a massage or her hair and nails done on Sundays. At first the trade slang made no sense to me and I felt like it was some foreign language. Gradually, I understood and quite enjoyed the gossipy news ground out each weekday by studios and press agents.

Sometimes she'd ask me to re-read some item about someone she knew particularly well and she'd add a few choice remarks. She'd laugh sometimes about how far from the truth some of the items were and comment on how some performers were so crazy to get their name in the columns that they'd have their press agents scheme up the most ludicrous stories. Some of the things I read to her she said were just downright lies because she knew the real story or she'd also been at the party and seen the original incident firsthand. It was an education in itself reading those columns and hearing her change the entire coloration of the printed story from her own personal storehouse of knowledge.

Mother made it her intensively serious business to keep extremely well informed about what was going on in town. I was amazed by the "skeletons" she found out about and did not hesitate to use when the moment suited her. She had an uncanny sense of how things worked in her special world and I always thought she'd have made a great spy. She never tired of the innuendo, the inference and put the pieces of the puzzle together in a masterful fashion.

There were two subjects, however, that she would never discuss. One was religion and the other was politics. Religion was a purely personal matter in her opinion, and a discussion of it caused too many hard feelings and arguments. Politics was totally off limits in her house because of the current McCarthy inquisition. She wanted nothing to do with political trouble and refused to acknowledge her party choices or even if she was going to vote. She was absolutely adamant on the subject to the extent that unless it had something to do with the film industry, she didn't even allow any discussion of everyday current events or the news. She was pleased about meeting General Eisenhower and had her picture taken with him after he became president, but that was because he was a famous person, a president, rather than any political affiliation she might have had. We could watch political events on the TV news but she'd never discuss them with us. Many of her old friends lost their jobs and had their careers ruined because of McCarthy. The very mention of politics made her visibly uncomfortable. If anyone asked her opinion, she simply said she never discussed religion or politics and left it at that.

Chris and I were both at Chadwick now, but because he was four grades behind me in the elementary school, I didn't see him that much during the week.

My class had grown over the last three years. There were now about twenty of us. I had matured considerably and grown to nearly my present height of five feet, four inches.

Whether it was because I was growing so fast or because Mother's finances were feeling the strain of independence from the studios I don't know, but clothes were becoming a serious problem again. Thank goodness I now had more than the two cotton dresses I was entombed in the year before, but the selection was not large by any means. Chadwick continued to attract students from the Hollywood community and most of them were from very wealthy families. The girls were particularly fond of cashmere sweater sets and many of them nonchalantly chose from literally dozens of matched sets covering every color in the rainbow. At first I asked a couple of girls if I could borrow from them on special occasions, but that was embarrassing after a while, particularly since they knew who my mother was just as well as I knew who their mothers and fathers were. It didn't make any sense to them that a famous movie star's daughter entering high school didn't have a decent selection of clothes. I did have some nice clothes, but Mother made me keep them at home and wouldn't let me bring them to school. That may have made some sense to her, but it was humiliating to me. I only went home four days a month at the most, the rest of my life was centered around school. She was always *very* particular about how I looked when I was with her where her friends would see me, but didn't seem to give a damn what I looked like or how I felt the rest of the time.

She also didn't seem to realize that I'd grown up a lot and the baby dresses she chose for me were totally inappropriate. I was *never* allowed to go into a store and choose my clothes for myself. She picked them out for me and she bought them. The worst part was that sometimes she said she didn't have time to shop for me and the secretary or a fan like Betty would buy my things. Half the time I hated the style and the other half the clothes didn't fit properly because I wasn't there to try them on first. So, I'd get stuck with the ones that at least fit and inevitably they were the ones I hated the most.

It was a frustrating time because I was just at the age when it was important to fit in and not look like a total freak. For someone who had been so fashion conscious herself, who in fact, had built a public image on being beautifully dressed, Mother seemed quite content to have me look like the ugly duckling. She had her own ideas about what was proper to wear and those ideas were rooted back in the forties. She didn't change her hemline or her padded shoulders or her makeup or her anklestrap shoes.

When I was little I loved dressing up in her clothes once a week as a treat on the nights she went to work in the Hollywood Canteen during the war. But at thirteen years old in 1952 and 1953, I was not at all thrilled by her rigid ideas of what she thought was or was not appropriate attire for me at school.

Since none of my pleading or protests worked to solve the problem, I had to find another solution. Borrowing, it also became clear, was also not going to be an effective means of dressing myself. It was tiresome to the other girls and became humiliating for me. I therefore devised a scheme to get enough money to buy clothes for myself to wear just at school.

On the bar at home there was a three foot tall imitation scotch bottle with a slot in the neck that was used as a bank for donations to some charity. Whenever Mother had guests over for drinks, she would cajole them out of a donation that was put into the big bottle. In the bottom there was a lot of change, but on top there were numerous folded bills in various denominations. I figured a way to tip the bottle on its side without making very much noise and slide the folded bills up to the open slot. Once the bills were over the slot, I'd take a table knife and manage to pull them through the slot and out of the bottle. I never took much at one time and would replace whatever I got with a one-dollar bill so that it wouldn't look as though the bottle's contents were being emptied. Once I hit the jackpot, pulling out a one hundred dollar bill. After that I had all the skirts, blouses and sweaters I needed and quit raiding the money stash.

On weekends that I stayed at school, it was not unusual for one of the faculty members to be going down the hill into Redondo or San Pedro. I'd manage to get a ride with one of them occasionally and do my shopping. I never bought much at one time so no one would get suspicious, because everyone knew from the year before what a problem I had with my mother and clothes! But little by little and piece by piece, I managed to get just enough so that I didn't look like the perennial orphan in borrowed clothes and hand-me-downs.

I can honestly say that I didn't feel even a touch of guilt about stealing the money. I was always scared that I'd get caught of course and then I knew that the consequences would be awful. But at the time I was desperately trying to make a life for myself at Chadwick and there didn't appear to be any other solution. I was too young to get a job and I was at boarding school anyway so that possibility was out. Mother wouldn't give me any money, so that door was closed. The charity, whatever it was (which I never found out, nor did I ever hear it mentioned either), got most of the money intended for it, and I figure that in a way, I was a charity case myself!

After I managed to solve my wardrobe problem, it became obvious that there was a far more serious problem that needed immediate attention.

The school had grown quite a bit since my seventh-grade year. Though two years seemed like a long time to me, it was curious how the story of my pre-adolescent misadventure with the boy in the stables seemed to be transmitted anew to the incoming students. What I thought I'd long ago paid for, over and above what was necessary punishment for misjudgment on my part at eleven years old was apparently one of the better pieces of gossip that was passed along to the new students. In this way, I was continually having to fight the battle for my reputation and trustworthiness over and over again.

The boys were worse than the girls in some ways. The girls made up their minds whether or not they wanted to be friends with me pretty quickly and that was the end of it. The boys were different. Some of them simply made rude remarks or ignored me. That hurt my feelings and made me mad but there wasn't too much I could do about it. Others would pretend they liked me and I'd be all pleased and excited about having a nice boyfriend until the first time they'd ask me to one of the school dances and then take me out into the bushes and try to be fresh. When I said no, as I always did, they'd get mad at me and tell me they'd already heard the story so what was I putting on such an act about. Well, that would be the end of that "romance" and I'd vow never to care about any of them.

After about four months of ninth grade, one night before dinner there was a rather large group of us standing around the outside patio waiting for the dining room doors to open. There was a lot of laughing and joking going on as usual and I was talking to some older students who were in a group near the fish pond in the middle of the patio.

Next to me there were three or four guys from the eleventh grade who were new students that fall. It was impossible for me not to hear what they were saying although I was in no way trying to eavesdrop on their conversation. It began to dawn on me that I was the topic of their conversation and that one was telling the other the old, tired story of my seventh-grade mishap, only over the years the story had been considerably embellished. Since none of them had been at school at the time, the story was way out of proportion and bore no resemblance to what had actually happened.

I was so tired of fighting this battle time and time again that I felt sort of sick to my stomach hearing it like this. Even so I think I would have let it go as though I hadn't heard it, or just given the group of them a dirty look and gone into the dining room if one of the guys who'd just told the story hadn't tried to slide his hand over my bottom as a joke in front of everyone. He was standing with his back to the fish pond and I had my back to him during his telling of the story. When he had the nerve to try and feel me up as part of the punch line, I lost my composure.

It happened so fast I don't remember thinking it through. It was really two years of hassles and innuendoes and sly smiles and lost boyfriends and not being totally trusted by the faculty. It was two years of week after week proving myself capable and fighting to regain my own self-respect. It was two years of trying to make friends and working hard to build a place for myself. It was two years of anxiety and frustration and anger that went into my closed fist as I whirled around to face this young man who towered over me. Without a second thought or a moment's hesitation I carried through with my fist and belted him right smack in the gut. It was so unexpected that he lost his balance, staggered a few steps backward, tripped and sank into the fish pond.

While only two or three people had seen me slug him in the stomach, half the student body population witnessed his spectacular plunge into the fish pond. Water splashed everywhere and a couple of large goldfish went flying out into the patio. Everyone roared with laughter at him as he sat in the middle of the pond totally drenched and completely bewildered. After a moment, even I laughed. Neither he nor his two friends said a word to anyone about how he'd ended up sitting in the fish pond. He had to miss dinner and I walked away with a feeling of silent triumph.

I knew I didn't have to worry about him ever bothering me again, but I also knew that I couldn't go around punching guys when they said something I didn't like or that hurt my feelings.

It sounds funny to say now, given that at the time I was just thirteen years old, but I was getting so tired of fighting all the time. Not fist fights like Judy and I used to have in public school, but the constant pressure on me because of my mother's erratic behavior and the school's feeling that they had to watch me more carefully than most of the others. I was just tired of fighting for every little victory, every single accomplishment, each day's progress. I was definitely making progress. I was carving a place for myself and making friends I knew I could count on, but I needed to do better and I wanted a little rest from the pressure.

I knew what had to be done, but I didn't know how to go about doing it. I was not basically manipulative so it never occurred to me that what I needed was someone to help me.

I didn't have a brilliant track record as far as boyfriends were concerned though I was as attractive as most of the girls who were considered very popular. I was also sort of shy and tended to get those painful crushes on boys who never even knew I was alive. It just seemed to me that the boys I liked never liked me and the ones I didn't care much about were the ones I got stuck with. I did have some really good friends that I could laugh and joke with like Hoagy and Jim Fadiman, but while we teased and joked and talked a lot, we didn't consider one another "boyfriend-girlfriend" types.

It came as an unbelievable piece of information, therefore, when one of my girlfriends, who was very popular and was going with a senior, told me she'd heard that another senior classman was interested in me. After my initial shock subsided, I was convinced that she was playing a very cruel joke on me and decided not to pay one bit of attention to any of it.

A few days later, she came back to talk to me and asked why I hadn't even tried to see Walter or get to talk to him. I looked at her in total disbelief. I told her I thought the whole thing was a joke. She, in turn, looked at me like I was a martian.

Walter was a senior and I was only in ninth grade. Ninth graders were generally considered the babies of high school and just to be seen with a senior was a giant status boost. In addition, Walter was captain of the football team *and* student body president. He may not have been the most handsome man in the senior class but he was certainly the most respected, the most powerful and the best liked. Everyone loved Walter. He was built like a defensive lineman and nobody argued with him very much nor for very long. He was also a very nice person and always had a group of friends around him. He loved to laugh and joke and had a smile for anyone he met. I had seen him in school for several years but always at a distance. I think I'd only spoken to him once or twice and voted for him when he was running for president.

In light of all that, I found it very difficult to believe that out of all the girls in the school, Walter had even noticed me. But evidently this was not a joke after all, and one day after lunch Walter came up to me and asked me to go to the dance with him on Saturday night. I tried my best not to act like a total idiot and managed to nod my head and say, "yes, I'd love to." Then he smiled and walked me to class which in itself made heads turn and whispers start.

Even though I was hopelessly nervous, Walter and I had a wonderful time at the dance. It was one of those informal "sock hops" so popular during the '50s to which we wore jeans and sweaters. I was surprised how gentle Walter was with me despite his size and powerfulness. I began to feel comfortable with him and to notice a difference in the way other people were treating me. His friends were nice to me and smiled and talked quite naturally, even if we'd never spoken before. The faculty members seemed to approve of my being with Walter and they seemed to relax a little. I had a wonderful time. A wonderful time. I felt accepted and comfortable and nice.

Not long after that, Walter asked me to go steady with him and I accepted happily. I wore his ring on a chain around my neck and took my place among the "popular" girls.

When I walked hand in hand with Walter across some part of the campus, people talked to us and smiled at me. I really didn't care if they genuinely liked me or not, so long as they weren't rude to my face. Even when I was alone, no one bothered me anymore. I had Walter beside me whether he was physically present or not.

In a way, the rest of that year was a breeze. I sailed through the social events without a bit of trouble, doubt or loneliness and my schoolwork continued to get me good grades. I guess I was second in my class with nearly straight A's except in math. I was not in love with Walter but I cared about him and genuinely tried not to give him too much grief. I didn't have very much experience with romantic relationships but most of the time we got along fine. We had arguments but that came with the territory of going steady. I always thought that he cared more deeply about me than I did about him, but it didn't really get in the way of our having a good time together. So, except for some minor difficulties, the year was a happy one.

After school ended in June I went home. I had made arrangements for one of my girlfriends to take the clothes I'd bought myself home with her over the summer so my mother wouldn't find out about them.

Walter had graduated and I didn't know exactly how we were going to keep in touch, except that I was supposed to be coming back for summer school and I told him I'd call him. I didn't want him to write me at home because my mail was always opened and it was always touch and go with telephone calls. Sometimes I got in trouble for them and sometimes I didn't and I was never sure which way it was going to be.

Going home was always a challenge. I was away so much that when I came back everything seemed to be in sharper focus. I never minded the tour buses with their loudspeakers blaring away the brief history of each movie stars' home when I lived there all the time, but after having been at school for a while I found them a totally offensive invasion of privacy. Even though we had very high fences covered with ivy, I hated the way tourists in the buses would stand up and strain to peek over the fence. If I was in the front yard I'd always go inside the house when I heard them coming down the street.

A small group of women who were fans for years would come and spend the entire day sitting on the garage steps, waiting for a chance to see Mother. I couldn't imagine why they did that every weekend. It seemed so tiresome, but week after week, there they were sitting on the steps.

Chris and I got to know them very well because they were the same ones who were commandeered for the special work details that Mother ran when the garden furniture needed washing or the basement needed cleaning, or the fan mail had stacked up. These three women were secretaries by profession but all of them were single and I guess being a fan was more interesting than being alone, so they always jumped at the chance to work their asses off in the service and presence of their favorite movie star.

And work they certainly did. Manual labor and menial tasks . . . nothing was too small or too heavy or too dirty for them. I never did understand it. I hated doing those jobs with a passion and I worked right alongside them. They didn't seem to mind a bit. They almost never accepted any money, though upon occasion Mother did offer to pay them. Their total reward was serving their idol. They never spoke up to defend themselves when Mother heaped abuses upon the quality of their work, they just looked heartbroken and worked all the harder. They never disagreed with anything Mother said or did, even when she pushed them to the limit. They always said yes to whatever she asked of them, even if it meant giving up all their spare time and energy. They were like a small band of puppets moving and swaying to her every wish and whim. They served her with loyalty and devotion and were totally self-effacing about it. They wanted no money, no praise . . . they only wanted to serve.

That's really what Mother secretly wanted from everyone around her and it drove her into a blue fury that I wasn't like the fans. I hated doing the dirty work of the house when I came home from school. I hated being treated like a puppet. I had to say "yes, Mommie dearest" so many times that the very sound of it nearly made me vomit. And even when I dutifully said "yes, Mommie dearest" I often got in trouble anyway for the tone of my voice or the look on my face. She wanted me to be one of those puppet fans and I couldn't be that.

There were times when I thought the things she did were just flat out wrong and even if I didn't say anything for fear of getting my mouth washed out with soap until I gagged and choked or afraid of getting a beating, she knew by the look on my face that I disagreed with her and it made her totally crazy.

It was then that she'd fly into one of her fits of temper and accuse me of doing things I'd never done. Then she punished me for the story she'd made up. If I denied what she accused me of doing, she called me a liar and told everyone how she was at her wit's end with me because I lied all the time. It was like living with a lunatic. No one believed me. I guess it was impossible for an adult who had not been present to believe me. I guess it was impossible for an adult to believe that *she* was the one who was making up the entire story and I was the one telling the truth. She was always so convincing. She appeared to be so genuinely upset over the situation that in addition to believing her, there was also a certain amount of empathy for all her troubles. And she never hesitated to tell anyone who would listen what a difficult time she had with me.

The pendulum swung full circle and I had gone from being the golden-haired princess to the family scapegoat for all of Mother's pent-up hostility and anger and frustration with a world she couldn't fully control anymore. In me she saw so much of herself and yet so much that was separate. She couldn't force me to say "yes" anymore or to curtsey or to be the perfect and adoring child. I was slowly becoming a person with my own ideas and dreams and thoughts about what was right and wrong.

～

At school we were encouraged to think independently, even though the social rules were strict. Thinking for yourself, at least on an intellectual level, was a virtue at school and forbidden at home. At home Mother was the only one allowed to think for herself and the rest of us were expected to jump to her command. We lived by *her* rules without discussion whether we were her children or her fans or her servants or her friend. She told everyone what to wear and what to eat and tried to tell them what to think.

By now the domestic help problem was acute and the fans filled more and more of the void. We'd already had one of the fans for a nurse. Mother had been unable to keep anyone, even the temporaries. The twins were still very young and they at least needed constant supervision. The fan whom we all liked the best quit her secretarial job and came to live with us as our nurse. She was not nearly as strict with us as Mother wanted but when Mother was at home she made us keep all the rules intact. When Mother wasn't there, she was more lenient but made us promise not to tell anyone. We grew to love her and she became our friend.

Unfortunately, she was too good to last very long. After about six months, Mommie dearest became aware that we really loved and cared about this fan-turned-nurse and she was fired on some trumped-up charge. Luckily for her she got a job right away as a secretary again and never mentioned being a nurse at Crawford's asylum.

Years later when I saw this same woman in New York she told me the rest of the story. She said that she was always sorry about leaving us because she felt that she'd been able to make our lives a little easier, which was true. At the time I met her again I was about nineteen and going through a really horrendous time with Mother. After I'd unburdened my troubles to her for several hours she told me the real reason she'd had to leave our house years before.

I knew it had been a bad time for Mother because she was trying to get another film to do and kept complaining about always being in debt with bills piling up and the house under a second mortgage. I knew she was having a hard time but I never quite understood why we supposedly didn't have any money because I'd heard her say before that she was making $150,000 to $200,000 a picture. Even at one picture a year, that was a hell of a lot of money in the 1950s.

Nevertheless, it was a bad time for her generally. She didn't have a steady boyfriend and complained about having to pick up the checks at restaurants all the time. She didn't have her next job lined up yet and that always made for difficult times in the house because she was there so much and didn't have enough to do to keep us from being the focus of her anger.

In addition I knew very well that her drinking was getting worse. The surest way to recognize Mother's drinking was her temper. Alcohol unleashed so much anger in that woman that it was sometimes very frightening to be around. She was never easy to deal with when she was under stress or tension but when the situation was compounded by her drinking she was impossible. She wouldn't listen to anybody and she'd find something to focus her anger upon. When I was around it was usually me, but when I wasn't there Chris or someone else got it. I know that she'd done it for years with men because I'd heard the fights since I was about six. I knew she drank too much when she was alone because I'd helped the nurse carry her to bed. Now there weren't too many men around except for the assortment of homosexuals she'd known for years who served as "dates" when she had to make public appearances or wanted to go somewhere and couldn't go alone because it wouldn't fit in with the image of the glamorous movie star. Since she had no man, no job and said she was running low on money, the image of the movie star was about all she had left to hold onto. She protected it with all her energy, imagination and every dime she could get her hands on. Most of the money went for show . . . the house, the parties, her clothes and jewelry.

The former nurse then told me that after she'd been with us several months, Mother started drinking very heavily at night after we'd gone to bed. The woman said that one night Mother came into her room and wanted her to have a drink. The woman said no. Mother got angry and stormed back into her own room, slamming the door behind her. A few nights later the woman was already asleep and woke up to find Mother standing next to her bed. She said Mother must have been drinking for hours and was unsteady on her feet. Then she said that Mother made a pass at her and wanted her to come into her room. The woman said no again and after a few choice swear words, Mother left. After that the woman closed and locked the door to her room at night. However, when Mother got drunk she'd come and pound on the door cursing and telling her to unlock the door immediately. The woman said nothing and didn't move from her bed. Finally Mother left and the woman decided then and there that she couldn't stay with us any longer.

Even though I was nineteen years old when I heard the story and knew by then to take everything I heard with a liberal grain of salt, what she told me made me sad. It didn't shock me because I'd already seen so much my mother had done that having someone tell me they thought she was also a lesbian made little difference to me at this point.

What I did think about was the pieces of the puzzle of my own childhood. I thought about the night raids which this woman knew about because she'd been there for the rose garden and orange tree decapitation. I thought about the loneliness of the famous movie star with no job and no man, who drank herself into a solitary fury and vented her rage on the household or whomever was closest at hand that couldn't do anything to protect themselves. I thought about the drunken arguments and the irrational anger, the fabricated stories and the lies about me and what I'd done. And then I thought about how excruciatingly ugly and sad it was for Mother to get drunk and crazy and make passes at the servants.

However, during early summer of 1953, I only lasted a few weeks at home. It wasn't long before I was on my way back to school with a sigh of relief. I went back to Chadwick house after summer school since there wasn't anywhere else for me to go.

I had been in touch with Walter and he'd come to see me on campus a couple of times. We'd even been to the movies in Redondo. I guess we were still sort of going together even though it was unofficial after graduation. He was going to college at Claremont and I knew he'd find lots of girls there, so it was nice to be able to still be special for him even for a little while longer. He came to see me one day at Chadwick house when Commander and Mrs. Chadwick were away. The only person besides me in the house was a young Japanese woman the Chadwicks had sort of adopted unofficially as their daughter and she helped with the housework in addition to working and going to college. She was quite strict with me and tended to boss me around when the Chadwicks weren't there. When she told me that Walter was at the door, I was delighted. I had to work hard at the house and it was a lovely surprise to be seeing Walter. He stayed for about an hour and we sat outside with some iced tea. He was getting excited about going off to college and I enjoyed hearing about all his plans. He told me that he'd keep in touch with me and try to see me. I smiled because it was nice to hear that he cared, not because I thought that would be the case in reality. He kissed me goodbye and left. After I walked him to his car, I went back to finish my work.

It, therefore, came as a huge shock to me when Mrs. Chadwick was furious with me when she found out Walter had visited. I was completely baffled because I hadn't made the arrangement, I hadn't called to ask him to come over, I hadn't opened the door to let him in and I knew I hadn't done a damn thing wrong. For once I stood up to Mrs. Chadwick and told it to her exactly like that. She countered by saying that I wasn't supposed to have any visitors without her permission. I asked point blank, "since when?" What was I supposed to do? Tell Walter to wait outside while I called Mrs. Chadwick to ask if I could see him, when we'd gone steady for almost a whole year at school and he'd been student body president. It was all absurd. I told her that we just sat out on the patio with some ice tea and he left after about an hour. The Japanese woman had told Mrs. Chadwick that Walter had kissed me goodbye. I didn't see one thing to be ashamed about and I told her so. She and Commander went into a conference right after she spoke so sharply to me and I think he must have calmed her down somewhat because I didn't hear anymore about it that evening.

It was decidedly bad timing that my mother called the next night for her weekly report on my behavior. Mrs. Chadwick made the mistake of telling Mother about the Walter incident of the day before and Mother flew into one of her rages. In no time at all they had me on the extension phone and Mother was screaming that I wasn't to be trusted and she was going to have to bring me home since I was causing Mrs. Chadwick so much trouble. After the phone call I saw Mrs. Chadwick crying. As terrible as I felt, it hurt me to see her cry. Mrs. Chadwick was such a basically good person that she never learned to second guess Mother and she just never got used to how Mother could made any molehill into a mountain of her own choice. This time Mrs. Chadwick knew that she'd been responsible for getting me into much more trouble than I deserved and there was nothing that she could do about it now.

I never understood why she wouldn't recognize the problem with Mother's drinking and kept falling into the same trap, taking me with her. I knew Mrs. Chadwick loved me and wished me no harm of any kind. I knew that she was a very well-educated woman who had a brilliant mind. But many times I wished that she'd had a little more sophistication about the rotten side of the world we all lived in so that these blunders of hers wouldn't disrupt my life for months on end. I think the trouble was that she tried to talk sense to Mother and she was intimidated by her. That's a trait she shared with many. Most people were intimidated by Mother in one way or another.

About 10 o'clock that night Mother showed up in the station wagon with her secretary as a companion. She'd been drinking and at least had the good sense not to drive by herself. I was packed and ready to go as soon as she finished talking with Mrs. Chadwick. Mother wouldn't speak to me except to order me into the back seat of the car. But before we left the Palos Verdes area, she asked the secretary if there was a liquor store in the area. The secretary said she didn't know anything about Palos Verdes. I volunteered from the back seat that there was a liquor store about two blocks away once we got to the main street. Mother slammed on the brakes which nearly sent me into the front seat and the secretary into the windshield. Mother slapped me across the face and growled, "You *always* know where to find the boys and the booze, don't you?" As I opened my mouth to explain, she slapped me several more times and ordered me to shut up. I sank down into the back seat and didn't say another word during the drive home. When we went into the house I went upstairs to my room to go to bed. I never wanted to say another word to her ever . . . period.

The next few days were just terrible. She wasn't talking to me, so she'd order the secretary or the nurse to tell me what to do. She kept me working ten or twelve hours a day. I ate my meals in silence and went to bed. There was to be no television, no radio, no books, no unnecessary conversations with anyone.

Toward the middle of that week, things eased off a bit and settled into just the normal bullshit routine of whispering in the mornings and abiding by the rules.

Mother had a friend who was visiting from the East and she'd invited the woman to have dinner with us one night. The woman's name was

Dorothy and when the evening arrived, Mother decided that she'd take Dorothy and me to Don the Beachcomber's. Under normal circumstances that would have been good news, but I was extremely nervous about being with Mother for any length of time, particularly in the evening. I'd found that staying out of her way and saying yes as pleasantly as possible was my only salvation. Everything I did seemed to irritate her immensely and I simply tried to be as inconspicuous as possible. An evening alone with her was not welcome and I hoped fervently that the lady would be talkative so that I could keep my mouth shut.

Going to Don the Beachcomber's and being with Mother was enough of a treat for Dorothy so that she felt obligated to entertain Mother for the duration of dinner. I sat furthest away from Mother and tried my best to do nothing to bring attention to myself. I smiled and nodded and was conscious of my most precise table manners . . . offering everyone the food before I took any, taking small portions when I helped myself and only speaking when I was directly asked a specific question. In other words, I was a nervous wreck the entire time. Dorothy seemed oblivious to anything except enjoying herself as Mother's guest and chattered happily for several hours. Dinner went smoothly for me, though I noticed with some trepidation that Mother was drinking a number of vodkas on the rocks.

We were nearly home and I was literally counting the minutes until I could safely escape to my room when Dorothy asked me how school was going. I had been sitting silently in the back seat until then, seemingly unnoticed by either of them. I replied that I liked school very much.

Dorothy asked me about several people's children that she knew who were also at Chadwick. One of the students had been expelled. I told her that I thought one of the students she mentioned had some trouble and had been expelled. With that Mother turned halfway around to momentarily face me, while driving full speed ahead, and icily inquired who was I to say anything about anyone else, since I'd been expelled too.

I was so taken aback that I didn't have any answer for her. I had *not* been expelled from school. She'd created a scene and taken me away from the Chadwick's house when school wasn't even in session. I could see that Dorothy was embarrassed and I didn't utter another word during the remainder of the drive.

Once we were inside the house I went to my mother when I found her alone and asked her why she'd told Dorothy I'd been expelled when it wasn't true. Mother hauled off and hit me across the side of my head so hard it made my ears ring. She told me in no uncertain terms that she'd decide what the truth was and that considering how much I lied no one believed me anyway no matter what I said. All I said was "That's not true" and she slapped me across the face again.

I was so mad I didn't cry even though it really hurt. I just stood there staring right back at her, determined that I wouldn't give her the satisfaction of seeing one tear. She slapped me hard several times again and then stepped back saying, "You love it don't you . . . you just love to make me hit you." By this time her friend Dorothy was in the room and saw the last time she slapped me.

Only because Mother didn't want Dorothy to have any more information about our happy Hollywood home, Mother called me into the bar to finish our conversation. I followed her into the little room where the drinks were fixed. She sat on the counter top and asked me why I insisted on arguing with her. I answered that I didn't wish to argue, but that I also didn't appreciate her telling people that I'd been expelled from school, which wasn't true. I said I thought she was supposed to be the one who was more understanding since she was the parent and the adult.

From the distance of this much time, it may not sound like it now, but this was the wrong thing to say to my mother at that particular moment in the time and space of our lives. It triggered something in her, the likes of which I never saw before and hope never to see again. It struck at some volcanic trauma in the center of her being that erupted with a violence, a hatred and a suddenness that plunged us both into an instantaneous struggle for survival.

She leaped off the counter and grabbed for my throat like some mad dog . . . like some wild beast . . . with a look in her eyes that will never be erased from my memory. I was caught totally defenseless and staggered backward, carried by her momentum. I lost my footing and fell to the floor, hitting my head on the ice chest in the fall. The choking pain of her fingers around my throat met the thudding ache of the blow to the back of my head. She banged my head on the floor, tightening her grip around my throat. Her face was only a few inches away from mine and she was screaming words at me I couldn't even hear. Her mouth was twisted with rage and her eyes . . . her eyes were the eyes of a killer animal, glistening with excitement. I gasped for air and felt myself sinking into unconsciousness as I tried desperately to fight back . . . to free myself. All I could think of was that my own mother was trying to kill me. If something or someone didn't help me very soon I was going to die. I tried with the last bit of my strength to struggle free of those choking fingers and managed to wedge one of my knees between her body and mine and push upward on her ribs with my hands which loosened her grip slightly. It at least allowed a trickle of air down my throat and kept me from losing consciousness. Now I fought back harder. I didn't want to die. I completely forgot that she was my mother. She was trying to kill me and if I had the strength I would try to kill her first. She was terribly strong and all I could do was concentrate on loosening her grip on my throat.

The next thing I knew the door opened and the secretary Billie burst into the small room, no larger than a hallway with counters on both sides.

"My God, Joan . . . you're going to kill her . . .," Billie yelled. She tried to pull Mother away from me. Though Billie was also a strong woman, it took her some time to separate the two of us. When Billie had succeeded in pulling us apart, Mother continued to hit me across the face. I felt her ring cut my lip and saw some blood on her hand.

"Joan . . . *Stop* . . . *Stop* . . . you're going to kill her!" Billie yelled again. Finally Mother allowed herself to be pulled away from me and sank into Billie's arms sobbing. I lay on the floor several minutes trying to catch my breath and get my bearings. My head was throbbing and I had a hard time swallowing, but nothing seemed to be broken. I raised myself to a sitting position slowly to test whether or not I was all right. Through her tears Mother ordered me to go up to the middle room and get into bed. Someone would be up to lock me in there.

The "middle room" was one of the servants' rooms off the back stairs, now used primarily for storage although it still had a bed and dresser in it. It had only small windows, no trees outside and no bathroom attached to it. Having to sleep in the middle room was a form of punishment for either Chris or me. It meant that we were not being trusted to stay put. I had tried to run away only once a long time ago but my brother Chris had successfully made the break several times already even though he was three years my junior.

Up I went to the middle room and put myself wearily into bed without brushing my teeth or washing my face. Since I had no pajamas or nightgown I just took off my clothes and left on only my underwear. I lay in the darkness for a few minutes before I heard the key turn in the lock outside the closed door to the room.

Strange to say that although I ached all over there was no real sensation of pain. I felt a peculiar numbness throughout my entire body and mind. I briefly thought about trying to figure out just exactly what had happened, but the image of the look in Mother's eyes flashed across my memory and I decided to just fall asleep.

It must have been several hours later when I heard a knock on the door and someone's voice telling me to get dressed and come downstairs to the bar. I had no idea what was going on but I followed the orders.

Still half asleep I descended the back stairs into the large living room we called the bar.

Not all the lights were on in the room so it was not very bright and outside it was pitch dark. Seated on the couch were my mother and a man I'd never seen before.

When I entered the room the man stood up and Mother introduced him to me, adding that he was a juvenile officer. I had no idea what a juvenile officer was doing in the house but while I was trying to figure out this new turn of events, the man asked my mother to leave the room so that he could speak to me alone. That surprised me because no one had ever said anything similar to her in my presence. Evidently she'd already spoken with him at some length, so she did not seem taken aback by his request.

I was still standing in the doorway but, after she left, the man asked me to come and sit on the couch with him. When I was seated he looked at me carefully for quite a long time without saying anything.

"She beat you pretty badly, didn't she?" he said rather softly.

I looked down at the floor and nodded my head yes. I didn't know what she'd told him. I also had no way of knowing what I looked like since the room I'd been locked up in didn't have a mirror.

"Your mother's told me her version of the story . . . now I'd like to hear yours."

I looked at him carefully. He was a man of about forty, not particularly handsome but nice looking in a plain way. His eyes were straight forward and direct. He seemed concerned but not particularly sympathetic and he looked tired.

I told him the events as simply and honestly as I could. I told him about going to dinner and the drive home when Mother had told her friend that I'd been expelled from school, which wasn't true. I told him about her hitting me and then telling me to come into the bar, pointing to the service area as I talked. I then told him about saying that part about how I thought she ought to be the more understanding one since she was older, the parent and the adult. I looked him directly in the face and said, "That's when she tried to kill me." I told him also that if it hadn't been for Billie's help, she might have succeeded.

That was the end of my story and I sat in silence with him for at least a minute.

When finally he started to speak, it was slow and deliberate. I knew he was choosing his words very carefully. He said that there was nothing he could do to help me. He said that I'd have to try harder to get along with my mother because if she called the authorities again, he'd have no choice but to take me to juvenile hall as an *incorrigible*.

He talked to me longer and tried to explain the situation more fully to me, but I could hardly hear anything more he said. What kept racing around in my mind was being taken off to juvenile hall as an *incorrigible*! What kind of a world was it that allowed my mother to nearly murder me and then make me take the rap as an incorrigible? What kind of world was it that let her off scot-free and punished me for her insanity? It was totally crazy. It was a crazy world. What power did she have that everyone believed her or at least acted like they did? Was it true that even the juvenile authorities believed her and would really take me to juvenile and put me in some detention school for incorrigibles?

"I'm not going to take you to juvenile hall tonight, even though that's what your mother has requested."

I had no words. I stared at him totally speechless. I couldn't believe this nightmare was happening to me.

"I'm going to tell her that we've had a long talk and that you're going to try harder to get along with her and not cause any more trouble in this household. But I have to tell you honestly that if she calls us again, I'll have to take you down to juvenile hall."

I didn't say a word but tears streamed down my face. I couldn't get it through my head that the world of adults and justice would take me to juvenile hall like some delinquent or criminal when it was Mother that had committed the wrong. My brain understood the words he was saying but I couldn't stand the cruelty and the injustice of it all. It was clear that I was all alone. There was no one in the world to help me. There was no one in the world to take a stand against her. The cards were all stacked in her favor. I just had to live with whatever chaos she chose to visit upon me whenever she got drunk or crazy.

Looking at him I knew he was trying to be gentle with me but it didn't help. I hated him and all the others for being too weak to stand up to her. And I hated her for what she did to people, for the way she bullied them with her stardom and her money. I hated the institutions that allowed this woman to live outside the rules of common decency and the law. It seemed to me there was a conspiracy of the famous who thought they were above the rules of the rest of society. By virtue of their fame, they were above the common people and didn't have to abide by the common people's ethics or values. Their money and their public image entitled them to make their own rules and then force everyone else to play the game their way. I felt myself bringing the cloak of my own body around my inner self for some small measure of protection. I decided from now on I would not show anyone how I felt. I would not ask anyone for anything. If I was to be totally alone, so be it . . . but I would not give any of them the satisfaction of knowing how much it hurt. I would simply learn not to care.

"I wish there was something more I could do to help you, but there isn't. You don't want to go to juvenile hall, do you?" He waited until I shook my head no, then he said, "Then remember what I told you and try to get along here and at school."

He called Mother back into the room. I left to go back to bed after they'd both had their say. I never looked at either of them again, even when I had to shake hands with the juvenile officer as a goodbye.

The next morning I got up and got dressed after trying the door to see if it was locked. It wasn't, so I went downstairs and through the house to my own room. When I got into the bathroom to wash up, I had quite a shock. It was the first time I'd seem myself in the mirror and I understood why it took the juvenile officer so long to start talking to me. Even in the dimly lighted room he must have been able to see my battered face.

I had one black eye and a cut on my upper lip that was swollen and covered with dried blood. My whole face was sort of puffy and I had a perfect handprint bruised across one cheek. My eyes were also swollen from crying during the night and I looked a mess. As I stared at the battered and bruised image of my face in the mirror I started crying again. My god . . . I looked awful. *How* could I be declared the incorrigible one?

I couldn't allow myself to think about it now. I turned on the cold water and plunged both my hands into the icy wetness, splashing it generously over my face. I had a sick and shaky feeling all over. I realized that just washing my face wasn't going to help much, so I decided to take a shower.

I turned the shower on hot and stood under it trying to rid myself of this clammy, chilly, shaky feeling. I washed my hair and gingerly felt the lump on the back of my head. Finally I turned the water colder and colder until there was no hot water left at all. It stung but it got rid of the sick feeling inside me.

I dried my hair and got dressed. The sick feeling came and went in waves, but I drank some cold water and that seemed to help. Later I took some aspirin for my headache.

Everyone in the house looked at me sadly when I went down to breakfast, but no one directly referred to my black eye or asked me what happened to me. I could see that just having to look at me was scary for them and they tried to act as though everything was normal. The nurse told me Mother had left word for me to stay in my room except for meals. I thought maybe someone would take me to a doctor, but no one did.

A few days later I was on my way back to the Chadwick's house. Mother had told them that I was incorrigible and she couldn't handle me any longer. They asked to have a chance to straighten things out, so back I went.

I still had vestiges of the black eye but the rest of my face had returned pretty much to normal. I was actually glad to be back with them even if I was a virtual prisoner in their home. I wasn't allowed any personal phone calls or mail or visitors. Since I was still being punished, I had to do extra work at the house and wasn't allowed to go anywhere except to church on Sunday with Mrs. Chadwick.

One of the many jobs I had to do was clean out all the outside closets and storage areas. I used to have nightmares about the bugs and the dead creepy crawlies in those closets. Sometimes even in the heat of the summer I'd be covered with goosebumps while I was doing the work. But no one bothered me and even though it was very lonely sometimes, it was better than being at home.

During those days alone while I worked I tried to sort out the mysteries of my life. There seemed to be times of total chaos followed by punishment and days of being all by myself. As the thing that originally caused the trouble faded away with time what was left for me was a state of "second chance." That meant that I had to watch every move I made, every word I said. It meant that everyone watched me more carefully than usual to make sure I did my work without a slip and toed the mark day after day. Human nature and time itself eased the situation somewhat, but there was always that tension, that silent expectation of the "next time." After a while it all melted into a lifestyle of troubled times, of never feeling totally at ease, of always being on the alert for the first signs of renewed outbursts from Mother over some infinitesimal slight, some unpremeditated oversight, some minute infringement of the rules that constantly changed according to whim and alcohol content in her blood.

I began to be rather adept at skirting the fringes of her recurrent insanity and at walking the tightrope of my own loneliness. Even though I did not feel I was a bad person, even though I didn't believe I had committed any serious crimes against humanity, I began to understand how parolees must feel being constantly watched and monitored with everyone waiting for the first telltale signs of a slip, living under the threat of incarceration.

The juvenile officer instilled in me a terror of being locked up in juvenile hall. I didn't really know all of what that meant in reality, but the threat of it was enough to terrify me and make me feel cold all over. I retreated as far into myself as I could go without completely losing touch with everyday reality. I lived in daydreams of the moment when I would be free to go my own way and live my own life. I made up stories about where I would go and what I would do when I grew up. I could amuse myself for days with these daydreams that were ongoing dramas I wove around the little I knew about the world outside.

Since I was not allowed to go to the movies or to watch television, I read books for entertainment. I would read far into the night until I was tired enough to go to sleep and hope the nightmares would not recur tonight. Maybe if I were tired enough I'd sleep soundly. Sometimes it worked and sometimes it didn't. I'd wake up in a cold sweat thinking something was trying to get me. After several nights like that, I'd sleep with the lights on and hope that would work.

Toward the end of that summer, the Chadwicks took me camping with them for a month up in the high Sierras.

I lived at Chadwick house during my tenth-grade year with my brother and a girl named Sandy. The circumstances had changed since my last stay a year before. Mother had spoken with the Chadwicks about her financial condition, which she indicated was in sad shape. She was only doing one film a year now and told the Chadwicks that although she fully planned to pay the tuition for Chris and myself, it might be a little slow in coming. Therefore I was put on partial scholarship and had to do extra work in order to get the money to pay for the things Chris and I needed such as school supplies, toothpaste and the various other little necessities of our lives. We were both expected to work at the Chadwicks' house and I worked at school also. What that meant was that I made breakfast for everyone in the morning and then Sandy and I made all the beds while Chris helped Mrs. Chadwick with the dishes. We all went to school together staying until after dinner and study hall. During the late afternoon I would also help in one of the offices or wherever extra work was required. On Saturdays we worked all day doing the laundry, cleaning the house, the yard and the patios. Since Mrs. Chadwick was a stern housekeeper from the old school and there were five of us living in the house, there was always a lot to be done. Sandy and I even had to wash the blue third-floor carpeting on our hands and knees with a smelly solution of soap, ammonia and bluing. On Sunday mornings we finished up the ironing that hadn't been completed the day before and were usually allowed to have Sunday afternoons to ourselves once the work was done.

Saturday lunch was always the same. Mrs. Chadwick would start soup stock in a big kettle on Friday night. Saturday morning while we were doing the laundry, she would clean out the icebox and everything that hadn't already spoiled went into the kettle. Around noon we all gathered in the kitchen and Mrs. Chadwick ladled generous portions into large bowls. Chris, Sandy and I sat in a small room adjacent to the kitchen and ate at our own table. Chris gave our Saturday lunch its name, which stuck with it for the duration of our stay. He called it "gristle soup" and it was often only too appropriate! Fortunately, Commander's German Shepherd named Bart was allowed to lie on the floor of our little room and we figured out ingenious, lightning fast ways to sneak large portions of the more inedible parts of the "gristle soup" into the eager jaws of the dog. If it hadn't been for the presence of Bart, our lives would have been difficult indeed. Mrs. Chadwick insisted that we finish all our food and there was no avenue of escape other than the dog. Many times we were silently convulsed with laughter at the expertise with which Chris rid his bowl of the gristle and fat.

The Chadwicks paid me $30 a month for my work. With that I bought Chris whatever things he had to have, including socks and sneakers. Since we were on such a strict budget, my provisions weren't exactly the lap of luxury but we both managed to get by without feeling totally deprived. We never received a penny from Mother nor did she pay our entire tuition that year.

I went to visit her on the MGM lot several times while she was filming *Torch Song*. The school bus would drop me off at the studio and I'd stay with her on the set until she drove home. It was interesting to watch the dance scenes that she'd been rehearsing with the director Chuck Walters since late summer. She did most of her own singing too, although it was later over-dubbed. It was the first time she'd been back at work on the Metro lot in about twelve years and she received a royal welcome from all the people who were still there from the old days. It was a time filled with nostalgia for her but it was nostalgia mixed with anxiety and very hard work. She was forty-five years old by public reckoning but, if Grandmother's version of her age was correct, she was in reality nearly fifty. She had been working on the choreography with Chuck Walters for months before the picture started shooting and had also started singing lessons again. She was determined to have the dance sequences look convincing and she worked long hard hours to ensure professionalism. The picture was only mediocre but she got a lot of publicity out of her return to Metro and the dance numbers.

Evidently she had slipped further into debt than she'd told Mrs. Chadwick because even after the picture finished shooting, she was unable to pay the rest of our tuition or give either Chris or me any allowance. She said it was good for us to have to work for what we got. She'd had to work her way through school scrubbing floors and waiting on tables, she said, and it wouldn't hurt me a bit to have to do the same. She thought that thirty dollars a month was more than adequate for what little we needed. After all, she said, how much could some school paper and pencils cost? When I tried to explain to her that there were other things we needed like toothpaste and gym clothes, she simply said that it was about time I learned to budget my money better. She didn't want to hear anymore about it because she was having a hard time herself. She told me that she was going to have to take out a second mortgage on her house if she didn't get another picture soon and that she had money problems beyond what she was going to tell me about. The picture she painted was one of debtor's prison just waiting for one false move on her part.

I never could figure out where all the money went. We certainly didn't get the benefit of any of it. Even with two of us at boarding school, it just wasn't that expensive. We didn't eat at home and certainly she didn't buy us lavish gifts or shower us with extensive wardrobes. She sent us no allowance money and she wasn't paying the school tuition which was under $2,000 a year for each of us . . . so where was all the money going? I don't know, but it certainly wasn't being spent on us even though she made us feel as though we were an interminable drain on her meager resources.

That might have been possible to believe if we had been in different circumstances. But at Chadwick the average student was from a prominent family either in the film industry or the general business community so we had firsthand knowledge of what standards our peer group

held to be the norm. Their expectations far exceeded ours and the two
of us were sort of pitied as poor relations. Indeed, Chris often looked
like a ragamuffin but part of it was because he was just at that age when
he was very hard on clothes and growing faster than I could afford to
get new jeans for him. He went through sneakers in a matter of a couple
months and they always seemed to have holes in them. Because he was
not adverse to getting in fights or playing ball in the dirt, his jeans were
unusually prone to rips and worn spots. I managed a bit better because
I could borrow clothes from Sandy and once in a while someone would
give me sweaters or blouses they didn't want anymore. At first I was
embarrassed about taking the hand-me-downs, but they were better
than nothing, so I accepted.

Although I was not in any trouble at home, most of that year I spent
weekends at the Chadwicks. I had become part of the family now and
they had become my surrogate parents. Because of their age they were
more like grandparents but they were kind to me and there was a consistency about our relationship that gave some stability and order to my
life. It's true that I worked very hard at their house and I wasn't allowed
to participate in the normal Saturday activities on campus because of it,
but I even got over resenting that after a while. As Sandy and I worked
together we became good friends. She had a bad time at home too, so
we were able to commiserate with one another, which helped. She had
a wry sense of humor and more often than not we got into trouble for
giggling and laughing instead of doing our work. It gave the drudgery
a perspective though and we'd managed to lighten the whole situation
with our kidding and some harmless practical jokes.

I had already decided what I wanted to be when I grew up. After realizing at about the age of ten that there was no future for me as a cowboy,
an accidental turn of events made the new decision easy. Each year the
school put on a Gilbert and Sullivan musical. My first year the elementary school was doing *HMS Pinafore*. I had auditioned for the lead role
of Josephine but didn't get it. However, after months of rehearsal and
just about a week before the performance, the girl playing Josephine
got the flu. Since I was the only soprano who could fit into the costume, it was decided that I'd step in as Josephine. The music teacher,
Mr. Stewart, worked privately with me for hours every day. By dress

rehearsal I knew all the songs and what I was supposed to do but I was scared to death. All I could think of was my total failure as the mother in my Brownie troop's production of *Hansel and Gretel* some years before. Mother had been asked many times to let me be in pictures like *Cheaper By the Dozen* all during my childhood but she had always refused, so I had practically no experience acting.

The day of the performance for the school and parents finally arrived and I had butterflies in my stomach from the time I got up in the morning. We had a final rehearsal, then went to get ready for the show.

By some miracle, everything went wonderfully well during the entire performance. I didn't make even one mistake and my voice sounded clear even without a microphone. I knew the pale lavender dress and matching bonnet looked very pretty on me and the show was a great success with students, faculty and parents. Afterwards everyone rushed up to me with congratulation and hugs. I knew then and there that being an actress was going to be a lot better than being a cowboy.

So, having decided that I was going to be an actress, I lost no opportunity to perform in the plays or musical reviews the school produced.

I was in everything during the regular school year and each summer school. I sang in all the chorus programs, spoke in the Christmas pageant and I gave speeches in class projects. At last I'd found something that I enjoyed and could do well besides my regular schoolwork. Mother had seen me in the sixth-grade performance of *HMS Pinafore* and didn't come to another school play until my crowning achievement as the old woman in *The Mikado* at the end of tenth grade. The part was very difficult because it was not only a character role but also supposed to be comedic. I'd done lots of things on stage that got laughs, but not all of them intended. Now I had the challenge of doing a real comedy part and again I was scared to death. Part of me felt like a total fool rushing around the stage with the exaggerated characterization that Mr. Stewart said was required. In addition, I had to manage a black Japanese wig that was about a foot tall and a kimono that was wrapped about me so tightly that I could hardly move, much less breathe. We only rehearsed with the wigs and costumes once, so I was none too sure of myself when performance time arrived. Mr. Stewart had staged a dramatic entrance for my character and from the instant I hit that stage, singing my lungs out in my ridiculous wig, exaggerated movements and funny walk caused by the kimono, the audience never stopped laughing. They laughed so hard and so long that I was sure something dreadful had happened. But I went onward, never skipping a beat and they kept laughing at each new development. After a few moments, I realized that they were laughing with me . . . not because I was making a fool of myself and I began to ride the wave of that laughter, spontaneously adding little touches that kept the wave from dying away. It was the most totally exhilarating experience I'd ever had. I could almost feel a physical connection between me and the audience and sensed when the laughter would hit again.

The play was funny anyway and the performance was a huge success. Afterwards, students, parents and faculty members alike went to Mother to tell her how much they'd enjoyed my performance. I didn't know it then, but most of them received a rather icy reception. When I had changed out of my costume and came out into the auditorium to see her, I asked how she liked the play. She said she'd enjoyed it and I had done a good job, even if I did overact a great deal. She said I was going to have to learn more subtlety if I was going to be a professional and most particularly not to use my hands so much. *Good* actresses didn't gesticulate any more than absolutely necessary.

I forgot to ask her if she'd laughed like everyone else because I was crushed by her criticism. I hardly heard the rest of the people who came up to congratulate me and tell me how terrific I'd been. Mother's stinging criticism even blinded me to the fact that she was being cold to my friends and their parents who came over to introduce themselves. She announced that she had to leave immediately or she'd be late for her appointment. I kissed her on the cheek and she drove away. I was heartbroken. Only a few minutes before I'd been on top of the world, thinking that I'd done a wonderful job. But I guess I should have known, because it was rather like my report cards. Instead of congratulating me on getting nearly straight A's, she only questioned why there were any B's at all. I never got anything lower than that but I didn't get many rewards for my good grades anyway.

Fortunately, everyone else loved the show and in a few hours I'd gotten so many compliments that the pain of Mother's reaction was dissipated.

Mother gave me a surprise party for my fifteenth birthday. She'd invited my boyfriend, Hank, who lived in San Mateo, to stay at our house for two days just to be sure he'd be able to attend. We had dinner at Mocambo's night club with two of my school friends. She'd also invited Jennings Lang and his wife. They lived just down the block from us and Jennings was one of her agents from MCA. Joe E. Louis was the headliner and his show was hilarious. Because we were all there at a ringside table, he made a lot of references to Mother and my birthday. There was a beautiful birthday cake with fifteen candles and the entire club sang "Happy Birthday" to me. Somehow Mother had also arranged for us to have champagne, even though my friends and I were all under age. We had a wonderful time laughing at the show and then dancing until nearly midnight to the songs we requested from the band. It was a perfect birthday. Nothing in the world could have indicated to a casual acquaintance that there was a problem in the world for our family. Mother was gracious and beautiful. She had the photographers take lots of pictures and was the most charming hostess you could imagine. I was thrilled and totally delighted by her affectionate attention and the fact that she'd planned everything so considerately.

The few weeks I was home went better than ever before. Mother gave a large party and asked me to be her co-hostess. She'd gotten me a very pretty dress for the occasion and I was excited about being included.

Since it was summertime, the party was being held outdoors in the garden. Abbey Rents came in the afternoon before and started setting up a large tent canopy that covered the whole back lawn. A large portable dance floor was constructed over the badminton court. Then the day of the party, the trucks came with the tables, chairs, the portable bar and buffet tables and all the table settings including dishes, glasses and silverware. About two o'clock, the florist truck arrived and the individual table arrangements began to line the dance floor, waiting until the tables were set in place. All day long the delivery people scurried back and forth transforming our large backyard into a party paradise. By late afternoon most of the delivery people were gone, only to be replaced by the servants who started arriving dressed in their black and white uniforms. There were several bartenders, maids and butlers and some cooks' helpers. Some of the food was catered and some was being prepared in our own ample kitchen. The cook was getting nervous by now, but there was, nevertheless, a seemingly endless array of hors d'oeuvres coming out of the ovens and being arranged carefully on trays in the kitchen.

I'm not exactly sure how many people were invited but there were easily 150 who actually arrived.

I was dressed and ready when the first doorbell rang and was delegated to greet the early arrivals. Mother, as usual, was not finished dressing and the first guests were shown upstairs.

I had a great time helping with the drinks and chattering with our friends. There were a lot of my favorite people at the party and they were always very nice to me. The first half-hour was a little slow, but as if by magic, the people then began to pour into our house and out into the garden in a steady stream. There were now far too many people to meet each one individually, so I just went around looking to see if anyone had empty glasses and took drink orders as I'd been told to do.

In the process I met just about everyone. The MCA group was there and I had known Lew Wasserman and Jennings Lang for years. They were not just Mother's agents, they were included in most of the social events around our house. Kay Spreckles, who later became Mrs. Clark Gable, was just in from Texas. She loved parties and had a delightful way of telling off-color jokes while remaining every inch a lady. Some of the *Sudden Fear* cast showed up, among them Touch Conners who was a young, handsome actor just getting his first breaks in the business and hadn't yet changed his name to Michael Conners. My "date" for the evening was a family friend, the man who wrote *Spiral Staircase* among others, Mel Dinelli. Mel was a darling, kind man of whom I was very fond. Mel helped me through many a difficult social situation while I was growing up by being considerate enough to really talk to me and answer many of my naive questions concerning what was going on around me. He was in no way a father figure and too many years my senior to even remotely be a romantic interest. He was just a dear man and a kind friend who was for many years a talented screen-writer. Mel also saved me from being a wallflower because he would always ask me to dance and I was free to say yes or no as I desired.

Later that evening Judy Garland arrived with her husband, Sid Luft. Judy was noticeably pregnant at the time and dressed in something that looked like a printed tent. Mother didn't like Sid Luft for a variety of reasons, not the least of which was that she privately blamed him for Judy's drug problem. Other than that, she just didn't like him as a person. Judy was a definite attraction at a Hollywood party because later on in the evening after everyone was feeling mellow if not drunk, Judy could usually be persuaded to sing for a while. That was a feather in any hostess's cap and would be talked about for weeks both in the columns and at other local show biz gatherings.

After dinner and dancing, Mother told me it was time for me to go to bed. I was reluctant to leave the festivities just when they were really starting to get rolling, but I was also tired. I said good night to the people I knew best and left.

After I'd gotten ready for bed I went into Mother's sleeping porch and sat down in front of the window overlooking the garden. I turned out the lights so no one could see me and sat there for at least an hour watching the individual people mingle and dance and kiss. I knew that a large number of the guests were well on their way to getting drunk and for some perverse reason I enjoyed watching the changes that took place in people when they were drunk. I learned a lot about people that way. I also got a lot of unexpected information about how people really thought when their guard was down. Since I was not considered an adult yet, I guess most of Mother's friends thought I was too young to understand most of it anyway.

Sure enough, after about an hour sitting in the dark and looking out the window at the lights and the people and listening to the music, someone in the garden persuaded Judy Garland to sing. The band had microphones, so I had no trouble hearing clear as a bell from my second-story hideout. She sang *Over the Rainbow* and followed that with almost the full repertoire of Garland favorites. It was magical sitting in the dark watching her and listening to the familiar songs. She sang for quite a while and when she was finished the entire party gave her a standing ovation. I applauded too, even though I knew she couldn't hear it. A few days later, I heard Mother say that the party cost over $5,000.

The rest of that summer passed quickly. After summer school, I went up to Douglas Camp again but this time it was as a junior counselor. I worked for two weeks on a pack trip through the mountains and down to the ocean. My love of riding and horses and camping had not diminished a bit so it was an enjoyable experience.

CHAPTER 16

When school started again, I was still on scholarship and still living at the Chadwick's house. Mother was not able to pay our full tuition this year either.

During the past year I had finally become a totally accepted part of school life. I had also joined the swimming team. Initially I joined because I detested field hockey and softball. The swim team had meets all year long and the members didn't have to participate in the other seasonal sports programs. I'd always liked swimming and was good enough to qualify. We had a new gym teacher named Nicki. She was intent on expanding the team's competitiveness and entering us in more meets than in previous years. Chadwick was her first full-time teaching job after graduating from UCLA and she was only ten years older than me when we first met.

If I'd had any inkling that we'd have to work so hard on the team, I probably would have put up with softball practice instead. In addition to regular gym class practice, the members of the team had to swim an extra two hours every afternoon. First we had to swim against the stopwatch to try and improve our speed and then we had to swim laps to increase our stamina. There were many afternoons I didn't have enough strength left to walk out of the pool at the end of practice and would flop myself on the deck totally exhausted. As tough a coach as Nicki was, she was just as understanding as a friend. She saw very quickly that my biggest problem was my own self-confidence. I had none. Nor did I have an overabundance of patience. Between those two shortcomings lay most of my defeats. Nicki worked with me for hours, pushing and prodding and yelling and forcing me back into the pool each time I was ready to give up. There were times when I was seriously on the verge of quitting, but I knew it was too late. There was nothing I could do but grumble and work harder.

The first meet we went to, everyone on the team was scared. Everything was so formal with roped off lanes and officials. The start of each race was so quiet you could have heard a pin drop before the gun went off and all hell broke loose. Once in the water, you could hardly hear the yelling and screaming but you swam for all you were worth. I came in second in the backstroke and did a lot better than I thought I would in the medley.

After that first meet, I worked like a demon with Nicki on my tail every minute. She was relentless and her encouragement knew no bounds. She did whatever she had to do to keep me going. She praised and goaded and yelled and joked. She was wonderful.

At the next swim meet a phenomenal thing happened in my life. I *won* the 50-yard event. I won the race by the distance of one hand . . . mine hit a tenth of a second sooner, but that was all it took. I didn't realize I'd won at first because I was still trying to catch my breath. But in an instant Nicki was kneeling on the deck above me laughing and crying at the same time. "Tina!!! You won!!!" She was hugging me and getting soaked and I could hardly believe it. Then the announcement came over the loudspeaker: "First place . . . Crawford . . . lane three . . . Chadwick." The times and other places were announced and the score was entered on the big board. Chadwick was now ahead in the meet because of my race. I was elated. I'd won! I'd worked and worked and now I'd actually won. It was one of the greatest days of my life. Nicki and I have been friends ever since. Over all the years that have passed in between then and now, the lessons she taught me have never stopped helping me. She was the first person that took the time and cared enough to help me learn how to win and I've never forgotten it.

Of course, I joined the swim team again in eleventh grade. But this year I also wanted to be a cheerleader. Everything was going extremely well for me at school. My grades were better than they'd ever been thanks to the steady competition of Jim Fadiman and the encouragement of our homeroom teacher Bob Martin.

Bob was a fiery teacher who not only encouraged us to think independently but insisted that we do so if we wanted to get top marks. His classes were more like running debates on the merits of any given idea rather than authoritarian dictates on the theory of right and wrong. Originality, inquisitiveness and hard work were combined into exciting classes and we all loved him. He needled us and disciplined us and even Jim Fadiman's lightning quick mind was challenged. Bob was also a young teacher and had the energy to match his own enthusiasm.

Mrs. Chadwick was sure I'd be able to get into whatever college I wanted because of my outstanding scholastic record, the very high scores on the IQ tests and the fact that I was well prepared for the upcoming college entrance exam. She was also very pleased with the rest of my conduct. I'd managed to stay completely clear of any trouble either at school or home for months and months. We were both convinced that it would be clear sailing from here on out. I'm sure also that she felt a sense of relief after the stormy years we'd had together. I'd been at Chadwick nearly five years now and even though the unpaid tuition was beginning to amount to a sizeable debt, Mrs. Chadwick assured me that she would let me finish out high school even if I had to go on a total scholarship. I was really touched by her generosity and concern for my well-being. She and Commander and the school had become my home. I had struggled a long time for a place and a sense of belonging there. In fact, I was becoming a model student in every respect and one that would be a credit to the school itself.

I decided to go for another brass ring . . . I wanted to be a cheerleader. In order to do that, you had to get together at least one other girl and work out several full routines. Then, during one pre-announced day, everyone had to audition in front of the whole student body. You had to go through the entire routine, in matching costumes complete with pom-poms and then the student body voted on which girls they thought were the best. I held my breath after the auditions while the votes were counted. Sandy and I had worked very hard for several weeks but the other girls were good too, and in some respects this was also a popularity contest. When the votes were counted . . . I'd won a position as cheerleader. The confidence I'd gained on the swimming team and in the classroom had enabled me to take the next step. I was very pleased because this accomplishment required the voice of student opinion and for me it was a long awaited vote of acceptance.

My college entrance exam scores were in the top ten percent of the national average though I was only a junior. That meant I didn't have to take the test in my senior year and could apply early to the finest colleges.

Everything I did these days seemed to turn out in my favor. Not that I hadn't worked for my success, I certainly had worked as hard if not harder than anyone in the school. But it was such a new feeling, such a new experience to be successful that it still had all the earmarks of strangeness.

After being elected as a cheerleader, though, I began to ease into a more casual acceptance of my position. I made friends among most of the new students, was elected an officer of my class and was thinking of running for a student body office next year. I had also begun exploratory talks with Mrs. Chadwick about which colleges would be the best bets for early application.

Mother had followed her musical with a western called *Johnny Guitar*. It wasn't a very good movie but it was good publicity and an adventure to make since most of it was on location. She'd brought Chris out to Arizona to visit her during the summer while I was at camp. He liked Nick Ray, the director, very much and had a good time around the cowboys. Nick's son, Tony, was also at Chadwick so Nick had no trouble relating to my brother Chris. There was a young actor in the picture named Ben Cooper who befriended Chris as well. My brother had a good time with the cast and crew. It was also good for Chris in another way. He was the only family member included in this visit and it was an important event for him to feel special. Chris had his share of problems with Mother and growing up in a house full of women. He'd run away from home numerous times, once for almost a week during which he lived down at the Santa Monica pier.

Mother was entirely too strict with him. She made no allowances for him, for the normal energies of a growing teenage boy. Chris stood nearly six feet tall by the time he was thirteen and still she treated him like a baby. He had to be the perfect gentlemen with proper manners and a quiet demeanor. All the spirit of boyhood got bottled up in him and exploded momentarily beyond his control.

The Chadwicks, particularly Commander, worked with Chris. They tried to make him feel a part of the family both at school and at home. Commander was the closest father figure Chris had known. Phillip

Terry left when Chris was so young he barely knew him. As part of the divorce agreement Phillip had agreed to give up all rights to see Chris or participate in his future development on the condition that a trust fund be established to send Chris to college and assure that he had some financial security when he grew up. Once Phillip left the house, it was fifteen years before Chris saw him again.

The week before Thanksgiving vacation, I called Mother one afternoon to find out if I should take the school bus home or if someone was coming to pick me up. I knew immediately that she was in a foul mood and wished I hadn't called. She was being picky about minute details and generally irritable. Just as I was about to say goodbye to her she asked me about my Christmas card list. That stopped me short. My Christmas card list? I honestly had to say that I hadn't even thought about it yet. That was all she needed. She launched into a tirade about how thoughtless I was, how disorganized, how sloppy. *She* started planning Christmas six months in advance, she said, and I couldn't even get my Christmas card list prepared without her having to remind me.

First of all, it wasn't true about her starting six months in advance for Christmas . . . it was one of those things she made up that sounded good to anyone who didn't know any better. It was just like those publicity stories about how she scrubbed her own floors on her hands and knees. Bullshit! I scrubbed the floors . . . Chris scrubbed the floors . . . the fans scrubbed the floors . . . all she did was give the orders. All this turmoil over the Christmas card list was ridiculous. Things had been relatively peaceful for months. I hadn't been home for a while but there had been nothing other than glowing reports from Mrs. Chadwick about my progress. There was nothing wrong, at least not on my part. I'd made sure I called her several times a week and was careful not to get into any arguments with her. But there was nothing I could do about this.

The Christmas card list was one of those leaps into insanity that plagued my life and my relationship with Mother. They sprung out of nowhere and there was nothing you could do to protect yourself against them because there was no way in the world to anticipate them. There was no warning except a tone of voice. It was like a tidal wave destroying everything in its path.

I had known the moment she said her first words over the phone that this was going to be a precarious conversation. I tried to walk the tightrope of politeness and deference in order to avoid anything unpleasant. But here it was anyway. This was just another unpleasantness which always made me feel as though I'd done something wrong even though I knew in reality I hadn't. This was a direct confrontation. It slowly dawned on me that she was setting up a direct confrontation . . . a fight. It didn't matter that I didn't know why. It only mattered that I found some way to deal with it and fast. I told her that I'd try to have my Christmas card list made up in the next two days. She said I'd better have it done tomorrow. Okay . . . I said, tomorrow then . . . I'd have it done tomorrow.

I didn't have to tell Mrs. Chadwick about the conversation because when I saw her that evening, she'd already gotten her own phone call from Mother. Things had been going so well that Mother's rage over the list caught even Mrs. Chadwick by surprise.

That night I sat down and tried to make up an appropriate list. I didn't have most of the addresses, but I thought that the names would be sufficient. There wasn't enough time to get all the addresses anyway because most of them were at the Brentwood house.

When I called her the next day she was still furious with me and ripped the list into verbal shreds. She told me that if I didn't have the *right* list with *all* the addresses by the next day, I couldn't come home for Thanksgiving. At this point I was beginning to feel a sense of hopelessness. No matter how hard I tried, no matter how many months went smoothly, there didn't seem to be any way to get along with her.

That night she and Mrs. Chadwick and I had a three-way phone conversation that degenerated into a total disaster. Even Mrs. Chadwick couldn't hold her temper with Mother. Mother was drunk and crazy and angry. She had deliberately caused this whole turmoil and now she was using it as an excuse to unleash venomous insults at both Mrs. Chadwick and myself. It had started out awful and was getting progressively worse. It was one of the only times I ever heard Mrs. Chadwick raise her voice or express any real opposition to Mother. She was trying to explain the situation over and over again to Mother who was too far gone on her own track to listen.

Finally Mother yelled at me that she didn't want me home for Thanksgiving or any other time. "Fine," I said . . . "That's fine with me." Under the circumstances I'd rather be almost anywhere other than home.

My reply sent her into a new fit of rage. She accused Mrs. Chadwick of turning me against her. She absolutely couldn't stand it that Mrs. Chadwick was trying to help me, or that the Chadwicks had come to genuinely care about me. I'd been at the school over five years and it was where I felt I belonged.

Then Mother dropped the final bombshell. *None* of us were coming home for Thanksgiving. Cindy, Cathy, Chris and myself were *all* staying at school over the vacation. After that . . . we *were all leaving Chadwick*. She would decide later where we were going to be sent . . . but she was taking all of us out of that school.

At that point I hung up. In that moment I hated her so much I wanted to kill her. I think I would have tried to kill her if we'd been in the same room. It didn't even matter to me that I'd have to spend the rest of my life in jail. Just the thought of being able to rid the earth of her evil should be enough satisfaction. I hated her so much I was shaking all over.

Mrs. Chadwick met me halfway down the stairs. Her face was ashen and I could see her hands shaking. Commander was with her.

The three of us sat in silence in the large Spanish living room. It was a cool November evening and the room had a chill to it. I looked carefully at each of their faces. This was not the usual meeting between us. Commander and Mrs. Chadwick looked different than I'd seen either of them before. It was as though the three of us were family and the enemy lurked all around us. The room was in semi-darkness and no one spoke for a long time.

Finally, Commander said in his gruff voice, "Tina . . . I don't know if there's anything we can do to help you, but we're going to try." Mrs. Chadwick was near tears but she was a woman of great inner strength, determination and courage. "This is wrong, Tina . . . this was not your fault." We talked about what had happened until there was nothing left to say. I wondered if, indeed, the Chadwicks could do anything to help me. No one else had even been able to, that much I knew. Evidently they were working toward some plan that would have allowed me to remain in their custody until I finished high school, which was another year and a half. Through the parents of various students at the school, there was a considerable community of influential people, not all of who was show business.

Two days later, it was Thanksgiving. My sisters had been staying in the Cottage where I'd lived when I fist arrived at Chadwick. Commander picked them up and Mrs. Chadwick tried to make it as festive a day as she could for all of us. We did our best to enjoy the meal, but every bite of food stuck in my throat. As I looked around the table at my sisters, my brother and the two elderly people that had come to be my parents, I could hardly imagine life without them. I could hardly imagine another school, new people when I'd fought so long and hard for a place here. I belonged somewhere now . . . I had friends and people who respected me.

Someone came to take my sisters home before the weekend was over. I didn't see them again, after that Thanksgiving, for almost a year. Then someone came to get Chris. I had tears in my eyes the entire time I was helping him pack his things. I think I felt worse for Chris than I did for myself. We'd been so close and I felt badly about leaving him. I also felt that all this was my fault and that they were being punished for something they didn't do. Mother was making all of us pay for what should have been just between her and me.

During these few days, Commander and Mrs. Chadwick were rarely off the phone. I think they must have called half of Los Angeles trying to find a way to keep us in school. I remembered the name of the juvenile officer that had visited me the night Mother had tried to kill me and I talked to him at some length. I even tried to be made a ward of the court, released in the Chadwicks' custody, but he said he couldn't help me.

In desperation, the Chadwicks called Martin Gang, a prominent attorney, to see if there were any laws or legal proceedings that might be able to help. If I'd been sixteen, there would have been a few avenues to pursue, but since I was just fifteen and a half, I wasn't old enough to go out on my own.

Mother owed the Chadwicks an enormous amount of money at this time. She hadn't paid full tuition for Chris or me in two years. She also owed the money for my sisters' first year. The Chadwicks had been carrying all of us on credit for years during which Mother had consistently cried poor and been unable to pay. Evidently there wasn't much they could do about that either except sue her.

As the days of Thanksgiving vacation ebbed away, I saw my sisters and then my brother taken away. I knew the time for me wasn't far off. It seemed ominously close. Mrs. Chadwick was getting frantic as the hours ticked off and the realization that no one was going to help us became clearer. I seriously thought about trying to run away. The trouble was that I knew I'd be hounded until I was caught and then it might be even worse for me.

So when I went to bed Saturday night, I couldn't sleep. I dreaded what would happen the next day. Late that afternoon, the secretary had called to say that she would pick me up Sunday after lunch. I was to have everything packed. I was going home.

Sunday morning I woke up with a dull, sick feeling in my stomach. There was still a part of me that couldn't come to terms with the facts as they now were. Outside it was cool and crisp, a slight breeze was blowing through my half-open window. Lying in bed, the cool air blew across me but it didn't matter. I felt an oppressiveness . . . a heaviness that made me feel as though I could barely breathe. I couldn't believe this was the end. It still didn't make any sense to me that what had started out as a minor flurry over something as unimportant as a Christmas card list could have turned into a major catastrophe for me.

I tried again to follow the slim threads of reality through the events of the past week and each time I ran headlong into the abyss of insanity. That black hole where nothing followed logically, where fabrication and anger and turmoil ruled supreme. That place where there was no help and no peace . . . no escape from the juggernaut of chaos. From her throne in the eye of the hurricane, brandishing her magic wand of obsession, ruled the queen of chaos herself: my mother.

I could find no reason, no logic, no justice, no solace. Powers far beyond my control seemed to have taken possession of my life, my future. I was a being without volition, without a voice in my own future.

I thought about the years I'd struggled to overcome the shame of my childhood folly. I thought about the hundreds of hours of manual labor and mental anguish. I thought about my slow, gradual, determined climb to a place of respect, trust, admiration and accomplishment over the past five and a half years. One third of my entire life had been spent with these people in this place. These were the people who loved me, who had spent years helping me, encouraging me to excel, working with me to assure a successful future. The Chadwicks had become my parents and the school my extended family, my home. At long last I knew I belonged here . . . and now, through a chance misspoken word, a few bottles of alcohol and a lot of tears, it was all being whisked away. We were all powerless to stop it. Our thoughts, our feelings, our years of hard work were being swept away while we stood by helplessly watching with horror and disbelief.

Legally she had the right. Questions of morality or cruelty held no sway. Legally she had the right and no one could stop her.

At breakfast I could see that Mrs. Chadwick had been crying. Commander was more gruff than usual, but I knew that was just his way of trying not to show undue emotion. I couldn't say much either and we ate in silence.

Strangely, it wasn't an uncomfortable silence. It was the silence of three people in pain. It was the silence that happens when someone dies and no one can find the words of solace. It was the silence of sharing a moment of mutual anguish. It was the silence of defeat too.

I finished packing and took the sheets off my bed. I cleaned my room thoroughly so Mrs. Chadwick wouldn't have to go to any extra trouble. I could hardly manage the last of the ordinary little tasks of leaving. My eyes were filled to the brim with tears. Every once in a while they would fall randomly on the sheets I was carrying to the laundry room or the dresser top I was dusting. My tears fell onto the clothes I was packing in the suitcase and on my own hands as I put on my shoes. I didn't try to stop them now because I was determined not to let anyone see me cry when the time came to leave.

The morning hours flew by faster than any I remember. I couldn't hold back the time any more than I could change the situation.

When lunchtime arrived, the three of us reassembled in the kitchen but no one could eat and we didn't even really try. There were no more words. Each of our minds was racing in different directions wondering how we would manage the final moments of our togetherness. Finally, Mrs. Chadwick suggested that I might want to say goodbye to the next-door neighbors who were good friends. Their daughter, Paulette, had been at my fifteenth birthday party just five months before.

More for something to do than any real desire to start saying the goodbyes, I walked the short distance to the Frankel home. The big Spanish house looked as gracious as ever and the Frankels themselves were lovely people that had been very kind to me. As I walked in and saw the sorrow on their faces it was nearly impossible to hold back the tears. I said a few halting words before they both embraced me. Now I had to fight hard not to just break down and weep. They must have realized that this wasn't helping even though it was well meant and they initiated their goodbyes.

As much as I'd tried to prepare myself for the moment, it came as a terrible shock to see that the station wagon had already pulled up in front of the Chadwick house. I had one last fleeting urge to run for my life . . . to run anywhere . . . to escape this dreadful moment. It took all my will power and courage to continue walking down the road toward Chadwick house.

As I approached I saw three people standing by the car. Betty, of course, was there. Betty, the fan who had finally cajoled her way into our household and over the objections of many, had made herself indispensable as Mother's secretary. There was a man who was evidently the driver since he wore the cap of a chauffeur and a nondescript blue suit. But there was another man whom I'd never seen before, standing apart from the rest looking ill at ease. He was slightly heavy set and had eyes that continually darted from one face to the next. Mrs. Chadwick was standing at the front door and Commander was talking to Betty.

I walked past all of them and into the house without so much as glancing at the group around the car. My knees were shaking as I descended the long flights of stairs to my room. A moment later as I was just gathering the last of my things, Commander and Mrs. Chadwick appeared in the doorway. I knew they were there, but I could hardly bear to turn and face them. I pulled my lips inward and held them between my teeth to keep from crying. I felt immobilized. I couldn't believe this was actually happening to me. At last I turned to face Commander and Mrs. Chadwick. I went to her first and put my arms around her. I was always surprised that she was such a small woman. Then I went to Commander. Ordinarily, Commander handled all situations with the same gruff authority he must have had in the Navy. But in this moment he was just a wonderful, kind man in his middle sixties who was feeling the pain of a battle lost and the casualty count beginning to come in.

Commander insisted on taking my suitcase. I tried to refuse, but he marched stalwartly up the two long flights of stairs ahead of Mrs. Chadwick and me. I felt as though I was dying. I think part of all three of us died that November day.

Just before we reached the landing of the second and last floor Mrs. Chadwick told me that the other man was a private detective and was carrying a gun. I looked at her in astonishment. She said that Mother was afraid there would be trouble. She was afraid that Commander and Mrs. Chadwick would interfere with my leaving and she'd ordered this armed guard to accompany Betty and the chauffeur. She whispered to me to be careful and remember they loved me like their own child.

I kissed her on the cheek and she kissed me. We held each other for one last moment. I couldn't bear it any longer. "Oh . . . Mrs. Chadwick . . .," I moaned. My throat ached from trying to hold back the sobbing. She gave me a Kleenex. I blew my nose and wiped my eyes and took a deep breath.

Commander had put my suitcase in the back of the station wagon. I saw the three hired abductors standing silently around the car. I took another deep breath, pulled myself up straight and tall and walked out of Chadwick house for the last time.

Betty said something to me which I totally ignored as I opened the back door and took my seat by the window. The driver and the hired gun got in the front seat. Betty said goodbye to the Chadwicks. I sat silently looking straight ahead as the long station wagon made its turn in the driveway and headed down the hill. I never turned back to catch a last glimpse or to wave goodbye. I looked out my window and didn't say one word. Betty introduced me to the driver and the gunman but I did nothing to acknowledge that I'd heard a word she said.

The Chadwicks and I had been told that I was being taken home. But within about fifteen minutes of driving, I knew that where ever they were taking me, it definitely wasn't home. If anything, we were headed in the opposite direction. Very shortly, I lost my sense of direction without any familiar landmarks to guide me.

So . . . I'm not going home, I thought. Where am I going? I guessed that it was to another school, but I wouldn't have been a bit surprised to have pulled up in front of juvenile hall or jail, for that matter. Everything was so out of hand that I could no longer trust my own past experience or intuition. Since I was damned if I was going to ask any of these abductors where I was being taken, I had no choice but to wait it out.

We drove for quite a long time during which I saw nothing familiar. Since it was obvious I wasn't going to say a word to any of the people in the station wagon, they started talking among themselves. Since they couldn't say anything revealing, the conversation was boring.

After over an hour of steady driving, the station wagon swung onto the Pasadena freeway. The numbered exits sped past without meaning anything to me. Finally the driver chose an exit and we started through a residential district. I fleetingly thought about opening the door and jumping out, but figured that would either get me shot or run over and I didn't really want to die like that. So I kept my eyes glued to the outdoor scenery, hoping for some further clue as to our location. In a few minutes, the driver made a sharp left-hand turn and we began climbing up a winding mountain road. There were a few houses scattered on either side of the road at first and then there was nothing but scrub brush and empty spaces.

Wherever we're going, it must be on the top of this mountain. We climbed further and further around hairpin curves on this small two-lane road. At last I saw a sign that said "Flintridge Sacred Heart Academy" and an arrow pointing to the left fork of the narrow road. We turned and continued another few blocks until a huge, old Spanish fortress-like building came into view. The station wagon pulled into a small parking lot at the bottom of a long, wide flight of cement stairs with wrought iron railings. There were no people around but the main entrance to the building was completely obvious. The secretary, driver and armed guard got out of the car, stretching themselves after the long, tiresome ride. The driver opened my door and then went around to the back to take out my suitcase. I sat immobile for a minute looking at the foreboding building which sat alone on the top of this mountain.

Betty and the driver walked up the long stairs with me. The entrance had huge iron and glass doors, one that was standing open. The driver put down my suitcase just inside the entrance and told Betty he'd wait for her in the car. It was sort of dark inside and my eyes had to adjust for a moment. Directly in front of the entrance was an enormous statue of Jesus holding a bleeding heart. I stared at it, horrified. *Where was I?* After a moment I looked at the rest of the entrance. Except for the huge statue, it looked rather like an old hotel lobby. It had dark red carpeting, wooden floors, large leaded glass windows and a couple of old-fashioned, over-stuffed armchairs directly out of the 1920s.

"Miss Barker?" a soft voice inquired behind me. I turned around to see a woman dressed in long, white robes with a black veil over her head standing behind what could have been a hotel check-in-counter. Every part of her body was covered except her face and her hands. I knew from the movies that she must be a nun, but I'd never seen such a person in real life.

"I'm Sister Benigna," I heard the woman say as the secretary walked toward the counter. I stood staring at the two of them as they talked for a minute. When I was introduced, I simply said, "Hello."

Sister Benigna showed us to my room, introducing me to my new roommate whose name was Marilyn. After Sister left, Betty told me to take out what underwear and personal items like a toothbrush that I'd need because she was going to take the rest of my things away with her. I looked at her with all the venomous hatred I had stored inside of me, but I said nothing. I took the essentials I needed, closed the suitcase and still said nothing. She indicated that my school uniform had already been ordered along with the shoes and that I would find them in the closet. I made no move, I stared at her silently.

I think she actually expected me to pick up my suitcase and take it back to the car for her. Here I was, being left with the clothes on my back and a school uniform and she expected me to participate further in my own slaughter. At that moment, hell could have frozen over before I'd have lifted one finger. I stared at her, daring her to ask anything more of me. She'd never once done anything to help me, quite the contrary, and I was damned if I'd let this small moment pass in docile subservience to her. Technically she may have had the upper hand and I was totally powerless, but not for all the money in the world would I back down.

It was only an instant. It was only a small, minor instant before she reached down and picked up the handle of the suitcase. Then, mercifully, she left.

Marilyn sat speechless on the edge of one of the beds. The room was plain but not too dreary and it had it's own bathroom.

"What is this place?" I asked my new roommate. Marilyn was surprised to learn that I knew nothing about the school, or even exactly where I was. She explained it was a Catholic girls' school in Flintridge, near Pasadena, run by the Dominican sisters. The nuns were a semi-enclosed order which meant they lived a more restricted life than some of the orders which devoted themselves to social work or nursing. This was, in effect, a convent school that had the reputation for scholastic achievement, since the Dominicans were a teaching order. It also prided itself on the fact that it was considered strict and none of its girls had ever successfully run away. The last part I could easily understand having just driven up the long, lonely and deserted mountain road leading to the school.

Marilyn seemed like a nice girl so when she asked me why I was transferred in the middle of the year, I related a brief and bitter account of the past week. She didn't say much, except that she was sorry. By the time we'd exchanged that much information, she looked at her watch and said it was dinnertime.

It was all so unfamiliar and strange to me. We were supposed to pray before and after each meal. I didn't know the prayers or the routine here. All the girls were strangers and the general atmosphere of the building was foreboding.

After dinner, Sister Benigna asked me to come into her private office. She closed the door and we sat across from one another in two small chairs. I waited for her to speak.

In a soft voice she told me what the rules here were to be for me. My mother had told her that I was very difficult to handle and had gotten into trouble at my former school. Mother had requested that I receive very strict discipline and be allowed no privileges of any kind. Sister Benigna said that meant I would not be allowed to leave the school, or to use the phone to make outside calls. I was to receive no mail, no visitors and no incoming calls. Since all the outgoing mail had to be checked through the office, it would not be possible for me to send letters to anyone but my mother. In addition, I was not allowed to have any money. There was a school store where I could charge $5.00 per month for toothpaste, shampoo or school supplies and that was all. As I listened to

Sister, it became clear to me that I was being held a prisoner. I was under virtual house arrest in this convent. Since no one from Chadwick knew where I was and I was not going to be allowed any communication with the outside world, I was a prisoner. I was in total exile.

It was then that my will power and determination began to crumble. I couldn't hold it together any longer. I began to tell Sister Benigna what had happened to me during the last week . . . it was so fresh in my memory that I related every last detail including my drunken, crazy mother, the Chadwicks trying to save me and the final abduction scene complete with the private detective and his gun. As I poured out my story I was only semi-conscious of the woman who sat across from me. She was still a total stranger, but she was the only person I had, the only one who would listen. Half the time I was sobbing and trying to talk at the same time. A lot of my story, I'm sure, made no sense. However, as it unfolded, I saw the expression on her face change. I was sure she wouldn't believe me . . . why should she? So I gave her the Chadwick's telephone number and begged her to call them and ask them whether or not I was telling the truth.

It was nearly 10 o'clock by then and Sister told me to go to bed and try to get some sleep. I didn't know whether or not she'd call the Chadwicks and there was nothing further I could do. She did say that no matter what the truth was, it wouldn't change the restrictions Mother had placed on me. I understood that already.

Sister did call the Chadwicks in a few days. It didn't change the punishment I was receiving, but at least she now had a much better understanding of the situation.

As for me . . . something had broken and I just cried uncontrollably. I cried through morning prayers, through religion class, through lunch and on into the afternoon. Sometimes I tried to stop crying but it was too much effort. I'd given up being embarrassed about the other girls looking at me. During the day, I took a seat in the back row of the class and cried. I have no idea what the sisters talked about, nor did it seem important. I turned in no papers, did no assignments and spoke to as few people as possible.

After four weeks of this and numerous talks with Sister Benigna who was trying desperately to find some means of consoling me, it was time for Christmas vacation. I knew I wasn't going anywhere even before

Sister told me. I knew that I was a prisoner in this dreadful, strange place where I didn't understand the people or the religion or the prayers or the talk about hell and sin and damnation. Being brought up in Christian Science, I'd never heard talk like that. I'd never thought about sin, I'd known only the gospel of God's goodness and man created in God's image and likeness. I felt as though I'd been thrust through a time machine back into the Middle Ages and it scared me.

Christmas vacation came and most of the students went home. There were perhaps a dozen girls from Central and South America left at the school but they went shopping, went to the movies and occasionally visited friends.

It was cold on top of that mountain. The winter rains came early that year. It was gray drizzle outside, damp dreariness inside.

After four or five days of the vacation, crying alone in my room most of the time, I finally got a stomachache and told Sister I was going to bed.

I had no more fight left, no more anger, no more spirit of survival. My entire life, built over the last five years of pain, of anguish, of determination and finally of success had suddenly been wrenched away from me. I had cried my eyes and my heart out for a month and I was exhausted by the sheer onslaught of the sorrow. My eyes had no more tears, my body had no more strength. I was suddenly worn out with the years of doing battle and getting nowhere. I was drained of the last shreds of hope that if I just worked hard enough and long enough, things would surely get better. Everything I held valuable, everyone I loved, every bit of success was gone. It was all gone. It was all gone. . . .

I lay in the bed, vaguely hearing the rain outside and slowly felt myself slipping away. I was too tired to think anymore . . . too tired to move. I was overcome with total exhaustion. The world just faded away from me and I sank into a kind of limbo world where nothing hurt anymore. If I lay very still and kept my eyes closed, it didn't hurt anymore. Everything was muffled now . . . the world was at a distance from me . . . time slipped by unnoticed. Day melted into night melted into day again and it was all the same. At some point, either night or day but which night or what day I don't know, I was dimly aware of Sister trying to talk to me. Her face floated above me swathed in white with a black halo shimmering above it. Through the haze I notice her mouth moving but the sound was so faint that it didn't matter. I didn't understand what the words meant and I didn't make any effort to ascribe meaning to the wavering sounds. I closed my eyes again and the floating face with the black halo disappeared like magic. Once or twice in the total darkness, I got up and went to the bathroom. I noticed a small tray of food by my bed and stared at it curiously. I had no feeling of hunger, so it went untouched.

Somehow I knew I was losing my sanity but it no longer mattered. I didn't care anymore. I wanted to die. I lost all desire to think. I just sank away into peaceful floating where there were no harsh voices, there was no pain, there was no terror. It was very nice here . . . very quiet . . . very peaceful. Nothing hurt me anymore . . . it was all very far away . . . soft and muffled.

Once when I opened my eyes in the dark I saw a stack of envelopes on a small table right next to my bed. Christmas cards . . . Christmas cards . . . Christmas card lists . . . I sank away again, never touching the envelopes.

Time . . . people . . . voices . . . meant nothing. Nothing could touch me here. Nothing could touch me . . . I didn't care anymore . . . I melted into the darkness and floated through the space of darkness. I didn't dream, I didn't think. I heard my own breathing and floated on the rise and fall of the air. Air and space and darkness melting and drifting away.

I had nothing to eat, said nothing. I have no concept of the time intervals, but every so often a white floating face with a black halo held me upright and forced me to drink some water. Most of it spilled but some was swallowed. Then I melted back into the quiet darkness again.

The white faces with the black halos gathered around me from time to time. I dimly heard the heavy black wooden rosary beads rattling as the litany of their prayers wafted across the bed. After a while the black halos drifted away.

It was later that I found out I'd been lying in bed for six days. I had no personal sense of time passing or events taking place. For me there was only the fading in and out of the black halos and the occasional sound of rain.

One day I felt hungry. I sat up in bed and looked out the window at a gray dawn. Just sitting up was such an effort I would have given up again except for the terrible gnawing hunger. I managed to get into the bathroom and sort of wash myself. I found something to wear, but I had to rest before I could dress. It seemed like an Herculean effort to walk down the endless hall. Again, I had to rest several times before I wandered slowly into the empty dining room. There were some sounds coming from the kitchen. Leaning against the high-backed chairs to steady my shaky legs, I progressed slowly toward the kitchen door. Before I had actually gotten to the kitchen entrance, a sister walked out carrying a tray of food. Seeing me half-standing, half-leaning on the nearest chair startled her. She looked at me as though she were seeing a ghost. She called for one of the other sisters to help me. A younger nun quickly assisted me back to my room, assuring me that she would return immediately with a tray of food. It seemed like an eternity that I lay weakly in bed waiting for something to eat.

The oatmeal, toast and milk looked like a feast to me, but I was so weak that the sister had to feed me the few mouthfuls I was able to swallow. When I tried to talk to her my voice had a strange, raspy sound. I asked her to leave the unfinished milk when she took the small tray away.

I fell asleep. When I awoke, Sister Benigna was sitting on the edge of the bed, saying her rosary quietly. I looked at her and tried to manage a smile. When she realized that I actually recognized her, tears welled up in her eyes. She took my limp hand in hers and said, "We've been praying for you."

"Thank you, Sister."

"You've been ill for nearly a week. Today we were going to call the doctor."

"I don't think that would have done any good." I was incredibly tired again and soon fell asleep. However, when one of the sisters arrived with some food for lunch, I sat up and managed to eat about half of it by myself. Even though I slept most of the day, when I was awake I was fully awake.

It took me the remainder of Christmas vacation to regain any strength at all, but at least I was up walking around. The last day before school started again I decided I was strong enough to go through the stack of cards that had remained untouched beside my bed.

Miraculously enough, most of the cards and letters were from friends of mine at Chadwick. They contained handwritten notes expressing love

for me and sadness at the terrible circumstances of my sudden departure. People I barely knew sent me little notes saying how much I would
be missed. I had mixed emotions as I opened one after the other. I
was deeply moved that so many people had taken the time to send me
their good wishes and their love, but the sadness that overcame me was
excruciating. It took all of the little courage I had not to take to my bed
again. I didn't have much left in the way of defenses, so I just sat there
sobbing with loneliness and despair.

When the siege of my tears subsided, I washed my face with cold
water several times and then decided to take a bath.

Somewhat refreshed, I returned to the remaining unopened letters.
It was only then that I saw one addressed in my mother's handwriting. The stationery was imprinted with a green wreath across which was
embossed "Happy Holidays to You" in red script. I stared dully at the
familiar scrawling handwriting. The letter read:

> *Tina dear*
>
> Thank you so very much for the lovely sachet—how sweet
> you were to make one for me and the girls.
>
> Enclosed are your cards and letters—I would appreciate
> your thank-you notes for all the gifts I sent up to you as soon as
> possible.
>
> My love to you and hope the New Year will bring you great
> joy and happiness
>
> *Always—*
> *"Mommie"*

My hands were shaking by the time I'd finished reading. I looked around
the room to see where "all the gifts" were, but I only saw three small
boxes. I turned the letter over and reread it, even though it made me
feel ill. The irony of the last sentence . . . "great joy and happiness" . . .
great joy and happiness . . . how the hell was I going to get great joy and
happiness when I was locked up in a convent being held prisoner on
top of a mountain with every single shred of my life taken away from
me? Insensitive, cruel, monstrous bitch . . . the impotent rage inside
me welled up and overflowed into hysterical laughter. Tears streaming
down my face, I laughed and danced wildly around the room bumping

into furniture and waving the "great joy and happiness" letter above my head like a banner. My foot caught on a chair leg. I collapsed across my bed sobbing uncontrollably again.

I can't stand it any longer . . . I can't stand this goddamn pain any longer . . . I can't stand the snide letters from her . . . I can . . . not . . . take . . . it . . . anymore.

I went back to bed until the first students began to return from vacation.

CHAPTER 17

Slowly, slowly the bleak routine of the Catholic girls' school began to be my way of life too. I went where I was supposed to go, did what I was told and spent most of the weekends by myself reading. I had become numbed into subservience. The penalty for thinking was pain beyond my endurance. I walked in line and went through the motions of being alive. I cried by myself and ate candy because it was the only pleasure left. I had given up hope now, so one day or one week was the same as another. I was serving time in purgatory and no one could help me. I was serving my life sentence for crimes beyond my undoing. Institutional life, barren as it was, simply created the format of my constant penance. Punishment had become the ordinary course of my days. At least here in this convent the sisters were kind and no one beat me. Sister Benigna, particularly, took hours and hours of her evenings and weekends to talk with me, trying to keep me from slipping away again. I felt she genuinely understood, which was peculiar because she hadn't known me very long. She was a sister, a Catholic nun, sheltered from the outside world. Yet I felt she understood me and my circumstances better than anyone else ever had. She had a strength and courage that was quiet but steadfast. She began to bend the special restrictions I was supposed to live under. She allowed me to write and receive letters from my friends at Chadwick and even to make a few phone calls if I cleared them with her first.

On February 5th, I received another letter from Mother. This one was typewritten.

Christina darling,

Thank you for your sweet letter. I hope you received all the presents last week. I have a list of the people who sent them to

you, but do not have what the gifts are. Will you be good enough
to write your thank-you letters and send them to me as soon as
possible.

I hope you are feeling better.
All my love,
"Mother"

Her correspondence with me picked up and about a week later this
typewritten letter arrived.

Christina darling,

Enclosed are some Valentine's cards. I'm sure you will be
grateful for them and for everyone who has been thinking of
you.

Thank you for calling me on Valentine's Eve. It was very sweet
and thoughtful of you. I'm deeply grateful. I am glad you had
such a lovely evening and I hope your school term is happy and
that you are well adjusted.

My love to you always,
"Mommie"

I had now been at Flintridge Sacred Heart Academy three months. It
seemed like a year. I wasn't really interested in my schoolwork anymore
because it was so easy compared to Chadwick that I was far ahead of
most of my classmates. Not many of the girls were planning to go on to
college, so the same level of academic excellence was not demanded of
them. Many of the girls were from Spanish speaking countries and had
considerable difficulties with English.

In addition, I discovered that Catholic education contained unexpected
pitfalls. My first real shock came in English class during book reports.
There was no special list of books to chose from, so I picked one that
I liked from my past experience and a volume I'd happened to have
received as a Christmas gift. When my turn came, I got up in front of
the class and my report on the *Rubyiat of Omar Khayam*, complete with
selections of the poetry which I read to the class. When I finished, it
was usual to ask for questions. But I met with stunned silence. I turned

to look at the plump sister teaching the class and she was crimson! She managed to sputter that the book I had just reported so thoroughly was on *the index*! A gasp went up from the class, but I had no idea what in the world she was talking about. She went on to explain that the index was a list of books which Catholics were forbidden to read.

It was now my turn to be stunned. A list of forbidden books? I couldn't believe my ears. I knew, by the extreme state of agitation the teacher was in, that this was no joke. Sister asked me to sit down and see her after class.

There was nothing in my educational background to prepare me for this kind of thinking. I had been taught to question everything and think for myself, not to follow like a sheep. I couldn't even bring myself to apologize to Sister after class. All I said was that I was not a Catholic and that I'd never heard of "the index" before today. Sister told me that from here on out, I was only to report on books found in the school library. There was no further discussion, although I always had the feeling Sister didn't quite know what to make of me after that incident. She tended to stay clear of me when I raised my hand in class and gave me straight A's anyway.

The beginning of March, since I received no spending money, Mother sent me a check for the school annual which I had requested. Her check was accompanied by this handwritten note:

> *Tina darling*
> Enclosed is a check for the "annual"
> Loved your sweet letter—and I love you—forgive brief note but I'm rushing to Queen Bee script reading—
> *"Mommie"*

Queen Bee was a movie I found horrifying when I saw it a year later. The reason it was horrifying was that it was exactly like Mother when she flew into one of her tirades at home. I can honestly say from years of experience at that particular time in both of our lives . . . her performance in *Queen Bee* was not a job of acting nor was it a characterization of another person . . . it was Mother. It was the same person who went into fits of rage and beat us; it was the same person who refused to listen to any side of a dispute except her own; it was the same person who made up stories about me and then got everyone to believe she was telling the truth and I was the liar. It was with secret pleasure that I later read Bosley Crother's review in the *New York Times*, which said: "As the wife of a Southern mill owner whom she had driven to drink by her ruthless, self-seeking machinations and frank infidelity (Miss Crawford) is the height of mellifluous meanness and frank insincerity. When she is killed at the end, as she should be, it is a genuine pleasure and relief."

Some people said she overacted. I knew that she wasn't "acting" at all ... she was just being herself. Maybe not the "self" she put on for her fellow professionals or the outside world and the press, but certainly the "self" she was at home with us and the servants.

I continued to write to her and call her once a week. It's hard to explain why, but habit was certainly part of it. Also, I was afraid that if I didn't make some attempt to have a relationship with her, at least let her know I was alive, she'd get crazy again and transfer me to some-place worse. I'd heard rumors about the county detention homes and foster parent programs. However much I disliked being at Flintridge I knew there were places worse and I didn't want to be sent to one of them.

On March 28, she sent me this typed thank-you note for the small birthday gift I'd made her.

Christina darling

I just received your letter of March 14th. Isn't that odd? And the package with the tea towel that you did.

Thank you so much for the lovely, lovely gift, beautifully done.

Thank you for telling me about your roommate. Hope the new one is nice, too. I'm sure she is. You spoke of the weather being extremely extreme, but where we are, it's just extreme. Just hot. No air-conditioning no nothing, and, of course, as usual I'm wearing fur coats in the summer, and I can guarantee you, no matter where I am in January or February, I will be wearing bathing suits. But this is life, and this is what makes it interesting.

I adored your St. Patrick's Day poem. It's charming beyond belief.

By the way, darling, did you get the bras? And did they fit, because in order to get pink or black we have to buy them and then dye them, and I didn't want to go to all that expense, unless the other two fit you. Do let me know, please.

Thank you again for writing, darling.

All my love,

"Mommie"

Even though this letter was longer than the usual perfunctory notes acknowledging a card or birthday gift I'd sent her, they all made me feel like I was part of the fan mail. The paragraph about the bras was ridiculous. I had no money to buy anything and had asked her to send me some underwear, specifying the sizes. What she'd sent were two custom-made bras that were all wrong. I never asked for pink or black either. What would I have done with them? I was living in total isolation as a student in a convent school. I was not allowed to leave the school premises and I couldn't have anyone visit me. What on earth would I need with pink and black bras? All I wanted was some underwear, plain and simple and utilitarian and I couldn't even seem to get that. All the "darling" business was for the benefit of her own self-image and nothing more. She knew that the sisters opened all the incoming mail before the students got it and were free to read the contents. I got the feeling it was all a put-on job for the sisters' benefit, because she never called me "darling" over the phone.

Two days later, the following letter from my brother arrived. It was dated March 28, the same as Mother's letter about the bras.

Dear Chris,

I called Mother last night and asked her if the whole family would be there for Easter. She said, "you mean Tina too?" I said, "yes." Then she said, "Do you want happiness and fun or sadness?" Of course I said I wanted fun and then she said "that's why, Chris, Tina isn't coming home until she can bring some love and happiness to us."

So if you would please come out of your shell and give instead of take you will find that lots and lots more love and joy than hate.

So if you want to be a great success like Mommie is, be sweet
and loving and you will find that you will gain lots more friends
and have lots more fun. O.K.

Just try it and see.

Your friend and loving brother,

Chris

P.S. Write soon,

Love,

Chris

I felt like someone hit me in the stomach. It had only been four months
since I last saw Chris. Through his well-intended letter to me, I heard
Mother's propaganda machine grinding out the lies about me. I wasn't
mad at Chris, just terribly hurt that he'd believe any of the garbage. But
I knew he was even more dependent on Mother's whim now that I was
gone and couldn't take care of him. Though I knew he was just trying to be
helpful in his own way, that didn't keep me from feeling betrayed anyway.
I thought back over the years we'd been together. Surely that meant something. But he was still young and her influence was all pervasive. That was
her strategy; indeed the "Queen Bee." Why did she bother with all that
phony "darling" shit, when she said terrible things about me behind my
back. I was inexplicably tied to her, but my god how I hated her.

Easter vacation came and went. I never set foot off the grounds of
Flintridge. There was a short note from Mother wishing me a "Happy
Easter" and a few cards from fans I barely knew.

Easter was an important religious holiday at Flintridge, so the few of
us who were left at school had to go to mass every day. I was more familiar with the ritual by now but, even so, Good Friday and Holy Saturday
were depressing. Easter Sunday's mass was beautiful with the flowers,
the gold and white robes on the altar and the priest and the joyous organ
music. I was terribly lonely and felt like the outsider I was.

It was the middle of April before I heard from Mother again.

Christina darling:

Thank you so much for the lovely sachet. How beautifully it is
made. The monogram is just enchanting. I thank you so much.

How sweet you were to think of me.

I'll send your formal and your summer things to you. I'm delighted you are enjoying the blouses I sent at Easter.

We previewed Female on the Beach last night and it went just beautiful.

Forgive me, darling, I must run,

Love

"Mommie"

Right on the heels of her Easter letter came another, dated April 21.

Christina dear:

Congratulations on your fine report card. I am so proud of you, and I know, you are very happy about it, too. Thank you for your sweet letter. I knew you got your clothes on Sunday, as I sent them by City Messenger.

I do know that Mrs. Chadwick's birthday is on the 26th and I am glad you want to do something for her. Why don't you do for her, what you did for me—send her a telegram, or did you have something more extravagant in mind? Do call Miss Scheel and tell her what you would like done. I cannot tell by your letter whether you were asking for money for a gift, whether you want us to choose something, or what. So call Miss Scheel as soon as you receive this.

My love to you as always,

"Mommie"

I was furious. The telegram she referred to was something that happened a year ago. I didn't have any money to buy her a present and I'd misguidedly thought that a telegram would be more important than just a card. So I sent her a telegram for her birthday. She interpreted the telegram in the light of how she used them . . . for last minute remembrances the mail would have delivered too late for the occasion. She interpreted it as not thinking in advance or not caring enough about her. I had no idea when I sent it that it would displease her so very much. For years after that she brought up the birthday telegram over and over again. In fact, from that point on and for every one of the twenty-two years until her death, she sent me a telegram on my birthday. She was fixated on that birthday telegram, even though more than twenty years passed and I never sent her a telegram again. Over the next twenty years I sent cards and presents, and still I got a telegram from her on my birthday. I sent her one telegram when I was fourteen years old and I got birthday telegrams in return for the next *twenty-one* years!

The weird thing is that I know what happened. First of all Mother tended to become riveted on what she considered a personal slight or an insult. She would not discuss it with you. Later, she wouldn't remember what the explanation for it was or that it may have been unintentional. She silently brooded over the incident and carried it with her inside. She remembered the insult, however accidental or unintended, and it grew as time passes. Usually, a misunderstanding fades away with time. But for Mother the process was just the opposite. Whatever happened as the years went by such as presents, cards and phone calls, she clung to the image of the old hurt, to her own secret image as the deprived, somehow cheated and unloved person.

It was like the proverbial bottomless pit into which you could pour years of loving, kindness, attempts at reconciliation and it was never enough to erase the one mistake. It put you at a permanent disadvantage because of a totally unpremeditated error in judgment. An error that existed privately in the far reaches of her own childhood deprivation, her own alienation and loneliness, her own insatiable need for love. There wasn't enough love in the whole world to fill her need. She didn't allow enough space for another human being to be themselves. She demanded such constant assurances of devotion that it was humanly impossible to satisfy her. Over the years, most of the people who really did love her, in spite of her demands, were pushed away from her because she seemed unable to accept others as sovereign beings. So she was forced to settle for subservience and what she interpreted as total devotion. To her, total devotion meant saying yes. It meant dropping your life to serve hers. It meant inevitably being placed in a position of servitude, however subtle. Because you didn't have a relationship with her, you did what she wanted and said what she wanted to hear or you were banished. You treated her always like a "star." You behaved enough like a fan to make her feel comfortable. Under these conditions, she was generous, she showered gifts and thoughtfulness beyond anything remotely required. That was the price and those were the payoffs.

The other part of the twenty-two years of telegrams was just book-keeping. You went on a telegram list. Birthdays, anniversaries and other special events were noted on the secretary's daily calendar. Year after year those lists were updated and transferred. As the pages flipped, the secretary sent the telegrams or reminded Mother to dictate personal notes. I got on the Los Angeles list. No matter where I lived or where Mother lived, the telegrams originated from Los Angeles. The secretary simply copied last year's message, looked in the black leather phone book under Crawford, Christina . . . noted the current address and sent the telegram along with all the others for that particular day. Simple as that.

The next message from Mother, dated May 3, was brief.

Christina dear:

I sent you your Easter gifts, but as yet have not received thank-you letters to Cathy, Cindy, Chris, Aunt Bettina, Aunt Helen and Uncle Mel.

Love
"Mommie"

Cathy, Cindy and Chris, of course, were my sisters and brother. Ludicrous as it now sounds, I had to write formal thank-you notes to my own family and they had to do the same. Not only did I have to write them, I had to send their thank-you notes to Mother instead of simply mailing them from school. Besides checking up on me to make sure I actually wrote them, the maneuver was designed to keep me uninformed as to their location. I was not supposed to have any direct contact with either my sisters or my brother because Mother had personally declared me a "corrupting influence" on their young, tender, innocent minds. So I had to write the letters, put them in unaddressed envelopes and forward them to Mother.

The "Aunt Bettina" referred to was the fan-now-secretary named Betty. Mother had changed her name to a more gracious, endearing form, though neither of those qualities was particularly suitable as far as I was concerned. I never called her by the newly coined name implying family membership. To me she remained just plain Betty. The "Aunt Helen" referred to was also a fan of long standing, one of the original three including Betty who used to sit on the garage steps waiting for a glimpse of their idol. Uncle Mel was the writer mentioned earlier.

The next letter, in retrospect, is chilling. Not just for what it actually says, but more importantly for what it neglects to say.

May 9, 1955

Christina, my darling:

Thank you so much for my lovely Mother's Day present. Sorry we didn't get to talk on Mother's Day, but your first message at nine o'clock was, that I had to call you by one, or you couldn't be reached, and I was not available at that time. So I didn't try to reach you, since you said it was impossible.

Then, when you called later in the afternoon, I was being photographed for a layout in *Look* and could not call back then either.

You were sweet to call, and I send you all my love,

As always,

"Mommie"

It was never-never land again. However, notice the date on the letter: *May 9, 1955.* (Note: Every letter received from her during the past four months has already been included.)

On *May 10, 1955,* Joan Crawford married a man by the name of Alfred N. Steele in Las Vegas, Nevada.

I heard about the marriage over the radio. I was stunned. Of course, everyone in school wanted to know what he was like, but all I could reply was that I'd never seen him or even heard of him until this very moment. The radio said he was president of Pepsi Cola. That was all I knew.

Sister Benigna had a long talk with me that day. She recognized how humiliating the situation was for me and tried her best to calm me down. I swung back and forth between being mortified about hearing the news over the radio and being furious at the insulting behavior that considered me no more important than the general public getting their information from the news media. Since none of the broadcasts mentioned the newlywed's location, it was several days before I was able to reach Mother, though I left several messages with the secretary at home.

Mother never did call me back. When I finally called and she was at home, the instant she got on the phone I could have strangled her. She was pompous, condescending and every inch the consummate bitch. She icily inquired why it had taken me so long to congratulate her! I told her the radio hadn't given any location and I'd left messages with the secretary. Then she said something that is emblazoned on my memory forever: "Christina, *all* you had to do was call Las Vegas . . . the whole world knows who *I* am . . . it's *very* simple, the information operator would have been able to locate me. Obviously, you didn't try very hard. Hundreds of *other* people found us!" The tone of voice she used was so degrading it made you feel like you'd just publicly shit in your pants. "Fine," I said, shaking violently from head to foot. "I hope you're both very happy." With that I hung up. It was useless. Totally useless.

She runs off and gets married to a total stranger, without having the common courtesy or decency to inform her children or even have the secretary call them if she was in such a bloody hurry, then turns right around and berates *me* for not tracking *her* down. Call Las Vegas, indeed! I'd rather die first. Can you imagine . . . "Hello, Las Vegas information? My name is Christina Crawford. I heard on the radio this morning that my mother, Joan Crawford, married a man named Alfred Steele. You wouldn't happen to know what hotel they're staying in would you?"

I did not speak to Mother again for several months. She and Mr. Steele left for Europe on their honeymoon. She did take time to write me this note from Paris, Hotel Plaza-Athenee.

> *Tina darling*
> Congratulations on being made Vice President of the Student Body— I am so proud and know you are too—

Aunt Bettina will see that you get your skirts—

We leave Paris in the morning early for the south of France touring by car—will be back at Plaza Athenee on the 11th of July—sail the 13th

My love to you always—

"Mommie"

Sister Benigna, however, received quite a different letter from Mother which was handwritten on Hotel Hassler stationery and mailed from Rome.

Dear Sister Benigna—

Thank you so much for your sweet letter—I would rather Christina stay at school—since she cannot behave at home—I have no assurance she would behave when a visitor—

It will do her good to have time alone when you are all in "Retreat"—to be alone instead of having someone to show off to—It will give her a "thinking time" which she needs—She never ever says love in her letters to me—but to other people— she says—"my love always to your dear Mother"—knowing I will read the letters—

It also took her Aunt Betty to scold her after eleven days after her birthday for not thanking me—I would like Tina to go to Sacred Heart next year and graduate—since she is doing so well—I think she should finish her high school there— In case of an emergency please contact Betty Barker—day at Old-field 42500—evenings Normandy 21440—ask her to call me in Paris—she knows where—

Thank you oh so much for your kind helpfulness with Tina— and I hope you will allow Tina to be with you another year—I'll be in N.Y. the 18th of July—36 Sutton Place So.—home the following week. I would like Tina to remain with you till she graduates.

Thank You

Joan Crawford

The only reason I know about this letter is that Sister showed it to be and let me copy it. I feel compelled at this point to back track a bit.

I had been at Flintridge for seven months now. During that time I had never seen Mother, never stepped foot off the campus. For seven months I had been punished severely for the incident which started over Christmas card lists in November and resulted in her taking all of us out of Chadwick School. During those seven months of agonizing personal hell, I had never once done anything that could be remotely considered wrong.

My report card, even by Mother's admission, was excellent. I had been elected Student Body Vice President for my senior year. That was the highest office a non-Catholic girl could hold at the school. The position of President was reserved for a Catholic and I was, therefore, ineligible, even for nomination. I had not broken any rules, gotten in any arguments with Mother, strayed from the straight and narrow path in any way, shape or manner. Even under circumstances that depressed and discouraged me, I had become a model student with the honors the faculty and my peers could bestow upon me. I got everything the meager situation had to give.

You would never guess that in a million years from the letter Mother had just written to Sister Benigna. Sister Benigna knew the truth . . . I knew the truth . . . but the truth didn't make a goddamned bit of difference to Mother. She was off on a honeymoon, couldn't be bothered with me and trumped-up feeble excuses, mostly constructed of her own cruelty and paranoia to punish me further. By now it could no longer be connected even remotely to my behavior. *My* behavior had been exemplary.

It was excruciating for me . . . frustrating beyond what words can convey. There didn't seem to be any connection, any relationship, between what I did and what I got. No matter how hard I tried, no matter how long I worked it didn't seem to be enough to get me out of this everlasting punishment. It didn't make any sense anymore. She held all the cards: "Her will be done."

So I stayed at Flintridge that summer. There was no summer school and the days dragged by interminably. For two weeks, the Dominican sisters went on retreat. That meant, for two weeks, not one sister said a word. They prayed and listened to religious lectures, but they remained silent. It was eerie being around all these silent people. I no longer found the entire surroundings strange, but it was lonely and depressing.

In order to keep me from going totally stir crazy, Sister Benigna asked me if I'd work in the office during the retreat. I was glad for anything to occupy my mind, so I answered the phones and opened the mail for eight hours a day. The rest of the time I spent taking walks by myself, going for an occasional swim by myself and reading alone in my room.

If I'd had a notion of loneliness before, it was nothing compared with this summer. I was so lonely I felt hollow. I was so lonely, the office telephone sounded like a cannon. The closest thing to companionship I had was food. It was the one and only source of anything remotely resembling pleasure. I was so unbelievably lonely, I wondered if I was going to lose my mind. I thought about prisoners locked away in solitary confinement and marveled that they retained the will to live at all. I thought about hermits and the mountain men of the old west and wondered if they too battled the enticing seductress of insanity. I now knew how people went mad . . . they gave up fighting. They went mad because it was a hell of a lot easier. They went mad because it comes to be a far better place than dying from the slow pain of loneliness. You sink willingly into going mad . . . you ease into being crazy . . . it doesn't happen overnight. You get tired of the constant battle with no victories. You become exhausted hoping for the "cease-fire" . . . you loose your grip on the world slowly and drift into the chasm of your own hopelessness. The *now* of your grief stretches endlessly into the future . . . no hope, no relief, no rewards, no change . . . ever.

That summer I stood shakily on the tightrope of my loneliness. Each time I wavered I saw below me that chasm of madness . . . beckoning me to join the other lost souls who had given up the fight and slipped into a special world. It was a terrifying journey no one else knew about. I was the solitary traveler, somewhere during each day suspended just above the beckoning chasm, hovering unsteadily, feeling my grip slipping. I was just sixteen years old.

I had gotten post cards from France and Italy as the honeymoon progressed. Mostly they held glowing praise for the lovely countryside and fabulous meals Joan Crawford and her new husband, Alfred Steele, were enjoying. On July 8th she scrawled this letter to me.

Tina dearest—

Thank you for your sweet letter—I'm glad you liked your birthday gifts—did you receive the cable?

Aunt Bettina and I had a very bad connection so she misunderstood the school is not in Berne—you spelled it "Bern"—I'm not about to send you into the German part of anything—I'm very aware that you do not speak German and very aware too that you have studied French—remember me—I've been around since your birth and have taken very good care of you—watched your grades, etc.

The enclosed pamphlet and card will give you an idea that I've taken as great care in selecting this school as I have guarding your life—(or trying to—) The lovely child on the cover—blonde—is Bridget Hayward, Margaret Sullivan's daughter whom I saw—and she said she had never been so happy as at "Montessano"

You will stay at Flintridge for one more year—graduate—then we will decide whether Switzerland—London—or California—

Bless you—have a good summer—think good thoughts

My love always—

"Mommie"

The topic of conversation revolved around college. I wanted to go to college and the places Mother was talking about were the equivalent of finishing schools. I didn't want to go to school in Europe because I knew I'd just be stuck again, without any money, any friends. She actually considered that putting us away in schools counted as taking care of us. The business of guarding my life seemed like a non-sequester . . . it didn't connect with anything I could figure out. The "have a good summer and think good thoughts" part nearly made me throw up. It was facetious and cruel. She knew very well what my "good summer" was all about—after all, it was because of her orders I continued to be locked up without parole. Who did she think she was kidding? Who was she putting on the charade for . . . herself? Is that how she deceived herself so that she could go on playing martyred mother for the public? Is that how she managed her conscience, if she had one, so that she was free to behave any damn way she wanted? Why in God's name did she adopt all of us in the first place? Sure we served a purpose when we were adorable babies. She got a hell of a lot of publicity out of us. She built a public image on us. Millions of unsuspecting fans thought: "what a wonderful woman . . . to take *four* little orphans into her home." Hundreds of pages of movie magazine garbage were turned out on what a wonderful mother she was. We were paraded out, one by one, in our darling little starched outfits and pseudo-British manners . . . we were photographed from every angle and cooed over by pandering publicity hacks, we were sent presents from fans all over the world . . . presents we were never allowed to keep. We were the best mannered, best behaved, most perfect child-mannequins the queen bee could produce. And when we had served our purpose and gotten all the publicity that could humanly be turned loose on the adoring public . . . we made a fatal error: we started growing up. We started becoming people. It was no longer possible to control our every thought, our every gesture, our every move. We were no longer the perfectly manipulated, camera-ready puppets that spouted, "I love you, Mommie dearest" at the slightest indication of her whimsical displeasure.

Mommie dearest got her feelings hurt. Mommie dearest became distressed. Mommie dearest became enraged when she perceived that all was not well in mannequin-land. The children, the babies were in a state of mutiny! Mommie dearest has to punish bad babies . . . Mommie dearest beat bad babies . . . Mommie dearest try to kill bad babies . . . Mommie dearest doesn't want to have anything more to do with bad babies . . . Mommie dearest put bad babies away from her . . . Mommie dearest found a prison for bad babies and locked them up to punish them for being such bad babies.

On July 21, when the honeymoon was over, I received this note from Mother on Sutton Place South stationery. Mother called herself Joan Steele on the envelope's return address.

Tina darling,

We received the tie and thank you so much. Your father appreciated it.

The weather in New York is fiercely hot and the humidity even worse. Will call you next week when we get home. The director and dress designer have been in New York, so I go into production immediately upon return.

All my love,
"Mommie"

The picture she was about to make was *Autumn Leaves* with Cliff Robertson, directed by Robert Aldrich.

Though she was making the picture in Los Angeles, I didn't see Mother during the time she was in town. I barely spoke to her because she said her schedule was so hectic that she didn't have much free time. My "think good thoughts" summer was mercifully over and school returned to its normal routine which seemed bustling with activity compared with the last three months of my solitary confinement.

CHAPTER 18

In October the news came out of the blue that Mother was taking all of us to Switzerland for Christmas! I would be coming home for Thanksgiving vacation and would be getting new clothes for the trip. I'd have to miss some school, but that could be arranged.

I stared at Sister Benigna in total disbelief. This had to be some sort of trick . . . some sort of game I was just too stupid to recognize.

I had not seen Mother even once in more than a year. I had not been home in over one year. I had been *persona non grata* for a *long* time. What had changed? I racked my brain, but I couldn't find any answers. I still had not met Alfred Steele, her husband of some five months. I had not seen my brother or sisters in almost a year. What had changed?

Sister did confide in me that after Mother and Mr. Steele were married, all my back school bills started being paid. I took a chance and called Mrs. Chadwick. She confirmed it. The back bills at Chadwick were beginning to be paid as well. Since nothing else had apparently changed, I could only guess that Mr. Steele was also the reason we were all going on this trip together. Maybe he had begun to wonder why we were never around and maybe it didn't look so good. I didn't know exactly what the reason was and I didn't care. I was actually going to get off the top of this mountain and out of these buildings. I didn't care if they wanted me to turn upside down and walk on my hands backwards . . . I was getting out!

Just before Thanksgiving vacation, this letter from Mother was sent from Detroit, Michigan.

Tina, my darling angel,

I loved your letter. This is going to be a brief note as my day is scheduled as one of the busiest I have had. We have been up since 5:45 a.m., and my last appearance is at 9 o'clock tonight in the theatre lobby, and that means I won't get back to the hotel until after midnight.

I've been rushing so much from city to city. We leave tomorrow morning at 8:30 for Chicago, where we'll be only four hours. Then we go to Portland, Oregon, San Francisco and home.

I send all my love to you—and I'll see you on Thanksgiving.

Love,
"Mommie"

I was so excited by these sudden changes I could hardly think about anything else. I was getting out at long last. We were all going to Europe for Christmas. I was getting new clothes. I could hardly believe it.

At first I had been cautious about hoping, for fear it would all fall through. But as Thanksgiving vacation approached and nothing went wrong, I let myself be excited and happy.

Mother sent a car and driver to pick me up from school. I was very nervous during the ride home. As we got closer and closer the scenery once again became familiar and I started getting scared. What if something happens and I don't get to go? What if Mr. Steele doesn't like me? What if I do something foolish? I hadn't been home in such a long time. I hadn't been *anywhere* in such a long time I wasn't sure I'd remember how to act with people. What would I do . . . what would I say? Is the past year just swept under the rug and forgotten? Is it a trap? Thoughts tumbled one after the other through my mind faster and faster.

At long last we turned onto North Bristol Avenue. It was a beautiful, wide, quiet street just as I'd remembered it. Almost everything was exactly the same. There were one or two new houses but the rest was the same as before.

Chris and my sisters were home too. We rushed into one another's arms, laughing and hugging. They were just as surprised as I'd been to hear the news of our trip. Chris had grown more and was a little taller than I. The girls hadn't changed much except they were of course a year older. I was sixteen and a half, Chris was thirteen and the girls were almost eight.

I first saw Alfred Steele swimming in our pool. I remember standing on the steps leading out to the garden and asking Mother what I was supposed to call him.

"What would you call anyone who was your father?" she asked me. I had to think about that for a moment. It had been ten years since she'd been married before and I couldn't remember what I'd called Phillip Terry. In between there had been lots of her lovers I'd had to call "Uncle" but that didn't seem appropriate either. The problem was that it seemed positively weird to call a total stranger "Daddy." I'd never even been introduced to him as Mr. Steele. It was very confusing, but I wanted to be as polite as possible and do anything I could to please her, so I finally decided on calling him "Daddy."

Mother turned to me and said: "He's too fat, he wears glasses and he's slightly hard of hearing in one ear, but he's a nice man. Go introduce yourself." It was getting dark outside and I couldn't see her face too well. Fortunately, I realized she couldn't see mine very clearly either because if she'd been able to she would have noticed a look of shock. This was how she described her husband of less than six months? She'd used a tone of voice with which I was all too familiar to describe the man swimming in the pool. I'd heard that condescending tone of voice all my life. It was the one she used most effectively when she didn't want to be quoted as saying anything outwardly terrible but wanted to get the message of her disdain for the person across.

In the semi-darkness I walked down to the pool alone. When I got near the edge I stopped and waved at the man in the pool. He swam up to where I was standing and smiled at me. I kneeled down and stuck out my hand. "Hello, Daddy . . . I'm Christina."

He took my outstretched hand in his dripping wet one and I knew immediately that I was going to like him.

Alfred Steele was a very direct man. He'd started out as a geologist, of all things, graduating from Northwestern University in Chicago. By what path he went from geology to sales at Coca-Cola, I never quite understood. But from Coca-Cola eventually he went to Pepsi-Cola. When Alfred Steele took the job at Pepsi, it was a little more than a regional southern drink with a loosely knit group of family owned and operated bottling plants and not much national distribution. By the time he married Joan Crawford, he'd driven Pepsi into national prominence and distribution, second only to his former employer Coca-Cola. Pepsi was giving Coke a run for its money in every nook and hamlet of America. Al Steele welded a national network of bottlers together, standardized the syrup formula, introduced Americans to the Pepsi generation, brought the distinctive logo into mass conscientiousness and was on the brink of going international for the first time. He liked music, loved jazz, had a deep respect for excellence and told good jokes. He was a self-made man with an education who inspired the people around him to do their best and didn't need to resort to that driven quality so often the earmark of successful men. He did not stand very tall . . . five foot ten maybe, but Al Steele was a big man and people loved him.

Thanksgiving vacation went wonderfully. We had a family dinner in the formal dining room. All of us were on our very best behavior, trying very, very hard to make everything go smoothly.

The Saturday before I was to leave for school, Mother had a man come to the house and fit me for a fur coat. I wasn't allowed to open my eyes, so I couldn't see the fur but I could feel its softness. There were lots of new clothes too. The store brought them to the house where they were spread across the beds in our rooms. We were all getting new clothes, new shoes to match, the girls were getting new purses and Chris was getting totally outfitted in suits, casual wear and sport clothes.

It was better than any Christmas I could remember. We were all jumping up and down with glee. The girls and I had been in Catholic boarding schools and Chris had been in military academy. We were sick to death of uniforms and this was an unbelievable bonanza. It was two days of continual fashion shows and squeals of delight.

I went back to Flintridge bubbling over with the story. Sister Benigna was reserved and even skeptical, but she prayed for me and wished me success.

The next few weeks flew by. I had extra schoolwork to do before I left and homework to take with me on the trip since I would be a month late in returning.

At long last the moment had come. Mother, the girls, Chris and I were boarding the train for New York. Mrs. Howe was also with us to take care of my sisters. As a Christmas bonus, she was spending a week at home in Scotland.

This trip was such a monumental event in my life that I decided to keep a diary of it. I wanted to remember all the details, all the people and all the places we were going to visit. My brother and I also collected souvenirs during the trip and made a big scrapbook filled with matchbooks, menus, photos and samples of currency.

We boarded the train in Union Station, Los Angeles on December 8, 1955. We had been finishing the last minute packing until about 4 o'clock in the afternoon. Mommie had invited a number of friends over to the house for cocktails and most of them accompanied us to the station. At 5:30 that afternoon, two Tanner Limousines picked us up and drove us down to the station.

The group of well-wishers who came down to see us off included Liza Wilson, Elva and Bob Martine, Asher Hayes, Bill Seay, Louis Meltzer, Stanley Medieros and fans Milderine Mues and Florence MacDonald.

In Mommie's room there were baskets of fruit, champagne and various small gifts for use on the trip. Wherever Mother went there was a crowd. Some of the crowd she brought with her and some appeared to see what the fuss was all about.

I wasn't used to being around all these people. My life had been so quiet and solitary during the last year that all this excitement left me exhausted. I didn't quite know what to say to everyone and was trying so hard to be on my very best behavior and please Mommie with everything I did that I was constantly looking for a way to serve her or be helpful.

I was actually relieved when they left and we were able to settle down to our compartments in some peace and quiet.

It snowed the next day as we watched Arizona and New Mexico speed by the windows of the train. We stopped in Albuquerque where more friends and fans of Mother's met the train. My sisters were excited about seeing their first snow.

The next day we arrived in Chicago around noon and went to the Ambassador Hotel to have lunch in the famous Pump Room. Mommie had an old friend named Casey who met us. Casey joined us for lunch and stayed with us until it was time to go back to the station. After lunch, Miss Fields from a store called Bramsons came to the hotel with more clothes for me. Mommie bought me a suit and three more dresses. They had to be altered and Miss Fields said she'd send them to New York before we sailed.

Every time I turned around I seemed to be getting presents. I didn't know why and I didn't bother to question it. This whole adventure was like a dream come true. Mommie was in a wonderful mood, everything was going smoothly and we were getting tons of new things. It was better than any Christmas I could remember.

On the overnight train to New York City we met the director Danny Mann who had drinks with Mother. Then in the dining car we sat next to Sugar Ray Robinson and his family. We were all eyes. This trip was like something out of the movies and we were beside ourselves with anticipation.

We arrived in New York about 9:30 the morning of the third day. Daddy and the press photographers were there to meet us. We were all beautifully dressed and lined up for dozens of group pictures. I realized that I wasn't used to having pictures taken any more and my mouth began to hurt from trying to smile for the cameras. Not that I wasn't happy and more than willing to smile or stand on my head if necessary . . . I was deliriously happy. I just wasn't used to smiling on command anymore. I did my best though and prayed that Mommie wouldn't be angry with me for ruining the pictures when she saw the clippings from the newspapers. These were the first "family" pictures we'd had taken with Daddy. These were the first family pictures we'd had taken in almost four years.

That evening Mommie and Daddy took all of us to dinner at Voisin and afterwards we went to the Stork Club. I slept soundly that night for the first time in a week.

We had acquired another voyager . . . Daddy's valet-bodyguard named Jimmy Murphy. Jimmy was as wide as he was tall and an original character right out of Damon Runyon. Jimmy had an accent you couldn't believe and a vocabulary to match. Jimmy knew everybody from the dockworkers to the maître d's to the royalty of Europe. He was a walking encyclopedia of information on any subject you'd care to name, from baseball to stock prices with everything in between. He knew about skeletons in family closets that the family didn't know and he *loved* gossip with a passion other men reserved for gambling, horses and women. Not that Jimmy didn't like those things too, but information was his passport to the world. Jimmy could find out anything. If he didn't know, he knew ten guys who would and he'd get the information fast as a computer. Jimmy was great and we all loved him. I should also add that Jimmy Murphy drove Mother wild. He made her totally crazy with his irreverence for convention and his street talk. Jimmy could have said, "Yes, Mrs. Steele" for the rest of his life while bowing politely and it wouldn't have made any difference to Mother. There was just something about Jimmy that got her crazy. They had their run-ins, true enough, but Mother never got into an all out war with Jimmy. She never overstepped the bounds of nagging him . . . she never took him on as an outright enemy, toe to toe. So, while there was evidently no love lost between them, Jimmy was always polite and Mother remained civil to him most of the time. Jimmy had been with Daddy for years and Mother knew better than to try to get rid of him. Our second day in New York City, Jimmy took Chris to get a haircut and then took him shopping for a hat and gloves. Chris really felt ridiculous in his formal getup because he was only thirteen years old, but he was quite pleased with all the attention he was getting.

Mommie, the girls and I went to Bonwit Teller . . . for *more* clothes! I couldn't believe it. Where were we going to put all these things? During the past two weeks, Chris, the two girls and I had been totally outfitted with brand new wardrobes. Not one thing in my suitcases or trunk was from the past. From the skin out, we were in newly bought outfits.

After Bonwit's, we met Daddy and Chris at the "21 Club" for lunch. Mike Stern, a friend of Mommie and Daddy's, joined us at the big table. We were allowed to order whatever we wanted from the menu. The waiters and maître d' hovered around our table like bees. In fact, it occurred to me there were nearly as many people waiting on us as there were people at the table! Of course we were a rather large group, but we were also seated in full view of the entire restaurant.

That evening we had dinner in the Hampshire House Hotel alone. Mother had to be an usherette at the benefit premiere of *Rose Tattoo*. But before she and Daddy left, they'd invited Sonny Werblin from MCA to join them for drinks. I liked Uncle Sonny very much. I'd known him since I was a little girl when Mommie and I used to visit New York. He was always kind to me, but tonight he took some special time with me to discuss college. I wanted to go to Carnegie in Pittsburgh because I'd heard that their drama department was one of the best in the country.

The Werblins invited us to dinner the next night at the Colony Club after which we went to see *The Lark* with Julie Harris. It was only the second Broadway play I'd ever seen and I was very excited. I'd already decided that I wanted to go into the theater, so I watched everything and everyone with a very special attentiveness. (My diary carefully noted that her performance was very exciting and that we met Leslie Caron and Henry Fonda when we went backstage afterwards.)

On Wednesday, December 14, our third day in New York . . . Mommie took us all shopping again! This time we swooped through Saks Fifth Avenue, Mark Cross, Bergdorf Goodman and Verdura. Part of the justification for this trip was Christmas shopping. At Saks, the four of us kids pooled our money and bought Mommie a huge leather travel bag.

That night we went to "21" again for dinner. We were obviously regulars there and because Mommie and Daddy knew everyone, Uncle Bob Kriendler was always there to greet us and everybody always made a big fuss over Mommie and Daddy. After dinner we went to see Maurice Chevalier at the Waldorf Astoria.

It was an absolute whirlwind of a time. This was just like the fantasy *other* people always had about what it was like to be a movie star's daughter! It was all right here . . . it was all happening right now . . . the beautiful, expensive clothes, the long black limousines, the best table in the best restaurants . . . the photographers wherever we went . . . the shopping sprees and the seemingly endless stream of money. I saw Daddy tipping $20 and $50 at a time . . . I saw Mommie signing for hundreds and hundreds of dollars of clothes and accessories. I saw the world at our fingertips . . . everyone smiling and bowing and doing our bidding. I saw more money and the things money could buy than I'd ever seen in my life. Mommie had always spent a lot of money on herself and the house, but I'd rarely seen the bills . . . I'd only seen the results. Now that Daddy was paying the bills, the pace picked up considerably.

Maybe it was all the time I'd spent alone in the convent . . . maybe it was the years of not enough clothes, no money at all, no privileges of any kind that created these extreme contrasts. Maybe it was the speed with which these changes had happened that made me begin to feel uneasy. Maybe it was just too much, too fast that unsettled me.

Whatever it was, I welcomed a quiet day of just packing and being with the other kids. Uncle Sonny and Aunt Leah Ray Werblin went with us to dinner at Pavillion and afterwards to the Stork Club, but our last day in New York was quiet in comparison to the previous four days.

Friday, December 16, 1955, we sailed aboard the Queen Mary for Europe. Mommie and Daddy had a party in their suite of staterooms. At 10 o'clock in the morning everyone who'd come to see us off was drinking champagne and having lots of fun. There were more photographers so, we smiled and waived for dozens of photographs.

Once the ship had sailed and we'd passed the Statue of Liberty, Jimmy took Chris and me for a tour of the ship. Without Jimmy, I'm sure we would have been bored to death before the trip was over. He was wonderful to us, kept us amused with various activities and always kept us laughing.

We were told that this particular time of year, the north Atlantic was rough and we were soon firm believers. In fact, it was the worst crossing in five years according to members of the ship staff. It was so rough that they put up handropes along all the passageways and stairs. In the dining room, all the chairs were fastened down and the sides of the tables turned up to form boxes so the plates wouldn't slide right off. However, despite the best precautions, one day at lunch it was so rough that the long buffet table collapsed and a huge roast turkey rolled by our table with the chef brandishing his long-handled fork in hot pursuit! Shortly afterwards, there was a fire in the kitchen and they had to evacuate the entire dining room. I don't think any of us were in real danger but the whole dining room was in such complete shambles that it was impossible to finish lunch anyway.

Chris played in the ping-pong tournament and did very well, especially considering that the tables were on a 45-degree angle most of the time.

Mommie asked me to do her thank-you letters for her so that they'd be ready to mail when we arrived in France. She paid me what I considered the extravagant price of $14 for my work and I didn't complain a bit.

After five days of rain and stormy seas, we arrived in Cherbourgh, France. There was a boat train waiting which was taking us to Paris.

It was a beautiful ride through the French countryside watching the farms, fields and little villages roll by outside the windows. To my amazement, we had two complete railroad cars to ourselves. Daddy and Mommie had their own car and we had separate but adjoining lounge car reserved for Mrs. Howe, the four of us kids and Jimmy. Shortly after we boarded, a steward came into the car to serve us. Though my French was pretty good after nearly five years of taking it in school, I was grateful that the man spoke English. He told us that lunch would begin being served in about an hour and asked if there was anything he could bring us in the meantime. We all agreed that we'd wait for lunch and settled down to play cards and watch France speed by the window.

That "lunch" the steward casually announced turned out to be a seven-course gourmet feast that lasted nearly the entire journey to Paris! I'd never seen anything like it in my life. The tables in our lounge car were set with linen clothes, linen napkins, silver, crystal and beautiful china. Then little bouquets of fresh flowers were brought to each place setting.

Finally we all sat down and began eating. Each course that was served had it's own china, it's own proper piece of silverware. Fortunately, Mommie had taught us good manners and we all knew to start with the outermost piece of silverware in the place setting and work our way in, course by course. There were so many different kinds of forks and knives and spoons for this meal that it could have gotten very confusing. With each new course, the steward brought a different bottle of French wine. My sisters who were not quite eight years old weren't allowed more than one glass of wine, but the rest of us had a perfectly wonderful time drinking our way across the country to Paris! I learned that in France there are no minimum drinking ages, and that children were often given wine to drink. I thought that was very civilized . . . the only unfortunate thing was that we weren't better able to appreciate the connoisseur quality of the wines . . . but had a grand time drinking them! In fact, if it hadn't been for Jimmy's consumption of several glasses of wine out of each bottle and the never ending dishes of food, our carload of travelers would have passed out cold long before the train reached Paris.

We took the waiting limousines to the Georges V Hotel to bathe and change our clothes. Before we got on the next train for Switzerland, Daddy had us taken on a driving tour of the city of Paris.

The overnight train was absolutely elegant. All the rooms had polished wood paneling and deep red carpets. Cathy and I shared a compartment and spent half the night with our noses glued to the cold windows. Early the next morning we had to change to one of the narrow gauge trains for our final ascent into the Swiss Alps.

The entire country looked to me like a Walt Disney movie. The white snow covered everything and was even suspended in the trees and over the rooftops. The Swiss chalets looked just like picture post cards.

When the train stopped at St. Moritz station there were horse-drawn sleighs waiting to take us to the Palace Hotel. The bells on the horses jingled just like Christmas carols and there were big furry lap blankets to protect us from the cold. The sky was crystal clear blue and the entire valley sparkled.

It was so magnificently beautiful that I was sure I was dreaming. I was sure I would wake up soon, back in my room at the convent. I was in a daze it was so wonderful.

The Palace Hotel was something out of another era, another century, another time. All the elegance of the last century had been captured in its spacious halls, antique furniture, gracious formal dining rooms and well-trained staff. My room again looked like a movie set. The bed had mountains of feather pillows and down comforters. The windows overlooked the little village covered with white snow and the furniture was all antiques.

During the next few days we barely saw Mommie and Daddy. Chris and I went skiing in the morning, ice skating in the afternoon, wandered around the village to our hearts content. We visited Mommie and Daddy at lunchtime, but were on our own the rest of the time. That afternoon I met some of the people we'd met on the slopes earlier that day. One of the young men invited me to a party that evening. I was delighted. But . . . I had to tell him that I'd have to let him know and asked him to call the hotel around seven.

Now I was faced with the first dilemma of this glorious trip. I knew I had to ask Mommie if I could go out. Even though I was sixteen and a half, I'd never gone on a real date. The only dating I'd ever done was school at Chadwick. Because I'd been in boarding school since I was ten years old, the subject had never arisen before. I was scared to death to ask Mommie. I had no idea what she'd say or how she'd react. The very last thing I wanted was to do anything wrong, no matter how inadvertent, and I debated several hours before I got up the courage to talk with her.

We were not supposed to disturb Mommie and Daddy in the afternoon until around five o'clock, so I sat in my room waiting for the appropriate time to call on the house phone. Their suite was right down the hall from the adjoining rooms Chris and I had, so it didn't take me long to knock on the door once she'd said it was all right to come and visit with them.

I was nervous and unsure as to how to broach the subject of my date, but Daddy unexpectedly solved the entire problem when he asked me if I'd met any nice young men! It was as though he'd been able to read my mind.

I smiled sheepishly like a kid caught with their hand in the cookie jar, and said, "As a matter of fact, I did meet a very nice young man who's invited me to a party at Chesa Vega tonight." I watched carefully to see what the reaction from them would be and held my breath. Mother frowned slightly, but before she said anything, Daddy laughed. They agreed that I could go on two conditions: First, I must introduce my date to both of them, and second I had to be home by midnight. I nearly danced for joy! I was going to be able to go out! The restrictions were so reasonable that I was astounded. I ran to hug and kiss both of them, bubbling my thank you's amidst the kisses. As I was about to leave, Mother added that I was also to knock on their door when I returned home, and it better not be one second after midnight! I nodded my head in complete and total agreement and skipped happily out of the room.

I followed their instructions to the absolute letter and I went out every single night. I went dancing and to lots of parties. It was my first international "jet set" experience and I had a wonderful time dating the wealthy, attractive young men from Spain, England, Australia, France, Italy and Austria.

On Christmas Eve the whole family gathered in Mommie and Daddy's suite for presents. They had ordered caviar and champagne for everyone. We had a wonderful time opening our gifts and watching them smile. Daddy was a terrific story-teller and regaled us with his own skiing escapades in the Austrian Alps years before. Mommie was quieter than usual and seemed happy to open her gifts and preside over the family evening.

Christmas day was a peaceful one. My brother and I went skiing all day, then met the rest of the family for dinner in the main dining room.

Chris and I had discovered the formula for staying out of trouble quite by accident. We went skiing all day and simply stayed out of the way. I was a terrible skier, but took my lesson in the morning and sat around with a group of friends in the afternoon. Since the ski slopes were a long distance from the hotel, we didn't come back down for lunch after the first day. We checked in with Mommie and Daddy around five o'clock, then I'd go out and Chris would play games after dinner with some other boys he'd met in the hotel.

The day after Christmas, Daddy had planned to take us to the Olympic ski jumping trials, but when Chris and I returned from the morning ski lessons it didn't take us long to figure out that something was beginning to turn sour in paradise. My guard went up immediately and I nudged Chris secretly to stay quiet. Daddy was plainly aggravated as he told us that "your mother prefers to stay at the hotel this afternoon."

Daddy's spirits picked up during the sleigh ride, which took us to the jumping trials. Chris and Jimmy and I had a great time with Daddy, laughing most of the afternoon at his jokes and watching the skiers jump off the side of the mountain with amazing speed, skill and courage. It was the first time we'd been around Daddy without Mommie and he seemed much more relaxed after he got over being aggravated. Chris and I stood on either side of him, watching the trials and once he put his arms around us. I remember looking at Daddy a long time, as long a time as I could without just staring at him and making him uncomfortable. I thought about how wonderful it was to have a father at long last. I thought about all the people who simply take it for granted that they have a mother and a father . . . a daddy who helps you and takes you places and maybe even loves you. I thought it was probably too soon to expect Daddy to love me, but I was hoping with all my heart that someday he might. He was always very kind to me and sometimes when he looked me directly in the eyes, I thought he just might understand something about the person inside me, but I never tried to say anything about it. Though it was very cold in the bleachers set up on the side of that mountain in Switzerland, I was basking in the happiness of being with my daddy, even if it was a sort of instantaneous father-daughter relationship and even if we didn't talk too much with one another and even if we didn't know too much about one another. It was a daddy . . . a nice daddy and that was the hope of having a chance for a real father as time went by.

During the sleigh ride back to the hotel, we sang Christmas carols until Jimmy broke up the song-fest with one of his off-color limericks.

We were still laughing when we got back to Mommie and Daddy's room bubbling over with stories about the afternoon and just dying to tell Mommie about the exciting Olympic time trials.

The moment she opened the door a cold chill ran through me. I knew before the rest of the group that Mommie was in the midst of one of her rages. I suspected that she'd been drinking while we were all away and had gotten herself into a full-fledged temper. It had been evident from Daddy's mood when he first met us that afternoon that they'd had some sort of disagreement, and in our absence, the situation had not improved.

From years of past experience, I knew my only salvation was to get the hell out of there as quickly and unobtrusively as possible. I managed some fast pleasantries and took my brother out with me.

Before we had gotten any distance down the hall, the door behind us slammed shut. Just as I had predicted, Mommie and Daddy launched into one hell of a fight. Chris and I stopped momentarily to listen to the first part of it, but then scurried back to our rooms for fear someone would catch us eavesdropping.

Except for "checking-in" around six o'clock each evening, that was just about the last I saw of Mommie and Daddy until New Year's Eve. It was a festive, gala evening with wonderful food, a terrific band, dancing and finally noise-makers and confetti at the stroke of midnight.

The next evening, which was our last in St. Moritz, Mommie gave a dinner party for Paul Gallico. Paul had been a friend of hers for many years and she was delighted to play hostess again. She had arranged for a private dining room in the hotel and had it decorated with a huge cow bell as the table centerpiece. The guest list read like an old European movie cast with the Baron and Baroness von Faltzfein, Prince Constantine and Princess Monica of Liechtenstein in attendance. I had asked an Englishman named David Bennett to be my escort. To my horror, I realized only an hour before the dinner party that Mother had gotten confused and invited another young man named David to be my escort.

She'd gotten the two David's mixed up so while I was inviting one, she was inviting the other! Well, there was no chance of stopping either of them from showing up by this time, so I had two young men, both named David, as dinner partners that evening. It was terribly funny but also very embarrassing!

The next morning Chris and I went up to the ski slopes to say good-bye to all our friends. We were very sad to be leaving this beautiful village after having such a wonderful time, but in my diary I wrote that Daddy promised we'd all be back.

The overnight train took us back to Paris where we checked into the George V Hotel again. My room was enormous and the bathroom was as big as half the main room. The only thing I couldn't understand was why they had *two* toilets in the one bathroom. It seemed very curious to me. I decided to flush both of them to see what the difference was, and did I get the shock of my life! Oh well, these French . . .

Chris and I went with a chauffeur that Daddy had hired on a tour of Paris. During our three-day stay, we went through the Louvre, Versailles, Malmaison, Sacre Coeur, Notre Dame and the tomb of Napoleon. I bought some French religious cards, a few small religious medals and a lovely hand-carved rosary for the sisters at Flintridge. The rosary was intended for Sister Benigna although I wasn't sure that she could keep a personal gift.

In the evening we went to the Roland Petit ballet and our last night in Paris, of course, it had to be Maxime's.

A friend of Mother's, Peter Railly, had been kind enough to take me to the Left Bank where we had lunch at a little cafe and then walked through the art galleries. So, although we hadn't been there very long . . . we had certainly "done" Paris!

That night we took the Blue Train for the south of France. The Ted Michelle's were there to see us off. Ted was working for Pepsi in Paris and was a great friend of Daddy's.

Early the next morning we arrived in Cannes and went to the Carlton Hotel to spend the few hours until we boarded the boat. Mommie didn't want to go anywhere, but I begged Daddy to let us have the car and driver so we could see a little of the Riviera. He good-naturedly agreed that it was foolish to have the car and not use it, so the four of us kids and Mrs. Howe set off. I told the driver to head south and we drove along a seaside road that took us along the Riviera, through Nice and down into Monte Carlo. We walked around Monte Carlo and I was quite pleased with my ability to speak French well enough to do some bargaining for the souvenirs we bought. On the way back to Cannes, we noticed that there were a number of beautiful villas overlooking the Mediterranean for sale . . . how we wished we could buy one!

After a rather strained luncheon with Mommie and Daddy, we drove down to the docks and boarded the small boat that took us out to our ship, the *Andrea Doria*.

The *Andrea Doria* was the reigning queen of Italian luxury liners. She was beautifully appointed with murals, plush furniture, glorious food and overall a magnificent ship. When she ran into a freighter and sank several years later, my sisters were aboard the Ile de France which rescued many of the survivors.

But in January of 1956, there was no hint of the ill fate destined to befall this beautiful ship. It was luxury and service and elegance personified.

The next morning we stopped in Naples, Italy to pick up more passengers. Since there was enough time to leave the ship, I again badgered Daddy to take us to Pompeii. He and Mommie agreed since we were so close it would be educational for all of us, so Daddy ordered two limousines for the journey.

I was not prepared for what I was to see during my brief stay in Naples. All we had seen of Europe up until this point was the luxury hotels, the ski resorts and the beautiful restaurants. It never even dawned on me to think of the devastation of World War II, or of hunger and poverty. I was stunned by the sights that met my naive eyes that cool, rainy January day. As we stepped off the small boat that brought us to the docks I saw groups of thin, shabby men milling around outside the high fences that circled the dock area. I asked the driver why those men were here and he replied in broken English that they were waiting for work. They came and waited every day for the half-dozen or so extra jobs that might be parceled out, doing sweeping, unloading or anything that might pay a few lira.

Mother was upset when she saw the "limousines." They weren't regular limousines at all. They were two strange old rickety jalopies that had been painted black. But the drivers excitedly explained to Daddy that there weren't any better cars in Naples. That seemed hard to believe, but since we just barely had enough time to get to Pompeii and back before lunch, Daddy didn't argue with them. Mother complained about the car most of the way to Pompeii, but I didn't pay any attention . . . I had my eyes glued to the countryside, as usual.

We were outside of the town of Naples in just a few minutes. The countryside was bleak and flat. Along the road I saw ruins of buildings that had been bombed during the war which had ended more than ten years before. Most of the buildings had no second floor left, none of them had glass in the windows and many had no doors. To my total and complete astonishment, I realized after a few miles that people were living in these places. I asked the driver if that was so and he confirmed my observations. As we drove further into the country along the bumpy road, I noticed something like haystacks dotting the fields, only most of them had small, smoldering fires in front of them. Again I asked the driver for information, and he told me that those were like tents made out of thatch or straw and that there were entire families living in those straw tents. "Why?" I asked. He simply told me in a very matter-of-fact way that those people had nowhere else to live, they had no money and no jobs . . . so they lived in the fields under the straw tents and burned dung in their fires.

Mommie and Daddy were talking, but I really didn't hear much of what they said. I was shocked by the poverty and the bombed buildings and the people burning dung . . . in 1956. I had no idea . . . I'd never heard anyone talk about anything like what I was seeing with my own eyes. I was quiet . . . thinking about the odd state of the world . . .

Pompeii surpassed everything I had read about it in books. It surpassed even my own imagination about what an ancient Roman city would look like. The temples and the open forum were so beautifully symmetrical . . . you could almost hear the ancient orators across the echoes of thousands of years. We walked down the little narrow cobbled streets and peeked into what the guide told us were shops and then houses. We went into the baths and there I was really impressed. The guide explained how the Romans had a hot water heating system that ran through all the stone benches around the edge of the baths and under the stone decking. I found it miraculous that the Romans had *hot* running water and so many of the other amenities that modern civilization has only enjoyed over the last fifty years!

Word had gotten around that Joan Crawford was visiting Pompeii. When we left the protected part of the ancient ruins to return to our "limousines", there were nearly a hundred people gathered at the gates . . . yelling, "Joan Crawford . . . Joan Crawford . . ." It was sort of startling to see these people materialize out of nowhere, waving and yelling. I had an uneasy feeling about it. They weren't the usual crowd of fans I'd seen all my life . . . there was something different about them.

Our drivers came to the entrance to escort us back to the black jalopies. They insisted on hurrying us and kept Mother between the two of them, trying to protect her. Mother naturally wanted to give the crowd autographs, since she thought that's what they wanted. But the two burly Italians who were our chauffeurs of the moment propelled her briskly toward the car. The crowd was upon us in an instant. They didn't want autographs. They wanted money . . . jewelry . . . anything of value. People were pulling at us now and the drivers were yelling at them in Italian. One man in the crowd tried to pull off Mother's gold earrings and the biggest driver hit him. We were running for the awaiting cars now . . . all of us . . . Daddy, Mommie and the rest of us running for the frail safety of the old black jalopies. Once inside, we slammed the doors, quickly locked them and rolled up the windows. It was only then that we appreciated the skill of our drivers. They managed with amazing speed and skill to get us out of that crowd without hurting anyone. Once we were safely down the road with the angry crowd a good distance behind us, Daddy thanked the man and said he'd appreciated the quick thinking and the help. Mommie was quiet the rest of the drive.

We did make one detour on the suggestion of the driver. It was to a small factory out in the middle of nowhere. A nondescript building stood alone on a side road and that was where the cars stopped. Inside, there were dozens of workers making cameos and coral jewelry. We watched one woman carving a small cameo and then Daddy bought me a lovely cameo bracelet with scenes of Roman mythology.

We were all rather glad to get back to Naples. We had a lovely lunch in a restaurant overlooking the bay and my only disappointment was that they didn't serve pizza. After lunch we took a short walk to look at some paintings on display in the small square across from the restaurant. Again, a crowd started to gather, only this time there were small, dirty, barefoot children among the crowd begging for food.

I was beginning to feel very strangely about the contrasts of this part of the trip. Here I stood in a fur coat having just finished a sumptuous lunch big enough for several people, and outside there were barefoot children shivering while they begged for bread. I had some lira left that I was certainly never going to need and I gave it and all the coins I had to the children while Mommie and Daddy were looking at the paintings.

Once aboard the *Andrea Doria* again, the ship's photographer dutifully chronicled our every move . . . dinner with Captain Calamio, the whole family up on the bridge, in the engine room, on the dance floor, at the parties.

I had lost my convent school shyness during the last six weeks. I was now quite the young lady, dressed in all my fine new clothes, having my hair done and a manicure once a week. Mother had my hair cut short in Paris. I wasn't thrilled with the way it looked, particularly after Mother said I reminded her of Norma Shearer. I knew that was no compliment. Mother didn't care for Norma Shearer. In fact, Mother herself told the story of sitting on the set just beyond camera and microphone range, knitting furiously the entire time they were shooting Norma Shearer's close-ups when they made *The Women* together at Metro in 1939! Yes, indeed, I certainly knew that Mother's reference to Norma Shearer was definitely *not* a compliment. But there was not much I could do about it until my hair grew back, so I tried to laugh it off and make the best of it.

January 15th was my sisters' birthday. Before dinner they opened their presents in Mommie and Daddy's stateroom. Each of them received beautiful real pearl necklaces as their main present from Mommie and Daddy. We had dinner in the main dining room. The menus had pictures of Cindy and Cathy and special dishes prepared by the chef which were named after them to celebrate their birthday.

Two days later we arrived in New York City. There was a large crowd on hand to greet us. Some of the photographers and a few Pepsi people came out on the tugboat and were on board before we actually docked.

The reporters and photographers worked feverishly to get their pictures and interviews, then dashed off to file them the moment we landed.

We were staying once again at the Hampshire House on Central Park South. Daddy had a big apartment on Sutton Place, but Mommie didn't like it there. She said the rooms were too small and that it was too cramped to be comfortable for all of us.

Daddy took Chris and the girls to the airport the following day but I was to stay on in New York for another week. Mother had told me just the last day aboard ship that a magazine called *Woman's Home Companion* wanted to do a layout on us and that I would be able to miss a little more school without any problem. Naturally, I was thrilled. It sounded very exciting to me. Mommie said that they'd heard I wanted to be an actress and thought it would be a wonderful story to see Mother and me together. Mother helping me to learn "the ropes."

So, during the following days, Mother and I went to buy clothes while the photographers snapped pictures of me trying on beautiful Tina Lesser and Ceil Chapman dresses. The irony of it was that by now, new clothes were just more of the same thing. If I'd gone to a party every night for a month, I couldn't have used them all. We went to the Actors Studio where we met Lee Strasberg and I saw Marilyn Monroe sitting way in the back of the class observing the scenes being done.

The first play in the series of Broadway hits I was taken to over the next week, was *Hatful of Rain* with Shelley Winters, Ben Gazarra and Anthony Franciosa. It was a chilling, realistic portrayal of addiction done in a style of acting that was so life-like I was totally demolished by it. In fact I was speechless during the rest of the evening. I couldn't say much of anything to anyone during supper at "21" . . . I just kept thinking about the play and the actors and the power of the story. I decided then and there that kind of work was what I wanted to do.

During the next day, I helped Mommie with the Christmas mail and what a job that was! There were stacks and bundles of mail everywhere. All of it had to be answered personally, so I opened it attached the notes and cards to their envelopes and sorted it according to personal, business and fan mail. In the afternoon I read trade papers to Mother while she had a facial and massage in her hotel room.

~

One evening we went to see her friends Lynn Fontaine and Alfred Lunt in *The Great Sebastians* and I was sent to a matinee of *Chalk Garden*, starring Cliff Robertson.

The layout and interviews for *Woman's Home Companion* were finally finished. I was getting tired after two months of this whirlwind activity. Most of it had gone amazingly well, but I was beginning to feel the strain and I desperately didn't want anything to go really wrong.

Mother and I had only one brief upset on the *Andrea Doria* returning to New York. She and Daddy hadn't been getting along very well in private since that day Daddy took us to the Olympic trials without her. You'd have never known that they were having terrible fights by their public behavior though. As long as there were people around and especially if there were photographers or press with us, they were the picture of the happy newlyweds with the perfect children in close attendance. As soon as the doors closed behind them though, it was a different story.

On the train back from Switzerland I had the room next to theirs and I lay half the night with my ear stuck to the wall listening to them berate one another. They called each other terrible names and finally I heard Daddy hit her and things quieted down after that. But on the *Andrea Doria*, things had not gone so smoothly. Mother was drinking quite a bit again . . . she always had her 100 proof vodka with her in flasks. We'd brought a couple of cases of it with us to Europe, stuck in all our trunks. I don't know why she bothered to spread it out like that, because I know that Jimmy made the appropriate arrangements at every custom inspection we had to go through and not one piece of luggage was ever opened in either the United States or any of the European countries. Maybe it was just a precaution like having us wear all the jewelry we'd been given instead of packing it.

Whatever the reasons, one night Mother had been drinking steadily since before dinner and when I finally came back to the stateroom to say goodnight, she was not in a good mood. I said goodnight to her, kissed her on the cheek and turned to leave. Daddy came into the room and I went to him to kiss him goodnight too. She whirled me around and slapped me across the face. "I got my man, now you damn well go out and get your own."

I didn't know what to do. I just stood there in stunned silence. Daddy started to say something to her but she told him to shut up. I just left both of them there arguing with one another and hurried to my stateroom, locking the door behind me. It was totally inconceivable to me that she considered *me* a threat. It was the furthest thing I could ever have imagined. It made absolutely no sense to me. All I wanted was a father . . . I certainly had no designs on her new husband . . . I barely knew him. I wanted a father . . . I wanted a father very much . . . I had hoped that eventually he would think of me as his daughter . . . but that was all I wanted. However, from that point on, she never allowed me to be anywhere with him alone.

On Friday, January 27, 1956, I flew back to Los Angeles by myself. Betty picked me up at the airport and took me home. I was exhausted from the flight that took all day and from the non-stop activity in New York. When she took me to school on Sunday, I was actually glad to see Sister Benigna's gentle smiling face welcoming me back.

The pictures in this photo section are all selected from my own scrapbook, which was compiled over many years by my mother and sent to me when our Brentwood house sold. This was the first photograph of Mommie and me. I was two months old according to her note on the back.

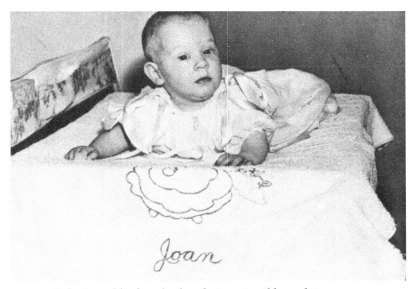

Baby Joan (that's me), already in satin ribbons, lying on my monogrammed towel.

Snuggled with my giant Panda.

A definitive 'first Christmas' snapshot.

On our visit to Helen Hayes, her son James welcomes me with a rose.

Mother-and-daughter portrait. I am about one year old.

In my nursery with new building blocks.

With Mommie and my new daddy,
Phillip Terry, shortly after their
marriage.

A quick snapshot for the fans.

Listening to fairy tales.

A typical day in my Hollywood childhood, posing for the cameras.

Mommie making sure I did just as my piano teacher instructed.

A wonderful view of our backyard with the theatre on the right and pool house on the left.

This adorable monkey was the hit of my party.

Even with my father to protect me, I was still quite shy with the clown.

This particular photograph is the essence of my Hollywood princess upbringing. It is evident that my expectations of the world were clearly formed when I was barely six years old.

The birthday party feast in our formal dining room. Mothers left to right are: Margaret Sullivan, Mrs. Gary Cooper, Mrs. Henry Hathaway and Mrs. Roger Converse.

With my baby brother, originally named Phillip, whose name was later changed to Christopher.

It's lonely at the head of the table.

Entertaining the soldiers during World War II. My curtsey by now is perfected.

Evidence of rare talents displayed during bedtime exercises.

With Mommie in our matching red-velvet mother-and-daughter outfits.

A room called the butler's pantry, where the children and nurse ate all meals.

With my brother wrapped in our father's jacket.

With Mommie on the Del Monte Lodge lawn.

On pebble beach in Carmel.

Posing for fans outside our back door. Now my brother and I have matching trim on our outfits.

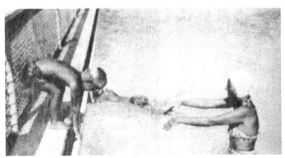

My brother learning to dive.

Backstage at the circus, totally awestruck.

Visiting Mommie at the studio during the filming of Mildred Pierce.

Going down to the docks to see Mommie off on her trip to Hawaii. Both my brother and I had to wear white gloves whenever we appeared in public.

Outfitted in full regalia at the height of my cowboy craze.

My brother and I shared a room and bath until I left for boarding school.

*With Mommie at Union Station boarding
the train for New York in 1946.*

At a toy store opening in Beverly Hills that was just for show.

Dress time! I loved going through all her closets and choosing ingredients for an outrageous outfit such as this one.

Mommie playing director for my Brownie troop's production of Hansel and Gretel.

With my newly adopted sisters in the nursery.

I had progressed to the Girl Scouts at about the age of ten.

On one of our 'dates' to a Hollywood première.

The last of the matching outfits for my final piano recital.

Visiting Mother on the set of The Damned Don't Cry. *I am wearing one of the plaid dresses.*

One of the rare photographs of my mother really laughing was taken while we were working together on a charity telethon in New York City. It is the last picture I have of the two of us.

CHAPTER 19

I had a terrific time during the next few weeks telling everyone about our fabulous whirlwind tour of Europe. My stories were the absolute center of attention, since almost none of the other girls had ever been there. I told them in great detail about the different countries, the grand hotels, the wonderful food and the beautiful clothes Mommie kept buying me. Of course, I didn't have any of those clothes at school because I didn't need them. They were being kept at home until I had some further use for them.

On February 4, this letter arrived from Mommie who was still in New York at the Hampshire House.

Christina darling,

Thank you so much for your sweet letters. The one to Herb Kenwith has been mailed.

I hope you enjoyed the Cliff Robertson show on TV. Yes, darling, you can go home with Gay White if the parents will pick you up and bring you back. Please show this letter to Sister Benigna so she will know.

I am going to Jamaica with your Daddy. He is going on business and I will go to try to get rid of this awful cold I have had for a week. I'm trying to pack up all fall clothes. My summer clothes have been sent to me, so I will lie in the sun and rest.

Enclosed is a sweet letter to you from Paul Muni, also one from Shirley Booth and Claudia Franck. Be a good girl and I send all my love to you as always.

"Mommie"

Herb Kenwith was a director friend of my mother's we'd seen briefly in New York. The letters to me from Paul Muni and Shirley Booth were in response to notes I'd written them after seeing plays they were in while on my nightly round of the best of that Broadway season.

In reply to my Valentine's cards to Mommie and Daddy, this letter arrived.

Tina darling

Thank you so much for the heavenly Valentine card—I love you so for thinking of me—I hope you received your Valentine I sent—also Edouard's bag—did you thank them?

The climate and island are beautiful beyond belief—I'm sunburned and tan—the cold has gone and just as I was getting unwound—Christopher was expelled from school again—California and I have been talking three and four times a day for a week now—I don't know what to do with him —

I sail from here March first arrive Hampshire House March 6th—work a week then home—I love you —

"Mommie"

I had gone home with my friend, Gay, several weekends between the time I'd returned from Europe and the end of February. Gay's mother had married Myford Irvine a few years before and they lived on the original Irvine ranch in Tustin, California. Gay and I had been friends when we were both going to Chadwick and before we'd transferred to Flintridge for different reasons, at two different times. It had been a year and a half since I'd seen Commander or Mrs. Chadwick and I really missed them. I didn't think anyone would be terribly hurt if I visited them just once, especially if none of us said anything about it. It wasn't like I was running off with some boy for the weekend. I just wanted to see the Chadwicks again and tell them about the trip and that things were finally beginning to go all right for me again.

I really believed that things were going just fine for me. There was absolutely nothing to lead either Sister Benigna or me to believe otherwise. I didn't tell her about planning a trip to see Commander and Mrs. Chadwick. I wasn't trying to be sneaky so much as I was trying not to give her any reason to lie for me. If she honestly didn't know, she wouldn't be put in any position to wrestle with her own conscience. It seemed like the best way at the time.

I had a wonderful time with the Chadwicks. They were so pleased and delighted about the trip and genuinely happy that we were all one family again. I told them how wonderful Daddy was and all about the interesting places we'd been. Mrs. Chadwick said I seemed very grown up and that she was pleased about my choice of Carnegie as a college. She did take me aside before I left and cautioned me about going easy on my make-up, but I laughed and told her that I'd worn it with Mother and Daddy and they didn't say anything. I guess I just chalked it up to the fact that Mrs. Chadwick was sort of old-fashioned, but I loved her and I didn't let it spoil my short visit. I was only with them two days.

At first I didn't know how Mother found out about my visit. Later on I put the pieces together and was totally dumbfounded by the complete stupidity with which Mrs. Chadwick continued to approach my situation. She had written a letter to my brother Chris, in response to his correspondence with her, and had told him about my visit! Mrs. Chadwick had no way of knowing before she mailed that letter that Chris would be expelled and the letter forwarded to the house at 426 North Bristol. However, through all the years she'd dealt with our family situation, I couldn't believe she didn't realize that to put my visit in writing where someone else could get hold of it was taking an enormous and unnecessary risk with my personal well-being. I couldn't believe she could be so thoughtless. I knew in my heart that it wasn't malicious on her part, but I was still shocked by her lack of forethought.

Mother was still in Jamaica when Mrs. Chadwick's letter was forwarded to her. The shit hit the fan, all right.

Christina dear—

I'm shocked beyond belief that you would go to the Chadwicks'—I forbid you ever to go there again or see them—if you do—I will not sent you to Carnegie or anywhere else—you lied to Sister Benigna—you lied to me, in a sense, by not telling me you had gone—

I see I cannot trust you any more than I ever could—all of your enthusiasm—your loving attention is surface and as false as ever—you pour it on only to get what you want, and if you think I haven't recognized that all during our Christmas holiday—then you have another thought coming. Your Dad and I both saw it constantly and remarked on it. I really feel sorry for you—you are cheating yourself because you are so artificial—you will never be a warm real human being—

You promised if you could come home for Christmas I would see "a new you" you would prove to me you have changed—you haven't changed one iota Tina—you are as artificial as all that make-up you constantly wear—obviously I'm not the only one who thinks so—as Mrs. Chadwick's letter tells you—all the compliments you received in New York were to make you happy—but you should have heard what people really said—about your temper—your too much make-up—your sophisticated snobbish manners—

After you graduate I'll have something planned for you till college opens—you are not bringing your qualities into our home again—I will not have the babies subjected to them—and don't try to tell me you will change—because I won't believe it

And mind you if you do see the Chadwicks I will find out—and I mean it—I will not send you to college if it happens—

Between you and Christopher I think I've had it—

Please return Mrs. Chadwick letter to 425—as soon as you've read it

This handwritten letter had no signature. It just ended at the bottom of the last page.

Well, that was it. I'd made an error in judgment, to say the least. I thought things had changed and that no one would ever find out if I made a short side-trip to see Commander and Mrs. Chadwick. It never dawned on me in a million years that it would be Mrs. Chadwick herself who would blow the whistle on me.

Of course, I apologized to Sister Benigna and told her that I knew I'd been wrong for not telling her what I was up to, but I thought my reasons justified it. I knew Mother would never have given me permission to visit the Chadwicks . . . she now hated them and said terrible things about them. But . . . I thought I could do something I wanted to do without hurting anyone else in the process. It sure didn't turn out that way. The way it did turn out, I got hurt the most of everyone.

In reply to my letter attempting explanation and apology, Mother sent this on April 3, 1956.

> *Christina dear,*
>   Your letter of March 14th stated you went to the Chadwicks', and I quote: "Whether or not you believe it, I felt guilty not getting your permission, but as I imagined you would not grant it, I made the decision and resolved to take the consequences."
>   If you knew I wouldn't grant permission, then you should have felt guilty, and you should have stayed at your own school.
>   You wrote, "You see, Mommie, our trip to Europe, provided so generously and lovingly by you and Daddy, was the most wonderful thing that has ever happened to me, and I wanted to share this happiness with the people and the school that guided me through some hard years." If you wanted to share the lovely, lovely trip that your Daddy and I gave you, you could have done it by writing the Chadwicks a letter. All you wanted to do was go there and show off, and this in your heart you know, Christina. Well, you showed off.
>   And what do you mean—you wanted to "share this happiness with the people who guided you through some hard years"? And where do I come in? I did a bit of guiding too—guiding and providing.
>   You wrote, "It seemed so little to give in return for what they gave me, and it was a simple as that." And what do you give to me, Christina? Dishonesty, lies, going where you are not supposed to go without my permission—is that a real "giving"?
>   You wrote, "Unfortunately, my actions have caused unhappiness to you for which I'm truly sorry, because it must seem as though I'm very unappreciative for all you've given me." It does, indeed, Christina. It does seem that you are extremely ungrateful.
>   You say you're willing to take the consequences. The consequences are that you stay at your present school until it is time to go to college—as I told you in the letter I wrote to you while I was in Jamaica. And if you make one false move, you are not

going to college. I told you that before, and I mean it. It is entirely
up to you. I hope you enjoy the consequences.
  Love
  "Mommie"

  P.S. I'm sending your black coat please wear it if you go out in
  the night air at the Prom—

Well, I'd really done it this time! I'd just handed her all the ammunition
she wanted to use against me. Things were back to normal . . . she'd found
something to punish me for again. My visit to the Chadwicks took place
during the end of February and my punishment for that unthinkable
crime lasted until September when I was sent off to college. That entire
time I was under the threat of not being able to go to college at all if I
made one false move. All my new-found privileges were removed, and
I was confined to the school campus. I knew it had all been too good
to last. I was dreadfully sorry that I'd actually contributed to my own
downfall this time, but I still didn't think what I'd done deserved *seven
months* of retribution.

  You'd never know how grim the situation had become again if you
judged it solely by her handwritten thank-you note mailed April 4.

  Christina darling—
    Thank you so much for the lovely color photograph for my
  birthday—and for the lovely birthday card it was an enchanting
  one—
    Thank you too for calling me on Easter it was good to hear
  from you—
    I'm rushing to catch that train—your black dress was sent to
  you—have fun—
    Love
    "Mommie"

I don't know why . . . I can't explain it . . . but I continued to send little
gifts and cards and to call her on every holiday. Part of it was habit I
guess . . . she was my mother . . . I didn't know what else to do. I was
totally dependent on her. I couldn't do anything or go anywhere unless

she and she alone allowed me to. That lesson I didn't have to learn all over again, I knew it by heart. She held this tremendous power over my life. There was no one to intercede for me. There was no one to help me. Those little cards and gifts were attempted peace offerings, I guess. They were my attempts to soften the harshness of the conditions under which I had lived so many years now. I used to think that if Mother would only love me, my whole life would be different. I tried every way I knew to show her that if she would just love me I'd be a good daughter. But she didn't really know me anymore. I'd only seen her for *two months* out of the last *two years*! How could she know me . . . how could she know what I was really like, what I thought, what I felt. She didn't know me . . . not really. She only knew these pieces of me and what she made up in her own mind *about* who she thought I was when I wasn't even there to defend myself. She listened to other people before she'd listen to me. She didn't try to know me . . . she just criticized me and punished me for things that weren't that big a deal in reality.

But there was no escaping it . . . I was tied to her. My future depended on her and I tried to do whatever I could not to make things any worse than they already were.

The first good news in months came when I received this letter on May 3. Carnegie had accepted me! I was totally overjoyed.

Tina dear,

I'm enclosing a letter that arrived today from Carnegie Tech. I know it will make you very happy.

I hope you had a lovely time at the May Day party. Let me know about it.

Cliquot, Camille and little Chiffon are all well and happy. They get along beautifully together. They are so adorable. Chiffon just hugs me around the neck when I pick her up—just like a real baby.

God bless. Write to me soon.

"Mommie"

The names referred to in this letter all belonged to *dogs*. They were the miniature French poodles Mother had collected. That was what she really wanted . . . babies and dogs. They did just exactly what you wanted

them to . . . they couldn't talk back . . . they couldn't think for themselves
. . . they were totally dependent and totally loving. That was what she
really wanted and that was why she got so pissed off at us. We were not
dogs . . . we were not babies, even though she referred to my sisters as
"the babies" until they were nine or ten years old.

School was nearly over now. There was only a month left until graduation and we were beginning to prepare for our final exams. All the
other girls were very excited about graduation and their future plans.
Most of them were glad high school was over and looking forward to
being included in the beginning of adulthood. A number of girls were
planning to get married, some were going to get jobs, only five of us
were going on to college.

Walter, my boyfriend from Chadwick, was my date at the senior
prom. I loved him dearly for making this effort for me. I didn't know
anyone else that I really wanted to see and I certainly didn't want to
accept a blind date for the evening. Walter was as wonderful to me as he
had ever been when we were going steady. There was something about
him that just made me feel secure and happy. He was doing very well
at college and we spent most of the evening dancing and talking about
what we were both planning to do with our lives. I told him about Carnegie and he wished me all luck. But that was Walter; he was always kind
and considerate. I'd told him about the visit to Chadwick and all the
trouble it had gotten me into. He said he'd try to come and visit me during the summer. That was Walter . . . my perennial life-saver. I always
seemed to be grateful to him. He could also make me laugh, which was
more welcome than anything else he could have done that evening. He
actually made the Prom a memorable and happy occasion for me.

I sent Mother and Daddy an anniversary card. Mother had been
traveling all over the country on business trips with Daddy, opening
bottling plants and making public appearances for Pepsi-Cola. She dictated this thank-you note which was mailed from Los Angeles, May 17.

Christina darling,
    Thank you, darling, for remembering our wedding anniver-
sary, and for sending the lovely, lovely card to me.
    I'm sure you have received by now the Carnegie Tech ques-
tionnaire that I sent to you. Be sure to fill it out as soon as

possible, and send it back to me so that I can attach a check to it and sent it to Carnegie Tech. Send it to me at: 426 N. Bristol Ave., darling, because I'll be home in a few days.

I'm delighted that the May Day Festival went so well.

My love to you always, and I'll be talking to you soon.

As ever,

"Mommie"

I was constantly praying that nothing would happen to me before I got out of here and off to college. Her letters were so sweet and so filled with "darlings" that I sometimes wondered about my own sanity and judgment. Of course, during all this time I was still being punished. I was still not allowed to leave the school. I was still not allowed to go home on weekends. But, you never would have guessed that from the "darling" letters.

My friend Gay was having a huge graduation party. Her parents, the Irvines, had invited every girl in the senior class and their parents. The parents of the girls from Central and South America were traveling thousands of miles to see their daughters graduate. They were all invited to Gay's party and they had all accepted.

I had written to ask permission to go to the party. Gay was one of my very best friends and her party was definitely *the* event of the entire graduation day. On May 31, I received the following letter of reply from my mother.

Christina dear,

You are not to go to any of the graduation parties that are off the school grounds of Sacred Heart Academy, Christina dear. This includes the party given by Mr. and Mrs. Irvine. I've already written them that you cannot come—

Your graduation and birthday present from me was to have been airline tickets to go to London while I am making the film, Story of Esther Costello this summer, and you were to go on location with me to Scotland and Ireland as well as England. But since you disobeyed me and visited the Chadwicks, I am afraid this is out of the questions. You wrote me that you are willing to suffer the consequences. Do you really think it was worth it?

I would just like to remind you again that if you leave the grounds of Sacred Heart Academy before you go to Carnegie Tech., you will not be able to go to Carnegie Tech.

Aunt Bettina will take you to the dentist's this summer. We will talk about that later.

My love, always,
"*Mommie*"

I ran to my room and threw myself across my bed, kicking and screaming and crying. Mean goddamned BITCH!! She's just a mean bitch to the marrow of her bones. This goddamned letter is just to make me feel bad . . . she never had any idea in this world of sending me airline tickets . . . she already told me I had to stay in school alone again all summer. She's the meanest bitch in the whole world . . . she's the goddamned "queen bee" . . . Now she's writing this "See-how-it-could-be-if-you-were-a-good-girl" letter to me just to make me crazy. How I wished I'd never been so honest and straightforward as to say I'd take the consequences! What I meant was that I'd made a mistake, I was sorry and I knew I was going to be punished for it. But she took that and turned it into a knife and sticks it into my belly whenever she finds something new to hold out like the forbidden carrot and torture me with it. She knows goddamned well she never in a million years intended to send me any goddamned airline tickets. She's the queen bitch and she'd *never* forget something in only *four months*! Four months isn't nearly long enough to torture bad, ungrateful, artificial Christina. Four months? Just a drop in the bucket compared with what she really had in mind. Four months? Not nearly long enough to make the point that it is "Mommie dearest" who is the powerful one . . . who holds the only key to the future . . . who's will *must* be done. Four months was not an adequate punishment at all . . . didn't begin to make amends for the crime of disobedience perpetrated upon the "queen bee" by her dishonest, lying, untrustworthy daughter. There had to be other ways to make the transgressor pay . . . this letter was one of them.

When my friend Gay came back from the last weekend at home before graduation, she brought me the letter Mother had sent her parents on Joan Crawford stationery.

May 30, 1956

My dear Mrs. Irvine,

Thank you so much for inviting my husband and me to your party on Tuesday, June 12th, at the Huntington-Sheraton Hotel in Pasadena. We would dearly love to attend, but my husband will be out of town, and I have business commitments that I just cannot postpone.

I presume you know that several months ago, Christina told Sister Benigna that she was spending the weekend with Gay at your home. Instead, she asked Gay to take her to visit Commander and Mrs. Chadwick at Chadwick School, and Christina stayed with them for three days. I had told Christina repeatedly that she was not to see nor contact the Chadwicks in any way. She disobeyed me, and I have felt that she must be punished.

That is why Christina is not to attend any of her class graduation parties off the grounds of Sacred Heart Academy. I do hope you understand that I must deprive her of some of the things she likes best, for the time being.

Thank you again for your kind invitation. I send my best wishes to you, and my congratulations to Gay upon her graduation.

Gratefully,

Joan

What Mrs. Irvine understood was that all the stories Gay had told her about my mother's meanness was actually true. Fortunately, Gay had not gotten in any trouble over taking me to see the Chadwicks.

That was how Mother continually operated. She'd set the perimeters of the situation so rigidly, so tight that it was humanly impossible to live with and then she'd punish you all over again for "disobeying." I sometimes think she was trying to break me completely. I think all this punishment that lasted for years was her way of trying to give me a lobotomy. She tried every single way she could dream up to completely break my spirit and my independence. She nearly succeeded more than once.

Preparations for graduation on June 12th were accelerating. There was the dress fitting at Bullocks and the invitations to be mailed. Classes were just a formality by now, so the time was passing quickly and easily. I'd sent Mother an invitation and also asked for a strapless bra to wear under my sheer, white graduation dress. I had no money so I always had to make a special request for everything out of the ordinary necessities. Her reply was dated June 2, just ten days before graduation day.

Tina darling,

Thank you for your sweet letter. Thank you too, darling, for sending your Daddy and me the invitation to your graduation exercises, with your very formal card enclosed. One usually crosses off the name and writes her first name on those little cards to her friends, Tina.

You don't need a new dress to wear to the Baccalaureate Sunday service, Christina dear. You have enough dresses at school, and you must be able to find one in all of those dresses that I have sent you.

You don't need a strapless bra, Tina. Ask Bullock's to put little lingerie straps on each shoulder of your graduation dress, as I have on my dresses, and you can fasten your bra straps in them.

Love,
"Mommie"

I had to go to Sister Benigna and ask her to explain to Mother that the bra straps would show through the sheer fabric of my graduation dress. The top was lined, but only just up to the arms. It was so embarrassing to have to always ask Sister to intervene for me, but I had no choice.

As for "all those dresses" . . . I didn't know what she was referring to because all my good clothes were still at home and all I had at school were just some regular clothes, nothing special.

I still didn't know from her letter whether or not anyone was coming to my graduation. All the other girls were excitedly making plans with their parents for parties and trips and all the other festivities. High school graduation was a big event for all of us. It was an important turning point for everyone, a moment every single person can remember for the rest of their life.

I remember my high school graduation as one of the most unhappy days of my life. It wasn't one of the worst days, but it was one of the most unhappy.

On June 11, the day before graduation and also my 17th birthday, I received this Special Delivery letter:

Tina darling,

I'm so very sorry, but I am working, and I won't be able to attend your graduation exercises. I have to work all day on Tuesday at the Studio to get my clothes ready, and then take your Daddy to the airport in the evening.

Aunt Bettina will bring your birthday and graduation presents out to you on Tuesday. She will also bring you a white strapless bra.

All my love,
"Mommie"

I crumpled the blue Joan Crawford stationery into a ball. I clenched the blue ball of paper in my fist. God . . . I hated her.

So . . . she and Daddy were both right here in Los Angeles . . . and no one but the secretary was coming to my high school graduation. The secretary wasn't even coming to the graduation; she was just delivering presents and a bra!

My mother and my stepfather were less than one hour's drive away from my school and neither one of them were coming to my graduation. She wasn't shooting a picture . . . she was trying on clothes! She couldn't find any better excuse . . . so she was trying on clothes at the Studio . . . all day? And, since when did she drive Daddy to the airport? They had limousines do that.

So that was to be the story. The reason that neither my mother nor my stepfather were coming to my graduation was that she had to try on some clothes and he had to catch a night flight?! That's the reason they couldn't take three hours out of their busy lives to come to my high school graduation? One was trying on dresses and the other had a plane to catch, *at night*? My graduation was scheduled for 2 p.m. in the afternoon. This was just another way to let me know I was being punished.

Betty arrived early the next day bringing me three small, gift-wrapped boxes, some cards and a white strapless bra. She stayed through graduation.

When the graduation ceremonies were over, I met many of my classmates' parents. There was a short school reception immediately following graduation, then the majority of the girls left with their parents.

I went back to my room about 4 o'clock. I took off my pretty white graduation dress, hung it up carefully and sat down on the edge of my bed. I sat there crying for some time. Everybody knew that I was the only girl in the graduating class without any family in attendance. Everybody knew that I was being punished. Everybody knew, and I could see the old look of pity in their eyes. How I detested that look. It made my skin crawl with humiliation and anger.

That night while the rest of my class was enjoying the big Irvine party, I ate dinner alone in one corner of the empty dining room. I watched an hour of television in the recreation room and I went to bed. Two days later, this letter arrived from my hard-working mother.

Christina darling,

Aunt Betty told me about your beautiful graduation ceremonies, and how exquisite you looked. I am so proud of you. Also, I am delighted that you received the Scholarship ribbon and the Legion of Honor medal from the American Legion.

You are a good, sweet girl, and you are behaving beautifully now. I want you to know that I love you very much and am proud of you.

Christina dear, be sure to write thank-you letters for all your birthday and graduation gifts and cards, and send them to me. I will mail them from here.

"Mommie"

I seriously wondered if Mother had written that letter. It sounded more like the way Betty talked and I wouldn't have doubted it if Mother had said "you were there, you write the letter and I'll sign it."

Actually, among the cards was a very sweet note from my Aunt Helen Hayes and another from Eleanor Powell. They had both sent gifts.

I was very surprised that they had remembered me and tried to write really nice thank-you notes to them.

That I still had to send the finished letters to Mother galled me. I was seventeen years old for heaven's sake and still treated like a nitwit.

But to Mother personally, I wrote a dilly of a letter. The final crowning blow of that miserable graduation day was when I opened the so-called birthday and graduation presents from her. There were two small, matching boxes that had been separately gift-wrapped. Each box contained *one* gold earring! One box had a birthday card on it and the other box had a graduation card on it. She had given me *one* earring for my birthday and *one* earring for my graduation! And that was it . . . nothing else. I was so furious that I couldn't find words for it until several days later. Her reply, dated June 20, is one of the classic letters in my collection. I had really gotten to her. I had touched some of the buried triggers. She replied at length and in true "queen bee" style.

Christina dear,

Thank you for your sweet letter. I am glad you liked the earrings. The reason I had them boxed in two boxes was that one was for your birthday, and the other was your graduation present.

You say "I'm sorry you weren't at my graduation because it was an experience we should have shared as it happens only once, and can never be recaptured." Christina, if you could only know the many moments we could have spent together that we can never recapture. You would not have written this letter if you had fully understood. There have been years of moments that you have failed to share with me—for your good, and for your life; so your sarcastic criticism of me for not being at your graduation made me feel awfully sorry for you. If you really understood about my work, you wouldn't have bothered to criticize me. It so happens I stood for seven hours that day, having fittings for a film so I can pay for your education.

The children and I are fine, thank you for asking. They will be home for a long weekend this week.

I'm not sending your letter to Christopher, because he didn't send you anything, not even the cards. And it isn't sad that he wasn't at your graduation. He has to earn the right to go out, and he has to behave in public before he can attend a graduation. I am sure you can understand why I am not sending your letter to him, as he would wonder what he had sent you. He is so thoughtless that he shouldn't be thanked until he has really done something, and has improved as a human being; and until he thinks of others first, for a change. Like you—

I don't know when I am leaving for Europe yet, as we are having a lot of costume problems and story problems.

I noticed you had "Room with Bath" marked on your Carnegie Tech, application form. I changed it to a room where you share a bath, as I cannot afford any more expenses.

Christina dear, will you please send me a list of the relics and other museum pieces that we took to the Chadwick School from the Museum in Carmel, and which were put on display in their "Science Room." Please do not contact the Chadwicks about them. I just want you to list them for me from memory.

You thanked Aunt Betty for the eleven pairs of stockings. They were given to you by Jennie and Jimmy and a birthday card from them was attached to the gift. Would you please write thank-you letters to them? As it should be.

Love,
"Mommie"

P.S. Please see next page.

Christina dear,

Since I talked to you tonight about Kathy Edwards, I would like to know where else you have been. I would like to hear it from you rather than from someone else. How did you know Kathy's name and address—and where to go—and what did you go for?

I don't care how silly you think the questions are that I have asked—or how ridiculous—I want an answer to them.

If I don't hear from you within one week, I will cancel your enrollment at Carnegie Tech.

Love,
"Mommie"

Mother had taken us to the lunatic fringe again. Working backwards, Kathy Edwards was a friend of my brother's. He told me where she lived and what part of town it was in. I'd never been there but Mother wouldn't believe me and I didn't feel like arguing with her anymore. It was all too stupid. I wrote her that I'd never been there or anywhere else that she didn't know about and left it at that. She was just going to have to deal with the rest of her paranoia by herself.

But the first part of the letter was something else. From long years of experience I knew that somewhere in her being Mother felt guilty. She couldn't stand any kind of honesty outside of the narrow confines of her work. She couldn't tolerate personal honesty. She interpreted any kind of honest reaction from someone else as criticism of herself. This time she'd been flat out wrong and she knew it. Her answer always to hide behind her work . . . to play the martyr . . . to try and make us feel guilty for receiving an education . . . to make us feel guilty about being alive. It was bullshit . . . We cost her almost nothing. Flintridge tuition was $1,200 a *year*. That included room and board as well. I had never been home except those four days of Thanksgiving. Chris, Cindy and Cathy were all in boarding schools. *She* was the one who put us in boarding schools . . . *she* decided we were all to leave home . . . not us. *She* put me in boarding school when I was only ten years old. My sisters started Chadwick when they were in second grade. She could have left all of us in public schools, but *she* chose differently, not us. We never asked her for any of it, but she totally ignored that and tried every way she knew to make us take the responsibility for her decisions. We were supposed to be forever grateful for her bountiful provisions . . . her care and concern for our well-being . . . the sumptuous manner in which she had provided for our wonderful and privileged life-style. It was all bullshit . . . right down to the last syllable.

Indeed, Mother and I had missed *years* of shared experience, but who's doing was it? I never asked to be sent away from home and locked away in boarding schools. I never asked not to come home. I never asked not to see my own brother and sisters grow up. She sent us away because she wanted to. She made the decisions about our lives and we had no choice but to live with them.

I thought back over the last two or three years of my life. What was it that had brought two years of punishment upon me? Well, let's see . . . one year of punishment was for not preparing a list of Christmas cards fast enough to suit her and the seven months of punishment were caused by a two-day visit to a couple in their sixties who had been my foster parents for five years.

Those were my "crimes." A Christmas card list and a visit to a couple in their sixties. For these heinous disobediences, I received a sentence of one year, seven months in solitary confinement.

However, while serving this sentence, I was supposed to feel unending love and deepest gratitude for the benevolence of my long-suffering, hard-working mother. My mother who believed in a philosophy of "take away what she loves most . . . and she'll learn giving." A philosophy of "maximum punishment for all disobedience . . . she'll learn to behave."

The truth of the matter was that I had nothing to be grateful for! I had spent approximately three months out of the last three years off the campus of a boarding school. I had no money, few clothes, none of the normal privileges given to other kids my own age and no home. I had been orphaned twice. Once by my own biological parents and the second time by my adopted parent. Since the age of ten I had grown up in institutions and foster homes, even if they went by other names. And, I had received better treatment, more consideration and basic understanding, compassion and fairness at the hands of comparative strangers than I ever had in my own home. For all this, I was to be eternally grateful.

It is no wonder that I had suffered from migraine headaches for the last year and a half. The headaches had gotten so bad last year that Sister suggested to Mother that I should be taken to a doctor. First I was taken to an eye doctor who checked my vision thoroughly and could find nothing wrong. Then, when I was told I was being taken back for a final eye examination, I found myself instead in the offices of a psychiatrist! I was furious with the deception, not with the fact that I was being sent to a shrink. I took the battery of tests the lady doctor gave me, stacked up the cards in yes and no piles, and gave my interpretation of the Rohrshalk pictures.

When all these were concluded, the woman asked me to come into her private office. She seemed like an understanding person, she seemed genuinely interested in helping me. I told her about the terrible headaches and when they had started. She asked me a few questions about my answers to the Rohrshalk test and then she asked me if I had any idea what might be bothering me . . . what might be causing my headaches.

I looked her squarely in the face and said to her directly: "Yes. I hate my mother."

That was the end of the interview. That was also the end of my visits to any doctor. That was not the end of my headaches.

Before she left for England, Mother sent this letter, the last I was to receive for nearly two months.

Christina dear,

I am returning your letter to Andre Fleuridas, Jr. It is a sweet letter, but you haven't mentioned the gift that he sent to you. It was in a little square box, Tina. Perhaps that will help you remember which gift he sent to you.

Also, please write thank-you letters to Jennie and Jimmy, and send those, with Andre's letter to me.

Love, "Mommie"

Jenny and Jimmy were the cook and her son. Andre was the son of one of Mother's jewelers, the man who made most of her specially designed matching sets of diamonds, rubies, sapphires, topaz and emeralds. I had known his son since I was about eleven.

During the remainder of that summer after graduation, I did what I could to help Sister Benigna. I worked in the office, answering the phones, typing transcripts, processing the applications of prospective students. I tried to lighten the enormous work load Sister had in her dual role as principal and administrator of the school. She had been very good to me. She had stayed up many, many nights talking with me when she knew she had to get up every morning at 5 o'clock. She had taken responsibility for bending some of Mother's restrictions and letting me go to an occasional movie. She had obtained permission from Mother Superior to allow me on one of the outings the sisters took to Lake Arrowhead where they had a small cabin. She had done everything within her power to make life bearable for me. She had extended herself way beyond any call of duty or technical responsibility for my well-being.

I realized during the quietness of that summer that I had also learned a lot from the sisters and the special life of the convent. As much as I had originally hated it and the circumstances that had brought me here, I had learned some lessons that perhaps could not have been attained any other way. I had come in contact with myself, with my own loneliness, my own craziness, my own hatred and impatience. Before, I had never known the kind of pain I'd felt during these long months of solitude. There was no escape for me . . . I had to find a way to face myself . . . learn to live with myself . . . and begin to be patient with myself. Patience. I had come face to face with my own Nemesis. Patience. The curse of the young. Patience. The secret weapon of survival.

I thanked Sister for her understanding, her many kindnesses toward me. I was a difficult person. I tended toward brooding and turned inward upon myself. She had met me with gentleness, with wisdom and with love. I admired her deeply.

Shortly before I was to leave for college I read an article in the Los Angeles Times about an auction. It was with great sadness that I realized it was the contents of *our* house that were going up for sale. I wrote Mother a letter inquiring about that auction and received this handwritten reply on August 27 from Great Fosters, Surrey, England.

> *Tina dear*
> Thank you for your two letters and sweet card—I know you called Aunt Bettina thinking I had left earlier than I did—but as I told you—the papers had me leaving every day for two weeks before I actually left—It's strange you never cared about the house or the running of it—until you saw an ad for auctioning— the house will be sold soon I hope—because there is no more love in it
> Yes dear I know about the doctors-dentists the bills—come in even before you arrive for the appointment
> We start shooting this coming Wednesday—with no script—as usual—the weather is glorious for me—its cold— rainy—and not the blistering heat of Calif and New York—No

refrigeration—no air-conditioning—the food is horrible—its fish with flies or steak—so thin you cannot find it—Everything is cooked in mineral oil—its a laxative every meal—I'm in the Suite of Henry the Eight and Ann Bolyn—the beds sink to the floor in the middle—the spiders are as big as tarantulas—and they are every where—we check our beds each night—

The babes leave soon for school again—next week before I shoot—Everything has been paid for first semester—except your allowance—I used my two months allowance and food checks—so you have to wait for your spending money for a while but I'll get it before you get to school.

Love
"Mother"

I got the picture that she hated being in England. She was obviously miserable and being forced to live under sub-human conditions just to support us. Just look how grateful that should make us, how she sacrificed for us. The two months allowance checks and food checks had been spent by her, so I'd just have to wait. It didn't surprise me particularly. I didn't expect much any more. What I cared about was that nothing major had gone wrong and in a few short weeks I was off to college and a new life. I didn't care about her nightmare. It was interesting, however, that this was the first time she'd signed any of her letters to me as simply "Mother." Always before she had signed them "Mommie" and she had always put the quotation marks as though it were a pseudonym. Perhaps it was.

A car and driver came to pick me up from Flintridge one week before college started. As I said goodbye to Sister Benigna I felt a genuine sadness in leaving. I knew she wished me well and I promised I'd write her. I was not sorry to be leaving the top of this mountain, however, and breathed a sigh of relief as the limousine descended the hill for the last time.

I had called my grandmother to say goodbye. I knew that I'd be closely watched at home and didn't want to give the secretary any unnecessary ammunition. I told Grandmother that I'd write her from college to let her know how I was doing and where I was. She was a dear old lady and always thanked me for my sweet phone calls and for thinking of her.

When I arrived at home, I found out that a big trunk was almost packed for me. Elva, Mother's wardrobe woman, had already finished most of the work. I liked Elva very much and thanked her for helping me. She had worked with Mother for years and also traveled with her upon occasion to make sure that all of Mother's clothes for personal appearances were properly packed, ironed and ready for Mother to just step into.

My brother and sisters were home from their respective schools. I knew it was the last time I'd be seeing them for a while and we spent a good deal of the time talking about the future. I spent hours talking to Chris. I gave him my address at college and asked him to try and stay in touch with me, no matter where he was sent. I told him that I didn't think they'd censor the mail at college and not to be afraid to write me.

I did call some of my old friends and told them that I was going back east to school. Since I wasn't allowed to leave my own house and yard, a few of them came to say goodbye to me. My coach from Chadwick was getting married and I'd managed to save a few dollars out of my extremely meager funds for a small wedding present. Nicki and her fiancé, Jim, made the trip out to the house and I gave them their wedding gift. Nicki was her usual energetic and positive self. I enjoyed seeing her again so much. She brought me up to date on all my friends at Chadwick during the couple of hours we were able to talk.

Finally it was time to leave for Union Station. Betty was going with me on the train to Pittsburgh and I wasn't particularly looking forward to spending two or three days alone with her. I walked from room to room through the entire house, trying to imprint the memory of how it looked in my brain. I told Mrs. Howe that I didn't think I'd ever see this house again. She looked at me a little oddly, but didn't try to dissuade me from my final tour of 426 North Bristol . . . the home of my childhood. I walked out into the yard where I could almost hear the echo of those long-ago birthday parties . . . the clowns and the organ-grinder music. I could almost catch a long forgotten glimpse of the big parties, the happy people and Judy Garland singing far into the summer night.

I walked around the pool where Chris and I had played "king of the mountain" and learned to talk to one another under water. I stood beneath the big olive tree where once we'd hung a big stuffed toy in effigy, scaring Mother half to death when she thought we'd executed one of the twins! I looked at the flower beds and the little vegetable garden we'd gotten one of the gardeners to help us with years ago. I went into the theater where I'd seen Mother walk into the ocean in *Humoresque* and gotten hysterical because I thought she'd really died. I looked at the chair where Phillip had given me my spankings and then I gazed at the little empty stage upon which I'd made my disastrous debut as the mother in *Hansel and Gretel.*

I tried to look at every corner and every piece of furniture. I stood under the trees and knelt beside the new rose garden. I knew in my bones that I would never see any of it again. I knew these moments were the last ones of this part of my life. I stood on the steps leading down into the garden, the same steps I'd stood on so many evenings wishing on the evening star . . . "star light, star bright . . ." wishing for a horse of my very own . . . wishing for the strength to stay alive until I could grow up . . . wishing for . . .

REFLECTIONS FROM NICKI BAILEY

Tina was fourteen when I met her at Chadwick School. She was an overweight tenth-grader who excelled academically but was very unsure of herself as a person. I was a young physical education teacher on my first assignment, fresh out of UCLA and I wanted to help Tina because she seemed so sad and unrealized and because I liked her as a person.

She was bright, hard-working and seeking approval in a family-like structure, which she considered "home." Through her physical education classes, she demonstrated good swimming ability and I convinced her to join the swim team. She proved to be very coachable, a beautiful performer and she found friendship among the girls on the squad who became her support system. This gave her a sense of belonging and acceptance.

She won her swim events in competition several times and for her it was a new and heady feeling! A sense of self-worth began to surface. She had never before been a winner!

I remember a time when Tina's mother took nearly all her clothes away because of a disagreement and Tina was left with almost nothing to wear to school. She had to "make do" with whatever we could collect until she could regain her own things. Through all of this difficulty, Tina maintained great dignity.

Her status as a valued member of the school community increased greatly when she performed the lead in a school production of *Mikado* before students and parents one evening. She was brilliant and her star was shining brightly that night until her mother, who was in attendance, crushed its glow. It was a private moment which occurred between Tina, her mother and me. Happily, no one else knew of this as she received countless congratulations from an admiring audience on her acting and singing performance. You see, I made the mistake of raving to Miss Crawford about Tina's presentation, remarking that she, Joan Crawford, must be terribly proud of her daughter, at which point she turned her back to me and there was absolute silence. However, from that time on we all knew that Tina had come to the realization that she was loved, accepted and very much respected by her teachers and her peers because of her achievements.

Nicki Bailey, M.A.
Former Chadwick faculty member;
Retired athletic coach, El Camino College

REFLECTIONS FROM ROBERT MARTIN

It was a warm California evening. A Chadwick School dance was in progress. My wife, Monica, accompanied me to chaperone the students, as they seemed to be having a good time talking, dancing and laughing. That is, everyone except Christina. She was stylishly dressed but walked about somewhat aimlessly with a blank look. She was an outstanding student, attractive and popular with her classmates so I wondered why she had no escort and why she was not dancing. I asked her to dance but she politely refused, offering no reason. After some pressing on my part, I learned that she was being punished by Joan for some trivial infraction such as not writing a letter on time. Christina had to wear a lovely outfit, attend the dance without dancing, refrain from mixing with her friends, and remain until the end. After hearing this, I tried to downplay such an irrational dictum and again suggested we dance, but Christina was concerned that someone would report back to her mother. As always, she did not whine or solicit sympathy, but simply accepted her circumstances as stoically as a young person can.

On another occasion I met Joan Crawford for the first and last time. Christina appeared in the school's production of *The Mikado* and Joan attended. I was struck with the maturity and professionalism of Christina's performance and in talking with Joan afterwards I mentioned this. Joan passed it off with a wave of her hand and a shrug that clearly communicated negative criticism. As Christina's homeroom instructor I thought Joan might be interested in her daughter's studies, but it was difficult to discuss much with Joan. She was beautifully dressed as if ready for the cameras but I got the impression that she was a person playing the part of a person and the lines did not come easily.

Suddenly, around Thanksgiving 1954, Christina and her brother were gone. No one knew where. Months went by until one day Monica got a phone call. The caller said softly, "Mrs. Martin, this is Christina Crawford. Please don't say anything. I am at Flintridge. I am not supposed to make this phone call but would Mr. Martin call Mother Superior and ask permission to visit me. I need to talk to him," and hung up.

Subsequently I called, explained that I had been Christina's teacher for two years. She recited some of the strict rules laid down by Joan but also mentioned how concerned she was about Christina's depression because she was cut off completely from friends, from Chadwick and was confined to the campus weekends and vacations. Finally I was given permission to come visit with Monica and our two young children, but was required to come to her office upon our arrival.

The next day we drove to Flintridge. After promising Mother Superior that we would not tell anybody about our visit, we were allowed to see Christina.

After warm hugs, we talked and walked outside in the garden. Christina had changed. Her wonderful, hearty, infectious laugh was gone. She was pale, dispirited, vulnerable. I could see that her confidence had been shaken and in its place was confusion and disarray.

After that visit, my wife and I were able to keep in touch with Christina, offering our encouragement. Of course, it couldn't substitute for what she really needed: love, affection, family, friends, and a return to her class at Chadwick, but I had no means to bring that about.

The following year when Christina graduated from Flintridge, we were present. Christina told us that Joan's secretary had come and that if asked, we should say that we were there to see Gay White, a former student of mine, graduate. Sure enough, the secretary confronted me and wanted to know who I was and why I was talking to Christina. Overlooking this rudeness, I gave her straightforward answers that precluded any reply and resumed conversing with Christina.

In summary, the person I remember so well from classes and from English papers was a young vibrant student, eager to learn, warm-natured and not afraid to ask challenging questions in class. She had no difficulty expressing her ideas on paper. She hid her troubles well and never once complained about her mother.

When *Mommie Dearest* was published, I knew instinctively that long pent-up emotions were finally surfacing. The book articulated what Christina and Joan's relationship was actually like. It squared with facts I knew. From long years of friendship, I also knew that this act of writing must lay bare old wounds and scars, but in the end would have a healing effect and help Christina come to terms with the past so that a future would be possible.

I admire her courage and positive outlook despite subsequent vicissitudes that would defeat most of us and engender bitterness. Christina has persisted and survived by self-reliance, hard work and stubborn spirit.

Robert M. Martin, J.D., former Chadwick Faculty member;
State Director, California Department Social Welfare;
Deputy District Attorney, Los Angeles County;
currently civil law practice, Donahue, Donahue and Martin

CHAPTER 20

College surpassed whatever expectations I might have had about it.

One of the Pepsi men met us at the Pittsburgh train station. Betty took me to the girls' dormitory on campus the following day. There was a big stir over the rumor that Joan Crawford's daughter was coming to Carnegie and my arrival with the secretary and the trunks did nothing to dampen student fantasy. My new roommate was understandably dismayed to discover that my things took up nearly our entire shared living quarters but I tried to assure her that I'd be unpacked in no time at all.

The fraternity boys discovered my presence immediately and I had dates lined up for a week in advance before my first full day at college was complete.

When I was told the rules of the dormitory, it seemed like total freedom to me. We had to sign in and out at the desk. On week nights, freshman girls had to be back by 9 p.m. but on Saturday we didn't have to sign in until midnight.

Class schedules were tight, but the better part of the afternoon and evenings were free.

Coming from nearly two years of being cooped up in one place, living under the convent restrictions and Mother's strict orders, this freedom all of a sudden nearly overwhelmed me. I was completely unprepared to handle it. So, at first I ventured very slowly into this new-found world of personal responsibility.

Of course I went to the fraternity rush parties and all the other campus activities I was interested in, but I stuck very closely to the rules.

Mother had sent me a "Happy first day at college" telegram from England where she was still shooting *The Story of Esther Costello*. I felt very much away from her and very much on my own.

My first day in acting class I was just as scared as everyone else. We had come from all parts of the country to go to this school but none of us had experienced college before and many had never been so far away from home before.

The teacher introduced himself and then called roll, asking each of us to raise our hand when he called our name so that he could begin to identify us personally. When he came to my name, he said, "Oh yes, you're the movie star's daughter with all the reporters following you." I was mortified! Stupid teacher obviously thought the whole thing was a big laugh and I knew then and there that I was going to have to get a lot tougher if I was going to make it here.

After roll call, we were given our first assignment. He had each of us walk across the stage alone and then gave us an individual critique. No one wanted to go first. Everyone was terrified.

Since there were no volunteers, the teacher went alphabetically. He was not kind with his remarks to the people that preceded me and I had no idea what to expect from him after his opening joke at my expense. Fortunately, for years Mother made me practice walking with stacks of books on my head. If any of them fell, I had to start all over again until I could walk completely across the room with the stack of books intact. Surprisingly enough, his only remark to me was that I'd have to loosen up a little but other than that I was fine.

I had only been at Carnegie a few days when the first letter from my mother arrived. It was dated September 14.

Christina darling,

Thank you so much for your sweet cable. I am sure you are having an exciting time. I loved your letters. Glad you had such a good time at home and also that you saw the babies. They are pretty wonderful, loving, sweet, kind, attentive and unselfish. Glad, too, that you enjoyed the garden with the zinnias blooming; they were bursting when I left.

I asked Aunt Bettina to see that you helped in the household and did your packing—what was left that Aunt Elva did not do, and the next thing I hear is that you are entertaining every day and going to the Ice Follies. Would you mind telling me how that happened?

You say you will try hard to be an actress and that "there are many questions I would like to ask, and so much I don't understand about the way I feel." Just ask the questions, darling, and I will try and answer them.

Yes, darling, the house will be up for sale, since, with you at college and Chris at school, it seems ridiculous to keep it since I will be living in New York some of the time.

Please let me hear from you about college, your roommate, and how things are going.

The picture is going slowly. Don't know where we will all be for Christmas.

God Bless and know that I love you.

Your

"Mommie"

Loved your other two letters en route I'll write more later as I'm signing this on the set—

Love

"Mommie"

I guess I hadn't come much a great distance after all. I knew that it had to be Betty that told Mother about the people coming over to say goodbye. There was nothing wrong that I could see in spending a little time with your friends before leaving to go east, but the way Betty told the story was obviously different. That happened all the time. Betty told Mother every move that was made in the house and we always ended up getting in trouble even if we were innocent of any intentional wrong doing. Betty had also gotten in touch with me during the first month of college, nearly hysterical and accusing me of *stealing* my own silver dresser set! I told her I didn't know what she was talking about and that I didn't have it. Even if I did bring it with me, I would hardly considered it stealing . . . since it was mine to begin with! As things turned out, the maid had packed it away in one of the dresser drawers and Betty had to apologize to me.

I wrote Mother at least once a week. I was so genuinely happy at college, making friends, going out on dates and working hard at my classes that I tried very hard to let her know in detail. It was still hard for me to believe that everything had suddenly changed so much for the better. Carnegie was a wonderful choice. I'd looked through hundreds of college catalogs and this was the only one that allowed you to begin your major in the freshman year. I knew I didn't want to go to any other college the minute I'd found that out. I didn't apply anywhere else, which was taking a terrible risk, but I just had a feeling I'd be accepted at Carnegie. I certainly didn't want to go to any of the eastern women's colleges . . . I'd had quite enough of girls' schools to last me the rest of my life.

September 17, 1956

Christina darling,

I am sure you are having a "ball." I hope everything is going well and you are over your apprehension on your classes. I am sure the excitement of meeting all new people and going to the fraternity dances will counteract any nervousness you might have.

As I said before, the working is going slowly but, I hope, well. It is a different kind of part for me. Heather Sears, the twenty-year-old girl, is just fabulous in the part of Esther. She is always on time; is as professional as can be; takes direction magnificently; is a joy to work with; and, of course, so is Brazzi.

I hope your roommate is nice. I am sure she is.

Did you ever do anything about learning to sew?

Please don't wear your evening dresses to classes. Save them for dinner parties. Dress simply, and watch the make-up—play it down, not up. And please make me very happy by not using eye shadow.

Love,
"Mommie"

I really had to laugh though it was always frustrating to have Mother think of me like an idiot. Just the thought of anyone being so lunatic as to wear evening dresses to classes made me laugh, though the fact that it even crossed her mind didn't particularly thrill me. The eye shadow business, of course, was an old holdover.

But she wrote back often and it made me very happy to see the tone of her letters changing.

September 19, 1956

Christina darling,

I am so delighted to get your letters. You sound very happy, which makes me, in turn, very happy too.

This is just a quick note between scenes to say that I love you. Please continue to be happy.

All my love,

"*Mommie*"

At one of the fraternity parties I had one of those college drinking experiences that remain with you forever. I was not used to drinking at all, needless to say, since I'd just come from a convent school. Usually I stuck to just beer and felt pretty safe with that. But one party was unusually dressy and they served mixed drinks. To this day I don't remember what the drink was called, all I know is that it was made with gin and tasted deceptively like lemonade. Nothing terrible happened at the party, but on the way home, in the car, I realized that I was going to be violently ill. I had to ask my date to stop the car immediately. We were in Schenley Park and it was quite dark in between the street lights. Thank god it was dark. I don't ever recall being that sick, or that embarrassed. But there I was in my lovely cocktail dress, on my hands and knees throwing up in the darkness. It was a totally dreadful experience. I never went out with that poor guy again, but I never touched another drop of gin either. From that point on, I made some attempt to watch what was being served very carefully.

September 27, 1956

Christina darling,

I loved your letter of the 20th. Your college career sounds very exciting, and I know how happy you must be. The stage craft and technical workings must be fascinating. How I wish I had had all that training before I started my career.

Did you finish your Stanislavsky book before you entered college? And remember one thing always, darling—don't take the books literally because you become nothing but a technical actress, and there is nothing duller. Most of the Actors' Studio people are technical, too technical, Cliff Robertson being one of the rare ones who have maintained his own identity.

I am delighted that you like your new skirts and sweaters. Also, happier than I can say that you like your new roommate.

The picture is going just as slow as usual. We are threatened with a walkout and strike on the part of the carpenters tomorrow. Some productions will close down until they have negotiated with the carpenters which could mean a wait of one week to five months. If we don't wait for the negotiations our company may have to finish the picture in Rome. Of course, I will let you know where I am at all times.

I understand Aunt Bettina let you have $50.00, so that for the next two months I do not think you will need any further allowance from me. This means you will have $25.00 a month, enough to last to the end of November, and whatever you save out of it for Christmas, I will double the amount.

All my love, darling,

Always,

"*Mommie*"

No matter how you figure it, Mother was not good at math. Betty gave me the $50 because the $50 that Mother had given me before school started went for books and supplies the first day I was there! That left me with nothing . . . not a dime. But, I'd explained that already to Mother, and in this case Betty had too. Putting the first $50 aside, there were *three* months, not two months between September and the end of November. So it was not the paltry sum of $25 a month that was supposed to be my allowance, but something in the neighborhood of $16.66, which ended up being about $4 a week. Inflation was not a serious factor in the fall of 1956, but nevertheless, four dollars a week was a totally hopeless amount to try and make it by on. It was no use arguing, though. It was a quirk of Mother's that she failed to understand small amounts of money and their relationship to everyday life. I was to meet that quirk many times over in my life and I never really understood it. She would spend thousands on a mink coat or a piece of jewelry or a fancy dinner party but when it came to my allowance she didn't seem to have any sense at all.

October 2, 1956

Christina darling,

Your letters are such fun. Your "Thought and Expression" class must be fascinating. I am so glad you are enjoying it so much. Life can be very exciting if we give to it, and we only get back what we give. I am only sorry about one thing—the interview you gave and the very corny picture that you took for the newspapers. I am sure if you saw the picture you were not happy with it and that is why you did not send it to me. The important thing to know during an interview is what not to say. Next time, why don't you say "See me in six years when I have started on my own," and not give out interviews.

Thank goodness we did not have the strike, so we can continue the film here.

Forgive the brief note, darling, but I have to run.

Love,

As Always,

"Mommie"

This was the first of many discussions Mother and I were to have about the press. The Pittsburgh papers had been calling me nearly every other day since my arrival in town and I got sick and tired of putting them off. I agreed to do *one* interview if they promised to leave me alone after that. The interview, I had thought, went well. They took a couple of photos and left. They had asked the usual questions about "how does it feel to be a movie star's daughter" and dumb stuff like "are you following in your mother's footsteps" to which I replied "not really, because I'm studying for the theater." I did the best I could, but I made some mistakes. I wasn't sophisticated enough yet to realize that once you became a public person, some of the control over what is printed about you is transferred out of your own hands and into the hands of strangers. It is possible, I found out, to say something perfectly innocently and have it taken out of context, so that the resulting printed article makes your original statement *seem* quite different than you intended. Mother should have known that better than anyone. She'd been dealing with the press for years. But it was like money versus my allowance; when it came to me, she seemed to forget how hard the lesson was to learn. However, I had already taken her advice and didn't allow any more interviews.

I really had more than I could handle just trying to get through my own classes and deal with regulating my social life so that one didn't conflict with the other. I'd given up the fraternity parties after a month or so, mainly because there was so much drinking and I had found out rather painfully that I couldn't handle alcohol very well. I was sticking closer to my own drama department. At night we had begun working "crew" which for the freshman girls meant primarily sewing costumes. But it also meant that we didn't have to be back in the dorm at 9:00 p.m., so there was a decided bonus in it for all of us.

The fall season was beautiful that year. The leaves turned brilliant colors just like picture postcards of the East. It was only the middle of October, but Pittsburgh was beginning to get cold. The wind blew fiercely across the campus and you had to struggle against it to walk. My California clothes were not nearly heavy enough for this weather, but I was afraid to tell my mother that I was getting cold. I thought maybe in a few more weeks I'd get more used to it. I had enough sweaters but I had no muffler, no heavy coat, no boots and no winter gloves.

October 25, 1956

Tina darling,

Loved your letters of the 4th and 9th. I haven't been so good about writing for the past week or so, but all of a sudden all hell broke loose on production and things have been very hectic. I loved hearing about all your classes and am very happy indeed that you are enjoying everything so much. I am sure you find that, being so occupied, the days and weeks fly by. It is true that you will have moments of discouragement, but they will pass and something will happen to give you renewed encouragement. This happens to all of us, whatever we do.

(Classmate's name deleted) has written asking if you may visit his home for a couple of days during the Thanksgiving holiday, and he will no doubt show you my reply.

I am sure you are making some nice friends at school. Which of the boys do you like best now? Times do change affections, or should I say, my darling, some people do not wear well.

This coming weekend will be a very busy one for me because of all the activities in connection with the Command Performance. There is even a rehearsal on Sunday morning! It will be an exciting evening, and I cannot have any time off the next day in order to recover.

The weather here in England is beautiful at present and the countryside is lovely, though I do not have much opportunity to see it since it is dark when we leave in the mornings for the studios, and the same in the evenings going back to Great Fosters.

Was the party a lovely one? Do tell me all about it, won't you. Keep well and happy, darling, and till next time all my love.

Your

Mommie

I already knew that Mother was going to be in England and that I had to make some arrangements for Thanksgiving vacation. I didn't mind staying in the dorm just four days and I didn't particularly want to stay in someone else's home because it was always sort of like being on "show." Not that anyone meant any harm, but I'd found out it was just sort of irresistible human behavior.

Except for the money and nearly freezing to death a couple of days, college was going well beyond my wildest dreams. I'd begun to make some very good friends among my classmates. There were two people in particular with whom I became extremely close. One was a very bright girl named Myrna Coburn, "Mickey" was her nickname. She came from Brooklyn and her father was a CPA. She wanted to be a writer, but she had to take all the acting classes anyway. My other special friend was Lloyd Battista. Lloyd wanted to be an actor with every fiber of his being and in fact had already worked for several years in the Cleveland Playhouse near his home. Lloyd wrote too, but I think it was more like music than literature to him. I loved Lloyd from the moment he sat down next to me in class. He was an outrageous and wonderfully funny man that could be electrifying and silly at the same time. I never figured out how he did that, but I loved him anyway. Lloyd was like quicksilver to me. I never felt I could really catch him long enough to see what made him tick, yet he was always right there whenever I needed him. I never figured out how he knew that about me, either. It was just one of those friendships that lasts from the first moment through all the years that follow.

In the weeks that passed so quickly I made other friends too. Jim Frawley was an actor in the class ahead of me and I was so fascinated by his classical style of acting that I used to go into his rehearsals and sit in the back watching. He had a wonderful voice and later on would help rid me of my California "twang." Jules Fisher was a technical major, wanted to be a lighting designer, which he very successfully became. He did the lighting that first year for a special dance performance which was magnificent. Everyone just sort of knew that Jules would be a big success.

November 11, 1956

Christina darling,

Enclosed is a copy of the letter I sent to (Classmate's name deleted).

Loved your last letter. I was terrified of the Command Performance but got through it all right.

The tea breaks are still going on and I don't know when we'll finish the film. Sorry we won't all be together at Thanksgiving; and I hope I'm still not stuck here for Christmas.

I can certainly understand why you don't want to spend Thanksgiving with Dennis, and of course I won't let him know. You will see from the copy of my letter that I handled it—I think—quite well.

You sound as though you are very sad that (boyfriend's name deleted) is not around. Have you gotten over it, or do you still get lightning streaks up and down your back when he walks in a room? The right person, my darling, will let that wall he had around him dissolve. So take it easy; don't press; and if you feel you love him, make him love you by your sweet consideration, kindness, and ladylike manner, and your understanding.

Keep well and happy, and know that I love you.

Your

"Mommie"

(Note: Some of the names are deleted so as not to infringe on their privacy.)

It was wonderful to feel the kindness, the understanding Mother showed in these letters to me. It made me feel close to her even though we had not seen one another in almost a year. I knew she was having a difficult time on this picture and yet she was taking precious moments to relate to me. Slowly she seemed to be dropping the old notions of me as a wayward child and beginning to respond to me as an adult. Her little bits of advice and personal thoughts on my problems were sweet. I felt as though she loved me and cared about me.

I doubled my efforts in class. I was getting good grades even in the boring classes and my acting was progressing well. My favorite drama instructor was Allen Fletcher. He was a tall, slender, intellectual type and something of a local guru as far as acting teachers went. He was definitely special for all those of us who wanted to become involved with "the method", which is basically what he taught. Mary Morris and Charlie Moore were more stylized in their approach, which of course we interpreted as "old-fashioned." I sort of fixed myself to Allen Fletcher's coattails and hung on with the rest of my crowd. I listened to his every word as though it were the living gospel. After seeing *Hatful of Rain* on Broadway the year before, I already knew the direction I wanted to head and Allen was going to help me learn how to get there. I worked for the man, for the instructor and not so much for myself. Perhaps that's the pitfall many young actors face. The actor is so dependent on the teacher at first and the director later on that it's hard not to make these people into minor guru's of the moment. Whatever the trap, I fell into it hook, line and sinker.

November 16, 1956

Christina darling,

In the first letter I wrote you at school I asked you how much money you had, and how much you thought you would need monthly, and you have not ever mentioned it, and now you are out of money. I know Aunt Bettina gave you $50.00, which I reimbursed her for in September. What have you spent it on since I am paying all the school bills, including laundry. Enclosed is a check for $50.00.

By now you have my letter I wrote last week about (boyfriend's name deleted). How sad he is going with a girl that makes him so unhappy. Since you see his mother, have you told her how you feel about her son? That might be a help only don't try too hard, honey. (Name) sounds like a mixed-up kid if I ever heard of one. Apparently, (boyfriend's girlfriend) has only one hold on him— which is not a lasting one; and with that temperament he will never make a director because no actor or actress would ever work with him. Why is he 26 and only a junior? Is he retarded? (You know, darling, that I'm only kidding.) You must know in your heart, darling, that if (name) is right for you God always has a way of working those things out. If you don't win him it means he isn't for you.

I will be in this Godforsaken land for Thanksgiving.

Please, darling, try to give me an idea of how much you will have to have every month in allowance, as I have to put that aside out of my own.

Have you gained weight? Have you lost weight? Or are you the usual size? I must know immediately because of Christmas, and it takes so long to get letters back and forth to the states and order things.

I have no idea, darling, where I'll be at Christmas with the way the picture is going—or not going. I have had to be off two days, one time with a tremendous mosquito bite on my eye when my whole face was swollen, and last night again one bit me on the lip. They attack me like dive bombers. I am just allergic to the nasty things and they are as big as bees over here.

In case I am not back for Christmas what shall we do about you? Let me hear as soon as you can, darling.

All my love,
Your
"Mommie"

I was so thrilled to get the $50 that I didn't bother to tell her that she had told me in the first letter how much I would be getting for an allowance . . . not asked me how much I needed. I simply wrote back thanking her and saying that $50 a month would be sufficient.

Christmas was going to be a dilemma. The dorm was closing for most of the vacation, so I wouldn't be able to stay there. My friend Mickey invited me to come home with her to Brooklyn. Mother wouldn't let me go because she said it was too expensive and she didn't know Mickey's parents.

Finally I worked out an arrangement with the dorm where I could stay until they closed it and return the day it reopened. That left only one week that I had to find a place to stay. The boyfriend Mother and I had been writing back and forth about heard about my predicament and told his mother. She insisted that I stay with them, which I did. They lived right in town, near the campus and within walking distance of the dorm. His parents were absolutely wonderful to me and I had a great time with them, his brother and sister-in-law. The only uncomfortable moments were when he brought his present girlfriend home with him for Christmas dinner and we all had to sit at the same table like one big happy family. I couldn't stand the sight of his girlfriend, but in spite of ample advice to the contrary, he let himself be talked into marrying her and they've been living unhappily together ever since!

Toward the middle of January 1957, Mother and Daddy returned from England. I was very disappointed in the Christmas gifts she'd sent. They were cocktail dresses, which I certainly did not need. What I needed was a winter coat, boots, winter pants and skirts. Although I'd told her all this over the phone, I received cocktail dresses instead.

Christina darling,

I am having your Christmas gifts mailed to you in Pittsburgh. Would you please write thank-you letters for all of them, and send them to me? Leave the envelopes unsealed, dear. I will address and mail the letters for you.

Please send the thank-you letters to 426 North Bristol Avenue, dear. Aunt Betty will forward them to me.

Love,

Mommie

P.S. We just arrived on the Queen Mary two hours ago and found your Christmas gifts your Daddy adored his Moustache

cologne and soap—and I love my stoles and sweet fur topped booties—more later darling—
All my love
Mommie

(The "P.S." was handwritten at the bottom of the typed letter.)

Somehow I always hoped that Daddy would write me himself, but he never did. I never heard from him except through Mother's letters, I never talked to him on the phone when I called them. We were translated to one another only through Mother.

I laughed about the absurdity of still having to send *unsealed* thank-you notes home just like a little kid. After all, I was in *college* and I was seventeen and a half years old. To all intents and purposes, I was on my own. There wasn't any secretary or nurse following me around checking up on my every move. I may not have become exactly adult yet, but I certainly wasn't some infant that had to send notes home for approval.

The letter didn't make me feel as badly as similar letters from Mother made me feel in the past, but I wondered seriously about who it was that she thought she was writing to, who it was that she had in mind when she was dictating. I wondered if she even thought much about me at all except when she had to answer one of my letters to her. I hadn't seen her in over a year. She had never been to Flintridge or Carnegie. She didn't know exactly what I looked like anymore and she couldn't really know much of anything about how I felt or what kind of person I was.

I'd been through a lot of changes during the first five months of college, but I think that happens to most people. It's your first real taste of growing up and being responsible for your own life. You meet so many new people. People whose ideas may be very different from your own. You are exposed to so much new information, so many new situations.

Most of my classmates had difficult Christmas vacations at home for just these reasons. Suddenly, they were not the same people their families remembered and it was unsettling for everyone. But Mother hadn't seen me since I left New York after finishing the magazine layout in

January of 1956. I could tell she really didn't know me by the presents she sent. They were nice, but they weren't appropriate for this time and this place in *my* life. She didn't even choose them. She put in orders and the store sent the closest thing they had in stock. The clothes weren't the right size and they weren't the right style, but there wasn't much I could do about it, because the price tags had been removed and I had no way to return them. So, I wrote the thank-you notes and put the things in the back of my closet, untouched until it was time to pack them in the trunk.

Spring vacation was at hand shortly after Christmas. Again my friend invited me to her home in Brooklyn. Again I asked Mother if I could *please* come to New York. This time I knew Mother and Daddy would be there and I wanted to see them.

   We talked several times on the phone and finally it was agreed that I could go home with Mickey and come into the city to visit Mother and Daddy.

   I was very excited about going to New York again, with the prospect of seeing more plays and getting to know the city better. Mickey and I got reservations on the same flight, which landed at the old La Guardia airport.

Her home in Brooklyn was on a quiet dead-end street lined with trees. Mr. and Mrs. Coburn were totally loving and parental people whom I called Aunt Min and Uncle Ben after the first few hours. They had one son at Cornell, Mickey at Carnegie and a younger son yet to be Bar Mitzvahed. They made me feel like part of the family immediately. Aunt Min was always putting food out on the table. Uncle Ben told funny jokes and tried to maintain some order in the boisterous household. Their little three-story house was always filled with people . . . friends, relatives and kids from the neighborhood. It struck me then that their hospitality was in sharp contrast to my own family. Here they were with two kids in college, another son preparing for Bar Mitzvah, Uncle Ben the only wage earner (an accountant) and still they had room in their home for one more. Five miles away in New York City, Mother and Daddy had an eight-room apartment on Sutton Place South and they didn't have enough room for their daughter to spend a week's vacation from college. They didn't have an extra bed or a spare couch where I could sleep and they hadn't seen me in a *year*. Yet these strangers, this Jewish family in Brooklyn with their little house bursting at the seams, they had plenty of room for one more kid.

My parents had no place for me to stay with them, but they put on a big show for the Coburn family. I'd gone into the city a couple of times to have lunch with Mother and Daddy at "21" Club, taking a taxi both ways because I was terrified of the subway system. Several times, Mother had gotten tickets for Broadway shows, which someone took me to see. Then, before vacation was over, she invited the entire Coburn family to have lunch. We all got dressed up and took a cab to the Sutton Place apartment where we met Mother and Daddy. They were very gracious to the Coburns who were understandably impressed. Then we went to lunch at "21", Mother and Daddy's regular hang-out. Daddy talked to Uncle Ben and Aunt Min and my mother talked mostly to my friend Mickey about her aspirations to becoming a writer. I could see the charm all around me, but there was no way for me to warn Mickey not to believe everything Mother said about wanting to read her work. I'd been in this situation as many times before that I knew it was graciousness, not instantaneous friendship . . . but how do you tell someone else who wants to believe in the reality of it that it's just ordinary operating procedure? How do you tell them that it's nothing special. You don't. You just have to let them find out for themselves.

Mother had given me $200 when I first met them for lunch by myself. That money was for taxis, for taking the Coburn family to dinner at Sardi's and for a house gift before leaving for school. I spent most of it on just those things. Taxis were nearly $10 each way and dinner at Sardi's was about $70. Compared to the allowance I was supposed to be getting, it was a lot of money. Compared to what things cost and commuting into the city from Brooklyn every other day, it barely lasted until the end of the ten-day vacation.

After the first visit, neither Mother nor Daddy asked me very much about myself. When I saw them it was usually in a restaurant and they were usually talking business with their friends or saying hello to the other people in the restaurant who dropped by the table. It was all very chic and all very expensively pleasant but it was also very impersonal. Coming from my college atmosphere where everyone was involved in the process of "discovering" who they really were it seemed very superficial to me. I also thought that it cost an absurd amount of money. Lunch alone usually cost nearly $100 and I thought wistfully about struggling to get along on my monthly allowance. Just one of those lunches would have made my life so much easier when I was at school. Just one of those lunches would have bought me a winter coat and boots. But it was useless to think in those terms. I learned long ago that when it came to money there were two distinctly different standards . . . one for Mother's needs and one for mine. Whatever Mother wanted, Mother got. Whatever I wanted, I had to beg for and usually didn't get. She'd give me $200 for a showy ten-day vacation designed to impress a family in Brooklyn, but no money for allowance when I was away at school. It was definitely a case of "out of sight, out of mind."

February 14, 1957

Christina darling,

Thank you for your sweet Valentine—it is just darling, and for the "Thank-you" notes.

I received your report card and am very proud of you.

Darling, please is it possible to let me know if the (family I stayed with over Christmas) received their carafes. I know how busy you are, darling, but just drop me a note, or call.

Incidentally, if you ever hear from the Blakes again it is not Flo, it is Florence and Joyce Blake.

All my love, darling, and I hope you are happy.

Your,

"Mommie"

P.S. Darling just received your letter today and honey I just cannot give you more money this month—you figure out how much I gave you while you were on your vacation down here and the dress the shoes—The gifts for the Coburns I bought too—so you will just have to wait for you March allowance

Love—Mommie

I kind of knew that I wouldn't get any more money, but I had to ask anyway. As for the report card, it was the worst I'd ever gotten, but I was saved by the belief that college was more difficult the first semester. Actually, I ended up with a straight B average, which meant a couple of A's and a couple of C's balanced each other out.

Since I had no money at all by this time, I started typing term papers at 25¢ a page. Each floor of the dorm had a living room and I'd stay up half the night typing while the other girls studied and then went to bed, leaving me working alone. I hated the term papers and I wasn't the best typist in the world, so it seemed to take me forever to finish. But I did them faster than most of the other girls who did typing so I had a steady clientele before long.

February 25, 1957

Tina darling,

Thank you for your letter and I am glad your Director is so good. I am also glad you are working so hard, and delighted about the part in *Cymbeline.* This experience will stand you in good stead when you get out into the world and really have to work. You know, Tina, most people think that college is the toughest part of it. It isn't nearly as tough as when you get out and have to do your own job by yourself. This probably won't make any sense to you now, but in a few years it will.

Did you ever get the other dress from Bramson's in Chicago? Please let me know.

Hope everything went alright with the dentist.

All my love,

Your,

"Mommie"

I thought a lot about getting out on my own during those hours typing late at night in the quiet dorm. I was getting bored with being in school for so many years. It's not that I didn't like Carnegie, because it was great for me. I was beginning to improve in my acting classes and starting to get a good reputation for the scenes I did. I had no trouble getting a partner to work with and we worked hard. I was learning to take the inevitable criticism without feeling that I'd totally failed. I was starting to understand some of the fundamentals of working on stage with others and taking directions more easily. Some of the other classes were boring to me, but not acting. It was just that I was so tired of being in schools all my life. I was tired of never having any money, any proper clothing, any normal freedom.

Since I'd never had a real paying job, I had no idea what it would be like, but I began to dream of the day when I'd be able to find out.

In the meantime, I typed term papers and wrote Mother for money when she always "forgot" to send my allowance. With the money I earned, Mickey and I would go down to the delicatessen once a week, usually on Saturday, and she'd teach me about Jewish food. I ordered matzo ball soup once, but it wasn't terrific. My favorites were corned beef, pastrami and poppy seed strudel. We'd all sit and talk for hours about life and our careers after school. Both of us were convinced that we were talented enough to become very successful, and though there was no such thing as women's lib yet, we were both convinced that marriage would have to wait . . . maybe forever. We talked about what it would be like to be on our own, about maybe living with someone if you loved them, what we'd tell our parents and much more. Since neither of us had even one day's real experience with any of these subjects, it was mostly conjecture on our parts.

Mickey had read more of the philosophy books than I had, but we'd both discovered *The Prophet* by Gibran. That little book was passed from hand to hand throughout the entire drama department, I think. It made an enormous impression on all of us and was my first introduction to an alternate philosophy of living. Since we were all searching for the meaning of life, which was a popular pursuit, we ran into a lot of different ideas. None were immediately discarded.

The late fifties were the tail-end of the dark period of literature and underground lifestyles. We were swept away by Camus and Kerouac, by Thomas Wolfe and Eugene O'Neill. We wore jeans to school, which was almost unheard of then, and dressed in black dance leotards. The drama department was definitely set apart from the rest of the primarily "ivy league" school and people could spot us immediately by the strange way we dressed. The difference in clothing originated form having to go from a dance class to English and from there to learning fights in acting class. We were constantly getting dirty and sweaty and you just couldn't wear regular clothes to do what we did. But, soon, the weirdness became a sort of department trademark, a sign of individualism. Long before it was in fashion, we all let our hair grow and wore funky clothes. The guys used the excuse of being in classical plays but the girls didn't feel any excuse necessary. We thought it was great.

That spring I had to have my wisdom teeth pulled and Mother decided I should have the dental surgery in New York. However, Daddy was also in the hospital and she wrote me this letter a few days previous to my trip.

March 13, 1957

Tina darling,

Thank you for your letter to Miss Elsye.

I wrote to Mrs. Stuart asking for the doctor's telephone numbers, but there is no sense in me calling them until the X-rays are taken and in front of them.

When I offered to come up to be with you for the extraction I thought your father's operation would be over. We are in the hospital now, but they can't operate for another week or so, and we must stay here until he is ready for the operation. But please do see that I get the doctor's names correctly spelled, and the telephone numbers, and when they will have your X-rays in front of them. I think you should plan to have the extraction on the 22nd. I love you dearly, and so wish I could be with you, but I know you understand.

Please feel free to call me if you have any problems, or any fears.

All my love—
Your
"Mommie"

I was nearly eighteen years old now. Whenever I thought about her it was as "Mother", but what I called her was still "Mommie." It always made me feel like a little girl to be writing to her as Mommie and calling her Mommie when I called from school. She still signed her letters to me with quotation marks around "Mommie" as though perhaps it was strange to her as well. But that's the way it went, without any change for many more years.

She did come to see me in the hospital. I'd had all four wisdom teeth removed and was very uncomfortable. I went from the airport to the hospital and from the hospital to the airport and back to school. The whole thing was a very unpleasant experience for me. My face was very swollen and I couldn't eat anything for almost two weeks. It was a great diet, but a hell of a way to lose weight.

Every freshman drama student was assigned someone from the sophomore class to coach them in voice and speech. My "big sister" was Peggy Hughes. Peggy was a special friend. She always cheered me up. Because she also lived off campus, it was always fun to walk over and see her. She lived in one of those Victorian Pittsburgh mansions on Fifth Avenue that had been turned into a boarding house. It was an eccentric place, to say the least. Peggy could always be counted on to liven up the dullest environment, she just had a way of finding the amusing out of any situation. She was a perfect friend for me because I tended to be rather shy at first with strangers. One of Peggy's best friends in this peculiar but interesting boarding house was a painter named Balcom Green. We used to go and visit him often because he was older than us and usually had some food and a bottle of wine handy. Peggy was never shy about saying anything to anyone, so the three of us spent many a cold winter afternoon laughing and talking about outrageous things.

April 1, 1957

Christina darling,

Thank you so much for your beautiful birthday card, and also for the lovely photographs of yourself.

I do hope you are truly feeling alright and that your gums are healing rapidly. I was so proud of you when you were in the hospital, you were so brave—a real good trouper!

I am busier than the proverbial bee, and have so much to do in the way of preparing for the trip to New Orleans. However, I expect I'll get through it all somehow.

Stay well and happy, and till next time all my love.

Your

"Mommie"

I knew from the times I did speak to her over the phone that she and Daddy were planning extensive travel to various Pepsi bottling plants, sales meetings and the like. Mother could be counted upon to draw the crowds since she was just about the only big Hollywood star yet to make the transition from filmdom to the business world. In the '50s no big stars did commercials for television, no stars were permanently associated with only one product.

Pepsi Cola was getting more publicity, more overall press coverage from Mother's personal appearances beside Daddy on these well-planned business trips than they could have ever bought with regular advertising dollars. Mother had bottles of Pepsi back stage at talk shows, she had a bottle of Pepsi next to her at press conferences, she mentioned the company name whenever she was interviewed for any purpose whatsoever. As Daddy pushed the soft drink company ever closer to the number one market spot in the nation through expansion and promotion, Mother drew the crowds and got the media attention. But behind all of it was the product . . . the soft drink that would mark an entire era . . . the "Pepsi generation" was coming of age.

Mother had only made one film in the last year and a half. She would not do another one until after Daddy died, but she had no way of knowing that yet. She was on the Pepsi trail with him most of the time. They covered every part of the United States with public appearances. No occasion was too insignificant to warrant a whistle-stop visit. It was during these hectic days that Mother had to start flying. Up until now she had insisted on taking the train. But with the schedule Daddy had mapped out for the two of them, it would have taken a year to do what they normally did in several months. Besides, Alfred Steele was now chairman of the board of the company and he had a business to run from the offices in New York.

Though Mother complained the usual about being so busy I knew she loved every minute of it. For the ten years previous to marrying Alfred Steele, she had barely left the state of California. She hadn't been to Europe since her honeymoon with Douglas Fairbanks, Jr. and she'd only made a couple of trips to New York. She'd struggled alone with a faltering career, four children and mounting debts. By the time they were married, she'd had to sell the apartment house she owned in

Beverly Hills, she'd taken a second mortgage on her house, she'd borrowed against her insurance policies and she didn't have a job. After the marriage, someone else paid the bills, bought her jewelry, paid the rent and took her anywhere she wanted to go. Her own income barely got the insurance policies paid and the back debts cleared up. Now she didn't have to worry about where her next job was coming from, because she considered the work for Pepsi just like a continuing performance, which it was. She knew the people were coming to see her and she gave them a show befitting the queen of celluloid. She always made a little speech and signed endless autographs. She changed her clothes two and three times a day so that all the photographs taken at different events wouldn't show her in the same outfit. She was every inch the visiting movie star and the media covered the glamorous couple wherever they went. Mother made sure that the Pepsi name was either in the photograph or in its caption. She was always a perfectionist.

In April they went to Ottawa, Kansas and from there to Tulsa, Oklahoma and Joplin, Missouri—hardly the major metropolitan areas of the country.

They were going to be on the road for part of my Easter vacation, so once again I went to Brooklyn with Mickey. This time we managed to get a ride with some other students who were driving to New York so I told Mother I didn't need the plane fare. She had promised me some money and the day before vacation started, this handwritten, special delivery letter arrived.

> *Tina darling*—
>   Enclosed is $110.00 one hundred and ten dollars—and honey please don't go back to school broke—try and keep an accounting so I'll have an idea where it goes—it would be helpful to both of us—as I'm rather low on cash with your hospital and the two doctors bills—I'm sure you understand—
>   *Love always*—
>   *"Mommie"*

This check I received on April 14th was the first money I'd gotten from her since semester vacation in February. Somehow during her busy schedule, she'd forgotten to send the March allowance. It seems so petty after all these years, but it was much more than a nuisance at the time.

Mickey and I had a wonderful time during the short Easter vacation. We spent most of the time around her neighborhood in Brooklyn, going into the little stores and meeting her family friends. There were family dinners and long talks with Aunt Min while she prepared the meals. I had sort of envied Mickey at school because she seemed so close to her parents. They sent her boxes of homemade goodies about once a month and we'd all gather in her room to share the bounty. Her parents gave her $50 a month in allowance with which she was very careful, but she never was totally broke. It seemed ironic to me and peculiar to Mickey that she received *double* the money I did. Better still, her parents didn't forget to send it. After all, her father was a CPA in Brooklyn and my mother was a movie star! It didn't make much sense to her or anyone else that I never went home and I didn't get enough money for normal college activities.

When we returned from the Easter holiday, I think I got a chronic case of spring fever. The winter had been so cold and dreary that spring seemed too beautiful for studies and the normal routine. I did my best to keep up in all the classes but the only one that continued to hold my full attention was acting. I began skipping some of the lecture classes and copying other people's notes. I met a rock 'n' roll singer and started going out with him. I had to laugh when all the girls stared at his shiny new white Cadillac sitting in the driveway outside the dorm. Sam *was* a little flamboyant, but he was also great fun and very good to me. I enjoyed going to the clubs and meeting the other guys he worked with in the group. We just had a good time, that's all. It was spring, the countryside was lush green, everything was in bloom and it was far too pretty to be stuck indoors. I came very close to flunking one lecture course. For the first time in my life I had to stay up all night cramming for a final exam.

In my acting class, however it was an entirely different story. I was one of the only two females single-cast in our final projects! It was an enormous honor to be singled out like that. I was going to play the part of Luba in *Darkness at Noon* directed by Allen Fletcher. I could hardly believe my good fortune. The only thing that marred the entire end of my first year at college was the news that Allen was leaving Carnegie. At first, no one could believe it. Then Allen himself confirmed the rumor and we were all terribly dismayed. But I figured if I only had this one opportunity to work with him, I'd put everything I had into it.

Final projects were open to the entire department. It was a very exciting time, because word had gotten around that *Darkness at Noon* was one of *the* projects to see that year. The little theater was packed—standing room only. By performance time, even the aisles were jammed.

It went wonderfully well. Afterwards I cried and everyone congratulated me. Allen was wonderful when I asked if I'd disappointed him in any way . . . he was supportive and kind to the young actress who hung on his every word.

I had asked Mother several months before if I could apply as a summer apprentice at the Westport Country Playhouse in Connecticut. Mother's friend, Bob Shear, had assured her that Westport was one of the very best summer stock theaters and was helpful in making the arrangements for me. A lot of theaters made the apprentices *pay* to work the summer, but Westport didn't. We didn't get any salary, either, but that wasn't so important at the moment. Mother and Daddy were going to be away on business most of the summer, so I guess my suggestion was as good as any others. It was decided that I'd come into New York for a couple days, stay with them and go on to Connecticut as soon as possible.

CHAPTER 21

I was in New York on June 11, 1957 which was my eighteenth birthday. Totally unexpectedly, Mother and Daddy gave me a *car* as my birthday present. They also gave me the portable typewriter I'd specially requested. I had absolutely no idea about the car, though it came as a total shock. I couldn't even drive a car . . . I had no license! After I hugged and kissed them, we went down to the street in front of their apartment on Sutton Place and there it was, parked at the curb all shiny unbelievable. It was a 1957 Thunderbird, painted turquoise blue and had the spare tire mounted in the back. It had been Daddy's car, but Mother wouldn't let him drive it any more. It was a sports car and she preferred the limousines. It was gorgeous! I couldn't believe that it was really mine. The whole thing was so unexpected that it didn't really sink in until the next day when Daddy got someone to drive me up to Westport in it and left me with the car keys at an inn called the General Putnam.

Daddy had arranged for a policeman in Westport to give me driving lessons, get me a learner's permit immediately and make sure I got my license before the theater opened for the season. That meant I had about ten days to learn to drive and pass the test. I was scared to death I'd make a mistake and wreck Daddy's car . . . my car. I applied myself with diligence, however, and everything went fine.

Mother was paying my weekly rent at the General Putnam Inn in Norwalk which was about five miles from the theater but my allowance was to pay for everything else. I had carefully figured out what I thought I would need, since I'd never had to pay for all my meals before nor ever had the responsibility of a car. I labored over the amount for hours and tried to check around the local places to see what representative prices for food might be. But in response to my carefully calculated request, I received this handwritten note from Mother on "Mrs. Alfred N. Steele" stationery.

> *Tina darling*
>   You say you need $43 dollars a week. Your father has figured $26 a week for food—$6.00 gas and oil—and $5.00 for incidentals—which would make $117.00 a month—
>   Enclosed is $117.00 which should last till the 12th of July— if you find it doesn't stretch that far—let me know—I should be back in New York around that time but of course we will be talking before I leave for Calif—and during our stay on the coast—
>   *Love*
>   *Always*
>   *"Mommie"*

Now, I knew I wasn't very good at math, but it came as a shock to me that "your father" was a lot worse! Maybe it wasn't Daddy at all . . . maybe that was just an excuse. I was quite sure that Daddy couldn't run a multimillion dollar company on that kind of accounting.

First of all . . . I was going to starve to death! Twenty-eight dollars a week for food is only $4 a day. I wasn't sitting around on my ass at the beach either. I was working a minimum of ten hours a day at the theater . . . doing whatever had to be done to get the place ready for opening. We swept the grounds, painted the lobby, cleaned out the johns, ran all over the county looking for props, loading them into the pickup truck. It was fun because we were all young and foolish, but it was damn hard work. Okay, so it was going to be donuts, coffee and hamburgers for the summer, but what about the rest? No matter how I tried to add the amounts up, they didn't come out to $117. The $6.00 apparently was supposed to be for gas and oil for an entire *month* and the $5 just didn't exist. Four weeks of food alone at $28 a week was $112. *That only left $5 for everything else.* Obviously I had to drive my car for transportation to and from the theater and it was about as far from being an economy car as you could get. That only meant one thing . . . fewer hamburgers. It really pissed me off this time. What the hell was I supposed to do? I'd already told them the minimum I had to have to stay alive on my own and it wasn't a staggering amount by any means. Then Mother pulls a cheap shot like this and expects me to smile and say "Thank you Mommie dearest for your great generosity." They'd given me a beautiful car. Big deal . . . I couldn't afford the goddamn gasoline for it!

I had to get over being furious with both of them, because it didn't do me any good. I just threw myself into the work at the theater, making new friends and getting as much experience as I could. I started to lose weight and tried not to eat any more than was absolutely necessary. After a few weeks, my stomach began to shrink and I didn't notice being hungry so much.

Westport Country Playhouse was a class act among summer stock theaters. It was the special project of Lawrence Langner and Armina Marshall who ran the prestigious Theatre Guild in New York. The "green room" was filled with Theatre Guild posters going back thirty years or more, a chronicle of Broadway success. The Langners had an estate in Westport and spent many weekends there, generally overseeing the theater's operations and coming to most opening nights. They worked on the star system. The shows were packaged in New York, rehearsing in the city and then opening in Westport before going on to other theaters for their six-week run in other parts of New England. Sometimes the theater would book other packages already on tour, but most of our shows opened in Westport. Because it was so accessible to New York City, Westport Country Playhouse got the best shows of the summer stock season. Everyone wanted to play Westport because of the reviewers and the civilized atmosphere of the quaint town.

There were about ten of us apprentices that summer. We were a varied group, mostly from New York. None of us started out with many useful talents, so the first few weeks were devoted to sorting out the total incompetents and training the rest of us in a crash course of practical theater before the season opened.

The person basically responsible for assigning apprentice jobs and making sure the jobs were completed was the property mistress, Mickey Mackay. There was also a master carpenter, gruff old Bill McGraw and a master electrician from the city, but the job of theater mother fell to Mickey. Her prop room became the general gathering place for all of us who reported to her every morning for our assignments. She was the fountain of information, assistance, consolation and generally our guardian angel. She trained and molded us into a crew . . . she advised us on problems and she interceded with management when the shit hit the fan. She worked like a Trojan and we followed suit. She was also a terrific woman. She'd been around theater most of her life and knew just about everyone. She'd learned to pace herself without ever getting lazy and she'd managed to deal with the temperament of stars, directors and summer stock with good humor and professionalism. She was a good friend to all of us.

At first I was an anomaly to the rest of the group. I had a flashy sports car and no money. I was a movie star's daughter who didn't complain about having to pick up cigarette butts from the theater grounds or clean out the johns. I knew hard work and I worked hard but I was essentially shy which translated initially into snobbery. People just couldn't figure me out.

Fortunately, that only lasted a week or so. After that everybody had too much work to do to spend any extra energy worrying about someone else. We ate at the little hamburger stand within walking distance from the theater and most of the time we slept on couches in the prop room. In the morning, I would stop at a donut shop out on the road from Norwalk to Westport and pick up fresh glazed donuts and several containers of coffee. Once at the theater we had about a half hour to talk before the days work began. From then until late at night, we worked.

I liked it. Each week there was a new show with different people and different problems. Inevitably there were proper changes once the show arrived for dress rehearsal, and everybody scurried in ten different directions until opening night. Closing nights, which were always Saturday, we worked until the old set was taken down and the new one up. Many was the weekend we worked two days straight without any more sleep than a brief nap on one of the old prop room couches. Then you could walk into the prop room and find bodies wall to wall.

If we had a relatively slow week, Mickey would get permission to use the Langner's pool and we'd all troop over there for a swim. The grounds of the estate were beautiful and the pool was built like a natural pond with an island in the middle of it. Once in a while Armina would come out on the lawn to inquire about how we were all holding up, but that was the most we saw of her.

A few weeks into the season I met Frank Perry. Frank worked for the Theatre Guild in New York, but he was from Westport and had been on staff at the theater in years past. He and Mickey were friends for years, so when I first met him it was because he came by the prop room to see Mickey.

Frank (who was to direct the film version of *Mommie Dearest* twenty-three years later) had the nickname of "Big Daddy" in those days, partly because he was somewhat overweight but mostly because of his way of taking people under his wing and becoming their mentor. We took to one another immediately and Frank became an important influence in my emerging life. He took the time to talk with me about the world that I aspired to work in, he helped me through the ups and downs of that entire summer. I looked forward to his weekend visits to the theater and our long talks sitting in the darkened theater wings before the evening performance. For me it wasn't a romantic relationship but much more like having a wonderful older brother rather than a boyfriend. We didn't go out, we didn't date. We talked and talked and talked. Frank sort of guided me through the maze of my initiation into adulthood, having to make decisions about real life for the first time. I was in a terrific hurry that summer and Frank talked some sense into my scattered plans for the future.

June 29, 1957

Christina dear,

I am enclosing your passport. Please take it to the State Motor Vehicle Department to verify your date of birth for your driver's license. Please, under no circumstances, leave this around. Send it to Faith Harrison in the enclosed addressed envelope. Take it to the post office, dear, and send it by registered mail. Buy some brown tape to seal it, as the post office will not accept it with Scotch tape on it.

Yesterday I sent you several of your dresses and some of your costume jewelry that was left here. You can have the skirt shortened on your graduation dress—then you can get some use out of it.

It would be nice if you would let us hear from you from time to time, and tell us whether you are still at Westport. We are twice as busy as you are. So get with it, gal.

Love,
Mommie

P.S. Tina, dear, I'm enclosing tape for you.
Aunt Betty

Mother and Daddy were in Los Angeles, and Mother was going through the house at 426 North Bristol getting it ready to be put up for sale later in the summer. I was terribly sad about the house being sold because it sort of signaled the end of my own ties to California. I liked the East and I particularly liked what I had seen of New England. It was lush and green. The old houses fascinated me and I felt very comfortable in my new surroundings. But I was still sad that the place of my childhood was going to strangers now.

Probably because I didn't ever have enough to eat, was working hard and kept such late hours after the work was over, I started getting sick. At first I got impetigo . . . which is an ugly, itchy skin rash that children often get from dirty sand boxes. I got it from the constant grime at the theater. I went to the local doctor and he prescribed treatment, but it lingered for nearly a month. It didn't do much more damage though than slowing me down a bit and hurting my ego because it was more unattractive than it was dangerous.

About a week after the previous letter, my second and last letter of the summer arrived from Mother who was still in Los Angeles.

July 5, 1957

Tina darling,

We loved your sweet wire wishing us a happy fourth of July, now please write us a letter and let us know whether or not you received your passport, and have sent it to Faith Harrison by now.

Your Daddy and I will be leaving here on the 11th and will be in New York on the 14th.

We hope your Fourth of July was a happy one. Be a good girl and let us hear from you soon.

Love,

"*Mommie*"

I'd returned the passport to Faith, Mother's secretary in New York already. My driver's license was in order.

I also had to laugh at the fact that Mother was still talking Daddy into taking the train from L.A. to New York instead of flying. It may have been a needed rest for him, but I could just imagine the conversations that preceded it. I guess she only flew now when it was directly connected to those short trips on Pepsi business and the rest of the time she got her way, which was trains or boats. I remember that Daddy had commuted to London every two weeks during the time she was shooting *The Story of Esther Costello* there. Good thing for her that Daddy wasn't so squeamish about airplanes.

Carnegie Tech required that all freshman drama students be individually invited to return for their sophomore year. After that it was generally clear sailing unless the student themselves flunked out. I spoke to Mickey Coburn several times during the early part of the summer to find out if she'd heard yet. We both discovered we'd been invited to return at about the same time. But shortly afterwards, I found out that a number of others hadn't been asked back. One girl took it so badly that she killed herself; she threw herself in front of an express subway train and was killed almost instantly. I was horrified by the news. She had not been a close friend of mine, but I knew her from the many classes we had together. I was stunned by the fact that she'd put such importance into the school and been so depressed by their rejection that she'd even think of killing herself, much less actually *do* it. I had to sit by myself a long time and just think about it. She was the first person I'd known even relatively well who had died. That she committed suicide at only nineteen years old really shocked me. I thought back over my own life and all the troubles I'd had. I could understand how she felt, but I couldn't understand why she'd kill herself over such a thing. Then I realized that for her, this must have been the worst thing that had ever happened to her and she didn't see any way to cope with the shame she felt. The public failure of not being asked to return was actually worse than flunking out. The sense of shame was rooted in the total rejection of her as a talent, not for her grades as a student. It was like saying she was a failure as a person. Being a failure as a human being and having all your dreams for a career smashed by so authoritarian an entity as a professional institution must have been too much for her to handle.

I was still horrified by the news of her death. I didn't admire a system that held life and death in the simple paperwork of a rejection letter. There was no follow-up counseling and I honestly don't think this girl had any idea that her ambitions were on such shaky ground. So, she killed herself.

Between the suicide and the fact that Allen was not returning the next year, I decided I didn't want to return to Carnegie. I was getting sick of school anyway and I very much wanted to get closer to being on my own . . . having the opportunity to begin getting work or at least being around the people that might eventually hire me.

When Mother and Daddy returned to New York, I called and had a long talk with Mother. I told her that I didn't want to go back to Carnegie, but that I would like to go to a professional two-year school in New York called Neighborhood Playhouse. It had a good reputation and it would be a way to live in the city and begin to look for work as well. Neither she nor Daddy were exactly pleased with my plans, but I tried to point out to them that I'd still be going to school, it would end up costing a little less and I'd have a better chance of getting a job sooner this way. I'd already talked to Mickey about sharing an apartment that fall in the city and she seemed agreeable, which I told Mother. Mother wasn't thrilled with the whole thing, but she said she couldn't force me to go back to college even though she wished that's what I'd do. I pleaded with her to at least let me see if I could get accepted to Neighborhood Playhouse and if I couldn't, then I'd go back to Carnegie for another year. That seemed reasonable enough to her and that was what we did. Of course, I was accepted to the new school and went ahead with my plans to move into New York.

Shortly after our conversation about schools, Mother and Daddy left for a tour of Africa and were gone for the rest of that summer.

I was offered a small part in *Witness for the Prosecution* starring Faye Emerson which would have gotten me into Equity, the stage union, but with Mother and Daddy away I decided I'd better stay at Westport. Later in the summer I was assistant stage manager for the rehearsals of an epic called *Back to Methuselah* with Celeste Home, James Daley and *Michael* directed by Phillip Burton. The production stage manager, Paul Leaf, taught me most of what I immediately needed to know but the first few days in New York rehearsals I mostly got coffee and ran errands. I'd been driving into the city every day for the first week, but the second week I stayed in Frank Perry's apartment in the village. Frank stayed with some friends, but we'd often meet in the evenings. It was my first introduction to the village and I was quite taken with the whole experience. I met and talked with so many other people living on promises and dreams that I thought it must be possible to find one's way through the chaos of New York and come out with a career.

Not long after that play opened, I came down with mononucleosis. I was so sick that I had to spend a couple of days in Norwalk Hospital. It was a most depressing illness, leaving you totally exhausted and devoid of any spirit. Frank visited me in the hospital and brought me Jack Kerouac's book, *On the Road*. When I left the hospital, I was still much too weak to do a full day's work at the theater, so I went back to the inn and rested for about a week.

As the days passed, I got more and more depressed. Part of it was being sick; the other part was a good deal of fear about what my big plans for the future were really going to hold. I was just as scared about moving into the "big apple" as any other nineteen-year-old kid ever was. I had about as much knowledge about how the real world worked as if I'd come from a rural farming community in the Midwest. Probably less than that, because except for the last year, I'd been in boarding schools and totally subservient to the rules and regulations set for me, not by me.

I'd found out during the summer at Westport that I really had no idea how to regulate my free time or properly take care of myself. There was, of course, the constant problem of money, but it was more than that. I just didn't know much of anything about the real world. What others took more or less for granted in terms of shared knowledge was a total mystery to me. I found that I had big gaps in my store of information about how things worked and how you went about getting things done. It was the practical side of life that I knew nothing about. It was very difficult for me to admit, as it was hard for me to bring myself to ask the necessary questions fearing that I might look like the fool I often thought myself to be.

My shortcoming in the area of asking questions relegated me to the position of an avid listener. I would listen to others talking about their plans or problems for hours, thinking that possibly I might get the necessary clues I needed for my own progress. It was a very insufficient way to go about life.

Mickey and I took several slow days to go into the city and hunt for apartments. We finally found a one-bedroom apartment on East 58th Street between First Avenue and Sutton Place for $175 a month. It wasn't very big but it was convenient and in a nice building. Neighborhood Playhouse was only five blocks away, so I could walk and Mickey could take the cross-town bus to work. I called Mother's secretary and told her all the details, asking for a check to cover my half of the first and last month's rent, so that we could take the apartment.

I still had my bouts with depression, but at least now they came and went rather than being a constant state. The summer was nearly over and we were involved in doing the little extra things that went into preparing the theater for its winter nap. Henry Jaglom, one of the other apprentices and I had become friends, and he was particularly close to Mickey. I told him that we were moving into New York together at the end of the season, and it was Henry who suggested we all stay in touch. He gave a number of wonderful parties during that winter so we did remain friends.

Mickey and I stayed until the doors of the theater were locked for the last time that season. I'd moved out of the General Putnam Inn the last week of the season and came to stay with her. We made several trips into the city with the pick-up truck used for hauling props and took most of her belongings into the apartment. She didn't have much, but she had a bed, a couple of chairs and some kitchen things. I didn't have anything but my typewriter and a suitcase of clothes. The remainder of my belongings were still in the trunk left at Carnegie in Pittsburgh and wouldn't be sent until the end of September. One of the apprentices lived with his family in New York and offered to lend us a rollaway bed until we could get some furniture and, since the bed was for *me*, I gladly accepted! We made arrangements to pick it up the first day we moved into the city and told him we'd call in advance. Mother had promised me some extra furniture from what she and Daddy had in storage, but they wouldn't be back until after we'd moved into the apartment.

When everything was finished at the theater, Mickey and I drove into Manhattan to begin our new adventure. It was Sunday, about a week after Labor Day and although the sun was bright, you could feel the first hint of fall in the air. Mickey had taken care of all the arrangements for the phone and Con Edison while I'd sat and listened. I didn't have the vaguest idea how one went about getting a phone installed or even who you were supposed to call for the gas and electricity. I was eighteen, but in those areas I was just like a kid.

Since the phone hadn't been installed yet, I walked down Sutton Place about seven blocks to my parent's apartment. I asked the doorman if anyone was home at the Steele apartment. I told him I was their daughter. He called upstairs, but returned shortly with the news that there was no answer on the house phone. I asked him if he had a letter for me, or a note from Mother telling me where my allowance check was. The doorman just looked at me with a blank stare. He didn't know anything about a letter or a note or a check. I just stood there with him for a moment while the information took hold of my brain.

Mother had told me she'd leave a check for me in New York and that it would be waiting for me when I moved into the city. She knew all the dates and we were right on schedule. I sighed and thanked the doorman. As I walked back up Sutton Place to my new apartment I was overcome by this sense of depression all over again. I was tired and hungry and I didn't have any money . . . maybe a dollar in change . . . and I was so sick of having to beg for every single thing from my mother and father. They had plenty of money, damn it. They were always going to the most expensive restaurants, staying in the most expensive hotels, buying the most expensive clothes and my mother had just gotten a completely new set of diamonds including necklace, bracelet, earrings, pin and massive wedding ring . . . but they wouldn't give me enough money to stay alive.

I just felt wave after wave of depression rolling over me. It wasn't like sorrow, it wasn't like feeling bad and crying and then feeling better. It was like some unseen force was draining all the hope and the energy out of your body. It was like being so tired you could hardly move or even think. I'd never experienced this kind of thing before and it was very upsetting.

Analysis, Freudian analysis, was *the* thing in New York, and I seriously thought that if this depression lasted much longer, I was going to have to find out about analysis. But when I discovered how much it cost per hour, it was the first good laugh I'd had in some time. I didn't have enough money for food, never mind analysis.

Anyway, Mickey and I between us had about three dollars that first Sunday. We went around to the corner store and got a can of Dinty Moore beef stew, some English muffins and instant coffee. That combined with the odds and ends from her Westport refrigerator, was all we had to eat for the next few days.

Monday morning I called Daddy's secretary at Pepsi. I went through my story again and asked if she had any idea where the check was. She didn't know any more than the doorman had the day before, but she very kindly offered to lend me $50 until she could wire Mother and Daddy in Africa. It would probably take a couple days to catch up with them, she said, and for them to reply. I asked her to wire them, but I'd call back. We still didn't have a phone yet, so that was all I could do.

Mickey borrowed some money from her friends, and with that she bought some more food but her borrowed money didn't do my situation a hell of a lot of good. By now nearly a week had gone by and I was in a state of rage. "Mommie dearest" and Daddy were off on a safari somewhere in Africa and she'd simply forgotten to provide me any money. I could understand her being off having a good time, what I couldn't understand was why in the world she hadn't made some arrangement with the secretary or the bank or someone for me. I was totally stranded in New York City without a dime to my name, because as so often in the past, my mother had simply forgotten me. She never forgot the slightest infraction of any of her rules, she never forgot to pester me about the stupid thank-you notes, but when it came to sending me enough money to live on, she forgot with a consistency that was astonishing.

The first night we were in New York, we'd picked up the rollaway bed for me. Mickey had made one last trip with the pick-up truck and we managed to get it up to the apartment by ourselves. Fortunately, we were still in jeans because it was kind of a dirty job moving all the stuff.

I started Neighborhood Playhouse about a week later. I walked to school that first day, not knowing a soul and wondering what it was going to be like. To my surprise, I met Jim Frawley in the hall. He'd also transferred from Carnegie and I was delighted to see one familiar face.

The routine of the school was quite different from college. There were no academic subjects. All the classes were geared to a professional training program, including voice, several dancing classes and two acting classes. I knew right away that I didn't like the dance classes, but I managed to struggle through them with the rest of the novices.

The first new friends I made were Betsy Farley and Eddie Garrabrandt. Betsy was lovely and we had a lot of classes together. Eddie was a bundle of energy and great fun. He talked enough for both of us, which was just fine with me because I was continually battling my shyness in new groups of people.

Mother and Daddy returned to New York toward the end of September from a side trip to Washington, D.C. I'd spoken to Mother several times on the phone and she'd arranged to send over some furniture we desperately needed.

One day when I got home from school, the man from the storage company was there arranging two small couches and a glass-top table with four chairs. The furniture was simple and modern. The colors were green and yellow. Mickey was standing in the middle of the room with a horrified look on her face. There was another man tacking up a trellis of fake, plastic ivy to one wall! She came over to me and said that I had to do something immediately . . . I had to *stop* the plastic ivy man right away. I nearly laughed right out loud, but she was so serious that I didn't dare. I went to the man and asked him to take down all the ivy he'd attached so far. He replied in a disdainful tone of voice that Miss Crawford had ordered it. I told him that I didn't care *what* "Miss Crawford" had ordered, he was to stop with the ivy immediately. Mickey sat down in a state of shock on the far side of the room. I went to the phone and called Mother.

When I reached Mother, I thanked her for the nice furniture and then told her that I didn't think we'd really be needing the ivy on the walls. I told her that our apartment was just too small, but thanked her for the extra thoughtfulness.

To my surprise, she was really angry with me! She said it had cost money to have the man spend that time. I tried to explain that we hadn't talked about any ivy and that I was sorry she'd gone to any extra expense, but it just wouldn't look right in the apartment. I didn't tell her that Mickey was probably thinking about moving to a place of her own at this very moment, and that if the ivy didn't go . . . Mickey would. Mother was very nasty with me and threw in some choice phrases about my lack of taste or sense of design or something like that. I didn't want any argument with her and I just took the abuse and tried to be calm about the whole thing.

The ivy man flounced out in a huff, trailing his plastic leaves behind him and slamming the door dramatically.

I turned to Mickey and started to laugh. She was still sitting in the same chair, eyeing the chaos with which she'd become surrounded. I apologized for the plastic ivy and said that sometimes I really wondered about my mother's good taste. Mickey was very New York, very New England. She liked old wood and antiques and pottery from Bennington. She did not like California plastic and bright colors and modern glass furniture. She did not like most of the furniture we'd been sent, but she could live with that, and was just as glad as I was to have something other than empty space. What she could not tolerate at all was plastic ivy climbing all over the walls. Eventually we both laughed about it, but she was not overly fond of Mother trying to impose her will over the two of us, particularly inside our apartment.

Mickey was five or six years older than me and she'd been on her own for quite a while. To her I was just a baby, but she was gentle and understanding about the areas of my emotional immaturity. What she was never going to understand about was the plastic ivy. I couldn't say I blamed her much, but I probably would have let it go, just to avoid any semblance of a confrontation with my mother. I would have just lived with the ivy and hated it every time I looked at it and wished I could stand up for myself better than I did.

A few days after the ivy incident, we had this letter hand delivered by the chauffeur.

September 23, 1957

Christina dear,

I am enclosing an item from Dorothy Kilgallen's column tonight. What do you think this makes us sound like?

When you go to school tomorrow, take the dirty blue jeans off, take a bath, and dress properly. Blue jeans are only to be worn when you paint, and not when you leave the house. You must take a bath every day, Christina, and wash you underwear every night—and *all* of it!

(The next sentence and the signature were handwritten, but by Betty Barker, not my mother.)

Dress for Neighborhood Playhouse tomorrow as if you were going to a premiere.

Mommie

The item in Dorothy Kilgallen's column was some innocuous two-liner about the bed moving incident when I first moved into New York. I don't know how she found out about it and I don't know why she chose to print it. It simply said that I'd been seen moving a bed in blue jeans.

As for *"What do you think this makes us sound like?"* if it hadn't been so serious on her part, it would have made me laugh. I was just doing the best I could to take care of myself without the benefit of any help from my family and without benefit of any money. I guess it made them sound like just what they were. Maybe *that* was what really made her so mad.

The item in the column was filler bullshit, drivel, nonsense. It didn't mean anything, really. It was the kind of stuff that columnists have always done, will continue doing as long as there's space to be filled in the papers. Of all the people in the entire business, Joan Crawford knew that better than anyone else. It had been her stock in trade for more than thirty years! But when it came to me, she took the attitude that somehow I'd been responsible for making them, particularly her, look bad. That I'd done it all with premeditation, that I'd done it on purpose.

It was useless trying to explain the simple fact that I had to have something to sleep on and that I'd been left without a dollar to my name because *she* neglected to leave my allowance check with anyone before she blithely took off for Africa! Now *that* was the truth. If the truth caused her a bit of momentary discomfort, if the truth bruised her carefully manicured public image, if the truth jarred her ego so easily, well then I couldn't be expected to take the blame.

But that wasn't her view of it at all. She believed that I had intentionally shamed the movie star and the chairman of the board. She never thought about the rest of it. She never once apologized for her own total lack of concern for my safety or well-being. She never once asked me how I'd managed to eat or how I liked sleeping on the floor. All she cared about was how it would look to others . . . what strangers and the fans might think. At any cost, the image must be maintained intact and that took precedent over the truth any day.

The rest of the letter degenerated into cruelty and insult. It hurt me. When she said things like that, it really hurt me. It was gutter talk without swear words. It was trash from the foul pits of her own mind. It was garbage talk she didn't have the courage to say to my face. She didn't even have the courtesy to call me on the phone and discuss it with me. She was living right in New York, less than seven blocks away from me and she didn't have the guts to talk to me. Instead she dictated these scathing chicken shit notes, and had the chauffeur deliver them. She even had the gall to add the last stupid line about dressing for school like I was going to a premiere, of all things, and make the secretary try to copy her handwriting. It was insanity. It was all just insanity!

I was getting so fed up with all of it. I was getting fed up with having to put up with these insults and tirades against me. She had no right to insult me like this. I had done nothing except try to take care of myself the best I could. She didn't give a shit about me . . . all she cared about was herself and her precious image.

I was so mad I didn't know what to do. I felt like throwing all the furniture right out the window. I felt like smashing the glass-top table into smithereens. I felt like going over to that apartment and punching her right in her dirty mouth.

The pathetic thing about all this is that she was still giving me $117 dollars a month allowance. With that I had to pay half the rent and half the other bills. Of course, it didn't stretch that far. Of course it meant that I *never* had any money left for food. Of course it meant that I was always in a chronic state of poverty. If it hadn't been for Mickey, I would have collapsed from sheer malnutrition. No matter how I pleaded, no matter how many times I explained the numbers, she still persisted in sending a check for $117.

Then she had the *nerve* to criticize me for having the initiative to find a bed to sleep on and the energy to move it, practically alone, so that I wouldn't have to sleep on the floor. Well, she could take her tirade about the jeans and the stunning edict about going to school dressed for a premiere and shove it!

I showed Mickey the letter. She was appalled and I was in tears. After we talked for a while, I decided not to answer it right away. I figured I'd be sorry later for what I said in anger now. I tried to swallow my rage and all that happened was that I became monstrously depressed again. I didn't go to school for the next two days. I called in sick and they believed me. I sat in the apartment and stared at the walls. I stared out the window onto the 59th Street bridge and wrote bleak, depressing poetry.

A few days later I finally called her and subserviently apologized for the incident with the blue jeans. I told her it was not intended to do anyone any harm, and I never thought such a trivial thing would make the newspapers.

I did not admire myself for being so weak and not standing up to her, but that was what I did. I was so scared of getting into more trouble when I was still totally dependent on the crumbs she threw me and the miserly allowance I managed to squeeze out of her that I dared not stray very far from subservience. In fact, I was so afraid of doing something wrong, something that would rekindle her wrath that all I did the first couple months I was in New York was walk to and from school. It was like I was still in the convent and prohibited from doing anything but go to school and come directly back to the apartment. I never explored the rest of the city. I never went to the movies. I never took a walk in Central Park. I just tread the trail down First Avenue from 58th to Neighborhood Playhouse . . . five blocks away.

The entire time I was depressed. I don't know whether that was from lack of food or whether the entire situation was beginning to be too much for me to handle, but I was continually depressed and feeling helpless.

That weekend she invited me over. Mother didn't like me to wear pants, particularly when I came to see her. I could never just dress casually and drop by the apartment to visit my own parents. I was supposed to dress nicely and I had to be specifically invited to appear. Mother didn't like surprises of any kind. She preferred to have life ordered and well arranged. We had to be invited for a visit, arrive at the specific time she indicated would be convenient for her and stay only as long as she decided was appropriate. It was all very formal. It was usually very strained. The conversation revolved around her. What she was doing, how she was feeling, what she was interested in. Most of the time there was also something she wanted that she couldn't get anyone else to do right away.

October 3, 1957

Tina darling,

I hate to bring up this subject, but I must sit down and go over your wardrobe with you. The other day you looked halfway decent in black, except for that horrible printed blouse. Yesterday I have never seen anything like that brown and white checked skirt, much too tight on you, and that charcoal sweater that Marlon Brando I am sure would have thrown away three years ago.

I know that I have given you many sweater and skirt outfits that are not only matching but have some color and line to them. I know too that probably your winter clothes are still at Carnegie Tech. When are they due to arrive here? If not this week, let me know, and I will send for them by plane, and help you go over your winter wardrobe, and help you pack your summer wardrobe for storage.

If you haven't any self-respect or pride for yourself, at least try and have it for the family tradition of being well-groomed. I have had several people call me to see if you would go on television, but under no circumstances, unless I supervise the clothes, the questions, and the hair.

Your wardrobe must be gone over before I leave for the Coast Thursday. I am going to get rid of those horrible outfits you have been wearing, and give them to the Salvation Army, but I am afraid not even they will wear them, but they'll put them to some use.

I love you very much, and you are a very beautiful young woman, but for heaven's sake, dress from the head down rather than from the lipstick up.

Please call me on this. Let's not be angry about it. Let's just discuss it as gal to gal. It's a very serious matter.

"Mommie"

This letter too was hand delivered by the chauffeur. She didn't call me on the phone. She preferred the insults to be written. As for the "wardrobe" she referred to, it was a total joke. I had three semi-winter skirts and matching sweaters that she'd given me the year before to go to college. One was black, one was baby blue and the other one was *pink*. They may have been all right for Southern California or Florida but they were laughable in New York. The rest of the "wardrobe" consisted of cocktail dresses and a couple of dressy suits she'd bought me *two* years ago when we went to Europe! That was the extent of the supposed wardrobe. Most of it was suitable only for going out to dinner with *her*. It bore no resemblance to what I needed for school, for cold weather, for the life I led. I had never been allowed to pick any of it, I had never been given any money to buy new winter clothes for this year in New York, I had never been given anything to supplement the few outfits which were technically usable but in which I wouldn't be caught dead. I'd far rather have looked like "Marlon Brando" than Betty Boop!

She wasn't offering any money for new clothes. She wasn't offering to let me go out and choose something more appropriate. She wasn't offering *anything*. I wondered seriously where her head was. If she thought about it at all where did she get these ideas? Was it just that they sounded good on paper?

I gave up trying to figure her out a long time ago, but it was getting *me* totally crazy to have her keep acting like my situation was perfectly normal, that I had all the things I needed to live my life with any kind of sanity and that I was the one who was always fucking up. It was making my whole life seem like some sort of house of mirrors. It was like going into the house of horrors and having things jump out at you. It was just totally nuts and I didn't seem to be able to do anything about it. I didn't seem to be able to deal with it in a way that made things get any better. Everything I did just seemed to make it worse.

Unfortunately about this same time, I really made a blunder. The car I'd been given was now in New York with me. The city had alternate side of the street parking regulations, and I had to go through the hassle of finding a parking spot every day before eight in the morning. One night Mickey and I had gone down to the village to hear some friends of hers who were jazz musicians in one of the little clubs. We'd gotten home late and I must have gotten mixed up about which side of the street was correct for the next day, because when I got home from school the damn car was gone! I was in a panic. At first I thought it must have been stolen, but Mickey said it was probably towed away because I parked it on the wrong side of the street. This was all I needed right now. I started calling the different car pounds. Finally I located it in lower Manhattan at the car impound area near the Brooklyn Bridge. The surly man at the impound area said that it would cost me $50 to get the car out *and* that since it wasn't registered in my name, I'd have to bring the registered owner with me. That was the end. The car was still registered to Alfred N. Steele. I was going to have to call him and try to get this worked out. I knew that my chances of fixing this mess were very slim, however, there was no other way out. By one of those positively weird quirks of fate, the doorbell rang at just the same moment I'd gotten the courage to pick up the phone and begin dialing the apartment on Sutton Place. I put the phone down and answered the door. Standing in front of me was John Coleman, a man that worked for Daddy and was a friend as well. I never really figured out what Uncle John really did, I only knew that when there was any kind of trouble, Uncle John usually appeared too. At first I was relieved to see him, thinking that perhaps he'd help me work out the mess I found myself in without my mother finding out and creating a big scene about it. To my horror he told me that the reason he was here was to pick up the keys and the car! Mother had decided, without telling me that I really didn't need the car in New York when all I was doing was going to school. That part was absolutely true, of course, however, the timing was freaky. I stared at Uncle John like a total idiot. I didn't know what to say or how to begin. Finally, there was nothing to do but tell him the truth. And the truth was that my car . . . Daddy's car . . . had been impounded and it would cost $50 and Daddy's personal appearance to get it out! After I finished my sad story, I just sat there waiting for the ceiling to fall in on me.

To my complete surprise, Uncle John was totally sympathetic. He understood immediately about the hassle of street parking in New York. He understood completely about the fine and he was even willing to try and help me. I was awestruck by this unexpected turn of events. He told me that there was a party going on over at the apartment, with lots of people and that he'd try to get Daddy alone and explain to him what had happened. As he was leaving, I told him I was eternally grateful and would do everything I could to expedite the details.

In less than an hour, Uncle John reappeared. By some magical process known only to him, he had a notarized letter from Daddy authorizing him to retrieve the car and a check for $50. Whatever Uncle John did to earn a living, he certainly was good at it!

The two of us took a cab downtown and after what seemed like hours, located the blue Thunderbird, paid the fine and drove off. By now, we were both laughing about the whole thing because that was about all one could do. He told me about the times this same thing had happened to him and how infuriating it was. I was really deeply grateful for both his sense of humor and his matter of fact attitude about something I'd considered nearly the end of the world.

He said he'd simply have the car parked in the 36 Sutton Place apartment garage where it had been until I got it and give the keys to Daddy. No one had to know anything about the incident and nothing more need be said about it. I gave Uncle John a big hug when he stopped to let me off in front of my apartment building and thanked him all over again. Uncle John was not at all prone to showing emotion, but he was kind enough to treat me just as though I was his own daughter. He told me not to worry anymore.

I fairly skipped through the hall and into the elevator. For once . . . for once the world didn't come to an end just because I'd made a mistake. Daddy wasn't mad at me either. In fact, Uncle John said he'd kind of laughed when John told him about the predicament I'd gotten into and how upset I was about it.

However, I hadn't been inside the apartment half an hour when the phone rang. It was my mother, in a rage. She'd found out about the whole thing because she wanted to know why John had been gone for over three hours when I lived only minutes away. I guess no one thought she'd make such a big deal of it since it was already fixed and there was an apartment full of people. They vastly underrated Mother. This was just the kind of situation she excelled in, this was just the sort of ammunition she used to the fullest. She went on and on over the phone about how irresponsible I was and how I couldn't be trusted. She then asked my why I hadn't put the car in a garage? I was dumbfounded by the question. All I could think to reply was that I couldn't afford $60 a month for a parking garage. "You should have asked me for the money," she said coldly.

I couldn't believe it. First of all, if she wouldn't give me enough money for food, enough money for winter boots . . . what in the world would ever have lead me to believe that she'd give me money for a garage? Secondly, the apartment they lived in had a garage and she never once mentioned it . . . she never once offered it . . . she never once gave it a thought until this very minute.

She then told me that she was taking the car away from me. I was relieved and glad to see the damn thing go. I didn't have the money for gasoline. I was sick and tired of trying to find parking places every day and I'd actually grown to hate the sight of that car. It was one of those situations where Mother and Daddy could get behind how wonderful and generous they were, what good parents they were, how fortunate a daughter I was . . . and the whole thing got turned around and used against me. They'd given me this huge present . . . they'd given me a car, something they did not want, and somehow that obliterated the need for anything further. Their generosity was established and I was the ungrateful, incompetent one. So, let them take the damn thing away. All I felt was . . . good riddance.

But things had their usual way of changing and not too long after that Mother told me that she'd accepted an appearance on the Jack Paar

Show for me. She told me what to wear and had the show send over all the questions I'd be asked. She made Jack Paar himself promise her that he wouldn't ask for any extemporaneous answers and then she coached me on what I was to say in response. The show was live in the East and delayed broadcast on the West Coast. Mother and Daddy would be in Los Angeles the night I was supposed to appear, but they'd be watching.

I didn't particularly want to do the show because it was some stupid segment that guessed who people were . . . I was going on as the daughter of a famous person. I didn't particularly like that part but I was so eager to begin a professional career that I swallowed my pride and did the show.

I was very nervous. I'd never done a live TV show . . . I'd never done anything professional at all. I'd been so thoroughly rehearsed that I'd memorized all the answers perfectly. I knew how to learn lines by then, and everything went smoothly. I even made a new friend. The NBC producer on the show was a young guy named David Sontag and he was so genuinely kind to me that night we became friends and saw each other for years afterwards.

After the Jack Paar Show was over and I was on my way home again, I realized for the first time that I'd made a fundamental personal error; one that was to haunt me over and over again during my professional career. I had no real credentials at all. I was on that program only as an extension of my mother. I was a movie star's daughter . . . one of the first of my generation and background to move into the public eye as an aspiring actress. I was a novelty, a curiosity. It was the old "What's it like to be a movie star's daughter?" routine again. The questions were about Mother, about Joan Crawford, not about me. I was standing in for her . . . I was important only by association and not because of myself.

Nobody had asked me anything about what I was doing or what I wanted that wasn't related always back to Mother. Was she helping me . . . was I following in her footsteps . . . what was it like growing up in Hollywood.

That was the first of those questions, but down through the years I came to know the pattern so well I could anticipate them long in advance. That was the first time I knew I'd been used and wasn't going to get anything but grief out of it. That was the first time I felt the monstrous lie I was telling in public by not being able to ever tell the truth. It was one of those awful trade-offs you make when you think that you'll be able to deal with the betrayal of your own value system later, but for now you'll do what has to be done to get ahead. The problem is that you never get to "later." The lies are always now, and have to be lived with in the present. The feeling about yourself, your own self-respect is always now, not later.

Mother and Betty both sent telegrams of congratulations. My TV debut was a "success."

Tina darling you were wonderful see you soon *"Mommie"*

Tina dear you were enchanting and divine on your television debut I adored seeing you and you looked lovely so poised and a great credit to your proud mother.
Love
Aunt Betty

I sure was a credit to Mother . . . I spoke only when spoken to, I said all the publicly right things, I was dressed in one of those outfits ordered for our European trip and there was nothing of me in that show except my physical presence.

I felt like I was a perfectly programmed automaton. There really was no Christina at all . . . there was just "Joan Crawford's daughter."

Up until that time, most of the other students at school didn't associate me with my famous parents because I never said anything about it and the name Crawford isn't uncommon. After I did the Jack Paar Show, I could see the attitudes of many change. I really hated what being known as "Joan Crawford's daughter" did to people. Suddenly they stared at me or became uncomfortable around me. It was not the old days of the elementary school kids wanting autographs and then disappearing. It was my peers, people who wanted the same thing I wanted, who had the same dreams and ambitions I had that suddenly related to me in all kinds of funny ways. It was as though the information alone changed something about me, something about the human being, something fundamental. It wasn't true of course, I was the same person the day after the show as I had been the day before. They were the ones who went through the changes. It was their fantasy about the information

that changed, not me. But because of it, I had to deal with them differently. I had to somehow reassure them that I wasn't a snob, that I wanted
to be friends, that I had to struggle just as hard as they did to get where I
wanted to go. All that was very hard for strangers to believe. The fantasy
was that I was being helped, that I had everything I could possibly need.
If I didn't quite fit the image then it was attributed to the fact that "slumming" must be chic. Thank god for Eddie. Somehow he understood, and
never changed a bit. If anything we became better friends. If anything
it opened the whole thing up and allowed us to talk about it. Then we
dropped the subject and continued being friends.

That fall I also appeared on the Arlene Francis morning talk show,
but Arlene was a very gracious lady and I thoroughly enjoyed myself.
She had a way of making everyone feel not just comfortable but welcome and special. After the show, she wrote me a very sweet note which
Mother forwarded to me.

November 4, 1957

Christina darling,
      Thank you for your wonderful letter. I was so proud of you on
the television show, and your letter was delightful.
      I'm enclosing your monthly allowance check, which is due on
November 15th.
      We send much love to you, my darling, and we will see you
very soon. We will be in New York tomorrow.
      God bless,
      Mommie

The house on Bristol was finally being sold to Donald O'Connor. Mother
said she was only getting $150,000 for it, but that was better than having
to keep paying upkeep and taxes. They were going to let the 36 Sutton
Place apartment go as well because Mother and Daddy had bought a
sixteen-room penthouse condominium on 70th and Fifth Avenue. Not
only had they bought this giant duplex overlooking Central Park in
the most expensive neighborhood the city had to offer, but they were
in the process of tearing the two floors down to the steel beams and
completely rebuilding. The apartment was redesigned. Where sixteen
normal rooms had previously existed on the two floors, there were now

going to be eight gigantic ones. Where walls had once stood there were to be huge windows and a panoramic park view. Where four bedrooms had existed, there were now going to be only two . . . one for her and one for him.

In this huge apartment they were only building accommodations for two people plus a small cubicle downstairs for a maid.

In the late fall of 1957, Joan Crawford and Alfred Steele had between them *five* children ages 18 and younger. She had the twins who were almost 11, a son 14, I was 18 and Mr. Steele had a son by his previous marriage. The architectural plans for the rebuilding of the duplex apartment at 2 East 70th Street called for two master bedrooms, two master baths and a maid's room. The cost of rebuilding this apartment and filling it with brand new furniture designed by William Haines, shipped from California and hauled up through the windows by giant cranes, was over $500,000. In fact, before it was all over, the delays and unexpected problems caused the price tag to inch dangerously close to one million dollars.

Construction went on for months and months, causing the other tenants in the building to complain and finally to try to sue the Steeles for completely disrupting the entire lifestyle of the other owners. There were numerous fights with the people who owned the apartments directly below. The constant hammering and pounding and heavy equipment tore at people's nerves and strained their patience.

When it was finally finished after more than six months of construction, my visiting sisters had to sleep on plastic covered couches in the den or at the Barbizon Hotel for women. This $500,000 tribute to success was designed to accommodate one person . . . my mother. Her pink and white bedroom was the larger of the two and her bath, dressing room and closets took twice the room allotted her husband.

Downstairs, the entire living room, den and dining room areas were done in white, yellow and green. There was nothing reflecting my father except a chess set and some carved ivory figures in a bookcase. The floors were polished to a dangerously slippery shine and where rugs existed, they were snow white. *All* the furniture was covered with fitted, heavy plastic that stuck to your clothes in the summer time. No one was allowed to wear shoes in the apartment, because Mother didn't want the white rugs getting soiled. Walking over those glassy, slippery floors in stocking feet was enough to get you permanently disfigured and before word got out in New York, many an unsuspecting guest was humiliated by smelly feet or a hole in their sock.

I had seen the apartment in its various stages of construction, but when I saw it's finished state, I was shocked. At first glance it was spectacular . . . the space and the view were unexcelled in Manhattan. But it was categorically the most uncomfortable, the most inhospitable, the coldest place I've ever been in. There was something totally barren about it. There wasn't one chair really comfortable to sit in and the plastic covers on all the upholstered furniture became clammy from the constant air conditioning. Everything was sealed up . . . the windows, the furniture, reality. In addition, Mother kept it so *cold* in there both winter and summer that it was like visiting a goddamn morgue! It was freezing in that place and everywhere you sat the plastic crinkled and stuck to you. It was really awful. There were none of the beautiful antiques from the California house, none of the old paintings. Everything was new and starkly modern and plastic. Even the flowers and plants were plastic! With all those windows and all that light, all the green plants in the rooms were plastic. Mother preferred them because they could be washed with soap and water and they didn't have any dirt.

When guests came for the first time, Mother always gave them the grand tour. She also showed them all of her closets. She'd proudly open the rows of mirrored doors and show off her endless racks of clothes, floor to ceiling, each garment carefully covered with plastic. She showed them an entire closet full of matching, custom-made shoes and handbags. Then there was another closet just for her hats. I always felt like I was back looking at Shirley Temple's costumes, but everyone else seemed most impressed.

Mother and Daddy spent the winter of 1957 at the Plaza Hotel on Central Park South while they waited for their apartment to be finished. They were still traveling a great deal. The beginning of November they were in Washington, D.C. and then went out to California for Thanksgiving with my sisters and brother.

I spent Thanksgiving with Mickey and her mother in Westport, Connecticut.

When they returned from California I was invited to have lunch with them at "21." I was to meet them at the restaurant because Daddy would be coming from the office and Mother had errands to run before lunch.

The meal was pleasant enough, with all the usual commotion over Mother and Daddy even though they went there many times a week. After lunch, Mother and I went to the ladies' room as usual. Just before leaving she looked in her purse and discovered she didn't have a one dollar bill to leave as a tip. Everyone else left quarters, but Mother usually gave the woman a dollar which of course ensured a big welcome the next time. Only this time Mother didn't have any singles with her. So she asked me to leave a dollar for the ladies' room attendant. Before she departed, I whispered to her that all I had was one dollar. She patted me on the shoulder and said Daddy would reimburse me. She'd said it loud enough that the lady was smiling at me, waiting almost with her hand out.

Long before I bothered to look in my own wallet, I knew that all I had was one dollar. I'd taken the bus from my apartment to the restaurant and intended to take the bus back. All I had in the wallet was a one dollar bill and some pennies, that's all the money I had. But, I thought, Mother did say that Daddy would give it back to me, so I'd be okay. I sort of grudgingly gave the woman her dollar and she, of course, said, "Thank you, Miss Crawford . . . you know your mother's a wonderful person . . . she's my favorite movie star." I smiled weakly, seeing her swiftly pocket my last dollar and left to join Mother and Daddy in the lobby.

They had their coats on already and were preparing to leave. Mother had just recently gotten a new mink which everyone looked at and Daddy was just putting on his hat. I got my own coat and caught up with them at the door to the limousine. I expected Daddy to give me the dollar in the car. But did I have a surprise in store for me. Mother was already in the car, Daddy was just shutting the door as Mother waved goodbye saying how nice it was to see me again, just like I was a fan or something. It happened so fast, I never got a chance to say one word. My heart sank as I watched the big black limousine pull away into traffic. The wind was blowing and it was cold. It looked as though it would begin snowing any minute now. I pulled my coat around me. The restaurant doorman asked politely if he could get me a cab. I turned to face him and managed to say nonchalantly, "Oh, no thanks. I think I'll walk." He looked at me like I was a bit strange, but off I went in the opposite direction.

It was a *long* walk across town from 52nd and Fifth Avenue to 58th Street and First Avenue. The wind was howling. People were hurrying alongside the buildings trying to get to their destinations as fast as possible. I was freezing cold. Every step I took I got angrier. How could they be so bloody cavalier? How could anyone be so unthinking, so mean as to take my last dollar and then not even offer me a ride home? How did she think I was going to get anywhere . . . fly? What was I supposed to do . . . wave a magic wand and will myself across town? I bet she never said a word to Daddy, either. I bet she just went out there to the lobby like a grand lady, allowed one of the men to drape her new mink coat around her shoulders and pranced out of the restaurant to the waiting limousine without a backward glance . . . or thought. It did start snowing before I reached the apartment. The walk had taken the better part of an hour and I didn't even have boots on that day because I was supposed to get dressed up. It's a wonder I didn't catch pneumonia or fall and break my neck walking through the freezing cold in high heel shoes. I was totally numb by the time I walked into the apartment. I took off my clothes and filled up the bathtub with hot water. I sat in the hot tub until I stopped shivering and then drank some hot tea. I did get a cold, but fortunately it was nothing worse than that.

Because it was a professional school, Neighborhood Playhouse didn't really have a Christmas vacation. We got about two weeks from just before Christmas until a few days past New Years.

I was doing all right at the school, but I wasn't in love with the place. My acting class with Sandy Meisner was going very well. I think it had to do with the fact that I'd already had most of the basics the year before at Carnegie, I'd already been in a number of plays and learned to handle myself at least adequately on stage. Sandy's criticism after scenes could be brutal, but he never landed hard on me. In fact I liked him and I didn't mind the sarcasm as much as some of the other students did. Of course, it was probably a little easier for me because I was rarely the brunt of his humor.

What I hated and detested was Martha Graham's modern dance class. At first I'd been rather in awe of her just like everyone else in school. She was famous all over the world and it was a great privilege to be able to study with her. But I grew to hate that class with a passion. Miss Graham would go around to each student in class while they were in the middle of trying to do one of the contortionist exercises and she had a miserable habit of slapping whatever part of ones' anatomy that wasn't performing correctly. She also made very personal remarks to both the men and women on the construction of their individual bodies. It was very embarrassing for everyone. We all blushed crimson when she singled us out individually. What made it ten times worse was that one whole wall of the dance room was mirrored, and Martha Graham was always right about our various physical flaws . . . those mirrors were staring right back at us. When she came to me she slapped my leg and said I had fat thighs . . . I'd have to get those legs working harder. It was the way she said "fat" that made me want to walk out of that class and never return. Miss Graham was thin as a rail from years of discipline as a professional dancer, what she said always had the ring of total authority. But the way she chose to conduct her classes made me never want to hear her name again. It may have worked with aspiring young dancers, but it had the opposite effect on me. I tried every way in the world to get out of that class, but nothing worked for very long until I decided to cook up a doctor's excuse for the remainder of the year. I still had to sit through the class, but I didn't have to participate in it.

Christmas itself came and went with little fanfare. I saw Mother and Daddy several times for lunch or dinner. They were getting ready to move into their new apartment and didn't have much time left over for anything else.

I got little presents for everyone in the family and delivered them myself. Mother sent nicely wrapped gifts over to me via the chauffeur.

December 30, 1957

Tina darling,
   Your Daddy and I thank you so much for the four beautiful, beautiful linen towels. They are so lovely, and will be so useful in our new apartment.

The twins are delighted with their new piccolos, and you were very sweet to think of them. We are all enchanted with the lovely pictured boxes of matches.

Darling, did you receive the gifts that we sent to you? We haven't heard from you yet, and I was just wondering.

We love you, and hope you are having happy Holidays.

Love,

"Mommie"

It didn't amuse me anymore that Mother wrote me formal thank-you notes when she lived in the same city, less than a dozen blocks away. The stationery was still from the Plaza Hotel, but the return address was 2 East 70th. It didn't amuse me that I had to get all dressed up whenever I was invited to see them and always had to wonder if my clothing would be acceptable. It didn't amuse me to see their palatial apartment, her endless closets of clothes, their $100 lunches and the ever-present limousines while I struggled to feed myself and could never pay all of my monthly bills.

It didn't amuse me that I was summoned to appear when it was convenient for them and forgotten about when it wasn't. It didn't amuse me that Mother would catch some ridiculous item in one of the columns that used my name for added readership value, putting me in places I'd never been with people I'd never met and she'd accuse me of being out all the time and not paying attention to school. It didn't amuse me that *she never* believed me when I told her the columns were just making these thing up, just like she used to tell me the trade papers made things up. She could never separate what she knew to be standard industry practice with everyone else from what she accused me of doing. She knew the restaurants and clubs got their names in the paper through the columnists. They'd find out who was in town, who wanted publicity and then they pair up the name of the restaurant with the names of the people. Whether it was true or not didn't matter, because under normal circumstances no one really got hurt by the small lies. It wasn't considered defamation of character and it was so fleeting in nature that it was forgotten immediately afterwards. No one really paid much attention to any of it except my own mother. She would never believe I had absolutely nothing to do with those stupid newspaper items and would have gladly stopped them if I could.

The irony of the whole thing was that I really wish I had been living such a glamorous, well-fed life! No one knew better than I did how heartily I would have welcomed those dates and that restaurant food. I was really getting nauseous at the sight of Dinty Moore beef stew cans and English muffins, though I started out this winter liking them both very much.

During these holidays I happened to see a Pepsi commercial on television starring Mother with just my two sisters. In the commercial, Mother said that she was here with her family! I didn't know anything about that commercial being done, I'd never been asked to be in it, though I thought I was still a member of the family, and the first I knew was when I saw it on TV. I was furious and felt totally insulted by the whole thing. Several of my friends had also seen the commercial and asked why I wasn't in it too. I had no answer, but I called Mother and told her exactly how I felt, asking why I hadn't been included too, since it was supposed to be a "family" commercial. She was clipped in her reply, but followed our brief conversation with this letter on Plaza Hotel stationery.

January 3, 1958
2 East 70th St.
New York, N.Y.

Christina dear,

Your sweet telegram, wishing us a happy New Year, made us very happy. However, your daddy and I got the sarcasm of "Mr. and Mrs. Alfred N. Steele and Family", particularly after our conversation when you said you feel excluded, because you were not included in the Pepsi-Cola television commercial.

I am going to explain something, and I want you to read this very carefully. Your father had Kenyon and Eckhardt, the agency, do three commercials for the Mary Martin show—Harpo Marx one, the Hans Conreid one, and another one. The third one came off so badly that your father was ashamed to use it. The agency's officials got together in a big conference, and Joe Lieb suggested I do the final commercial. Your father hesitated to ask me, since I was not getting paid for it. When I was told about it, I naturally accepted, because I had seen the three commercials and knew they were desperately in need of a final one.

So they sent for Charles Lang, the photographer, and the twins because of one thing (that I am sure you are not cognizant of). Your father is in a family business, Pepsi-Cola is a family drink—the bottlers all feel they are part of the Pepsi-Cola Family. All last year when we toured the States, and even in Africa, the bottlers all greeted us as friends, and said they were so glad to be a part of the "Family." Even in the "Pepsi-Cola World," the magazine for Pepsi-Cola, they embrace all bottlers' wives and families as the Pepsi-Cola Family. So when I said in the commercial, "I am here with my family," that did not exclude you, because there has been so much publicity that you are now living in your own apartment in New York (and as you know, the commercial was supposedly taken in California). Everyone knows that you are studying drama in New York and that you are on your own. Everyone takes it for granted that children, when they grow up, leave home.

The set designers tried to duplicate the California house the best they could, and everyone (even people who know us and have been in our house in California) thought it was taken in the drawing room in California, and I am sure you did too. As a matter of fact, it was filmed a week beforehand at MPO Studios in New York. If you remember, you came to the Plaza Hotel to see the twins while they were here on the Sunday night of their weekend. We tried to reach you on Thursday, on the Friday of rehearsal, and the Saturday it was filmed, but you had spent that weekend with the Fleuridases, and you were not available. We did not even hear from you until Sunday, and the film had been completed by then.

I want you to know I love you very much. You shouldn't be sarcastic, you shouldn't be envious.

I'm so glad that Dr. Nachtigall made you feel better, and that you are off for a merry weekend. In the future, please call him when you feel ill, because penicillin shots are not the only things needed to cure a cold. What Aunt Bettina tells me you actually said was "All he'll give me is a penicillin shot, and I'll get immune to them."

Now get the chip off your shoulder, the lead out of your heart, and the bitterness out of your soul. And have a wonderful 1958, with joy and love and gratitude. Save your vivid imagination for your acting, and not for daily living.

Love,
Mommie

The logic is difficult to follow, but it was not difficult to understand the result. I was eighteen years old. My brother, who was now having his share of difficulties, was just fourteen but he was over six feet tall. My sisters were almost eleven and still being dressed like little girls. It was not hard to see why a commercial for the "Pepsi generation" was better if it featured a glamorous movie star with her two little girls rather than that same movie star with teenagers who already looked like adults!

As for the rest of it, I could imagine just how hard they tried to reach me. We didn't have an answering service on our phone, but what happened all of a sudden to those hand-delivered notes Mother doled out in the past?

From New York Mother and Daddy went back to Los Angeles to finish the last of the packing and sorting before the house sale was final.

January 6, 1958

Christina dear,

We are sending you a supply of your "Christina" towels and wash cloths, which I am sure you would want in New York.

We sent some things to you yesterday, which included your Sterling silver toilet set. Take good care of them and keep them polished, as they are valuable, and will be a beautiful addition to your bedroom.

We'll send the linens to you tomorrow.

We love you very much, and will be back in New York next week. God Bless.

"Mommie"

Saying that she loved me and acting as though she loved me were two different things altogether. So, it hurt my feelings terribly, but didn't really surprise me deep down inside that all I was going to receive out of our house were those things which were monogrammed with my full name on them and totally useless to anyone else. Some towels, a silver dresser set, a few portraits of me as a child, a scrapbook and my baby rocking chair was the sum total out of the entire house. She didn't even send me my own collection of books or the small personal items such as clocks and knick-knacks out of my room. Everything was either sold at auction or given to charities to sell.

I'm sure the people around the house at the time got things, because that's the way Mother was about giving. If you were right there in front of her, doing what she asked and serving her, she was very generous. But I wasn't there anymore. So I got some old towels, a dresser set and a baby rocker. Strangers, fans, the servants and charities got the rest.

I knew I'd never see that house or anything in it again, and I was absolutely right. It's strange how you just sense some things without any real evidence or information to back it up. The last few days I was in that house I had this overwhelming feeling I'd never see it again, that I'd never be inside it again. That's why I told Mrs. Howe, just to have a witness. That's why I took my little tour all by myself, so I'd remember it correctly. Many years later Mrs. Howe told me she'd recalled what I said to her and when the house was put up for sale, she said she got a funny feeling hearing my words echo in her memory.

Mother finally raised my allowance to $200 a month because I simply could not manage on less. I couldn't manage very well with the new amount, but at least I didn't have to always borrow from Mickey and eat up all her food. One thing Mother was most generous with was theater tickets. She continued to send me two tickets to most of the major Broadway shows and I eagerly went to every one. I always wrote her a note thanking her afterwards. I tried to be grateful in all the genuine ways I could and to let her know I appreciated the kind gestures.

Mother and Daddy were always away so much that although I usually had lunch with them during their brief stopovers in the city, I rarely had the chance to sit down and talk to her at any length. Understandably, she was caught up in the new whirlwind of activity and the constant round of bottling plants, openings, sales meetings, board meetings where she was usually the star attraction after the meeting itself, stockholders meetings and all the rest of her activities with Pepsi-Cola. The work was paying off for her, Daddy, and Pepsi. The stock price was climbing and Pepsi was giving its only major competitor a serious challenge for first place in the soft drink market. She was still big news in small towns across the nation where most of the plants were located. Her normal fan mail letter writing campaign was expanded to include all the Pepsi people she was now meeting. Pepsi allotted her a personal secretary in New York in addition to the secretary she kept on salary in Los Angeles.

January 11, 1958

Tina darling,

I loved your sweet letter, which arrived today. By the time you receive this letter, we will be back in New York, as we are flying there tonight.

The twins are having a small birthday party today—just the Starr girls, Aunt Happy and Uncle Joe Lieb. It doesn't seem possible that they are almost eleven years old!

I'm so please that you saw *Cave Dwellers* and *Clerambard.* Have you seen your Aunt Helen in *Time Remembered*? It is an enchanting story ("tongue-in-cheek" type), and you would adore it. I'll get you the tickets—tell me when.

We love you—and please let us know if you have received the towels and various other things I've been sending to you.

"*Mommie*"

By the way Cindy did have quite a problem the night we went to *Ole Yellar*— she forgot her television and movie glasses—and get violent headaches when she views a movie without them. Thought you would like to know—

Love

"*Mommie*"

It seems that headaches tended to run in our whole family . . . for different reasons. For the last two years the twins had been living in Los Angeles, going to boarding school at Marymount in Palos Verdes and coming home on weekends. However, since neither Mother nor Daddy were in Los Angeles that much, the girls were being taken care of by Mr. and Mrs. Howe who both spent the weekends with the girls. The house in Brentwood was unoccupied most of the time with only a skeleton staff remaining. On weekends, the girls and the Howes would often be the only ones in the house. After the house was sold, Mother took an apartment on Fountain and at the end of the year the girls were transferred to an Eastern school.

This time when Mother and Daddy returned to the city for a short stay before taking their vacation in Mexico, I offered to help get things arranged and put away in their new Fifth Avenue apartment. I went over to the apartment after school and on Saturday. I never ceased being amazed at how much there was, how meticulously it had to be arranged, how spotless everything had to be kept. It was a full-time job just to keep things so clean. Between answering the mail and constantly cleaning and re-cleaning every single nook and cranny and physical possession, Mother could have arranged a complete daily schedule for herself and several servants.

I always felt exhausted when I left her. It wasn't just the work either. It was something else, something I couldn't quite define. There was such attention to minor details. Nothing was simple. Every single tiny job or process was an event in and of itself. It was sort of like your whole being depended on how well that little thing was accomplished. I was in a constant state of agitation over whether or not I'd make a mistake, say the wrong thing, do something that would cause me embarrassment. It was exhausting to be there any length of time. It was also freezing cold. I'd always have to bring an extra sweater to wear *inside* the apartment whether it was winter or summer. Even in the winter time there was never any heat. I used to make hot coffee or tea for myself just to try and stay warm. Mother, on the other hand, looked like she was ready for the beach! She usually wore a loose fitting cotton shift referred to as a "muumuu" without any sleeves and thong sandals. The apartment was kept at a temperature comfortable for her and the rest of us shivered in our sweaters and woolen winter clothes. I'd look at the contrast between her and the rest of us in total amazement. It was as though we were completely different sorts of human beings. She dressed for the beach while we dressed for Alaska! She must have had anti-freeze for blood.

Mother, Daddy and the twins went to Mexico for about two weeks.

January 29, 1958

Tina darling,

I adored your letter, and it was so sweet of you to write so

glowingly of our days together and our "chatty visits." It was such
fun working with you, and thank you for your wonderful help.

Your Daddy and I are having a peaceful and heavenly vacation here. We have an enchanting bungalow overlooking the
green lawns, waving palm trees, and the blue, blue Pacific in the
distance. The waves roll in pretty high, but we do venture forth
when the spirit moves us. In fact, we are just "letting our hair
down" and completely relaxing, and doing just what we want to
do, for the first time in fifteen months of constant working.

We found Tasco a fabulous shopping center, and I'll tell you
all about it when I see you next month. The shops are so quaint
and native, and the streets are made of tiny cobblestones. And if
you think San Francisco is hilly—just wait till you see the steep
hills of Tasco!

We will be in California around February 12th, where I am to
make a General Electric television film, then we are flying back
to New York on about February 22nd or 23rd, and we'll see you
shortly after that.

All our love to you and Mickey.

"*Mommie*"

That winter in New York was really cold. We'd already had several bliz-
zards that stopped all traffic in the city for a day or two at a time. The
sidewalks were icy and I hated trying to maneuver myself inch by inch
across their glassy surface. About once a week, I slipped and fell. I was
never really injured, but my pride took a beating. I'd made more friends at
Neighborhood Playhouse and spent the majority of my time with them.
I didn't see my roommate much these days. She was busy working and I
was busy with school and my new friends. We tried to work things out so
that we didn't collide in the small apartment, but more and more what I
wanted and what she wanted were beginning to conflict. New York is so
cramped for living space that it amazed me when people were able to get
along well so squashed together. Except for the streets and the park there
was nowhere to go to get away from one another. I'd had roommates for
years at boarding school, but that was different. In school, we were about
the same age, lived on the same schedule and were involved in the same
activities. Here in New York, Mickey and I had very different lives. She

was a night owl and I had to go to bed earlier if I wanted to be even half-awake for school. She had her group of friends and I didn't like some of them. She didn't like some of mine either, so there began to be a strain on the space in which we shared our friendship.

Earlier in the fall, I'd met a friend of Eddie's who was a good deal older than I, a man named Al Bouzide. Ali, as he was known, had gatherings at his apartment on Sunday afternoons and Eddie invited me to join them. The first Sunday I don't think I said three sentences. I didn't know anyone except Eddie and I was still very shy around total strangers. But that wasn't the entire reason for my silence. I was flabbergasted by the candor with which this group of New Yorkers approached ordinary conversation. I'd never heard people talk about reality, or reality as they perceived it, in such an outspoken way. I was fascinated by just listening to the rapid exchanges and unable to participate because I just never talked like that. I had no experience with life in the terms they addressed it. Most of the people had been friends for years, had known Ali for years and shared the New York experience in common. Most of them were currently in or had been through "analysis" and that formed a mutual basis for understanding one another. I'd only been in New York a few months at that time, had never been closer to "analysis" than the time I told the lady psychiatrist I hated my mother, and had no idea what these people were talking about half the time. But I was a fast study and I guess I didn't make myself totally obnoxious that first Sunday, so I was invited to become one of the "regulars." Ali became one of the very best friends I've ever had. He was the first adult I'd known who was absolutely straightforward with everyone and yet had a sense of humor that cut through most obstacles he ever encountered. He also had a grasp of the totally outrageous . . . he poked fun at all the hallowed traditions while using them to his own full advantage. He had no respect for money at all. Money was only useful if it got you a lifestyle that made you feel at ease, if it provided the clothes and restaurants and travel that made life exciting. He never saved a dime and never worried about it either. I adored him from the first moment I met him until his death twenty years later.

Ali was my first introduction to another adult world altogether, to another way of seeing life and dealing with it so that you got what you needed. Those Sundays were my initiation into a way of relating to others based on discussion of individual ideas where you could heatedly disagree with someone else and still remain friends. It was a proving ground for wit and intelligence and quickness. Not everyone agreed with one another by a long shot and at first I was always scared there was going to be a real fight, but that never happened. There were passionate debates on the merits of a play or a review or a political candidate. It was a whole new world out there where people actually discussed what they thought about politics or philosophy, where no one person was always right and everyone else had to bow to their ideas. In that group very few people agreed with one another and that's exactly what made it interesting. I could hardly believe it. It was just as foreign to me as if I'd been transported to another time zone or a distant planet.

February 2, 1958

Dearest Tina,

Thank you for your sweet letter. I'm so happy that you and Mickey enjoyed "West Side Story." You will find the Helen Hayes play even better, I'm sure.

We are having a wonderful time here. I thought I was relaxing and resting the first week, but yesterday, on the tenth day, I suddenly wanted to sleep after breakfast and after lunch, which I did but suddenly made it out to the beach at 6:00 p.m. with the sun going down at 6:30. Cindy and Cathy are getting freckles and a tan. The gin rummy score is going up and down like "Rock-a-Bye, Baby."

We will be home in California on the 12th, and I'm doing a "General Electric Theatre"—will rehearse on the 17th and 18th, and shoot on the 22nd and 23rd, and fly back to New York on the 24th or 25th because Daddy has a Board Meeting on the 27th.

We'll be seeing you soon, and we love you very much.

"Mommie"

Nobody could make a two-day shoot into a bigger deal than Mother. It was part of her particular genius, part of her star image that turned two days of shooting on a television show into a three-ring circus! My allowance check was late because she'd "been so terribly busy making all preparations and story conferences for the television show." She sent the check special delivery with a brief apology.

What others took in stride, Mother made into an event. What was normal procedure had to be changed for her. She was a dedicated perfectionist who made damn sure that everyone around her knew she was a real star, if only by the inconvenience incurred in the process.

February 21, 1958

Tina darling,

I loved your letter of the 17th. You have a nice choice of words and write beautifully.

It's hard to imagine New York ever being virtually paralyzed, but a twenty-four-hour snowstorm could do it! Fifty-eighth Street must have been a fantastic sight, with snow mounds all the way out to the middle of the street.

We tried to fly into New York on next Tuesday morning, but the flights are taken for that day, and the only thing we can get is a flight on TWA on Monday night. So we'll arrive in New York early Tuesday morning.

The General Electric film is going magnificently, Tina dear. Tom Tyron, John McIntyre and Sidney Blackmer are in the cast with me. I think you will go crazy when you see Tom Tyron. He is your type guy, and an excellent actor. He will replace IT in your heart.

So glad you enjoyed *Paths of Glory.* I've read so much about that film, but we haven't had time to see it yet. What a shocking story that is. Kirk Douglas is always great.

Please give my best to the Coburns and to Mickey when you next see them. I'm so glad Mickey is finding her niche at Carnegie Tech., and has changed her major, as I remember so well that she wanted so much to write.

Since I don't finish the G.E. film until Monday, I'll work right up to plane time that night, and we'll catch a 9:00 p.m. plane.

Bless you, and we'll see you very soon now.

"Mommie"

P.S. Call any time after Tuesday—noon—

CHAPTER 22

I called, I visited, I wrote, I remembered all the holidays and birthdays and anniversaries. I tried to be what she wanted me to be but I knew in my heart that my own life was beginning to change radically, and it was getting harder and harder to bicycle between the two.

Some months before, I'd met a jazz musician and started going out with him. I'd sit in the back of the clubs while he played with the group, usually on weekends. The clubs were in terrible parts of New York, mostly on the lower East Side at the edge of the Bowery. It was definitely "slumming" for me at first, going from the dingy clubs to the various lofts where there were usually parties afterwards lasting until daylight. It was the first time I'd seen dope passed around. I was very naive about almost everything connected with my new boyfriend's life, so once again I retreated behind watching and listening to the people around me. I guess it was because I was obviously such a green kid and obviously not a narc, no one paid much attention to me. I was just around all the time. No one offered me any of the goodies and I never asked, so I just remained a bystander though eventually accepted. Eventually I learned to step over the drunks and ignore the junkies just like everyone else in this strange night world. But what I saw as the evenings rolled by and the music played on was that dope was a dead end. I can't begin to even remember how many people I knew got busted that year and sent to Rikers Island. When musicians I actually spent time with got sick and when I heard about junkies dying, I decided that dope was not for me. My boyfriend tried to teach me how to smoke joints, but I felt so stupid and inept that my pride overtook my curiosity and I gave up. Grass was okay, but I was so scared of being locked up anywhere ever again that it simply wasn't worth the trade-off. I didn't think the cops would ever believe me if any of these places were ever raided and the whole thing was just so dangerous in 1958 that I started being a lot more careful. Finally we stopped seeing each other but the dope and the shooting up was only a part of it.

There was no going back into total innocence about what life in the big city was like. From this point on I knew as much about things I never even thought about before as I possibly could without actually being an experiential part of it. I was no longer just a casual observer, I had been initiated. These people weren't just statistics, some of them were my friends. I couldn't go to that cold white palace at 2 East 70th Street anymore not knowing there was any other world.

The concentricity of Mother's life, the absorption in herself, the lack of real concern for anything but my superficial well-being was beginning to be more than I could politely nod through. I couldn't tune it all out anymore and pretend everything was okay. The way she chose to live was so far removed from anything even remotely available to me that sometimes just that insight alone left me feeling quite helpless. How could I explain what was happening with me, when her main concern was the plastic covers on her closets full of clothes or making sure no one walked on her white rugs without taking their shoes off first? Where could I begin relating what I was seeing for the first time when she had such a screaming fit about my wearing jeans to move furniture? Sure, I knew she'd come from hard times . . . but that was so long ago for her . . . she'd done such an incredible job of erasing every single trace of it . . . she'd launched such a massive campaign into elegance and money and what was properly acceptable that there were no visible traces of the person that might listen to my discoveries. At least there were no visible traces to me at that time in my life. There was not one thing about my mother, her half-million dollar apartment, or her attitude that gave me a hope or a hint of understanding.

April 17, 1958

Christina dear,

I had a long talk with Mr. Meisner, who feels that you are getting along exceptionally well. There is only one thing that bothers me, and that is that you have not been taking dancing since December. Your dancing teacher says that you told her you were not allowed to take dancing lessons because of doctor's orders. I called Dr. Nachtigall, and he knew nothing about it, and he said certainly it was not by his instructions. I would like to know why the dancing has been eliminated, because it is certainly one of the most important things you could study.

I'd like to know what your plans are for the summer—if you are going back to Westport or not. I'm having some people check on other theaters for summer stock, where the younger players really get to act, and I should have this information in a week or so. However, you would not get a salary. The "New School" is definitely out.

Since my schedule and hours during the day are so irregular, and you are out all day in school, I think it would be better if you drop me a note explaining about the dance situation and your plans.

Love,
"Mommie"

That's what I really loved about Mother. She lived on 70th and Fifth, I lived on 58th and First. This letter was again hand delivered instead of being sent through the mail. She communicated with me through letters and chauffeurs or the secretary instead of picking up the phone or asking me to come over and talk. She didn't have the guts to work anything out with me . . . she didn't want to talk about it face to face . . . she hid behind doormen and secretaries and chauffeurs and her work. Anything to keep from being straight with me. She put the restrictions on our communication, on our relationship and on my entire life. I couldn't move, I couldn't breathe, I couldn't make decisions, I couldn't get free of this constructed, manufactured, phony, hype!

What she was saying was that she didn't want to talk to me. What she was also saying was that if I tried to call and talk to her about this, she wouldn't "be available." She never answered the phone herself and so she never had to deal with anything she didn't want to. She never had to come face to face with reality not of her own choosing like the rest of us mortals and were forced by life itself to do. She was above facing reality. If she didn't like the reality she blamed someone else for it. Because she always had to be right. She always had to protect herself by being the one who knew what the ultimate truth was. If reality and her truth didn't match . . . well then reality was a bad, ungrateful dirty girl.

I didn't answer her letter. I didn't call her. I didn't do anything but go about my own life for the next few weeks as best I could.

At school, we were beginning to prepare for final projects. That was much more interesting than the usual routine of scenes and acting exercises. It was the first time many of the students would be on stage in front of an audience and some were very nervous. Part of being asked to return to Neighborhood Playhouse and finish the second year was riding on how well you did in the final project, so there was a lot of anxiety running rampant among students.

My roommate and I were definitely not getting along now. She had her friends staying over at night and my space was getting smaller and smaller. Rather than face the prospect of losing the friendship completely, I decided to find another apartment and move after school was over for the summer.

As I started looking for a new apartment, it began to dawn on me that it was not going to be easy to find something I could afford by myself, without a roommate sharing half the expense. I followed leads in the papers and asked around the school if any of the other students knew of anything or heard of something that was available to let me know.

One afternoon, a girl I didn't know too well told me that she had a friend who sublet apartments. I found out that there was sort of a black market in cheap tenement apartments that were still rent controlled. The way it worked was that you paid "key money" to the person holding the legal lease and then paid double or triple the legal rent controlled price. The apartment mail box had to have the legal tenant's name on it and you just added your own name below theirs. Most of the places available were in wretched parts of New York. I looked at half a dozen of them, knowing full well that I could never survive in those neighborhoods. They were scary as hell during the daytime so I could just imagine what they'd be like by myself at night. I was getting very discouraged. I thought about having to go to Mother and ask her for more money. As unpleasant as that was, if I didn't find something soon, I'd have to do it. I couldn't afford the $175 a month rent on the apartment Mickey and I shared and I didn't know anyone else I'd be comfortable living with. So

I continued the seemingly futile search, hoping that I'd find something that was acceptable.

Just a week before school finished, I went to look at a cold-water flat on the ground floor of a building on York Avenue near East 72nd Street. The apartment consisted of three rooms. The front door to the flat opened directly into the kitchen which had the oldest working three-burner gas stove in New York City, a large sink like a laundry sink and a bath tub! There was a room of equal size to the left of the kitchen which was a living room with a fireplace that had been sealed up and didn't work and another small room to the right of the kitchen which had a closet in it and served as a bedroom. There were windows in each of the room but because it was on the ground floor, they let in neither much light nor much air. Although laws had been passed in the city many years before requiring heat and complete bathrooms in each dwelling rented, this particular cold-water flat had neither. There was hot running water in the sink and bathtub, but there was no heat of any kind and the toilet was in a small cubicle outside the apartment down the hall. The toilet also must have been there since the turn of the century, when the building was first built. It was a real old-fashioned water closet, with a pull chain flush! There was no lock on the door and only a hook latch inside. But, despite all these decided inconveniences the man only wanted $200 key money and $35 a month rent.

The only good thing about the entire situation was that the neighborhood was not a slum. All the buildings were definitely old tenements, but most of the people living in them were families with children and the area was one of the safest in New York. In the year or so that I lived there, I never heard of even one robbery. Everyone knew each other and looked out for their neighbors. It was mainly a German and Polish neighborhood, bordering on Yorktown, the large German shopping center of Manhattan. The East River was only a block away and the breeze from the river helped to keep the area a little cooler in the summertime. Most of the stores and shops were owned and run by local people so it had a small town feeling to it.

The end of April, another of the hand delivered notes arrived from Mother. I had not answered her original letter. I didn't intend doing anything about the dance classes I wasn't taking, except ballet which I liked. I had asked her about attending college at the New School for Social

Research in New York, but she didn't like what she'd heard about the school's political leaning. She said she'd been told there were socialists and even communists at the school and she didn't want me associated with it. I never did figure out whether it was for her sake or mine that she didn't want the association, but it didn't really matter at the time, because if she refused to pay the tuition I wasn't going. I decided to stick it out at Neighborhood Playhouse for the second year, if I was asked to return.

> *Tina darling*
>   I wrote you a couple of weeks ago asking for a note from you explaining the dance situation at school—
>   Surely you can be responsible for these little things I've been calling but there is no answer.
>   Daddy just received your birthday card as it was sent to the Coast and had to be sent back here—
>   Please let me know what your proposed plans are for the summer and the dance bit—
>   *Love*
>   "*Mommie*"

It is not entirely to my credit that I was becoming so stubborn with her. There were so few areas in which I could exercise any control over my own life that I chose the negative in many cases. It sort of became a battle over who would win these stupid "you will—I won't" confrontations. She wanted me to write a letter about a situation that I thought she should have enough concern over to talk to me personally. I thought it was insulting to be told to write her when she was right here in New York. I also thought it was a way for her to avoid me. Therefore, I didn't write the note. I waited to see what the silence would bring forth from her, knowing full well that it would make her mad. Then we would both be in the same boat . . . angry. Both of us thinking we were right and the other was wrong. Both trying to manipulate and no one really winning. She ultimately won in the sense that she held the trump cards . . . she held the purse strings. But I was getting so fed up with being the puppet on the end of those damn strings, jumping and begging and bowing on command that I was just about to the point of telling her to take her measly money and shove it.

The surprise of my life came on my birthday. I had already moved into the cold water flat. Michael Du Pont had borrowed a car to help move the furniture and some of my other friends had helped me move the few boxes of things and my suitcases on the bus! The bus fare was only 15 cents and we made several trips in a ridiculous caravan for less than one cab ride would have cost. I'd given Mother my new address and phone number, explaining that the apartment was small and in an old building but that the neighborhood was all right. I'd also told her the reason for the move, that Mickey and I weren't getting along that well and I couldn't afford to keep the apartment by myself. She said she understood, but she didn't offer any more money, so I just went ahead with the move. On my nineteenth birthday, I went over to the apartment to see her. She'd bought me a couple of summer skirts and blouses which were still on hangers. I thanked her and thought that was the end of it. It came as a complete shock when she handed me an envelope and told me that was the rest of my birthday present. I opened the sealed envelope and found a note from her saying that here were the keys to my car! I was being re-given the Thunderbird that had been taken away from me the previous fall after the disaster with the towing and impound ticket. I couldn't believe it. I had absolutely no more idea how I was going to care for it this time any better than I had the last, but I was determined to give it a try. Despite the previous experience with the garage discussion, Mother made no mention of making arrangements for a garage or giving me extra money to pay for a garage myself. All she told me was that I could pick it up in a few days because it was being serviced right now and they hadn't finished the work in time for my birthday. I didn't see Daddy that day because he was at the office, but I asked Mother to thank him for me.

As it turned out, I needn't have worried about the car or the garage. Before the time arrived for me to pick up the car, Mother called me on the phone. During the course of that conversation, she said that she and Daddy had driven by the apartment building, in their limousine, of course, and that she was shocked beyond belief by the building and the neighborhood. She wanted me to move out of there immediately and into something decent. She said that unless I did make arrangements to move, I was not going to get my car. She was extremely upset. She said how could I expect to get any decent man to take me out when he saw where I lived. Nobody decent would ever come to visit me. She wanted me out of there in a week. I tried to explain to her all over again what I'd told her to begin with when the situation initially arose. I told her that I simply couldn't afford anything better than this without either a roommate to share expenses or a raise in my allowance.

Since it was well into the evening by the time she called me, I don't even know why I persisted in trying to explain all this rationally to her. She didn't seem to hear a word I said. She just kept repeating that I had to get out of there or I didn't get to keep the car. Finally I couldn't take it any longer and told her I simply couldn't afford to move on the allowance I got. She told me to return the car keys to the *doorman* at 2 East 70th Street and hung up on me.

When she wasn't face to face with you and couldn't slap you, Mother's next favorite ploy was to hang up on you. It didn't matter if you were in the middle of a sentence, it didn't matter if you were trying to explain, or even trying to keep the conversation going until some solution could be reached. Slam . . . that phone went in your ear without so much as a goodbye. I hated it.

The next day I put the keys in a sealed envelope without a note of any kind and took the bus across 72nd Street to Fifth Ave. I left the keys with the doorman, saying they were for Mrs. Steele and without further explanation, I left.

During the last few weeks of school, I had auditioned for a number of non-Equity, non-union off-Broadway plays. To my amazement, I actually got one. It didn't pay anything, but the rehearsals were going to be at night, so I could look for other work during the day. In the meantime, Mother had arranged for me to see Uncle Sonny Werbling who was head of the New York MCA office. They'd arranged for me to get a job as a receptionist for the summer and were going to pay $45 a week. I didn't really want the job, but Mother seemed so intent on having me do it and had seemingly gone to so much trouble to arrange it that I didn't have the nerve to say no.

She seemed to think that it was an ideal way for me to meet people in the business and have access to scripts and directors. She said that when she started out in the business, she would do anything to get her hands on the scripts even if she had to steal them. She told me to try and take the scripts to read overnight or to read them on my lunch hour before I delivered them into the back offices. I listened to what she had to say, but I couldn't help thinking privately that it was a lot different for her when she started. She had nowhere to go but up. I had a famous, successful mother and there was a natural assumption that I'd already run into numerous times: the assumption was that certainly she would be helping me to get started in a business where she knew practically everyone. The assumption was totally erroneous. Once Mother arranged the job as a receptionist on the tenth floor of her own agency, she figured she'd dispensed with her help.

People continually asked me what I was doing as a receptionist for the summer, when they knew my mother was one of the biggest clients at the agency. They wondered why she hadn't helped to get me a job as an actress rather than as a receptionist. I couldn't explain and after a while didn't bother. I was the tenth floor curiosity. People would come by just to meet me and confirm for themselves the rumor that Joan Crawford's daughter was a receptionist at the agency. I was continually embarrassed by the notoriety, even though the people I actually worked with on that floor were always very kind and considerate toward me.

The best thing about working at MCA that summer was that it was air-conditioned. My apartment was like an inferno. I found out after the fact that it was located directly over the coal fueled boilers that produced hot water for the building. Late at night I could hear the superintendent shoveling the coal into the boilers and the heat they generated came right up through the floors. That heat coupled with the external heat and humidity of my first New York City summer made life nearly unbearable.

We rehearsed the play for two weeks. I didn't have much experience judging new plays, but it wasn't hard even for me to realize the play was a turkey long before we actually opened. The final straw was finding out that the producer had posters made, advertising the play starring "Joan Crawford's daughter." I flew into a total rage with him and said that if he didn't remove every single one of those posters that I'd quit before the play ever opened. Not having a union contract worked both ways . . . I didn't have written protection about how he used my name or my family but he didn't have any protection against me quitting at the very last minute and preventing the play from opening at all. He took the posters down, but the damage was done. The play opened to disastrous reviews which let me off the hook, mercifully, saying simply that I'd been caught in a bad play. We closed after three performances.

Mother, Daddy and the twins were in Europe but sent opening night telegrams from Brussels where they were visiting the fair and doing Pepsi business for the fledgling international operations.

When Mother returned from Europe someone told her about the posters. She had a total fit. Not with the producer . . . with me! I could understand why she was mad, I'd been furious myself. I'd had nothing to do with the whole shoddy thing and in fact, had threatened to quit if they weren't removed. I told her the entire story, but she wasn't in the least bit sympathetic. She continued to blame me.

To make matters worse that muggy, hot summer, my cat Eloise died. I felt terrible. Eloise was the first pet I'd ever had. Of course we'd had dogs all during the time I was growing up, but they weren't really ours. The dachshund Mother had when I was a baby got so old he finally had to be put to sleep. I cried but I wasn't all that sad to see him go. After that there was a succession of dogs. Two black standard poodles Mother named "Gin" and "Tonic." They were wonderful but they dug giant holes in the flower bed, so they went after about a year. A boxer who's name I forget also dug holes and didn't last. For a very short time we had a Dalmatian and then a lovely female cocker spaniel named Honey. Mother found something wrong with all of them until finally she got a little champagne poodle named Cliquot. He lasted for years until he too got very old. Mother didn't like cats so we never had one. But I'd found Eloise as a kitten at the theater in Westport and brought her into the city with me. When she died I was really heartbroken. I couldn't even think about her being thrown into one of the sanitation department trash bins, so I asked the veterinarian if there was any alternative. He looked at me a little funny, but gave me the name and number of a pet cemetery in Long Island. I called them and spoke to a very nice lady who understood my feelings immediately. She asked for the name of the vet and said they'd handle everything from that point on. All I had to do was come out to Long Island on Saturday between nine and noon to sign the papers and see the pet properly buried. I thanked her profusely and my conscience was much relieved.

The next problem facing me was . . . how to get to Long Island. The train didn't stop in the little town. I called a couple friends in the city to find out if anyone had a car I might borrow for the morning and my friend Jim Frawley said he could borrow his dad's car and would drive me out. He really came to my rescue. I called Eddie to tell him about all the plans and he said he'd come with me too. I was really touched by the response of my new friends. I thought it was enormously considerate of them to accompany me to Long Island in this terrible heat.

Early Saturday morning, Jim picked me up and we drove downtown to get Eddie. As it turned out, Eddie had told Al and he'd decided to come along for the ride. So there we were . . . the four of us on the Long Island expressway headed for a cat funeral! Jim was nervous about driving his dad's car, Eddie had a hangover, Ali was in great spirits as usual and I was on the verge of tears the entire time.

The directions were perfect and at just nine o'clock we pulled into the long driveway leading to the cemetery office. All along both sides of the drive there were burial grounds. Interspersed among the small markers were some huge marble headstones commemorating the heroic feats of many war dogs and lesser known beloved pets. I was very impressed with the beautiful park setting and the peaceful, quiet atmosphere.

In the office, everyone spoke softly and was very polite. I signed the papers and then a gentleman took me into see my poor Eloise. She was in a little metal box and looked like she was asleep. I, of course, started crying. Then the man closed the lid and I followed him out of the room and through the main office. My three friends fell into line behind me and we all marched out to the cemetery itself. The man gave the little box to an attendant who put it in the ground and started to cover it with earth. Eddie whispered from behind me. "Any last words?" I turned and gave him a dirty look through my tears. Fortunately, through my own concern with myself and Eloise I never noticed that Al was nearly doubled over with laughter. He never made a sound, although later he told me he had nearly choked to death trying to contain himself.

I thanked everyone for their kindness, took out a Kleenex and sniffled all the way back to the car.

The four of us sat in silence most of the way back to the city. It wasn't until we got to Al's apartment and he offered all of us a drink that I began to appreciate the lunacy of our journey.

After a couple of bloody Mary's, my three stalwart friends had me convinced that I had just provided one of the most bizarre events of their entire life . . . a story that would go down in all our personal histories . . . Evelyn Waugh would have been proud! As they each recounted their version of that morning, I started to laugh until I really cried. My knees felt weak, I laughed so hard. But that was nothing compared to what happened to them. Eddie rolled off the couch into the floor, holding his stomach. Jim was shaking his head in disbelief so vigorously he nearly gave himself a crick in the neck. Al said he was finished for the day, if not the weekend. I declined to come to the next day's Sunday gathering for fearing for my life! I knew there was no way on earth I'd ever live the story down, so there was nothing to be done but go along with the hilarity. It didn't matter a bit though, because I was relieved to know that Eloise wasn't in the sanitation trash bin and my conscience was clear.

I paid the annual maintenance fee on the numbered plot for the next ten years. By that time I figured Eloise wouldn't know the difference and I let it go.

August 11, 1958

Christina dear,

I'm sending your check to you now, but it's only for $200 for this month's allowance. I know I'm early with it, but I will be in Bermuda for three days on this weekend.

I hope you will understand why the check is only for $200, but with all my expenses and practically no salary coming in, and Daddy not on his salary yet, I just can't make it any more. Then, too, since you have a job, I thought maybe you could get along on this.

I'm trying to save a little for "Neighborhood", and unless I cut down with you now, I can't see "Neighborhood" this fall. The expense of Christopher has been so unbelievably exorbitant. If you can't make out on this, let me know. I'm so hoping it is possible for you as it would be helpful for me.

Love,
"Mommie"

I had gotten over being so angry every time one of these "I can't afford your allowance" letters arrived. There was a time when the letters coming from England, Mexico, Belgium and now a three-day weekend in Bermuda would have made me furious. There was a time when the $100 lunches and the new mink coats and the specially designed sets of diamonds made me feel sick to my stomach, knowing the entire time I spent complimenting her on the beautiful jewelry or the lovely new coat or the spacious new apartment, that I returned to poverty as soon as I left her. But after all the years, I had come to expect those differences as just a part of my strange, incongruous life.[9]

What hurt more than Mother's oblivious display of wealth was the public's delusion. I could almost predict the result of telling people the truth about my penniless situation. They just couldn't put together the fact of my parents living in opulence on Fifth Avenue and me living in poverty in a cold water flat. It didn't make any sense. Their fantasy created by all the publicity about movie stars simply didn't allow room for the truth. It was even exaggerated, I think, in my case because of the years of publicity in movie magazines featuring the story about us being adopted. No one I ever met could understand how a woman could adopt four children and then not provide decently for them. I didn't understand either, but that wasn't the point now. My primary concern was getting a career going without the assumed assistance of my family.

I knew the job at MCA was only a temporary replacement for the

---

9   In the mid 1990s, information came to me about Mother's jewelry which was a closely guarded secret for years.

Mother persuaded Alfred Steele to use her jeweler friend of many years when purchasing jewelry for her because it always had to be one-of-a-kind specially designed. She particularly delighted in colored gemstones such as sapphires, rubies, and emeralds, although diamonds were the standard.

Alfred Steele bought Mother *a lot* of new jewelry through her jeweler friend from California. How he paid for it is a mystery since he "wasn't on salary" for almost a year, but that's not the point.

Apparently, soon after Mother received the new set of necklace, earrings, and ring, she insured it for full value and supposedly put it in the vault for safekeeping. However, on the way to the vault, the jewelry took a secretive detour to the backroom of the jeweler's office at night. There, one man, and one man only, made copies of the stones, took out the precious gem and replaced it with an excellent fake. The real gemstones were given back to Mother surreptitiously and the piece of jewelry put in the vault fully insured at its original value. The fake stones were so well done that only another jeweler could tell the difference.

The subterfuge provided her with tens of thousands of dollars to spend without anyone else's knowledge. Basically, only she and one other person knew the secret process which had been going on for many years. She was a cunning woman and she took Alfred Steele to the cleaners in the brief three years of their marriage.

summer and the regular receptionist was returning mid-September. I found out that, once again, most of my best friends were not returning to Neighborhood Playhouse, among them Jim Frawley and Ted Bessel. I didn't know what Mother would say if I told her I didn't want to go back either, but that time was approaching.

As for the reference in this letter to neither Mother or Daddy having any salary, a peculiar thing had happened with them. The apartment Mother had Daddy build for her had over run it's original cost estimate in both time and money. I guess Mother had used some of the money she'd gotten from the sale of the Brentwood house, but it had been under a second mortgage and she told me she just didn't get that much from the $150,000 sale price after the existing loans against it had been paid off.

Alfred Steele made a lot of money but he had no inherited wealth. Then too, he was paying alimony and child support to his first wife who had custody of their boy, Sonny. So, when the building costs exceeded their combined funds, Daddy had to borrow against his future salary from Pepsi. That meant he borrowed against money he hadn't yet earned. That also meant that he didn't get the majority of his salary at the present time. I think it was a pretty well-kept secret, because it wouldn't have looked very good publicly for the Chairman of the Board of a "family" company like Pepsi to be so in debt that he had to borrow against money he hadn't yet earned. It just wasn't the kind of thing you wanted all those "family" bottlers and stockholders and consumers to get a hold of because there was no telling what they might think about that kind of financial arrangements within the company. He was only about 53 years old at the time, but what if something should happen to Alfred. Steele? After all, there wasn't any collateral for the sizable loan other than his own physical being. His health was generally good, although Mother said he was overweight; his reputation was impeccable; what he had done for the company in the last five years was extraordinary and undeniable. The private loan went through.

On the surface, Mother and Daddy continued to live as they always had. However in August 1958, nearly eight months after moving into their new apartment, Daddy was still "not on his salary yet."

CHAPTER 23

I hadn't seen much of my brother during this time. I'd heard that he'd had a bad time of it at his last several schools and been transferred to an eastern boarding school. I knew Chris didn't particularly like the military academies Mother had insisted he go to for their strict discipline. He'd either run away or been expelled from the last two and I wasn't sure of the exact details. Coincidentally, I'd met a black actor named Rupert Crosse at a party and he'd told me that he knew my brother because he supervised the athletics part-time at the school Chris was currently attending. Small world! Because Rupert went up almost every weekend, I asked him to take messages and some small gifts to my brother. It was indirectly through my brother that Rupert and I became friends.

What I didn't know until years later, thank heavens, was that after the trouble at Chris's last school in the west, Mother was so disgusted that she tried to find someone who would take Chris to Switzerland and leave him there without a passport. She was going to send him to some school in Switzerland and then, by removing his passport, prevent him from re-entering the United States. Chris was fourteen.

Fortunately for all of us, she was unable to find anyone who would go along with her scheme. Many years after the actual occurrence of all this, I was privately impressed that none of the people she must have contacted were willing to do such a thing to a fourteen-year-old boy, no matter how much money she offered them. I surmised that actually participating in such a scheme was somehow much more offensive than simply turning your back on practices you know are wrong.

I didn't know about any of this when it was taking place. All I knew was that my brother had been transferred and kept in touch with him through Rupert or personal visits when I could afford the train fare.

On August 14, 1958, my grandmother died. I might not have found out about it at all except that my friend who had promised to visit Grandmother, wired me about her death. I think Mother was still in Bermuda at the time, or perhaps had just returned to New York when she received the news. The doctors had advised her of Grandmother's serious condition well in advance, but Mother had not gone to Los Angeles. Mother did not call me to tell me that Grandmother died. She did not ask any of us to attend the funeral. She and Daddy flew to Los Angeles, made the arrangements for a closed casket and the burial. I don't know how long it had been since Mother had seen Grandmother. I think it was a least several years.

I quit my temporary job at MCA the week the regular receptionist was due to return. Shortly after that I had to tell Mother that I didn't want to return to Neighborhood Playhouse. I decided that in this case, it might be better to write her a letter about it, giving her time to think about it before she spoke to me. I wasn't looking forward to the result, but I didn't want to return. I was so tired of having to be grateful for the tuition and the measly allowance and I thought it was about time I tried to look for regular work.

She called immediately after receiving my letter. She asked me to come over to the apartment right away.

About an hour later, I arrived at 2 East 70th street. It wasn't the "right away" she probably had in mind because I had to either take the bus or walk and I chose the bus. It was still very much summer time and at least the bus was air-conditioned.

The minute I walked into the apartment, I realized that I should have taken a little more time and changed my clothes. I had on Bermuda shorts, a blouse and sandals. Mother had said something nasty about dressing for the beach instead of the city, but I didn't hear it clearly enough to reply.

I followed her into the small den she called her office and saw Daddy sitting on the opposite side of her large leather-covered green desk. I started to go over to him, but she ordered me to sit in a chair half-way across the room. I knew this was it. This was the show-down I'd almost been expecting. So I just sat where I was ordered and waited for the show to begin.

She started by saying that she was shocked I'd quit the job she'd worked so hard to get me at MCA. Before I could reply, she went on to say that if I couldn't finish anything, if I couldn't abide by my parents' wishes and stay in school, then I would have to go out on my own.

I looked from her face to Daddy's, but he was fiddling with a pen and didn't look up at me.

Mother continued, saying that they were both very displeased with my decision, very displeased that I chose not to continue school.

At this point Daddy spoke to me, half looking at me and half fooling with the pen. He said that he thought that he could arrange for me to get into his old alma mater, Northwestern, which also had an excellent drama department and that I'd only be one year behind, which wouldn't be too bad for me. I asked him point blank if I'd get enough money to live on while I was there . . . or was it always going to be me begging.

Mother cut in, saying that I had no concept of money, that I had no concept of gratitude for what had already been done for me, that I was obviously too irresponsible to stick with anything I started and that I was never going to make anything out of myself with that attitude. I started to answer back but Daddy started talking at the same time as I did.

All Daddy managed to say was "Joan, for God's sakes, give the kid a chance to . . ." Mother cut him off. She said, "Damn it, Alfred! They're *my* kids and *I'll* decide what happens to them. Just shut up and don't interfere! I don't interfere with yours and you don't have anything to say about mine."

She was yelling at him by the end and I could see that Daddy was getting mad because his face became quite red and then drained to a paleness that wasn't normally like him. He didn't say another word.

Mother asked me how much money I had. "About enough for one month," I answered. "Well," she said, "then I guess you'd better go out and find a job. You're on your own now."

That was it. That was all there was to it. I was dismissed without further discussion. Neither Mother nor Daddy got out of their chairs. No one said goodbye to me. In fact there was a silence so pointed that it was absolutely clear to me that I was expected to disappear now. I was expected to pick up my purse and exit. Of course, that's exactly what I did.

~

I didn't know what I was going to do. I tried to think of what sort of job I could look for and realized I was totally unequipped for anything other than perhaps a domestic servant! *That* I knew like an expert, but nothing else. I could type only adequately and I'd been a receptionist for three months, but other than that I didn't know how to do anything.

What I *didn't* know that awful hot day, as I was walking home from the penthouse duplex on Fifth Avenue, was that I wouldn't see my mother face to face again for nearly eight years. I didn't know that I'd *never* see my daddy alive again.

What I would learn almost immediately is that life works in very strange ways. When I finally got back to my little cold water flat, I fixed a glass of instant iced coffee and sat down alone in the living room to contemplate my very precarious future. I had no idea how to look for a regular job, nor even what I should be trying to get. I decided to buy the Sunday Times and start there. Perhaps it would give me a clue. Then I thought I'd call some of my friends and ask if they knew of anything. That chance was slim because most of them were just beginning to be out on their own and were hustling for themselves. Well, I thought . . . I'm nineteen years old and I better just get after it. I'm scared and I'm inexperienced, but I've got to make it somehow. The "how" was my major question.

I must have been sitting there for a long time, sort of daydreaming because when the phone rang I realized for the first time how dark the apartment had gotten. I answered the phone and turned on a light.

To my amazement, it was my friend Jim calling to see how I was getting along. It made me feel so good just to hear a friendly voice and know that somewhere in this great big city, a person cared about me. If that had been all he called about, it would have been enough to get me through the night. But, there was more . . . there was the strange quirk of life. What Jim was really calling about was to inquire whether or not I might be interested in a job at his dad's restaurant! I couldn't believe it. He said that they had a position open one night a week as cashier and that they'd train me. He said it only paid $10 a night but that I could also have dinner there. To me, the second half of the "pay" was almost as valuable as the cash and I told him I could start immediately. Ten dollars a week wasn't going to do any more than pay my rent, but it was a hell of a start, considering I'd only been out on my own a few hours!

Jim's dad gave me the job, however, the first night I worked for nothing except my dinner because there was an even $10 missing from the register at the end of the evening. I was horrified that anyone might think I took it, but the bartenders later told me that I was just being taught a lesson the fastest way possible. From that first night on, I was nicknamed "hawk-eye" because I never let *anyone* touch that register when I was on duty. It became a great joke among all of us who worked at O'Henry's, located at 18th Street and Irving near Gramercy Park.

Chris was never allowed to leave any of his schools, so he became somewhat of an expert at escaping them. Usually he ended up with his friends at my cold water flat, since I was the only person he knew he could trust. Usually I'd talk him into going back to school, but once the police were sent to pick him up. When that happened, he was taken to Bellevue Hospital as a juvenile runaway. That was awful. He was put in one of the so-called "non-violent" locked wards in the old Bellevue, which looked like a medieval fortress.

I was working at the restaurant more than one night a week now, for which I was very grateful. I'd also started group acting classes with a director from the Actor's Studio named Frank Corsaro . . . the same man who had directed *Hatful of Rain* a few seasons before. My acting classes were several afternoons a week and I was working several nights a week at O'Henry's. So in between, I would go down to Bellevue and spend time with my brother. It was then that I began to learn about the juvenile justice system.

I was one of the few relatives that visited and I was only a couple of years older than most of the boys, so they told me their backgrounds very openly. Many of them were not juvenile offenders. By that I mean they had not committed any crimes. The majority of the boys I got to know were from broken homes. It became ordinary to hear of mothers who were prostitutes, mothers and fathers who were alcoholics and junkies. It was also common among these boys to hear of beatings. Most of the boys had been seriously hurt at least once by another member of their family and most had witnessed their mother and father beating one another.

Running away was as normal on this ward as breathing. These boys ran away from everything and everyone. They trusted only their own age group, none of them believed anyone in a position of authority. They'd already been through the social workers and the probation departments. They'd been in regular schools and foster homes. The majority were now headed for county detention schools as wards of the court until they reached eighteen years old. It seems odd that under these conditions, we usually had a lot of fun when I visited my brother. But it was like one of the few positive events in their lives. I always stopped on the way down and bought candy and soft drinks. The boys would make up songs in the rock style of the day and sing in funny little groups with me as their only audience. I got to know all the attendants by first name and a good number of the boys.

After over a month, my brother was sent to another school in Connecticut. I went up there to talk to the head mistress and tried to explain the full situation to her. She seemed like a reasonable woman and we tried to work out some way to get my brother to stay put in this establishment. I visited as often as I could which amounted to about every other weekend.

I had gotten a roommate to share half of the expenses. She was my age, wanted to be a dress designer and her name was Lotte. We'd met when I was at Neighborhood Playhouse and she was attending a design school a block away. She had some mad story about being a Yugoslavian countess, whose family had fled the communists leaving all their worldly possessions behind. Half the family went to Turkey and Lotte went with her mother to Italy. The part about leaving Yugoslavia I think was true. The other part about being titled nobility I'm not so sure of, but there were a lot of nutty people running around New York those days claiming to be descended from royalty of one sort or another and it got so that you just didn't pay much attention after a while. They had a sort of spiritedness about them, very good manners and no money. So you learned to take it rather lightly.

Between the cold water flat and working nights in a restaurant, I was learning a lot about the bottom rung of the ladder in New York. I worked until 1 or 2 a.m., left alone and was scared most of the time. I learned about the numbers, about the payoffs, about the cons. I met the bookies and the hustlers, the struggling artists and the junkies. I learned which dark New York streets were okay to walk if you minded your own business and hurried along and which were worth your life to enter. If I had to live in this world of the bottom, I decided I damn well better learn enough to stay alive.

What fascinated me most was that everybody had a scam going. There wasn't anybody who worked with money and didn't short-change customers. They did it so well and had it figured out so perfectly that they even knew in advance who to pull it on and who not to. Most of them played the numbers or the horses or any other long shot with the big pay-off. That was what everyone was looking for . . . the big hustle with the big pot of gold at the end of the rainbow. I guess they almost had to do something to make the routine dreariness of the old apartments and the tiresome job, year in and year out, bearable. It was something exciting . . . something challenging . . . something more than their everyday lives could offer.

September 29, 1958

Christina darling,

Thank you for your sweet letter.

Am glad your acting classes with Frank Corsaro are coming along so well, and that you are so happy. Glad, too, your job at the restaurant is so interesting.

The twins have a magazine subscription drive again at school, so I have ordered "Seventeen" for you. I hope it is all right.

I am off to the Coast, to be gone just a couple of days to do a Bob Hope show, so if you need anything call Faith either at the Pepsi office, or at the house where she will probably be some of the time.

I had an idea. By eating my only full meals at the restaurant for free and saving every dime I could get my hands on, maybe I could go to Europe for a couple months and visit the friends I'd made on our 1956 trip. I wrote my friends in England and asked if I could stay with them for a while in the spring. They wrote back and said they'd be delighted. So, that's what I worked toward. I opened a savings account and every spare dollar went into it. I worked as many nights as I could and took some temporary typing jobs during the day.

Mother was very aggravated when my working at the restaurant appeared in one of the newspaper columns, but now I didn't care what she thought as long as my own conscience was clear. Now that I had a clear goal, the work became easier. Now that I had something to look forward to I didn't mind the scrimping and saving so much.

As hot as the summer had been, it was easy street compared to the winter. Lotte and I used to sleep in slacks and sweaters with our winter coats over the blankets. We had no heat at all except the antiquated gas stove. When the snow came I was glad to be living over the boiler room, but even that didn't warm the rooms up enough. Every night we heard the radio warnings about trying to heat with the gas kitchen stoves, about what a terrible fire hazard it was, but we had little choice. It was either leave the oven on and a pan full of water on top of the stove or risk freezing to death in your bed. It was miserable, to say the least.

This winter there was no money from my family at all. A few weeks after the confrontation with Mother and Daddy, there was a knock on my door one night rather late. I was afraid to open the door, so I asked who was there. A muffled voice replied, "Jimmy . . . open up." There before me was Jimmy, Daddy's valet and bodyguard. He seemed in a terrible hurry and was talking very fast, looking over his shoulder down the hallway as though he was afraid of being followed. He made me instantly nervous, but I asked him inside. He stepped through the doorway but wouldn't come any further. "Your dad sent you this," he said, thrusting something into my hand. Then he whispered, "Don't let anyone know . . . it's just between your dad and you. Don't say nothing about it!" I nodded, "Okay." In my hand there was a hundred-dollar bill. Tears welled up in my eyes and I was about to ask Jimmy to thank Daddy when he said, "Your dad says to tell you he sends his love and hopes you're getting along all right." As Jimmy was nearly out the door I grabbed his arm and said, "Tell Daddy I'm just fine and thanks."

After I'd closed and locked the door, I sat down on the edge of the kitchen chair staring at the money from my father. As much as I needed and appreciated the money, I appreciated the thought even more. I wished I could have called him and talked to him, but I was afraid to for fear it would cause trouble.

Then I started thinking about my father, chairman of the board of a major corporation, a responsible adult having to sneak around Mother to do something decent for me. She was relentless when it came to having her own way. She even finally got to him.

It never ceased to amaze me that people would give up so much of their own free will just to be around her. I couldn't do it. I never was able to do it. She was my own mother. She was a famous movie star. And there was no way on earth that I was going to live my life according to her dictates ever again if I could help it. Because, for me, that wasn't living at all. That was no better than being a slave. She always held out the promise of great rewards in return for your voluntary slavery. She always held out the promise of undying love in return for your total devotion, but in my experience with her it never happened. And now she had Daddy playing slave, too.

She's gotten him to buy her everything she wanted. She's gotten him into incredible debt. This made him give up his own salary to fulfill her wishes. She's gotten him to live according to her schedules and prerogatives. And now she's gotten him to sneak around behind her back for fear of her anger. But that's how it is with her. I knew the pattern well enough by now. She draws the perimeters of what was acceptable behavior according to her definition so tight, that in order to express any free will at all you have to sneak around trying not to get caught.

Poor Daddy, I thought. I wonder if he still thinks he got such a bargain. I wonder if he knows he's already sold his soul to the devil herself, in return for nothing. I wonder if he knows she'd already got him and he'll never get out alive. I bet he doesn't and there's no way for me to help him. There's nothing I can do but watch it all unfold like a movie plot.

October 13, 1958

Tina darling,

I'm so glad you had a nice day with Christopher and Mr. Coleman. I do wish, darling, that when you are in trouble and having a rough go of it, as you told your Uncle John, that, instead of telling other people, you would sit down and write me a letter about it. I'm having a pretty rough go of it, myself. I'm enclosing a check for you for $100.00.

Will be back in New York next week, and will talk to you then.

Love,

"Mommie"

The hundred dollars was welcome enough, the comment about writing her about my problems wasn't. That letter was mailed from Los Angeles because she was there doing another TV show. Most of the time now she lived right in New York. But she didn't ask me to talk to her about the problems or come to see her about the problems. She asked me to write her. That was Mother . . . always in control.

Thanksgiving I worked at the restaurant and had a wonderful dinner. I had the opportunity to work steady through Christmas and New Years which was good news indeed. My savings account only had about a hundred dollars in it and that was through Herculean effort. Lotte was going home for Christmas, so I'd be alone in the city and welcomed the opportunity to be busy. I was going to spend Christmas day with my brother at his school and try my best to make it festive despite the dreary surroundings. I remembered only too clearly being locked up in schools over the holidays and could still feel the crushing loneliness of those memories. I had to at least try to make it a little better for my brother.

November 26, 1958

Tina darling,

Loved your sweet letter. I'm rushing around like mad, because we are finishing filming the G.E. Theatre tonight, but I do want to get a note off to you, anyway, to send my love, and wish you a happy, happy Thanksgiving weekend.

Yes, we finally did get Charles Lang to film the G.E. Theatre. It will be on television on January 4th, so I hope you will see it and enjoy it.

I brought Mickey Coburn's work with me to the Coast, and will be writing to her about it in a day or so.

We are leaving for Cincinnati on Sunday, and will be returning to New York on December 5th.

Bless you, and all of us send our love to you.

"Mommie"

How like Mother to take a friend's work under consideration. How like her to help people who were practically strangers and not help her own family. My friend Mickey from Carnegie had continued to correspond with Mother and to call her once in a while when she was home on vacation. I couldn't blame her at all for that. I probably would have done the same thing if I'd been in her shoes. They carried on their friendship and their correspondence without me though. I guess it went way back to elementary school and the kids being nice to me in order to get movie star's pictures, but when I saw the tide begin to turn with someone I grew to realize that our friendship was coming to an end. It simply was not possible for me to continue trusting anyone who wanted to be friends with Mother that badly. Eventually, they'd have to face the conflict themselves, but I'd gotten myself in a lot of trouble even as a little kid by trusting people I thought were my friends only to have them tell Mother every single word out of my mouth just to have her praise them and tell them how wonderful they were. As I grew older I also found out that there weren't many other adults I could trust either, not when it came to Mother. So, long ago, I had made it my personal policy never to tell anyone who was friendly with Mother anything I didn't want to risk having her know. Not that I was actively engaged in anything sneaky, but I just couldn't take the chance of handing her any more ammunition than she already had acquired over a lifetime.

Mother wanted to know everything about everyone. That is one of the ways she survived so long in show business. She loved gossip, she loved to know anything that was supposed to be secret. She really would have been a marvelous secret agent or private investigator. She had miraculous ways of finding out what she wanted to know. Sometimes it was through fans of hers who had jobs in the studios. They'd hunt around virtually unnoticed until they found what she wanted, even if it was only a clue. She could piece the rest together and come up with a pretty good conjecture herself. Other times I used to think that she had a sort of network of informers throughout the country. That may be total paranoia on my part, but so much information came to her that way and not just about me, that I'm not sure it isn't true.

To my total fascination, I found out that she kept a file on me during all those years I didn't see her! There were press clippings, letters from people who'd seen me in various plays or on television and copies of letters she'd written to some other people mentioning me. It wasn't like a scrapbook, it was a regular file. I guess that's how she kept track of me even when she didn't have my phone number or address. I guess she figured that if I was sick or dead, someone would notify her. Meanwhile, if I managed to stay alive and get work, it would turn up in some paper somewhere in the country and she'd have it put right there in the file along with the rest. It was an odd feeling for me when I found out about the file. I sort of felt like J. Edgar Hoover was watching.

I did my Christmas shopping for the whole family as usual. I'd never yet missed a Christmas or a birthday or Mother's Day or any of the other holidays. I always struggled over what on earth to give Mother . . . who had everything. My brother and sisters were always easy, but Mother was always a trauma. I never had much money and always wanted to get something nice, so it was *always* difficult.

This Christmas Mother sent me one box from Lord and Taylors. It contained a black pouffy cocktail dress, two sizes too large. Not only didn't the dress fit, I wouldn't be caught dead in it! It was *the* ugliest thing I'd ever laid eyes on. The dress itself was like a sheath but it had puffs of material like old-fashioned bustles on each hip! I was not thin, I wore a size 10 or 11 at the time, but lord have mercy . . . that dress made me look like a Sumo wrestler in drag!! It was absolutely ghastly beyond belief. I looked at myself in the mirror and started to laugh until I had tears running down my face. Whatever joke this was by whoever picked this ugly thing out for me, I had no intention of keeping it. When I thought about how long I'd looked for something to give Mother and Daddy and I get this apparition of a dress, I couldn't believe it. Whatever possessed her to order a black cocktail dress, knowing bitterly well how I was living, was beyond me. What I needed with a cocktail dress at this time in my life was an almost ridiculous question. So, the day after Christmas, I folded the hideous dress neatly in it's box and got on the bus for Lord and Taylor. I had a bit of difficulty returning it because Mother didn't have a charge there and the dress no longer had it's price tag. But I finally convinced the sales woman to let me exchange it for a two-piece wool suit that was on sale for less than the price of the dress.

That was the first time I'd ever had the nerve to try and return a present from Mother. Always before I'd dutifully thanked her while feeling nothing but rage in my heart. I'd put the present away because either it didn't fit and I didn't have the money to have it altered or just because for whatever reason it wasn't something I could use. There it would sit in a drawer or hung in the back of a closet for years. And every time I'd move, I'd move all the useless things with me, scared to give them away for fear Mother would find out and get mad at me. I guess my real feeling was that I got so little from her that I had to keep *whatever* she gave me for fear there'd never be anything more. Even something totally useless to me was better than nothing. For the first time that Christmas I realized what a dreadful bargain I'd made, what a stupid trade-off I'd accepted. I liked my new suit very much. For the first time in just ages I felt quite pleased with myself. I felt a small hint of courage returning.

From Puerto Rico where Mother and Daddy were spending their holidays, I received the last letter of this eventful year.

December 27, 1958

Tina, my darling,

We just adore our book, *The Thrones of Earth and Heaven*. It is a fabulous history of art around the world, and I know we shall have many happy hours reading it. As you know, we are very much interested in native art, and this is a fabulous chronological history that I know will teach us much. It was so thoughtful of you.

We thought of you so often, and your gifts to all of us are greatly appreciated.

Bless you, my darling, and we hope the New Year brings you every happiness.

"Mommie"

I continued going to acting classes, making the rounds of all the casting offices and calling everyone I'd ever known in hopes someone would have a job. I didn't belong to any of the acting unions yet and it was like a vicious circle. You had to have a union card to get a union job and you had to get a union job in order to be eligible to join the union. Without any help from Mother or anyone who knew Mother, I would have to just be persistent and keep slugging away like everyone else.

It was a dreary winter. Lotte remained in Chicago with her parents because she couldn't get a decent job in New York either. It was right at the end of what they called the Eisenhower recession and jobs at the entry level were scarce indeed. I continued working two or three nights a week at the restaurant and managed to get by all right. I'd gotten a big boost toward my planned trip to England working all during the holidays and had put almost every cent in my savings account. I never bought any food for myself other than coffee and cottage cheese. Cigarettes were only 25 cents a pack, the bus fare was still 15 cents, so I could live on a dollar a day as long as I kept working at the restaurant. The cook down there would always slip me a small bag of leftovers and that would give me something to eat during the two days until I worked again. Sometimes after work I'd go out for a drink with one of the customers or a waiter. I never let any of them take me home, but most were kind enough to offer me cab fare. I'd gladly accept but I only took the cab a couple of blocks to the nearest bus stop going uptown. I'd pay the fare to that point, pocket the remainder of the money I'd been given and get on the bus. Fortunately for me, the buses ran all night long in New York. It was quite literally hand to mouth, each day a new challenge to try and stay alive in the city. I learned to walk as much as possible. I learned every cheap place to buy things. I went to all the free street fairs from Mulberry Street to 114th Street. You could spend days at those street fairs just for the price of the food you bought. When the weather was a little warmer, we had picnics in Central Park. We went to 50-cent movies in the middle of the night down on 42nd street and saw all the European imports that way.

There was a whole world of people in the city that had no money and were getting by with nothing. The difference was that none of us ever thought it would last forever. Tomorrow or the next day . . . soon, things would change. We had absolutely no sense that this condition of poverty would last forever. We were young and the whole world was available if you could just live through the next couple of days. None of us knew how we were going to make it, but none of us doubted that we would. We may have been stone cold broke but not one of us considered ourselves "poor." No one could get unemployment insurance money. New York required twenty consecutive weeks work. For most of us five months work in a full-time job was almost unheard of luxury.

There simply was no such thing as food stamps. There were no massive social programs, no uprising of social consciousness. This was not the Kennedy-Johnson sixties. This was the very end of the Eisenhower administration, this was the end of the entire fifties with a prolonged economic recession, the Cold War era, the McCarthy inquisitions, rock 'n' roll and suburban sprawl. There were all the elements necessary for a social revolution but they were still scattered. They existed primarily in small groups whose membership had stepped aside for a while and taken a good hard look at the chaos just under the surface of Cold War calm. People were scared of being blown to bits at any moment by the atom bomb. The constant threat of annihilation had consequences no one could have predicted. If, so the thinking went, I can be blown away at any minute and if there's nothing I can do about that, then I better do something important about *now*. This ferment was coming out of the blackness and the depressiveness of the bohemian or "beatnik" movement, which was just about the only major underground white movement I knew about personally.

The blacks I met through my travels in the city were just plain pissed off. They were angry beyond what any one of them could yet put into words. Their problems had not yet begun to be addressed but their strength and their numbers were increasing. They moved downtown from the Harlem ghettos into the tenements and that's how we strangers found each other . . . through the city's natural melting pot . . . the tenements. In the music world there were not so many color barriers; in the acting world there were a lot of them but that didn't keep out the hopefuls. Black faces weren't on Broadway or on TV in any numbers yet, but it wouldn't be long now.

March 7, 1958

Christina darling,

In a few days, you will receive some bras and girdles that are being sent to you. They are the best I can get for you. I know the bras won't fit perfectly. The best I can suggest for you to do is go see Mrs. Bea Traub (at Bonwit Teller's), and have her fit them on you. Be sure to have them separated in the middle so that your bosoms are not pushed together. I think it would be wise to have elastic put in the middle, between the bosoms.

These articles have already been paid for, so will you please
have Mrs. Traub have her husband alter them so they will fit you.
God bless—and we'll be home soon.
"*Mommie*"

I could not believe this letter. I re-read it several times. Before Mother
left for Los Angeles, she'd asked if there was anything I specially needed.
I said in a sort of off-hand way that I could use some new underwear,
never thinking she was serious. Instead of sending me to a New York
store and allowing me to pick out a certain amount to be charged to her
account, or even sending me a little money to go buy what I needed, I
got this weird letter and a package of things that didn't fit me! It was
unbelievable that after all these years, everything she sent me was too
big . . . nothing ever fit and she never let me go into the store and buy
what was appropriate. The whole adventure with her was a huge waste
of time and money. But, she was in control of it. The situation was being
handled her way. It was nearly irrelevant that it never worked out right
for me. It was unimportant that there were always far more efficient
ways to handle the entire effort. But it always ended up being a massive
inconvenience for everyone and I was supposed to be grateful. By the
time it was all over, I never was grateful one bit. I was always in a rage.

But that was only part of it. The other part was the incredible incon-
gruity of getting letters from Mother abut separating bosoms and fitting
bras when I knew the world was on the brink of a social upheaval. I
knew it because I was out there on the streets. It wasn't any great insight
or any inside information. Everyone on the streets could feel it, we all
knew it was coming. It was just that none of us knew how or exactly
when. But it was definitely coming. There were too many people left
out of the system now. There were too many people with an education
who didn't fit in anywhere. There were too many people thinking for
themselves and asking questions with no answers. There were too many
people who were tired of the same old story and the same old lies about
"keep your mouth shut and toe the line and in fifty years you'll get a nice
gold watch." There were too many people who didn't want that any more
and were not going to put up with it much longer.

I sailed for England toward the end of March aboard the old Queen
Elizabeth. It was a rough winter crossing. The North Atlantic was

turbulent, the winds blew and the old ship rolled mightily, heaving her way forward against the giant waves. I was traveling tourist class and had a cabin mate. The poor lady was seasick most of the journey which was decidedly unpleasant for both of us. I tried to let her have the cabin to herself as much as possible. I played cards, took long walks on the windy decks and even went swimming every day. That was an adventure in itself. The tourist class swimming pool was an Olympic size salt-water lake down in the bowels of the ship. The seas were so rough that the pool water sloshed from side to side creating something like indoor waves. I was usually the only one in it and had a great time riding the motion of the ship in what amounted to my own private pool. The food was wonderful, but the dining room was half-empty most of the trip.

When we finally arrived in Southampton five days later, a boat train was waiting to take us to London. Friends met me at the London station, which was just like something out of a 1930s movie. We had lunch and then I boarded another train that would take me to a country village just south of Cambridge where my friends, the Bennetts, lived. It was all quite an amazing adventure for me. I'd had the foresight and good advice to only bring one large suitcase that I could manage myself. No one helped you through customs, no one helped you on the trains except getting on and off.

At the end of my sixth day of traveling alone I finally arrived in the medieval village of Downham Market, Norfolk, England. My friends lived in a charming house originally built in the fifteenth century and even though there were now modern additions, they had retained the thatched roof. The village itself had cobblestone streets and ancient buildings. My friends were landowners, ran very large farms and were considered "gentlemen farmers" or landed gentry, but not nobility. Most of the people in the village had in some way or another worked for the Bennetts for generations. Everyone knew one another for generations also. It was a totally different environment from anything I'd ever experienced.

They were all wonderful to me. I went all over the surrounding area, and then down to Cambridge by train for a few days. We drove through the English countryside to Stratford-on-Avon, which was thrilling for me. I loved history, knew my English history fairly well, so to actually be seeing it firsthand was nearly unbelievable. It was spring and it rained nearly every day for a few hours but fortunately for my insatiable curiosity, it rained mostly at night.

After about three weeks, the whole family went down to London. I stayed in their club, the Farmers Club. It was also an incredible place. Hanging on the walls in place of the ordinary pictures, were oil paintings of prize farm animals dating back three and four hundred years! There were pigs and bulls and roosters, all done in oil color with huge ornate guilded frames. It was an extraordinary sight. The rooms were simple and the baths were down the hall. You had to "book" (that meant to reserve) time for your bath. At the appointed hour an attendant would meet you in the huge bathroom bringing towels and soap. She stayed with you while you took your bath and cleaned the room up when you were finished.

We'd been in London about three days when I had a very peculiar experience one night. I was sound asleep in the small single bed next to a wall. For no apparent reason I woke up with a start. As I opened my eyes, I saw a strange object lying on the bed between my body and the wall. As I focused my eyes on it, I realized it was the lamp shade! I turned over to reach for the lamp on the little nightstand next to the bed but in the darkness, I couldn't find it. My eyes were now becoming accustomed to the darkness and I got out of bed. To my surprise, there on the floor was the lamp. It was on the opposite side of the night stand lying on its side, but it was not damaged in any way. Several feet away nearly in the middle of the small room I found the ashtray perfectly turned upside down with its contents neatly contained underneath as though someone had deliberately, but carefully put it there.

I went over to the door and turned on the overhead light switch. I didn't know what to think about the state of my room. There was the lamp shade beside the wall on top of my bed, the lamp on the opposite side of the night stand on the floor and the ashtray neatly turned upside down on the carpet. It didn't make any sense. I tried the door to my room to see if it was still locked from the inside as I'd left it, and it was still securely closed and double locked from the inside. I checked the window, but it was still closed as well. I couldn't figure out what could have caused this upheaval. If I'd bumped the nightstand in my sleep causing the lamp and ashtray to fall to the floor, *how* did the lamp shade end up between me and the wall? If I'd somehow pulled on the lamp, why didn't it hit me in the head? None of this made any sense at all. I was totally mystified, but cleaned up the mess and determined to go back to sleep.

The entire next day I had an uncomfortable, uneasy feeling for no good reason. I was having a wonderful time with all my friends. We were sightseeing and going to charming, quaint pubs . . . there was absolutely no good reason for my strange mood. Finally, I couldn't stand it any longer and I decided that I had to tell them what had happened the night before, even if they thought I was weird. Being thought weird was better than having them think I was just sullen.

After my story was finished we sat in total silence. One of the woman, Marty, spoke first. She started telling me that in England there were many people who had very strong beliefs about the supernatural. She said that there were many beautiful old houses that could not be sold because they were believed haunted and no English person would touch them. She also said that because England was such an old country, and had such a long history going way back past the Druids who were believed to be a truly mystical people, that belief in spirits, ghosts, ESP and other paranormal phenomena was quite common. As I looked from her face to the others, I realized that they were quite seriously nodding their heads in total agreement with her. I got goose bumps all over my arms. She continued by saying that it sounded to her as though someone was trying to contact me, that someone was trying to get a message to me. I couldn't imagine who in the world that might have been. I'd never had any experience with this sort of thing and I didn't even know where to look for an acceptable answer. The conversation turned to the other's experiences with haunted houses or ESP and I listened quietly. I just didn't realize all this existed. It was quite unsettling for me, even though my group of friends had been most supportive and understanding, I felt weird about it.

About six o'clock the next morning Mr. Bennett called to say the news had been on the radio the night before that my father had died of a heart attack in New York City.

I sat on the edge of my little bed with my hand covering my mouth. My very first thought was, "My God . . . she killed him!" Then I got the goosebumps all over again. Was it my daddy who was trying to get a message through to me? Was that the explanation for the weird things that happened two nights ago? I had no information on the time of death until the next day when the papers carried a small story. When I read the story, I got those damn goosebumps again. The time of his death and the time of the chaos in my room were only one hour different! I had to take a long walk by myself to calm down and think all this through. Then, as now, I believe the circumstances of Al Steele's death were suspicious and a cover-up took place.

Mother had no way of knowing where I was, so I spent about six hours trying to get a transatlantic call through to her in New York. I decided that I could turn in my boat ticket for an airplane ticket and be back the next day. I'd already made the reservations by the time my call finally got through.

She was absolutely horrible to me on the phone. Her voice had ice dripping from every syllable. Nevertheless, I told her how sorry I was, and said I was planning to return right away. She said she didn't want me anywhere near the funeral! She said Daddy's funeral was for friends and family only and that since I was neither, I could stay put right where I was. I said I could understand that she was terribly upset, but that I thought I should be there and would do anything I could to help. She repeated that she didn't want me, that I didn't belong there and that she'd see to it I wasn't admitted if I tried to attend.

I was crying. My feelings hadn't just been hurt, they'd been shattered. After all, he was supposed to be my father . . . how could she be so cruel?

I hung up the phone. Neither of us had said goodbye. I went to my room and cried for about an hour. Then I decided there was nothing more I could do about any of it except continue to try and live my own life. Daddy would have understood that and probably would have wanted it as well. So that's what I would do.

I stayed in England another month. We went to the races away out in the country and I won a long-shot that paid twenty-to-one. I'd bet the entire amount I'd won so far during the day on that last race and won! It nearly paid for my entire trip. I bought some nice presents for my generous and kind friends, knowing I'd vastly overstayed my welcome. I did a little more traveling, went back to London and took the boat train down to Southampton to catch the Maretania, sailing for New York.

Even though it was now May, the North Atlantic was still rough. We had a lot of Irish immigrants on board this trip and a lot of them were sick. The ones that weren't were a wonderful group with whom I drank beer and played cards most of the way home. We ate like Trojans because again the dining room became nearly empty after the first day at sea. I cried a lot during those five days. I didn't want to leave England and my friends. I didn't have anything to come home to. I didn't have any money left and I had to get a job immediately. My daddy was dead and I didn't even know where he was buried. I couldn't even go visit his grave. Mother was being a total pig and I didn't care if I never spoke to her again in my whole life.

The day we landed in New York City, I spent my last pound notes on tips for the crew members who had served us. To my great surprise, Lotte and some of her friends were at the ship to meet me! I couldn't believe it. I didn't even remember writing her about my return. What good fortune it was . . . I didn't even have taxi fare home.

CHAPTER 24

It was a good thing for me that I'd had such a wonderful trip because what I found waiting for me upon my return was a disaster. My brother had gotten in some trouble before I'd left for England. He and some other boys had taken a teacher's car from school and gone on a joy ride. Chris was only a passenger and not the driver, but all the boys were picked up because they'd been dumb enough to cross a state line from Connecticut to New York. I'd gone up to visit my brother in the Westchester County jail where he was being held and talked to all the authorities involved. There was nothing I could do to help him. I was only nineteen years old, I had no money for lawyers and I had no personal influence. The boy who had driven the car was released in his parent's custody within forty-eight hours, the other boys released on probation shortly afterwards.

When I returned from England I was horrified to find out that my brother was still in jail. He was the only one of the boys originally involved still being held. I went up to White Plains immediately and tried to get some information from the head probation officer. What I found out horrified me even more. The reason my brother was still in jail was that there was no place suitable to send him. The school didn't want to take him back, Mother didn't want him, the foster homes had been turned down for one reason or another and there was as yet no place to take custody of him. It was several months now that he'd been sitting there, without a lawyer, without a hearing, without anything. As I delved further into the mess, I was told that Mother and the company lawyers were trying to get the judge to send my brother to Elmira! The very name sent chills through me. Elmira was where they sent juveniles who had committed a criminal offense. My brother had been in his share of trouble, but he was certainly no criminal. If he went to Elmira, that would all change. He'd have nothing to look forward to then. He probably would be a criminal, certainly he'd have ample opportunity to learn from the Elmira experts!

In that awful moment, I decided that I had to do something. I had to find a lawyer to help me and I had to somehow stop this terrible, unfair, totally unjust punishment that was about to befall my brother.

I returned to New York and began my search for help. I had no money. I was typing scripts at home for $75 a finished copy and working half the night to complete the jobs faster. I went to every existing agency seeking help. There was none available to us. I went to every law firm I heard of that did either legal aid work or handled child abuse cases. I told my story from beginning to end in one office after another until I was so discouraged I'd come home and weep with helpless frustration. After almost a month of this, I got a lead on a partnership with a young lawyer who'd handled some unpopular cases and might be interested in helping me. I called immediately and went to see them the next afternoon. I always had to tell them out front that I had no money, but begged them to hear me out. When I'd finished my story for what seemed like the hundredth time, the younger lawyer said that he'd go with me to White Plains and at least talk to the people about trying to get more information. I was so grateful I nearly forgot myself and hugged him. I nicknamed the young lawyer "Mr. S." and that's what I'll call him from here on through.

A few days later he drove me up to White Plains and we talked to each and every person involved with the case, including my brother. Most of the people were willing to be helpful since this situation was turning into an injustice even in their opinion. My brother had now been in jail without so much as a formal hearing before a judge for over three months.

As the summer droned on, Mr. S. and I made trips to White Plains every two weeks. Since the boy who had actually driven the car had been released on probation in the custody of his parents and no charges were being brought by the teacher after the car was safely returned, that meant there were no charges being brought against my brother. He should have been released months ago, but the problem was: where?

In my opinion, the judge who was supposed to be handling the case was dragging his feet unjustifiably. He was in line for a State Supreme

Court nomination and understandably didn't want his last days in Juvenile Court marred by a scandal. I understood that the company lawyers, on specific orders from Mother, were pressuring the judge to send my brother to Elmira and be finished with the whole thing. I asked for and received an appointment with that judge. Where I found the nerve I'll never know, but I told him in no uncertain terms that if he sent my brother to Elmira, I'd go to every newspaper and television station in New York and tell them the entire story. I would not rest until I totally discredited him and he'd *never* get his appointment. I told him that in his heart he knew full well that my brother didn't deserve this severe treatment. Maybe he did deserve to be punished for what he'd participated in with those other boys, but he'd already served a three-month sentence for God's sakes and the driver was out in forty-eight hours. Was *that* fair treatment under any law?

The next thing we knew, that judge had removed himself from the case and we had to start all over again with a new judge. The hearing that had been scheduled was now postponed. Another month went by before anything further happened.

Mr. S. was wonderful. He did everything he possibly could for the two of us and never took one single penny in return for his efforts.

It was an enormously frustrating time, during which I tried to keep busy. I met some people doing charity work for an organization called Boys Town of Italy and volunteered my services. I still had the family name and if it could be put to some good use, so much the better. Mostly I helped with fund-raising events and modeled dresses and jewelry at charity balls in New York and Washington, D.C.

The only correspondence I received from Mother that summer was a handwritten note on "Mrs. Alfred N, Steele" stationary in response to a letter I'd sent her. It was dated July 29, 1959.

Tina dear—

I'm delighted you met such nice people thru "Boys Town of Italy." Its a wonderful organization with lovely people—

Yes the Journal American article was very good—thank you

All this week I will be working with the Nigerian Delegation then I'm off—for two weeks—on business—back for one day then off for more business—

Knowing you I know you will do a good job—with the public
relations people—just remember to always make it dignified—
that's the secret of all good relations—public or personal—
Love

There was no signature on this letter. Mother had been made an honor-
ary board member of Pepsi in memory of her husband. She had also
been put on the official Pepsi payroll. She continued to do the same
work she'd done with Daddy only now she made the appearances alone.
The Journal American article was all about how she was carrying on
her husband's work now that he was gone and she was a widow. It was
quite touching and had some lovely photographs. I heard that his will
had been offered for probate and that his former wife was contesting
on behalf of their son. Beyond that I was totally uninvolved and uninformed. I simply assumed that I'd been left nothing and that everything
had gone to Mother. No one contacted me to the contrary.

The first week of August I received a letter from the probation officer in
White Plains. The letter was an urgent request for assistance. The judge
and Mother's lawyers had explored the possibility of my brother signing on with the Merchant Marines, since the school didn't want him
to return. As a result, an opening was found on a ship sailing immediately for the Orient. In the meantime, the school was re-approached and
finally agreed to take him back. My brother had his heart set on taking
the job offer and when he was told that the judge had ordered him back
into the school, he was extremely distressed. If my brother didn't obey
the court order, the probation officer's letter stated that he would be
committed to a maximum security institution. *Elmira.* The closing paragraph said: "You are perhaps the one person in the world who had the
full confidence of the boy and it is for that reason only that I write you
this letter, which you are free to show him if you consider it advisable."

I immediately called Mr. S. and read him the letter. We both called
the probation officer and asked him to tell Chris we'd be up the next
morning.

It was with a feeling of impending doom that we drove the now familiar
road to White Plains. We met with everyone we could get in to see. While

Mr. S. was with the probation officer, I tried to talk to my brother. It was a dreadful situation because he was so upset and disappointed. He had been sitting in jail *five* months now and things seemed to be getting worse for him, not better. He didn't want to go back to the school. He couldn't understand why the judge had ruled against his joining the Merchant Marines and neither could I. But all that didn't matter any more. What mattered was trying to find yet another solution and it didn't look very hopeful. The judge was running out of patience and we were running out of time. I begged my brother to try and hold on a little longer, assuring him that I was doing everything humanly possible. He knew that but it didn't seem to be getting any of us very far at the moment. I went and talked to the new judge at some length. He told me that Mother and her lawyers had told him that Mother was afraid my brother would harm her. I told the judge to just look at his history. He'd always tried to run *away* from her, not toward her. He did agree that was true. I begged him to simply make my brother a ward of the court. It was the only decent solution now. I couldn't take custody of him because I was under twenty-one years old and didn't even have a permanent job. But as a ward of the court at least he wouldn't be under Mother's domination any more. I told him I thought she might welcome having the responsibility she complained so bitterly about taken away from her, that she might just find it a relief. I begged him to at least consider it a viable possibility.

The formal and final hearing of this case was scheduled. I again drove up to the court house with Mr. S. We were allowed a final interview with the judge. When I entered the chambers, I could smell Mother's perfume still in the room. She and the Pepsi lawyers had just left their interview. I was scared to death. It was finally dawning on me what an enormous amount of power I'd been single-handedly fighting. Mother never spoke to me and I never spoke to her. Mother sat with her lawyers and the other men she brought with her in the first two rows; I had to get special permission to sit in the last row alone. Mr. S. was not allowed inside the courtroom with me. It was hot and still in that big room and I felt my heart beating the whole time. I had no idea what would happen and it was now too late to change the decision. I prayed to God for help as I had so many times before. I had tried every way I knew to buck the system, to turn the tide of money and power and influence. All I had was the truth and a fighting spirit.

~

To my complete and total amazement, the judge ruled favorably. My brother was placed on six-month probation and made a ward of the State of New York. He was sixteen years old and had been in Westchester County jail without bail, with no charges brought against him . . . for *six* months. When I heard the ruling, tears of relief flooded down my cheeks. We'd won! We'd actually won. I waited until my mother and her entourage left the courtroom by the side door. She'd never said one word to her son. That little blonde boy she'd adopted with Phillip Terry just sixteen years ago was being made a ward of the court in his own best interest and she never said one word of apology or goodbye to him. He never received the trust fund or the college education the divorce decree supposedly guaranteed him. From that day on he was an official ward of the court until he was eighteen years old. He'd ended up pretty much where he began . . . an orphan. The good thing was that she couldn't touch him ever again. The damage was already done, but she couldn't continue to make it worse. She could totally ignore him, which she did, but she couldn't hurt him any more than she already had.

I ran to my brother and hugged him. He was crying too. Mr. S. came down the aisle and shook his hand. I hugged Mr. S, thanking him over and over again. The judge had left, so I didn't get to say anything to him, but I'm sure he was relieved that he'd never have to see me again after that day. We were told that my brother would be transferred to a settlement house in Manhattan during the next week and they'd call to let me know.

My building had to have heat installed via an inspection violation and subsequent court order. Workman came to cut holes in the floors and ceilings of each apartment through which the steam heat pipes were fitted. You never saw anything like what happened after the mess was cleaned up and those pipes in place. It was the cockroach raceway . . . five stories high! Nothing you could do stopped them. It was revolting and disgusting. I decided I had to move out of there before the rats followed the cockroaches.

A few blocks away on 73rd street near Second Avenue there were two old brownstones being renovated into one new apartment building. I went to the building office on the first floor to inquire about availability. The woman put me on a list and said that the rent for a studio with kitchen and bath was $135 a month, first and last months rent in advance. I told her I wanted one and filled out all the papers, lying about my employment. I scraped together every penny I could get my hands on, illegally sold the "key" to my cold water flat for $150 and sent the building a check for the advance rent, guaranteeing myself a place in the building. The next week I carried my belongings through the streets of New York and into my brand new apartment.

I had a roommate but she didn't make much money so I only asked her for a small portion of the rent. I didn't care how we had to struggle, it was wonderful having new appliances, a real bathroom inside the apartment and an air conditioner.

Chris hated the settlement house and got permission to move in with me after a month. I got him a job in a college bookstore through my friend Eddie because we didn't get any money from the state unless he lived at the settlement house.

My roommate moved out after a few weeks, saying she couldn't afford half the rent and she didn't feel comfortable not being able to pay her way. Shortly afterwards my friend Lotte came back to New York and moved in again. That meant there were three of us living in a one-room apartment with only two single beds. Somebody always had to sleep on the floor. It was totally crazy and very crowded, but we were all still young and we managed to work it out. I didn't ask my brother to pay any rent but he did have to provide his own food and transportation to work. I couldn't give him any more than a place to live. I wasn't working and I still couldn't get unemployment, so it was touch and go every single month. Lotte received some money from her parents so at least I only had to worry about my half of the rent and the phone.

I started making arrangements to go out to dinner nearly every single night of the week. I'd order steak, rare, and only eat the outside edges. I'd finish the rest of my dinner and then ask for a doggy bag. I'd ask my date for money to tip the ladies' room attendant and usually get a dollar. I'd leave the woman a quarter and pocket the change. Then I'd ask for cab fare home if the man got drunk and pull my old trick of going around the corner and taking the bus the rest of the way home. My brother would be waiting up for his dinner, no matter how late it was when I got home. We'd warm the rare steak in the broiler and it would turn out a perfect medium rare by the time it was hot again. We had a lot of fun and got a lot of laughs out of our minor tribulations. He was an awfully good sport and I did the best I could. We managed.

Needless to say, I didn't see Mother. She was livid over my role during the court battle. She perceived me as the total traitor, troublemaker and instigator of the entire mess. All I had been able to see was the potential destruction of my brother's life. All I wanted was a fair deal for him. From what I could tell, it hadn't hurt her one bit. She was now relieved from all further expense on his behalf which meant that she now only had two children left to care for, since I'd been on my own for nearly a year. She was the one who got off easy in the long run.

CHAPTER 25

The only acting work I had done so far this year consisted of five days as an extra on a movie shooting on location in New York. I'd heard that the director was one of my former "uncles" from the old days at Brentwood and called him to say hello. He invited me for dinner and then arranged for me to get on the picture as an extra each day it was shooting in the city.

Lotte eventually went back to stay with her parents again. My brother got married after his seventeenth birthday and moved to Florida. The apartment was empty and seemed so quiet. It was well into winter now and I couldn't seem to get any work. With no roommate, the expenses skyrocketed into more than I could manage. I began to get really concerned. I just couldn't seem to make ends meet.

From Los Angeles, Mother wrote this courteous reply to the letter I'd sent her containing my new address.

October 14, 1959

Dearest Tina,

I'm happy to hear of your new apartment, and it sounds wonderful that it's a brand new building. You will have a nice, good, clean start at housekeeping now.

It's nice of you to keep me informed.

Bless you, and my love.

"*Mommie*"

Finally, I was a month behind in paying the rent and I had run out of food completely. I didn't have any money left at all. For three days I stayed inside the apartment having a massive anxiety attack about my whole life. I even thought about killing myself, but that seemed so ordinary and chicken shit.

By one of those miracles that happen in life, the phone finally rang. I had gotten an appointment through an old friend at MCA who was not my agent, to see the director of a winter stock theater in Milwaukee. I got dressed immediately and scrounged around for bus fare. When I added the change up, it was mostly in pennies, but I got to the appointment on time. The man offered me an Equity contract for the rest of the winter season and a minimum salary which was $80 a week. He told me that the theater had company housing at $10 a week that was only one block away and an easy walk even in the snows of Milwaukee. I accepted immediately. He told me he'd arrange to get me a plane ticket, that I'd be reporting to the theater in a week!

I walked home because I didn't have any more money for the bus. I called everyone I knew, asking if I could borrow enough to join the union. Between three separate friends, I managed to scrape together the $200, which was just enough to join the union and get me to the airport. I packed my suitcase, called the landlord to tell him I was going out of town to work, but that I'd send him all the money I owed as soon as I got paid.

Someone had given me a dog several months ago. It was a miserable, shaky little beast named Paco. It was a Chihuahua. That dog never liked me and I was not fond of him, but we were now stuck with one another. I had to take him with me or have him put to sleep. The latter is what I secretly wanted to do, but my conscience wouldn't let me. So, off I went with Paco under my arm to a city called Milwaukee and another adventure.

I am ashamed to admit that my basic knowledge of geography was so poor and my ego so misplaced when it came to asking dumb questions, that I was in the city of Milwaukee one solid week before I was able to discover what *state* I was living in!

The company apartment was a total madhouse. I was the only woman there, but given the sexual preferences of the male tenants, I was quite safe from molestation. I had my own large room at the end of the hall and it was thoroughly clean and comfortable. The second floor apartment boasted its own large kitchen and living room, so there was plenty of living space for the few free hours any of us had. Because I was so far in debt upon my arrival, it took me several paychecks before I was able to buy many groceries. The male members of the company were very good cooks, and thank goodness they invited me to join some of the meals. I suspect they knew I didn't have a dime to spare and was too proud to ask. Except for leaving poor Paco out in the snow on several occasions, life at the theater went well.

While I was in rehearsal for the second show, I got a call from some Carnegie friends who were doing their first full-length feature film. I'd met with them about the movie before leaving New York, but had forgotten all about it in my rush to get to Milwaukee. They told me they planned to start filming in Florida the beginning of February and offered me a small part at Screen Actors Guild minimum, but with all expenses paid and a guarantee of three weeks work. It was another union to join but the SAG minimum was $350 a week which sounded like a princely sum to me. I told them I'd love it and to let me know when exactly, because I'd have to give notice at the theater.

Lotte drove up from Chicago to see my first real play which was *Dark of the Moon*. I had one of the supporting roles but was on stage most of the time. She asked me if she could come back to the apartment after the first of the year which was great. She gave me some money for the rent and I gave her back the extra key. That way she could just make her own plans without worrying where I was and how she would get into the apartment. I was really delighted. At long last, things seemed to be starting. I'd been offered the lead part of Emily in the second play, *Our Town*, which was very exciting and now a part in a film which would also get me into the next union. Things were beginning to move right along for me. I'd be going from one reputable, paying job right into another one. I was very happy, getting good reviews and feeling greatly encouraged. Maybe I hadn't made a giant mistake with my life after all.

I spent the winter working in Milwaukee until my friends called to tell me they were definitely starting in February. I gave notice and said goodbye sadly to the wonderful friends I made at the Fred Miller Theater.

There was a slight delay in plans after I returned to New York, which aggravated me, because as it turned out, I could have stayed for one more play. But I had a month in New York with Lotte, getting ready to go to Miami for about a month. I had to borrow money again to join

Screen Actors Guild. Fortunately, because I already belonged to Equity, the new union SAG gave members a discounted fee, but I think it was still $150. I'd paid off all my previous debts, so I didn't have so much trouble going back to borrow the second time around. Off I went to Miami, taking great delight in being so chic as to go "south" for the last of winter.

The company was housed at the Cadillac Hotel on Collins Avenue right on the ocean. We had some deal where our rooms and two meals a day were paid in return for some publicity given the hotel by all members of the cast. That was the easiest free ride I'd ever gotten. We posed for some extra pictures, and that was about the extent of it.

Since I didn't work right away, I had time to see all of Miami, shop and go boating. I got a terrific tan within the first week, though I'd been pale as a ghost upon arrival.

After the second week of no work, we all began to get stir crazy. Something had gone wrong in planning this shoot, because half of us were now sitting around our rooms on twenty-four-hour call, with nothing to do.

The third week passed and we began to wonder if something was really wrong. But during the fourth week I did my entire part, checked out of the hotel without my last paycheck in hand and took the first plane back to New York.

I was one of the lucky ones. I reported my late paycheck to the union and left the rest to them. The stories that drifted back were like actors' nightmares. I was the first member of the cast to be finished and the first to leave Miami. I heard that everyone else either got stuck for at least part of their hotel bills or had to wait for their paychecks and finally the film itself was impounded for a while. I felt rather like I must have had a guardian angel on my shoulder to get out so literally in the nick of time. I'd actually had a very good time. I'd gotten a wonderful tan, eaten two delicious meals a day for almost a month and come home with plenty of money to see me through the next few months now that Lotte was back.

Mother had gone out to the Coast to do a cameo role in Jerry Wald's production of *The Best of Everything*. It was the first film she'd done since completing *The Story of Esther Costello* in 1956. Jerry and Mother had been close friends since they'd done *Mildred Pierce* together. Jerry had been one of the few who really believed in Mother and helped her make that comeback. He now must have realized what a difficult time it was for her right after Daddy's death and offered the small part to her. I thought it was really very kind and considerate of him.

Before leaving for Miami, I'd had several long talks with a freelance writer who was interested in doing a national magazine story on me. I was one of the first "Hollywood kids" to go into the business as an actress and there was evidently story value in that as well as my own personal experience. The money he talked about seemed like a fortune to me at the time, and he seemed reputable enough. He contacted *Redbook Magazine* and on the basis of a preliminary outline, received an advance. In retrospect, I didn't get paid a lot of money for the story and that was never my primary concern. I welcomed what I assumed was an opportunity to tell *my* story truthfully in hopes that it would help me set the record straight as to why Mother was choosing not to help me financially or professionally.

I turned out to be woefully naive. Mother found out about the magazine's plans and contacted one of the editors. She insisted on being able to see the final copy and to have her version included in the same article. The piece did not start out to be a joint venture, but perhaps because of libel worries on the part of the magazine management, she was interviewed and her quotes printed in the article. What the writer, who was by now caught squarely in the middle, attempted to do was investigate the allegations she made and to verify them. To my great disappointment, the story turned out to be a question of her word against mine. She even was quoted as saying that I had been expelled from Chadwick! When I read the article in its finished state, I couldn't believe my eyes.

The direct quote about my leaving Chadwick School was: "The whole story is a product of the girl's imagination. My relationship with the Chadwicks was always warm and friendly. Christina's behavior at school was not always what it should have been. She often dated and went away for weekends without my permission or that of the Chadwicks. I don't enjoy telling you this, but the real reason Christina left Chadwick was that she had been expelled—and I will not say why. I sent her to the convent because it was the only school that would accept her."

~

She's gone crazy, I thought. She's gotten it all mixed up in her head. One year and another are blurred together in her story . . . one school and another have been transposed. The business with the unauthorized weekend happened at *Flintridge* not at Chadwick and is easily proven by her own letters to me, to Sister Benigna and to Mrs. Irvine. The dating business is a total figment of *her* imagination. That never happened at all. Ever. If her relationship with the Chadwicks was always so "warm and friendly" then why did she forbid me to ever see them again, why did she punish me for seven months for going to visit them? Either she's just intentionally lying or she doesn't *know* what really happened any more.

The Chadwicks declined any corroborative interview, wiring their response: "From experience with Christina's Mother, we consider it unwise to involve Chadwick by making any public comment. Very sorry."

So, once more it was Mother's word against mine. I was telling the truth and she was lying and the magazine printed both versions, which was the only thing left for them to do. Of course there was no written record of any such expulsion on my high school transcripts, because no such thing *ever* took place.

Elsewhere in the article, Mother said that she recalled the family trip to Europe as a "miserable time" because she felt I intruded on her privacy with her new husband and allowed them no time together. She went on to say that Daddy was not enchanted by the continual presence of a sixteen-year-old girl.

I think I hated her more for that lie than the other. Jesus Christ, I thought will it never end?

The article was published in October 1960. It was as well researched and clearly written as was possible under the circumstances. Unfortunately, the title was not of my choosing and caused quite a stir. The magazine had finally decided on "The Revolt of Joan Crawford's Daughter." I had a dreadful sinking feeling. Not so much about the contents of the article and the false allegations, those just made me mad. What I resented terribly was not having a proper name of my own . . . I was growing to hate the phrase "Joan Crawford's daughter" with a mighty passion. It was the most giant hype in the world. I wasn't her blood daughter and I had none of the privileges or benefits of being her adopted daughter either. All of the words in that phrase made my blood boil, because all I seemed to do was pay through my whole life for them, never getting one damn thing in return. Okay, I thought. This is it and I can't change the title of the article, but maybe this time I can manage to get something out of it for myself. Maybe there's some way I can use it to my advantage.

I sent a copy of the magazine with a short note to Louella Parsons, saying that I hoped she'd be able to understand the spirit in which the article was written and not just its title. She wrote me back a sweet note saying that since she'd known me practically all my life, she was indeed aware of the intentions of the article and wished me all success in my career. Louella was an elderly lady by that time, but she still held control over a powerful column. She decided to help me in whatever way she could and started writing things in the column about me, my blossoming career and finally about the article I'd sent her with the note. There was a lot of publicity that was a direct result of her column and almost inevitably, a job offer.

The majority of my life I'd tried to be someone on my own. I'd tried to get work without using Mother or her name, though I never changed my own as she had asked me to do. This time, I was determined to do whatever the hype, which was not of my own making, demanded. I would give the interviews and do the talk shows and take the work that came as a result. This was a classic case of the hype working through publicity campaigns that began to have their own momentum, but which had originated with Louella Parsons' column. From there, lots of others jumped on the bandwagon and tried to get in on the act.

Not long afterwards, I received a wire from Jerry Wald, offering me a part in the next new picture starring Elvis Presley. I went to the 20th Century Fox offices in New York. I knew the Skouras family who still ran Fox in those days from my work with Boys Towns of Italy. They liked me and Spiros Skouras had me into his office for a brief interview. I was then offered a long-term contract with Fox, but I'd have to go out to the Coast for a screen test. It was just like all the stories you've ever read in movie magazines. I tried to remain calm through the whole uproar, but it was getting impossible. I was getting progressively more scared as each day rolled by. They gave me a first-class, round-trip ticket and told me to plan on staying in Los Angeles two weeks.

I had to borrow money for the first few days in California and the trip to the airport. Seems as though I *always* had to borrow money just to get out of town! The studio agreed to pay a per diem and pick up my hotel bill, but I wouldn't go on salary until the picture started.

Saying goodbye to my friends in New York was a mixed blessing. I was very sad to leave, scared to death about returning to Los Angeles and so excited about how well all this was going that I couldn't stand it.

I was very nervous during my screen test. It was all so formal, so many people scurrying around the big sound stage and so quiet when the work began and the cameras rolled. I'd been on sound stages all my life. I knew the entire routine. But, I'd never been there on my own. The film we did in Florida was primarily on locations, it was a low budget movie and we were all very informal. This was the "big time," for real. The next five years of my life depended on just one day, just one screen test.

When I saw the test, I didn't like it very much. There were a multitude of things I would have done differently the next time. But it was good enough to get me the part in Jerry Wald's picture and the studio signed my long-term contract renewable at their option.

I went to see my Uncle Jerry in his office to thank him for this wonderful opportunity. He was just exactly as I remembered him from the years he visited the Brentwood house: a round man with a moon-like face and a heart of gold. He was also a very good producer. We reminisced a while about the "old days" and I felt it was time to leave. He gave me a big hug and told me he was glad things had worked out so well.

Every time something had appeared in her column about me, I'd written Aunt Louella to thank her. Unfortunately, by the time I actually arrived in Los Angeles, she was too ill to have visitors. So I left messages and wrote her notes on my progress, thanking her again for helping to make it all possible.

November 5, 1960

Christina dear,

I saw your test, and I thought you were just lovely. I am glad you had the loving care of Jerry Wald, Bill Mellor, Perry Lieber, Don Prince and Phillip Dunne.

I am sure you will have great success, and nobody wishes it for you more than your—

"*Mommie*"

I was embarrassed to realize that she'd been on the studio lot the same time I had been there and I'd been manipulated so skillfully that I didn't bump into her or even know she was there seeing my screen test. It wasn't just embarrassing, it was downright creepy.

Almost every day I was at the studio doing wardrobe fittings, hair and makeup tests, publicity photos and having lunches at the commissary with the publicity department for interviews they'd arranged. I was now one of the stable of contract players on the lot and I just simply didn't ask questions. I gave interviews on the theme "I'm glad my mother disciplined me because if I'm to succeed in this business, I'll need it." I tried to turn the thrust of the questions into a positive image for myself. I tried to gloss over the years of estrangement, which were still going on and only emphasize my early, happy childhood years with Mother. It seemed like every time I turned around, I was meeting someone who said: "I'll bet you don't remember me, but I met you when you were . . ." I began to think that half the known world must have passed through the gates of our Brentwood house before I was seven years old. I didn't remember most of the people, but I tried to be polite about it. How could I be expected to remember someone I met only once at three years old? But, by God, they remembered me! I listened to their stories with that fixed, polite smile on my face so many times it's a wonder I didn't forget myself and curtsey at the end of them.

In my free time I contacted Sister Benigna and visited her at Flintridge. I called Nicki and she drove up to Hollywood to see me. I saw some of my schoolmates from Chadwick, most of whom were married now. I visited with Mrs. Chadwick and she told me the sad news of Commander's death. I even saw Walter again. He was very successful already and directly in line to take over the family business. He was wonderful to me as always, despite the years that had passed and all the changes we'd both been through. The only truly magnanimous gesture of my life was not allowing myself to marry Walter. He would have given me the world if he could and all I would have given him in return would have been total misery. Not because I intended to, but at that time of my life, I wasn't really capable of much better. It was because I loved him and cared about him that I had to stop seeing him, not because he wasn't important to me. There are just some people you cannot allow yourself to screw up with, and that's how I felt about Walter. He deserved better.

There was something about all of this that was like ghosts on parade for me. It was a weird homecoming. I felt uneasy.

In the midst of the notoriety that was beginning to surround me, I was nearly broke. After my test was over, I couldn't afford the hotel and I had to stay with a series of friends. I'm afraid I always overstayed my welcome, since I was an intrusion into their ordinary, everyday lives. I didn't have a car nor did I have a California driver's license. Getting from one place to another was an incredible hassle. I began to realize that I was doing something wrong, that I just couldn't seem to hold it all together.

When the picture finally started shooting, I was told that I'd only have two weeks work on it. The two weeks dwindled down to one week with some night shooting on overtime. It was a very small part with billing far beyond what the part itself required. It was the hype again, only this time I did recognize it happening. I was just being used in every way possible and in return I was getting one week's work. It was starting to make me feel very crazy. I was beginning to realize that I was no match for the experts. Certainly, they'd turned this hype around on me and gotten by far the better deal out of it.

I was going out with one of Elvis Presley's companion-bodyguards, who was very nice to me and invited me to a lot of the parties given at the Bel Air mansion Elvis occupied.

Before the small part I had in the picture was even finished shooting, I received word that Jerry Wald wanted to see me in his office. I didn't think much about it, since I'd been to see Jerry a number of times since my arrival.

Jerry had a habit of stuttering slightly whenever he was excited or agitated. As he greeted me, I realized that he was stuttering today. He motioned me to a chair in front of his desk and didn't get up to give me a hug as usual. I sat quietly, waiting for what he had to say.

He was clearly an uncomfortable man during these next moments. He didn't look at me directly, but at the floor, the ceiling and his desk. He told me he wanted to talk to me about something that had just happened that was very disturbing to him and which he hoped I would be able to clarify.

He then related to me the following story: Apparently, after my mother had finished the cameo role in his film *The Best of Everything* last year, he and Mother had talked about her appearing in his next film, after the Elvis movie, which was *Return to Peyton Place*. Mother had asked to see the script, as usual, and then agreed to do the film for him. They'd gotten so far that they'd worked out all the details right up to actually signing contracts, which was supposed to have occurred just about now. Jerry paused at this point, looking directly at me for the first time.

"Your mother has just informed me that she is unable to do the picture." He almost had tears in his eyes. He went on to say that she said she was very sorry, but other commitments prevented her from doing his film. He looked at me and said: "It was all set! What do you think could have happened?"

I honestly didn't know, since I had not seen Mother here at the studio. I hadn't seen anything except the back of her hat in the Westchester Court House for well over a year.

Jerry was extremely agitated now, and was pacing up and down behind his desk. He said that he got the impression that the reason she wouldn't do his next film, which had been all set, was that I was doing his current film. He had the distinct impression that she was angry with him for hiring and helping me! He looked directly at me again. I didn't know what to say. I just sat there like a big bump.

He repeated his impression differently. In other words, he said, if he hired me he wasn't going to be able to get her. But since he'd already hired me and since I'd nearly finished shooting my small part in the movie, there was nothing he could do about it.

"Are you and your mother on good terms?" he asked directly.

"No, we're not," I answered back just as directly.

"That's it," he mumbled, more to himself than to me. "I hired you and now she won't work for me."

"I'm sorry, Uncle Jerry. I didn't know anything like this would happen to anybody." I felt terrible, both for myself and for him. There was nothing I could do about it either. She was punishing him where it really hurt. She was showing him and the rest of the industry that she could give out hard lessons too. Once word got around, as I knew it would, that if you hired me, don't expect Mother to work for you. She was in the process of giving everyone a graphic lesson in what to expect. I don't think she realized that Jerry would tell me what had happened, or give me enough information to know why. It was innuendo and intimidation at its very best. It was the old hype at work full-time . . . full steam ahead.

I finished my part in the picture. With the salary I'd been getting, I finally managed to get an apartment on Franklin Avenue in Hollywood, but it was unfurnished. I sent for my few things from New York and let the apartment there go. My things had not yet arrived, so I was practically sleeping on the floor.

Thanksgiving was spent with my friend who had visited Grandmother. But as the holiday season approached, there were invitations to a lot of parties. No one yet knew what a small part I'd had in the Presley movie. All they knew was what a lot of publicity I'd been getting, courtesy of the studio interviews. I received invitations to a lot of parties that were given mainly for their own publicity value. It was sort of a circle. If your name was in the papers, you had ample opportunities to get your name in the paper over and over again.

I was invited to a holiday party at Presley's house as well. There were lots of people delighted to attend, since Elvis rarely went out and it was something of a status symbol to be invited to his house. Midway through the party, Elvis and I were seated side by side on the couch in the living room filled with people. What started out as just a joke involving his big cigar and my drink turned into an unfortunate scuffle. The contents of my glass were dripping all over his shirt.

Needless to say, I left immediately thereafter and had to apologize profusely to him before my faux pas was forgiven.

It was sort of all in keeping with the rest that was happening in my life. Just one screw up after another. A couple of days before, I received word that the studio was not picking up their option on my contract. I was to get my things out of the dressing room as soon as possible. When I arrived at the front gate to retrieve my few belongings, not two weeks after finishing the picture, I found out I no longer had a pass and was ushered through the reception office having to get special permission even to enter the lot. It was again, just like you read about in movie magazines, only now it was the flip side of the coin and it was happening to me. The official reason the studio gave was general cutback due to the cost of *Cleopatra* which was way over budget. While that may well have been true, I don't think the story Jerry Wald told me exactly helped my chances for continued success.

So, there I was in Los Angeles. I'd let my New York apartment go, I'd sent for my belongings which were midway across the country. I'd been counting on a steady salary when I signed the lease on my Franklin Avenue apartment and . . . now I had nothing.

My last paycheck just got me through the first of the new year. Then I had to move in with friends. There had been so much publicity about my being under contract to Fox, that it was difficult to explain why I was out looking for work. Ironically, the time lag was such that publicity stories were continuing to appear in print long after my contract was canceled. So, to the world at large, it appeared that I was continuing to do extremely well for myself, though in fact, I was again penniless and having to move out of my apartment in the middle of the night.

I'd made contact with Phillip Terry again. He took me out to dinner several times and filled me in on the story of his divorce from Mother. It was only then that I learned about the agreement he made with her at that time. It came as a shock to him when he heard that Chris had never received any trust fund or college education money, both of which were stipulated in the divorce agreement in return for her getting sole custody of the child he thought they had adopted together. In addition, he told me that after the divorce he had been unable to get a job anywhere in the business. He'd gone into real estate and done quite well. I told him I was really sorry about the way she'd treated him and the stories about her vendetta against her own brother, Hal. Then I told him about my talk with Jerry Wald and Phillip only replied that it didn't surprise him.

He was going to Mexico on a fishing trip and offered me the use of his apartment while he was away. Of course, I accepted gratefully and moved in the day he left. In fact, I drove him down to meet his friends in Newport Beach and also had the use of his car. The final irony was that his car was a turquoise blue 1957 Thunderbird, identical to the one given to me on my eighteenth birthday. I had some weird feelings about that too. The whole thing was like history repeating itself in almost spooky ways that were beyond my comprehension.

During the month of his vacation, my agents sent me on numerous appointments. I didn't get any of the jobs. I was out of money. I spent the last of my small reserve paying the shipping charges on my belongings from New York. When Phillip returned, I went to live with a man I'd met on the picture. I continued to try to get work for another six months. I never landed one of the jobs and finally even the appointments stopped.

Several people made veiled reference to the reason no one wanted to even see me for an audition, never mind hire me for a job. I had it hinted to me on different occasions that I'd somehow been "blacklisted" but there was no way to prove it. No one would admit anything outright. Hollywood is an exciting industry, but it is a town run on fear.

Everyone wants to be on the winning bandwagon and no one wants to even come close to anything that smells of trouble or fear they'll be next in line for the invisible axe.

One lady columnist had the kindness and the courage to lend me $200 with which to buy a used car, but she made me promise not to tell anyone, not even her husband! I paid back the money in full, eventually, as I had always repaid my debts.

It was too much for me to handle after about a year. I just dropped out of sight completely. I paid my union dues but let the agents go, which wasn't a hard decision for either of us. I ceased trying to get work as an actress and when all the money ran out, I went to work incognito. I took a job in the mailroom of a savings and loan in Hollywood and worked there for two years. The rest of my time I spent in my garden on a hillside in Laurel Canyon. I was very poor during those years, but I put myself back together again as a human being.

I'm forever grateful to the man who stood by me, who supported me, who helped me find some reality. My life was a total shambles when I met him. He was my first real love, he was my first real man. He was my first glimpse into another way of life. I guess we were living like "hippies" long before there ever was such a word. We grew most of our own food and we fished out at Paradise Cove. We loved each other and we loved our friends.

I learned about the ideas of reincarnation and karma. I thought a lot about that in the context of my own life. It was the first philosophy that gave me anything to hold onto. It was the first concept that seemed to make any sense in the light of my own life and my relationship with my mother. It was the first time I sensed some order to the universe, some meaning to my own lifelong pain. If my relationship with my mother was something to do with karma, then it didn't appear to be total absurdity. There was a reason I was put on earth . . . a life lesson I had to learn. I would continue to have to learn it over and over until the karma was resolved. Until there was peace in my life, I could go on no further. It was a time of inner speculation. It was a time when I was forced to come face to face with myself. I didn't always like what I saw in my own mirror.

During these years I made no attempt to keep in contact with Mother. I sent no gifts. I wrote no polite letters. I gave up making any pretense of being the good, dutiful daughter. She lived her life and I lived mine quite separately. I gave up trying to blame her. I also had to give up making excuses for either one of us. I honestly didn't care what she thought about me, or if she thought about me. I had to put my own life back together based on something other than total bullshit insanity. I had my journey to discover and to complete and that was my only concern. I think those years saved me from totally destroying myself.

I was on the bottom rung of the economic and social ladder but this time it was quite different. Now there were groups of people who helped one another. There were people banding together in communes who chose not to participate in a system they found corrupt and unjust. We all believed passionately in President Kennedy. We believed in the civil rights movement. We knew the injustices firsthand. There was no use trying to bullshit us through the media because we'd all been there. People made it on unemployment, by painting houses and fixing cars. They all wanted to be somebody, but on their terms and not the systems! The dissatisfaction ran very deep. It was the beginning of a social revolution that would last through the sixties.

The day John Kennedy was assassinated, I was working on the switchboard at the savings and loan when the news came through. I couldn't believe it was really true. At lunchtime I rushed to a friend's house to see the television coverage.

When he was dead I cried harder than when Daddy died. He represented the only real hope for the future my generation had ever known. His loss was devastating. We were all glued to the television set for the next three days. I went to church to pray for him. When I returned, Lee Harvey Oswald had just been murdered in real time, right there on television! The whole world was falling apart! The whole thing was just falling apart. Everybody was crying.

I don't think that anyone who was in their early years when Kennedy was murdered was ever quite the same again. A trust, a faith, a belief and a hope that things would get better left all of us.

I didn't start back to work in show business until nearly the end of 1964. I did a play in Los Angeles, one in Santa Barbara, summer stock in Chicago and a couple of small parts on episodic television, but nothing significant. Early in 1965 I auditioned for John Cassevettes' movie *Faces* and was hired.

Through the considerable efforts of a friend in New York, I was booked the entire summer doing various plays in stock companies and on tour throughout the Midwest. I was happy to return to Chicago for a month, where I'd gotten very good reviews the summer before and made some friends.

While I was still performing at a dinner theater about half an hour's drive west of Chicago, Mother arrived in town on Pepsi business. I'd heard she was staying at the Ambassador Hotel and sent her a note inviting her out to see the play. I had enclosed the glowing reviews we'd gotten. She never came to the theater, never called me. It so happened that, quite separately, a group of local Pepsi people had gotten tickets to see our play. I found out that they'd taken about ten tables and that night I arranged for small flower arrangements with a personal note from me to be placed on all the Pepsi tables.

After the play, I met some of the people who were most complimentary. They asked if Mother had seen the play and I had to say she'd been too busy.

When I returned to Los Angeles, this letter was waiting for me.

June 8, 1965

Christina dear,

Thank you so much for your note and the reviews. I am terribly sorry that they arrived the day after I had departed for New York. Fortunately, some of the Pepsi people were still in Chicago and sent them on to me.

I am delighted about your success. I am really deeply happy for you.

I don't know what your plans are, or how long you are running there, so let me hear. I am back in New York now.

God bless.

Love,
Mother

Except for my screen test at Fox, Mother had never seen anything I'd done. I guess she'd heard from fans in various parts of the country who had come to see me, but she really had no idea what I was like anymore. The last time I'd seen her was almost seven years before, when she told me I'd better go out and find a job. I'd spoken with her on the phone for several years after that and we'd written to one another periodically.

She'd had a great success with her movie *What Ever Happened to Baby Jane?* in 1962. I'd had to laugh when I read all the stories about her feud with Bette Davis, because I could just imagine the trauma of those two working together. How Bob Aldrich ever got that picture finished is a marvel of modern times. Bette Davis was probably the only actress alive who was an absolutely fair match for Mother. Years later, Mother would only have to hear Bette Davis's name mentioned to start into a complete tirade. I don't think it is possible to carry that amount of hostility for so many years without a secret admiration for an equal adversary. When you meet your match and can't come away with a total victory, there has to be a certain respect mingled with the anger, whether or not you choose to admit it.

My last stop on tour that summer of 1965 was a theater in an amusement park in the coal mining region of Pennsylvania. Before the week's run was quite over, I received word that I'd gotten an audition in New York. It was very exciting news. Saint Subber was looking for a replacement of the lead in the Chicago company of *Barefoot In The Park*.

The day of my audition, Sue Mengers went with me to the theater. I'd never auditioned in a Broadway theater and I was so nervous I was visibly shaking. I did the best I could in a sort of totally unconscious state. When it was over, there was dead silence in the dark house. I was on the stage and didn't know whether to just leave, whether I was supposed to stand there or find someplace to sit down. I was sort of immobilized.

Then a voice came out of the darkness of the house. It was the producer himself, St. Subber. He said, "That was probably the worse audition I've ever sat through. You haven't seen the play, have you?"

I thought surely I was going to throw up all over their pretty set! I managed to nod my head, "no," but I couldn't say anything. The voice from the darkness said, "See the play tonight and come back at 10:30 tomorrow morning."

I laughed so hard during the play that night, it was nearly impossible to see it and memorize the blocking in only one viewing. But I got the idea of what they wanted and I'd made a lot of little notes on my script. It was only then that I realized what good training I'd gotten over the years in summer stock. There, you only had one week's rehearsal at the most and everything was done very quickly. I stayed up half the night memorizing the lines and working out the blocking as best I could. Fortunately, there was only one set, so that wasn't very difficult.

The next morning I returned alone to the theater, and this time managed to be composed enough to remember the stage manager's name. I thought the whole audition went very well. It was certainly light years away from the disaster of the day before. They had me do three scenes, after which I was soaked with perspiration from all the running the character was directed to do. They said thank-you-very-much-we'll-be-in-touch, and I left, not knowing one thing about what my chances were.

I was back in Los Angeles almost a month before the agents called to tell me I was hired and to come to New York immediately to begin rehearsals! I would be financially solvent for the first time in my whole life. I was just 25 years old, but I'd been totally on my own for the last six years.

The stage manager I'd met at the original audition, Harvey, was responsible for directing the replacements. The first evening in Chicago we were taken by Harvey to meet the cast. Joan Van Ark was playing "Corrie", Dick Benjamin was playing "Paul" and Myrna Loy was playing the mother. Myrna was the star name in the package. Joan and Dick were gracious and offered to do whatever they could to help us. Joan and I had a rather long talk and she was just wonderful. Myrna Loy was polite as we shook hands and she mentioned something about meeting me as a little girl wearing white gloves and curtseying. I smiled back politely, not terribly amused.

I realized the first day of full rehearsal in Chicago that Myrna was not going to be particularly helpful to us. She simply didn't adjust to the fact that we were different people and try as we might, neither of us was going to be a carbon copy of the people she was used to seeing in our places. We didn't sound alike, we didn't look alike, but we were determined to give good performances.

I'd worked with my fair share of stars in summer stock and the most difficult ones I'd known were pussy cats compared with Myrna.

Harvey was wonderful to me, kept trying to reassure me that everything would be fine once the tension of our opening night was past. He told me I was superb in the part and not to worry one bit.

Opening night was the most exhilarating experience of my life! Everything worked magnificently. First of all the play was a brilliantly written comedy. Secondly, the original direction by Mike Nichols was what we were following and it was paced so fast that the audience never had a chance to fully recover from the waves of laughter that engulfed them after the opening seconds. It was the most thrilling acting experience with an audience I'd ever known. I'd done a lot of comedy, but nothing to compare with this. My part was on stage almost every minute of the play and was a thoroughly exhausting assignment. What made it so fantastic was the laughter.

August 25, 1965

Tina darling,

I'm delighted you are doing *Barefoot in the Park*. It should be a very exciting experience for you.

The Festival was just wonderful—25,000 people in the arena—and I was on Eurovision three times, which meant an audience each time of 50 million.

I'm off on the 7th for Atlantic City, to be a judge for "Miss America." Back to New York, then off to California to do a "Hollywood Palace."

Love to you and please give my fondest love to Myrna Loy. She is a great lady.

"*Mother*"

I gave Myrna mother's regards, but by now I did not share Mother's opinion, at least not based on my own personal experience.

What Mother had neglected to mention in her "itinerary" letter, was that she was also scheduled to be in Chicago on company business. Once again I learned from the papers that she was staying at the Ambassador Hotel. I sent a bouquet of flowers to her with another note inviting her to see the play. The Chicago critics had re-reviewed the play. If I'd tried to write a review of my own performance, I couldn't have asked for a more glowing accolade then I'd been given. In the midst of the growing tension at the theater those reviews were a much needed confirmation of my own instinct and professionalism, upon which I prided myself.

Mother did not come to see the play. She declined on the basis that her schedule for Pepsi was already brimming over and left her no free time. It was bullshit, of course, but I had to swallow it.

September 14, 1965

Tina dear,

So glad the play is going well. How long do you stay in Chicago and where do you go from there?

Didn't quite understand what you meant by "we all have such games." Personally, I don't have time for them.

Dearest love to you.

"*Mother*"

I had written her a very sarcastic letter after the "busy schedule" excuse. Her reply was only what I would have expected.

One night I was surprised to learn that Dick Benjamin was in the theater. I liked him very much in the short time I'd known him and admired his talent greatly. To my dismay, I discovered that the reason he was in Chicago was to redirect some of my scenes! Not only was that highly unusual, it was a terribly difficult position for him to be in. We all made the best of it, but it was a dreadful couple of days. Everyone's nerves were frazzled, mine along with the rest.

I called Harvey in New York to try and find out what was really going on. He'd heard that despite the great reviews and sold-out houses, our star wasn't happy. Management was trying to please her and it wasn't really directed totally at me, even though I seemed to be taking the brunt of it. We were playing to standing room only. The new reviews and the personal publicity I was getting because I'd become quite popular in Chicago, helped make our show a solid hit all over again. It looked as though it could play Chicago another year at this point.

Things went from bad to worse as the weeks went by. The New York office kept sending people out to see the show and report back on what they saw. Business was great and holding up solidly. The reviews were so good that I was subsequently nominated for one of the critics awards as best young actress of the season.

I started hearing a rumor that they were going to fire me! I couldn't believe it. I called my agents in New York but they said no one had said anything to them. Out of total desperation, I called my mother. I told her what I'd heard was happening and pleaded with her to call our star and help me get this thing straightened out. Mother listened to the entire story and then told me that she was very sorry. She said she didn't think she should *interfere*, and that she didn't think Myrna would really do that. She wished me good luck, and that was it.

The following morning, my agents called, terribly upset. The producers' office had called to tell them I was being fired. They had no cause, no reason that would stand up with the union, so they were going to have to pay me every cent they owed under the terms of the contract, which didn't expire until the following May or June. My agent said that the producers told him they were very sorry about the entire situation, but that it had come down to a choice of firing me and paying off my contract or losing their star. Naturally, I was the one to go.

I called Mother to tell her I was returning to Los Angeles, after my brief stay with friends. She vehemently objected to my being with friends. She said when things like this happen, you should be alone. Don't ever let anyone know how you feel, was her motto. Go off by yourself and don't come back until everything is all right again. I wanted to be with people who cared about me, who loved me. I needed that right now. Her way would have been to disappear until she figured the whole incident had blown over and not say a word to anyone in the meantime.

She kept everything locked up inside of her and wouldn't let anyone in to see what was really going on. She wouldn't admit to anyone that she hurt, wouldn't admit that she needed anyone. She wouldn't allow any help, wouldn't accept any kindness. She pushed people away, except when she was in total control. She handled life like a wounded animal. She didn't trust herself or anyone else enough to let the pain show through. In my opinion, that had caused her more pain, more failed relationships, more hurt feelings and more sorrow than the original pain she tried so hard to cover up and deal with all alone.

I don't think she ever felt really secure and comfortable in any relationship she ever had with anyone other than a person whose only function was to serve her wishes. But that was another kind of loneliness. That was the loneliness of the superior and the inferior, the mistress and the servant. That was not real friendship, not true companionship. But she never lasted very long in relationships where she was not in total control, calling all the shots and dictating all the other persons' behavior. Maybe she just never learned how, I don't know. She had learned how to be a dancer, she had learned how to be an actress, she had learned how to be a star. Maybe she just never had enough time left over to learn how to be a human being. Maybe she only felt safe within the rigid boundaries she set and only when she had a well-defined role to play.

I returned to Los Angeles after four months instead of one year. It was a very difficult time for me.

Harvey called nearly every day. He was wonderfully supportive and always made me feel happier. He came out to visit and we spent some time together. When he was back in New York, he wrote often and kept calling. Finally, he asked me to marry him and I accepted. I thought I loved him and I welcomed the prospect of moving back to New York where he lived. I was tired of Los Angeles and I seemed to have better luck professionally in New York anyway. Most of my friends were very pleased for me. I was almost 26 years old and never married. I guess I also had some fears about being an "old maid" which sounds very silly now, but was real enough then.

However, along with the thought of getting married, came the realization that I was going to have to tell my mother. I hadn't spoken to her since my emergency call from Chicago and I really had no idea what her response would be.

Several days after I arrived in New York, I called her. I had to go through the company switchboard since I no longer had her private number. When I finally reached her, what I said was: "Mother, I'm planning to get married. I'd like you to meet my fiancé. I'd also like you to be at the wedding. It just wouldn't seem right without you there."

It was a combination of many things, but I got so choked up that I could barely finish the sentence. I waited for her reaction for what seemed like an eternity. There were no guarantees as to how she'd react, and I'd gotten the "busy schedule" routine so many times over the last few years that no excuse would have totally shocked me.

What happened next was something akin to a miracle. My mother was delighted! Instantly she invited the two of us to come for drinks that very evening and to join her at a dinner party with Marty Allen and his wife. It was a total and complete acceptance in a turnaround that I never could have anticipated in a million years.

From that point on, Mother and I were in daily contact. She decided to plan the wedding, the reception, the whole thing. We wanted only a civil ceremony so she arranged for a New York State Supreme Court judge. She booked one whole floor of the "21" Club for the reception and luncheon. She talked to me about my dress and told me to register at Tiffany's and Georg Jensen so her friends would know exactly what to get us. She had the announcements engraved and her secretary made out the guest lists and sent the invitations. I was totally and completely overwhelmed. Harvey was slightly glassy-eyed at this point, but he handled himself admirably. In fact, he and Mother became good friends and liked one another's company.

Mother was superb. She had planned everything down to the very last detail. We were married on May 20, 1966. I was on cloud nine. People had flown in from Chicago and several other cities in the East. In addition to a large number of Harvey's immediate relatives, the guest list included: Uncle Sonny and Aunt Leah Ray Werblin, Herb Barnett, Mr. and Mrs. Mitchell Cox from Pepsi, Mike Nichols and Neil Simon, my friends, Eddie and Al, my cousin, Joan and her husband, some of the Pepsi people who were particularly close friends of Mother's and of course, the Kriendlers and Burns of "21." I couldn't invite my brother because he was still persona non grata and my two sisters weren't there either because of some minor altercation they'd had with Mother just before the wedding over dresses or some other such nonsense. I tried to talk Mother into allowing them to come, but rapidly saw it was useless. I spoke with them on the phone the day before the wedding and said not to worry about it, that I knew they'd be there with me in spirit and I'd see them when school was over. They were coming into New York for the summer.

Only a month after the honeymoon, I was hired to do a new play with Fred Clark and Tony Roberts, directed by Alan Alda. It was not the greatest play but it was a cute comedy. Fred and Tony made it work and the audiences had a good time. I almost had more fun watching the two of them than doing my own part. The summer passed quickly and happily.

While my husband was away on business, I spent many evenings with my mother in her apartment. For the first time in my life, I felt relatively comfortable with her. She seemed to feel the same and she went out of her way to plan fun things for the two of us to do together. I was included in most of her social events, met the majority of her friends and went over to spend quiet evenings with her just watching television and talking. There were some days when she was in a bad mood, and she was still drinking quite a bit during this entire time, but there was not even a hint of her old anger with me. She still flew into her fits, but they were never directed at me. She had a German woman working for her at the time whom she called "Mamacita" or just "Mama." Interestingly, the woman's real name was Anna, the same as Grandmother's name.

However, it was upon Mamacita that Mother vented her fits of temper and impatience, even though she loved her dearly. Mamacita took it for years and years, but finally had to quit because of ill health. I'm sure she never imagined she'd outlive her former employer.

Harvey sent for me to come to England just before his play was scheduled to open. It was a glorious opening with an elegant party afterwards and rave reviews. We traveled around England and then went to Paris for a weekend, staying in the fabulous Plaza Athenee Hotel.

When we returned to New York, I did some commercials and then had an opportunity to do two plays in repertory at a new theater in

Pittsburgh. I spent two freezing months in Pittsburgh working in a small theater that was barely any warmer inside that it was outside. We managed to have a good time and so some very good work, but I was quite ready to leave after the second show.

Christmas was wonderful. We spent half the time with my mother and then went to Connecticut to visit Harvey's family. My husband and I had hardly spent any time together since our honeymoon over six months earlier and we had some differences to straighten out as all new couples do. As it turned out, however, that was not so easy.

I decided that perhaps I'd better seek some help and started going to a highly recommended therapist one or two times a week.

That summer I did his package of *Barefoot in the Park* with Tab Hunter. We opened in Dennis, Massachusetts and then went on to Ogunquit, Maine.

In the fall, Harvey directed a pre-Broadway play written by Herman Raucher. It opened and closed in Boston. During the weeks of rehearsal, we worked very closely with Herman and shared the sorrow of closing night together.

My brother had gotten a divorce and moved back to New York. We saw each other several times a week and had great fun just being together again. The good times didn't last long, however. He was drafted into the Army just two months after his draft status changed. He went through the usual boot camp training down south and then returned to the city on leave before being transferred to Fort Ord in Monterey. Then one night he called and gave me the bad news. He was going to Viet Nam. My heart nearly stopped. I was scared to death. That was all you heard about those days, all you saw on the TV news. He told me he was coming home on leave as was customary before the army sent you overseas into a combat zone.

We spent most of his leave together, though he also went out to Long Island to see close friends who lived out there. We had one of those excruciatingly painful talks that millions of loved ones must have shared with each other before the battle begins. We had to talk about the possibility of death and what he wanted me to do in the event he didn't return. We sat up half one night crying and starting the conversation all over again, trying to talk about the very things that were our worst fears. I made him promise me that he would at least write his name on a postcard every week he was over there, so I'd know he was still alive. I followed the news of battles and studied the maps in the newspapers to see how close the enemy attacks were to the places he was stationed. I went to the peace rallies in Central Park and prayed for his safe return.

During these months Mother and I remained very close. The subject of my brother was off-limits at all times, however, once in a while when the two of us were alone in the room, she'd ask if I knew where he was. It would come out of the blue, for no apparent reason with no particular connection to anything that had been said before. She wouldn't look at me, but would always be busy doing something else, and her inquiry was almost casual as though it were not of any particular importance. At those times I quietly told her where he was located currently in Viet Nam. There was no further discussion. There was just the one question and my short, factual answer. She knew that we had remained close over all the years and I was the one person in the world she could ask for the information without ever letting it be known that she'd softened her position of total banishment. She had refused his every attempt at reconciliation. When he had come to New York with his young wife and little baby, Mother had refused to see them. They came to the apartment building and she refused them entrance. She ordered the doorman to turn them away. In fact, the last day she ever saw him was that day he was made a ward of the court. She never showed any signs of relenting. She never changed her mind. She never saw her only son after the age of sixteen years old.

We had so many moments together that were filled with real understanding and the beginning of a genuine friendship that it was a wonderful time for both of us. Something about my being married and her participating in the whole event had changed her attitude toward me. Now, it seemed as though she trusted me and even would look to me for my opinion on a range of subjects. There was one thing she knew about me that never changed. She knew that I would tell her the truth, as I perceived it. Many of the people she surrounded herself with would try to second guess the situation and tell her what they thought she wanted to hear. I didn't do that, I never had been like that. I tried to always show her respect, but I was no longer that afraid of her. I also tried to help her in any way I could, but I made it crystal clear that I was not her servant and that if she started treating me like that, I could always leave. We never actually discussed it, but she knew. To her enormous credit, I must say she was very perceptive in that area. If you were clear about where you were as a person, her intuition did not allow her to overstep those personal boundaries. If you were unclear she would push you to the limit and then smile when you fell on your face. Once she managed to get you on that tract, on her territory you just might not ever be able to get off. That was her game. She tried to control everything. She made up games of control and if you thought you could get something you wanted in return for playing the game by the rules, she let you. But just as soon as you'd mastered one set of rules . . . she changed them all and you looked like an idiot.

My only salvation was to be my own person and set my own limits of acceptable behavior. On several occasions, I put on my coat and left when the going got rough. She'd lived with me long enough to know I'd do the same thing again if she pushed me too hard. We evolved a sort of mutual understanding but we never had a real conversation about it. It just existed.

She was very giving to me in many different ways. In fact, I rarely left the apartment empty-handed. She'd give me food or some pillows, a statue or Daddy's chess set. Some gift was thrust into my arms nearly every time I visited her.

She began talking to me more and more when we were alone. She told me some of the personal difficulties she was having. It was the first time we'd had talks like this since I was a little girl and too young to fully understand. She'd never go into any great detail, but she'd outline what was going on, what she was worried about. She talked to me a lot about Daddy. On my wedding day she'd given me the pearl necklace he'd given to her. She later gave me the gold watch he'd given her. Mother never wore watches anymore and she wanted me to have something they'd shared together. Daddy had been dead seven years now, but the will was still being contested. She told me that after he'd borrowed against his salary in order to finish the apartment, they had some serious financial problems. They'd bought the apartment for $100,000 and spent another $400,000 on rebuilding and decorating. Neither his borrowed future salary nor the sale of the Brentwood house was enough to pay the bills accumulated by the new apartment and still have money to live on. Daddy then borrowed money from Mother. She'd done some television shows, but she was just able to pay current bills with that. So, she told me that she borrowed against her own insurance policies and he gave her his company stock as collateral. When he died suddenly, she gave me the impression that their financial affairs were in rather a mess. I don't think, from the way she described it, that he lived long enough to pay back the original loan on his salary. The loan didn't have any real collateral. Mother had borrowed to the limit on everything she had and if she hadn't been put on the official Pepsi payroll almost immediately after his death, she would have been in very serious financial trouble. However, when he died, she was holding most of his assets as collateral on the substantial amounts of money she'd loaned him. Therefore, there was really nothing much left over to be willed to anyone else.

I didn't say one word during this entire revelation. I must say I was stunned to learn that they'd been living so precariously. I thought back to all the presents Daddy had given her . . . the diamonds and the minks and the non-business trips, always staying at the most expensive hotels. I thought about those $100 lunches, heaven only knows what the dinners cost. I thought, they were just like two kids, for God's sakes. Money was just burning a hole in their pockets. He must have thought that she had money, since she was a big movie star and she must have thought that he had money since he was a big business executive, chairman of the board of a multimillion dollar corporation. Then they both proceeded to spend according to their fantasy about the other person, having nothing to do with the reality of either one's personal bank accounts. I guess they figured there was always more, a never-ending supply. Daddy always said you had to spend money to make money. It was a business philosophy of his but I guess it was also a personal philosophy as well. Mother had always spent money like it was water. She developed very expensive tastes. Long before she was married to Daddy, she'd nearly run her own family into impossible debt because of the way she spent money on life's luxuries. She told me that if it hadn't been for the deal she had on the picture *What Ever Happened to Baby Jane?* she'd have a much tougher time right now. She did that film for a moderate salary and a large percentage. The picture was a solid box office hit and she made a lot of money from her percentage deal.

I almost laughed right out loud when I thought back to the situation in my own life the year after Daddy's death. Macabre as it is, there was a rumor going around the social set in New York that since I was eldest daughter, I must be the next in line for the money. The probate had been kept very quiet and almost out of the papers entirely. I wondered why all of a sudden I was so popular with a group of people who barely knew me and with whom I had very little in common. There were always inviting me to the Hamptons for the weekend and out to dinner at the best clubs and restaurants. Then one night when the group was fairly drunk, I heard a comment about my being the Pepsi-Cola heiress! Ahhhhh . . . I thought. So *that's* what's been going on. Well, I could not help laughing. It was the hype at it's very, very best. Not one shred of the rumor was true.

The hype is the big lie. The big lie seducing unknowing souls into believing that for a few moments they can be associated with greatness . . . vicarious greatness, glamour, excitement. The hype is someone or something outside ourselves, more beautiful, more talented, richer than we can ever dare hope to be.

Maybe the lie is everyone's broken dreams, even the ones no one even allows themselves. People who don't know who they are, living in places they don't want to be, with people they don't particularly like, doing something they hate to earn a living. This is the fertile soil in which the lie grows best.

Somewhere in the vortex, everyone knows. But people have such a big stake in keeping the lie alive that no one dares tell the secret they all share.

It is real by consensus. It has nothing to do with fact. The truth is irrelevant. It is the care and feeding of the fantasy that is important, that is crucial.

All the lies have a curious way of fitting together. If you recognize one, the whole house of cards will come tumbling down. Perhaps that is why it is so well protected. Intuitively it is known that to expose one is to jeopardize the whole lot.

The great lie is bigger than one person, one system, one idol, one superstar. It is an ethic unto itself, a set of values and structures and organizations that are enmeshed and intertwined, working for a common goal and supporting others of their own persuasion. It is a way of seeing life, a focus on the world.

It is a consortium of the "musts" and the "shoulds" that people agree to live under. It is that creeping guilt superimposed on behavior and curiosity. It is the fear of making a mistake, of temporarily looking like a fool. It is all the lies we are willing to believe in order not to have to face what is real. It's the pain we live with when we know something is wrong and keep our mouths shut. It is part of the unspoken terror of our existence.

The big lie is not an innocent bystander. It requires more than just belief. You must do something, become involved. The more you support it with your energy, your belief, your dollars . . . even if you think it is totally innocent . . . the more impossible you will find leaving it behind.

The only way I know to get free of the big lie is to be straight with yourself. No bullshit, no excuses, no condemnations, no fake humility and no seeming to be all right when you're not. We've all been sold a lot of myths, false expectations about what's real and what's important.

The lie can only flourish through consensus. Sometimes the hardest thing in the world is to say "no" and walk away.

CHAPTER 26

In April 1968 I auditioned for my first part on a daytime soap opera. A few days later I heard that I'd been hired for one day. It was a test to see whether or not I could handle the pressure of a daily show that was taped in real time and only a major disaster like the set falling down was cause for a re-take.

A soap usually has five scenes in a half-hour show. I was in three of the five that first day. It was an initiation by fire. I think the only reason I was able to get through it was my extremely good fortune to be cast opposite a wonderful actor named Keith Charles. We were playing husband and wife in a marriage that was already falling apart. It was the most instant relationship I ever had. We only had a few hours together to meet, get to know something about the pace at which the other person spoke and learn our lines. Keith had only been on the show a short while himself, but at least this wasn't the first day for both of us. He was wonderful to me. We went over and over the scenes in every moment of what little spare time there was in the tight schedule. I'd never worked in front of three cameras except on talk shows where you're sitting down most of the time.

My heart was beating so fast when the zero hour arrived and the cameras started rolling for the opening of that day's show that I thought I was going to have a heart attack before I was able to do any of my scenes. By one of those miracles of professionalism and the considerable talents of Keith Charles, the scenes all went perfectly, although I think I did them by some kind of remote control mechanism, because I remember very little about it. After the show, Gloria Monty, our director, congratulated me on a good performance. I was elated, if totally exhausted. Keith and I laughed when I told him I had amnesia about the entire half hour.

I found out the air date for the show and told everyone I knew to watch. Mother was very pleased because she liked watching the soaps and often did see a number of them before her daily afternoon nap. We both saw my first show and she loved it. I was so thrilled that she'd liked it I could hardly speak.

Very shortly after the first show aired, my manager called to say that they wanted me to continue the character and were offering a long-term contract, renewable every thirteen weeks. It was the best news I could have gotten. I happily signed on as a running character in *Secret Storm* videotaping at CBS. I called Mother to tell her the good news and she asked me to keep a running list of the air dates so that she could see the show even if she was out of town on company business. She wrote some of her friends about the show and she received lots of mail from her own fans telling her how much they were enjoying me on the program. She was very proud of me.

Interestingly enough, the name of my character was Joan. She was a neurotic woman, jealous and suspicious. Later on in the part, she began to have a drinking problem. She was really a wonderful, bitchy woman— the epitome of the terrific soap opera part. She *always* had trouble getting along with people. She *always* had some trauma going in her life. She was always accusing everyone else of being wrong. I had a great time playing her. The crew used to tell me that they looked forward to the days I was working because it guaranteed the sparks would fly! The people on the show became like family. We worked so closely together, depended on the other actors in the scene so heavily and had to function under so much time pressure that you got to know people much faster and very differently than under normal working conditions. You had to pay so much attention every minute that you were on camera that you could tell when another actor was on the verge of forgetting their lines even before it actually happened. You had to have your mind focused totally in the immediate present not letting it wander even for a split second. In that split second you could forget your lines and a disaster would follow for everyone else.

~

I liked working at CBS too. It was a huge rambling complex on West 57th Street near the Hudson River. Fred Silverman had taken over as the new head of daytime programming and was beginning to make changes. His first major coup was installing a new soap called *Love is a Many Splendored Thing*, which had nothing really to do with the movie of the same name. They spent a lot of money on that show, which made the rest of us jealous sometimes, but the show was a hit.

My husband and I were not getting along very well at all. It was one of those situations that isn't either person's fault totally. We liked working together but we didn't seem to be able to live together. By now, the smallest incident turned into unpleasantness. I was still in therapy, trying to work out my part of it, but the clearer I saw myself the more I wanted out of my marriage. I didn't think it was ever going to work and I didn't want the unhappiness to drag on, hurting both of us more as time progressed and our relationship deteriorated. We'd been married just two years, but we hadn't spent more than a third of that time together. It just wasn't a good match.

As the time I worked on the soap increased to three or four days a week, my free time dwindled down to almost zero. We had a maid to clean the apartment and I managed to do the shopping, but I really wasn't able to spend much time or devote much attention to running a home, even one as casual as ours.

However, before our relationship had gotten to this point, we'd been able to have Mother over for dinner on a number of occasions. What I'd thought would be something of a trauma turned out to be great fun, if quite a challenge. We lived in a brownstone apartment in the east 60s near Park Avenue that was lovely but small. In fact, we only had one gigantic main room that had originally been the formal living room of the house when it had been privately owned. The living room had eighteen-foot ceilings, a large fireplace and floor to ceiling French doors with little iron balconies overlooking the street. Since we were on the second floor, the trees blocked any direct view of other buildings so it was rather like living in a greenhouse.

My kitchen, however, was the size of a normal closet! There was barely enough room to turn around in it. It was directly in front of the entranceway and we'd had a divider built for storage and work space.

It never ceased to amaze me that I could learn to create dinner in that closet without totally losing my mind or breaking every dish we owned. I got the whole routine down to a fine art which was crucial because no one could get into the kitchen to help me!

When Mother was invited for dinner, I took particular care to have everything planned to the minute. The table was set in advance and whatever could be prepared ahead of time was already finished.

Mother was as unused to being invited to a family dinner as I was to giving one! We just about died with laughter when she arrived the first time. Mother invited Cesar Romero to join the three of us since he was a very close, longtime family friend and could be counted on to lend moral support to the evening. We'd always called him "Uncle Butch" as kids and that's what I called him still. I adored him.

At exactly the appointed hour, Mother and Uncle Butch arrived in her limousine. When I opened the door to our apartment I saw the two of them carrying Pepsi coolers up the one flight of stairs to our landing, like they were coming to a picnic or a pot-luck supper. Mother had brought nearly an entire meal with her! There was smoked salmon, wine, her own vodka and stacks of other "goodies" from her own refrigerator. I had no idea where I was going to put this unexpected bounty and just had to pray it wouldn't spoil before I could find room in our tiny refrigerator for all of it.

It was so like Mother to be invited to dinner and then bring more with her than whatever she was going to receive. At first glance I felt a wave of insult. For a brief moment I thought maybe she was taking out insurance against what I might have forgotten, such as her special 100-proof vodka. But then I realized that it was just her way of feeling secure. It was her way of giving, it was her way of saying "thank you" in advance. She was trying in every way she knew to show that she loved me and was genuinely touched by the invitation, but even more so by the thought. If her way tended to be a little overwhelming, she'd never been in this situation before and neither had I. We were both finding our way in this relationship and doing the best we could. I dropped my misplaced paranoia and we had a delightful evening.

Uncle Butch was at his very best . . . witty and charming, just as I'd always remembered him. Mother was very fond of him. They'd originally met during their chorus days in New York and been friends over thirty years. As was her custom, Mother never stayed out very late at night. She preferred to be home no later than 10 p.m. My dinner was a great success judged by the compliments she gave me. We sat and talked for a while afterward and then she left.

It was a very happy moment in my life. It was one of the first times I felt I'd been able to give her something she really appreciated and enjoyed. It was one of the first times since I was a child that I'd felt any genuine sense of family in the traditional meaning of the word. Because it was so private an experience, Mother seemed to relax after a while and to enjoy herself.

Although I was now working very hard on the soap opera, I was not feeling terribly well. I'd been to several doctors who were not able to diagnose the problem. I was having a lot of trouble with my skin and thought perhaps I was allergic to the studio make-up. But that didn't seem to be the answer either.

Finally, I was sent to a gynecologist. The doctor gave me very bad news. She said that I had a large fallopian tumor, which required surgery as soon as it could be scheduled. She also said that I would not be able to work for at least six weeks after the operation. She was unusually forceful about the need for an operation, which scared me to death.

After the appointment, I walked for a long time. When I returned home, I cried for several hours. I'd only been on the show a couple of months. There was no way they'd hold my job for nearly two months. They'd have to replace me or write me out.

When my husband came home that night, I was in a dreadful state. I was scared to even think about having such a serious operation and I was just as scared not to think about it. He was very concerned, naturally. He told me that I couldn't even consider not following the doctor's recommendation, because no job was as important as my health.

During the next week, I made one of the worst decisions of my entire life. It was totally irrational and nearly cost my life. I decided to wait a few months before scheduling the operation. I decided to see how things were going on the show and broach the subject to the producers about writing me out for a month or so later on, if my contract was renewed after the first thirteen weeks. It was sheer stupidity on my part. I made my husband promise not to tell anyone, particularly my mother. I promised, in return, to speak to the producers right after my contract was renewed, since it was only a month or so away. It was a very bad bargain on my part.

Then, I tried to go on with my life as usual. Of course, I didn't feel well some days, my skin didn't get any better and my energy level was very low. I took extra vitamins and tried to keep going as though nothing had happened.

But, when I was alone the gnawing fear would sweep over me leaving me in a cold sweat and unable to sleep well.

My husband was away working most of that summer. For the first time I was really lonely. I went to visit his sister in Connecticut a couple of times, but mostly I stayed in the city. I was with Mother a lot of the free time I had. She was getting ready to sell the apartment because she said she could no longer afford it. She needed the money and she felt she would be more comfortable in something smaller. Also, there was the matter of the stairs. I never liked the design of those open stairs, I was always sure I'd slip and get my leg caught in the opening between each step. I did worry about Mother too. The apartment was ludicrously large for just one person and a maid. I knew Mother was drinking heavily again, as well as taking various prescription drugs from more than one doctor. She had sleeping pills and other medicine for her nerves and her chronic upset stomach. I worried very much about her in the house alone with only an elderly maid. I worried about her getting up in the middle of the night and falling as she already had done several times now, hurting herself fairly badly.

Up until recently, she'd received mainly bruises which could easily be covered with regular clothing. Lately, however, she'd begun to take pretty bad falls and had seriously hurt her back one time and her foot on two different occasions. She blamed the antibiotics or the other medicine. I knew she drank every day and then took sleeping pills every night. I was really worried that she'd kill herself accidentally, as I'd heard of other people doing. I spoke with one of her doctors but it didn't do any good. No one wanted to bring the subject out into the open with her. I didn't agree, but I wasn't a doctor.

She controlled her drinking primarily to certain hours. I'd see her drinking in the morning but she ate lunch and then took a nap. She'd drink in the afternoons and during the evening, but she'd usually eat dinner and go to bed fairly early. When she was working for the company, she kept it pretty much together, though everything had to be well scheduled and controlled tightly then too. I don't know how many people were aware that she had a serious drinking problem during those years. If they knew, they didn't ever speak about it in my presence.

By the middle of the summer, I'd decided it would be better for both my husband and myself if we got a divorce. We were not getting along at all and he was away the majority of the time. It was better, I thought, to admit that we'd made a mistake and separate rather than continue making each other miserable. We had no children to consider, we had no community property, we had only the contents of the apartment to divide between us. I spoke with Mother at some length. She was really quite wonderful. She didn't try to convince me one way or the other, but whatever I decided she wouldn't try to talk me out of it or change my mind. She gave me the name of her lawyers and they referred me to someone who handled a lot of New York divorces. I had a couple of special considerations to think about. First, the laws of New York were still rather antiquated when it came to divorce and secondly, I'd had to sign a "morals clause" in my CBS contract just like everyone else who worked for the network. It was a standard clause but it could be very widely interpreted. I didn't want any publicity at all, certainly nothing unpleasant that might jeopardize my job.

Fortunately, the entire thing was handled very quickly and quietly. Since my husband had lived in the apartment before we'd been married, I decided to move somewhere else and leave him with the apartment. I didn't ask for any money. I only wanted to be able to take with me what I felt was mine.

Divorce is a nasty time, no matter how the people involved try to remain civilized. There is something awful about dividing up mutual possessions, something about the whole process that brings out the worst in everyone. No matter how much the two people disagree on living together any longer, no matter how rationally they try to behave, it's a dreadful time. Part of it lies in the nagging question of failure. The relationship may not work at all, you may both be miserable, but that public admission of a mistake is always embarrassing.

It was always hard for me to admit that I'd made a mistake. I prided myself on doing an excellent job with whatever task I involved myself. I had to face the cold fact that I'd made a monumental error with my life and I didn't like it at all. Not that I blamed him, because I didn't. It was just one of those things you know in your heart doesn't work and you have to get out the best you can.

Mother was so understanding I could hardly believe it. I was ashamed to tell her at first, but she took it with such good grace that I was very grateful. Of course, she'd been through this situation before herself, and knew my feelings on all levels. We either saw or spoke to one another every day. I spent a great deal of time with her during these painful weeks. She listened patiently to me and offered what advice she could as far as my personal well-being was concerned. To her great credit, again, she was wise enough not to get involved at all in my relationship with my husband. She was helpful in every possible way, short of actually doing anything directly. She didn't feel it was her place and I totally agreed with her. In fact, it was far better if she didn't and we both knew that. She was supportive and understanding and deeply concerned. She was really like a true mother during these difficult times and I was so grateful to her that I did everything I could to be helpful with anything she asked.

I moved out of the apartment right before Labor Day weekend. Mother arranged for my things to be put in storage until I could find an apartment. I'd been looking for weeks but couldn't find anything suitable. I stayed with a girlfriend for a while and then moved into an apartment hotel on Central Park West.

Early September, Mother asked me to go to Philadelphia with her and do the Mike Douglas show together. My sister Cathy went with us, and all three of us ended up doing the show together. We'd just returned to the hotel when the New York secretary called. Mother was in the other room, so I answered the phone. It was very sad news.

I walked into the other room and asked Mother to sit down on the edge of the bed. Then I had to tell her as gently as possible that Franchot Tone had just died. She buried her face in her hands and cried. I held her in my arms for a few minutes. Then she asked if she could be alone.

We returned to New York the next day and Mother went to the funeral. Afterward, she arranged for Franchot's sons to receive some of the silver that Franchot had given her during their marriage.

I was working on the soap four days a week now. I didn't have a moment of free time except on the weekends. I spent Saturdays and Sundays helping Mother at least half a day and was at the apartment at least once during the week for dinner with her. The apartment hotel I was living in was clean and decent, but it was hardly a home. In fact, it was sort of depressing and I was glad I didn't have to spend much time there. I was still looking for an apartment, and for whatever reasons, was having a hard time finding one.

The beginning of October, I flew to Mexico to get my divorce. Mother had helped me make the arrangements and everything went as smoothly as possible. It was, nevertheless, a lonely time for me. My whole life was being rearranged after the upheaval. I couldn't find a place to live, my things were still in storage and my cats were being boarded at Mother's veterinarians at an astronomical monthly fee. If it hadn't been for my very well paying job, I would have been in an awful mess.

I had just finished doing a long and complicated courtroom sequence on the show, where I'd been in practically every scene of every show for the last three weeks. The amount of memorizing alone was beginning to be a strain. I had to learn nearly twenty pages of dialogue every day and by now one show was beginning to melt into another. I had thrown myself totally into my work, partly out of necessity and partly to avoid the pain of thinking about the current state of my life. I had just turned twenty-nine years old that June. My marriage, which had started out so joyously two years before, was now over. My personal and social life now revolved totally around my mother. I was not really interested in anything except my relationship with her and doing a good job at work. I went out on dates only occasionally. It seemed to take too much effort to meet new people right now.

I thought it was just the strain I was under with the divorce and the long hours of work, but I wasn't feeling well at all lately. I was constantly tired and had lost some weight. I knew that this sequence of the show had concluded and I'd have some extra time which I was looking forward to even though I loved my work and clung to it for security.

One morning I woke up at the usual time, around six o'clock. I felt very ill, but thought that a shower and washing my hair in preparation for going to the studio would help. It didn't. Before an hour had passed, I knew I was terribly ill, terrible pain which kept getting progressively worse. I went back to bed, thinking that perhaps lying down would help. It didn't. I was really sick. I broke into a cold sweat as the pain got worse. I wasn't going to be able to go to work. I was very scared.

The last thing I was able to do was call my mother. I waited until eight o'clock and then called to beg her to get me a doctor. I told her I was very, very sick.

The first person to arrive was Betty, her secretary from Los Angeles who was in New York to do some extra work for Mother. The second person to arrive was the doctor who called for an ambulance immediately and a surgeon to stand by at the hospital. The third person to arrive was my director, Gloria Monty. She stayed with me until the ambulance arrived. I lost consciousness several times during the eternity I waited for the ambulance. The pain was now so excruciating that I couldn't stand it.

After two of the longest hours I ever remember waiting for anything, the ambulance arrived. I was only semi-conscious but engulfed by pain so unbelievably awful that I was sure I was going to die from the pain itself.

I remember nothing except sirens and doors opening, closing and people in white moving me from one place to another. The doctor at the hospital was only a blurry image, though I could hear his voice. He told me I needed emergency surgery and that immediate preparations were being made. I had to give my medical history and sign some papers permitting them to operate. I could barely hold the pen. I kept fainting from the horrible excruciating pain. I begged someone to give me something for the pain, but they couldn't until closer to the time for the operations. It was nearly 3 o'clock in the afternoon before they took me to a room and prepared me for surgery. I was sure I was going to die. I couldn't talk. I couldn't see clearly. I silently prayed to God in heaven to let me live. I didn't think I could survive the pain. I prayed for my life until I got to the operating room. The table was cold. The room was cold. I was sure I was dying. I was terrified. I was all alone and I was dying. I prayed to God to help me. I never got to say goodbye to my mother. This was it. This was surely the end of my life. A tear trickled down my cheek. The anesthetic was administered and I slipped away.

I was on the operating table for three hours. The tumor diagnosed months before had entangled itself. Peritonitis had already set in, the poison working its way through my body. That is what caused the awful, unbearable pain. Gangrene.

In the recovery room, I dimly saw the face of a doctor I recognized. I managed to whisper: "Tony, am I going to die?" He told me I was very ill, but I wasn't going to die. The pain was too much for me and I slipped away again into unconsciousness.

I remember very little of that day. I was finally taken to a private room for intensive care. I had needles and tubes everywhere. Oxygen to breathe, blood transfusions, intravenous glucose, catheter . . . the whole works. My entire abdomen from pelvis to the bottom of my ribs was just one mammoth mountainous bandage. Now they could give me Demerol every few hours for the pain, but it didn't seem to be doing any good. My whole being was focused in pain. It was all encompassing. The shots didn't seem to help that pain at all, they just made it impossible for me to say anything about it or to move my body. The shots made me sleep most of the time, but even asleep, the constant pain was surrounding me.

Early the next morning I was transferred to a private room on another floor. I had twenty-four-hour nursing care. I was still in critical condition, but so relieved to be alive, so grateful not to have died, that even through the unrelenting pain . . . I felt at peace.

I couldn't do anything for myself. I could barely focus my eyes through the pain and the medicine they kept giving me. But near the middle of the morning I awoke to see the doctor with my mother and Gloria, my director. They were standing around my bed. My vision still had a surrealistic quality to it. The sides of my bed were still up, so I wouldn't fall out and they had put pillows around me so I couldn't move much. I looked at the faces through the bars of the bed rails and the bottles suspended above me. But somewhere it penetrated my very limited consciousness that everyone looked very worried. Mother stood somewhat in the background after she'd leaned over to kiss me on the forehead. Gloria came to stand beside me, taking my hand in hers. Very quietly she started talking to me. I could only understand a little of what she said. It took nearly a full minute for the information to penetrate the fog of pain and heavy medication. She was trying to tell me that . . . Mother . . . had . . . offered . . . to *play* . . . *my part* . . . on the . . . soap opera . . . and CBS . . . had . . . accepted . . . her generous . . . offer.

It came to me . . . very slowly. I tried to bring Gloria's face into clear focus with what little strength I had. I could feel her hand clasping mine tightly as one does with someone who is in great pain or sorrow. All I could whisper was, "what?" She thought I hadn't heard her, which was partially true and she repeated the information again in a soft but somewhat louder tone of voice. This time I managed to concentrate a little better on the words. It was true . . . what I thought she said the first time . . . but it was still coming to me in sort of a dreamlike floating state. Mother was going to do *my* part. Mother was going to take my part on the soap opera.

I couldn't think with all the medicine and the awful pain. My brain refused to assimilate. I got what she said by some terrible organic infusion of the words into my semi-conscious. I couldn't move my body but I turned my head slowly from side to side involuntarily. The doctor came to me immediately. There was a sense of deep concern about him. He told Gloria and Mother that they would have to leave right away. He said that I could not stand any kind of strain right now. He asked me if I was all right. I couldn't answer him.

I tried to signal Gloria through our clasped hands. She leaned very close to me. I barely whispered: "Gloria . . . take care of her . . ." That was the end of my ability to function. Again I slipped away into a nightmare of semi-conscious pain with my head trying desperately to float free of the agony in my poor body.

It was late afternoon when I woke again. The nurse was right next to my bed as though she'd been standing there for some time. She asked me to sip some water through a hard plastic straw sticking out of a cup she was holding near my mouth. It was very difficult. Any movement at all brought back the terrible pain, but I did my best.

I wasn't allowed any visitors or phone calls now because I was much too heavily sedated and too weak to do anything but rest. But when I focused enough to notice the rest of the room, I saw beautiful flowers everywhere surrounding me. The nurse had arranged the bouquets of flowers so they were directly in my line of vision, even lying down. I looked at the pretty shapes and colors and turned back to her, trying to smile. Then I fell asleep again. At night there was another nurse sitting reading quietly beside my bed. They were changed in eight-hour shifts, but they were present every hour of the day and night.

Time melted past me. All I wanted to do was sleep. I was grateful to be alive, but too exhausted to do anything but sleep. I couldn't believe it when the nurse told me I had to sit up and be transferred to a chair. The next day I had to start walking! I couldn't move, much less walk. But she was firm. I fainted twice in my attempt to be assisted into the chair not two feet away. I still had all the bottles attached and it was very difficult. But she told me that I had to start moving or I was in danger of complications like pneumonia.

The doctor came to see me several times a day. He was very kind and seemed consistently concerned. He said I was making good progress and urged me to do everything the nurses asked, since they had to get me on the road to physical recovery as soon as possible for my own sake. But, he said that the most important thing of all was my own will to get well. That was what he seemed most concerned about.

I was still getting shots every couple of hours during these first three days, so life remained mercifully at a foggy distance.

On the fourth day, Mother called me in the evening just after I'd tried to eat dinner for the first time. The doctor said I had to eat now, even if I didn't want to. The nurse made me finish half my food just like when I was a little girl. If I could have laughed, I would have.

Mother's voice on the phone sounded very happy and excited. She said the work was going very well, everyone was *so* helpful and there were just a few things she wanted to ask me about the part. She chatted on good humoredly, asking questions that I tried my best to answer. My hand started shaking and I had to transfer the phone but knocked over my water cup in the process. The nurse looked at me closely before she cleaned up the water and left the room for a minute. I tried to talk normally to Mother who sounded as though she was having a great time. She said Gloria was coming over that evening to work with her on the scenes for tomorrow's rehearsal. There were now going to be only four or five scenes that would be taped in sequence over the weekend and inserted into different shows during the following week. I told her I had to say goodbye because I was feeling very weak, but thanked her for sharing all this with me and I wished her luck on the show.

I didn't know whether I felt so badly because they were beginning to cut back on my pain medication or because of the phone call. I thought I was going to vomit. The pain was terrible again, after what had been the first fairly decent day. I had this awful, sinking feeling all over me that was making me shake involuntarily.

She's taken *my* job . . . how could she do that to me? Here I am so sick . . . so helpless . . . and she rushes to take *my job* away from me. No matter what kindness she may have thought she was doing . . . no matter how noble . . . to step in for me, she's really taken my job nearly over my dead body. That marks the *end* of my career on this soap opera. She's over sixty years old . . . what's in her mind to try and play a twenty-nine-year-old again? My God . . . what's in her mind?

I was getting hysterical sitting in this hospital bed, totally helpless to do anything to defend my life or my job . . . totally helpless to do anything but stay alive and . . . my God . . . she's taken the one thing I had left to hold onto . . . she's taken my job!

My God . . . my God . . . it's the big lie raising its ugly head and coming to haunt me again. She hasn't worked as an actress in a long time. This was *the* perfect opportunity, who could resist it. Certainly not CBS. Their job was to get ratings. This won't just get ratings, this will get more national publicity for her and for the show and for CBS than anything they could have ever dreamed up.

But she's an alcoholic. She can't hold up under that kind of strain and tension. That's what I tried to tell Gloria. That's probably why she doesn't get any more job offers. People are beginning to know. She has to have everything very carefully managed now . . . she rarely ever works full days anymore.

The doctor came to the doorway of my room followed by my nurse. He asked me if I'd like a cup of coffee. I had tears in my eyes, so I just nodded my head. He asked my nurse if she'd please get us both a cup of coffee. Then he came and sat by my bed.

"I think you'd better tell me about it," he said very gently. I realized for the first time that he knew. I also realized for the first time that he was good looking. I'd never really noticed his face that clearly before. But that was just a random thought that crossed my mind fleetingly before the flood of tears began. It hurt me so much to cry, it hurt so much to breathe deeply. I tried to stop, but I couldn't. It all started pouring out of me . . . Mother taking my job . . . Mother an alcoholic . . . how humiliating and helpless it was . . . she kept calling to tell me how wonderful she was doing . . . how wonderful all the people were . . . she was having such a good time . . . all the papers wanted interviews . . . it was going to be in *Time Magazine* . . . she was a star again . . . the focus of all the attention . . . it was *my* job . . . she'd taken my job away from me . . . my God . . . what could she be thinking of when she did that? She said it was to save my job . . . so they wouldn't replace me, but that was the biggest lie of them all. *She* replaced me. That was the end of the credibility to my part and credibility is crucial to the soaps. After the smoke cleared, I knew they'd have no choice but to write me out. No matter what they said to her right now or to me . . . that was the truth. That is what would happen.

Nothing in recent years gave Mother as much publicity as taking over my part in the daytime soap opera. It was in all the national newspapers, most of the national magazines and remembered long after my part in the show was over. It was one of those perfect publicity hypes. It was one of those events that overshadows all the rest of the work. Years later when people asked about my professional background and I'd mention doing the soap, they'd reply "Oh yes, I remember that . . . your mother took your part."

But for now, the doctor's only concern was for me. It was very important to my recovery that I had a positive attitude about getting well. It was very important that I retain the will to get better and stronger. I would have to work hard to regain my health and strength and return to normal living again. It would take several months of recovery and the key point was my own will power. He was most concerned about that at this moment. He sat with me for quite a while that night, talking to me and trying to cheer me up by putting these painful moments into the perspective of a future time of health and well-being. He tried to tell me that it was understandable I should be upset, but to try and not let it detour me from my own responsibility which was to get well again. He said there would be many other jobs in the future as long as I worked hard right now to recover my health. He said my body had been through a severe shock and that was bound to affect my whole being, but I was to rest now and he'd be back to see me again in the morning.

I thanked him for his understanding. I also asked him not to say anything about our conversation.

Whatever they gave me to sleep that night worked. I slept like a rock until my day nurse arrived the next morning. She told me the doctor said I could now have visitors, but only for ten minutes at a time. Also, she said that today we were going to start walking.

Before it was time for me to be released from the hospital, the first of the shows Mother did was aired on television. My nurse and I turned on the television a few minutes before the program began. I realized I had butterflies in my stomach, just as though it were a show of my own. Mother had said that everything went wonderfully well during the two days of taping and I prayed she was right. I had not spoken with Gloria or any of the rest of the cast and I had no other feedback.

At the very beginning of that day's episode of *Secret Storm* the announcer stated that my part was being played by my mother, Joan Crawford. Then the music came up and the show began just as it always did.

The moment her scene began, I had that strange sinking feeling all over again. I watched every move she made, my eyes glued to the television set. She was nervous, I could see that. Anyone is nervous under the strain of daytime television, but after a while you learn to deal with it. But as the scene progressed, my heart sank into the pit of my stomach. She wasn't just nervous. From years and years with Mother I knew there was something else reflected in this performance. Mother was not sober when this scene was taped. Mother had been drinking.

After the show, I called her. I was not at all pleased with what I had just seen, but the way she sounded on the phone was almost a pathetic plea for everything to be all right and I didn't have the heart to say anything but "Thank you." She seemed instantly delighted, but there was also a vulnerability to her voice that I wasn't used to hearing. She said, "I hope you're proud of me," and again I didn't have the nerve to say anything except, "Of course . . . I'm very grateful."

When I hung up the phone I felt ill again. I felt sick about what I'd just seen on television and sick about the lies I'd just told. I still wasn't very strong yet and this just exhausted me.

The national publicity hit that week and everyone was talking about her taking my part. I tried very hard to keep up the image and be gracious, saying to whoever asked that it was a very kind gesture on her part.

As the days progressed and the remainder of the shows in which she had taped scenes were aired, I sat in my hospital bed watching the television with a growing sense of horror. My mother was appearing on that show drunk! She was obviously and continuously drunk! She slurred her words and her movements were unsteady. She was drunk!

I couldn't believe it. I was in a state of shock. I felt growing rage and humiliation as the shows progressed. How *dare* she go on my show, working with my friends and humiliate me? How dare she allow herself to go on camera drunk? How dare she insult me, the show and the rest of the people she was working with? How was I going to face all those people again, now that they knew? If she couldn't handle it, she should at least have admitted it and gotten out. That would have been the decent and courteous thing to do. But no, she got nervous so she had a couple of drinks and that made her shaky so she got nervous about that and had a couple more drinks. By the time she was ready to actually tape the show, she was drunk. How dare she? Jesus Christ . . . this was a nightmare!

The doctor came in and watched the last show with us. Afterwards he just turned to look at me as tears were streaming down my face. "She's drunk," I whispered. He nodded his head and said, "I'm sorry."

I am not proud of the fact that I never told Mother how humiliating her performance was. I never told her how furious I was that she'd done my show drunk. It was on the tip of my tongue several times, but I couldn't say it. I just couldn't come right out and be honest enough to say the words. What I should have said to her was what I said to myself. How dare you humiliate *both* of us by getting drunk before the show. Jesus Christ, Mother . . . don't you have *any* self-respect left? But I didn't say any of that to her. I held it all inside and let it eat me up. What I said was polite. What I said was just, "thank you."

She only came to the hospital once and that was only for a few minutes. She did not come to take me home when I was released. She was scared of hospitals.

Jim Somerall, President of Pepsi, was kind enough to take me home in his limousine. I had a special relationship with big Jim Somerall. It was a private relationship. He reminded me in many ways of my stepfather, Alfred Steele. Jim had been sort of a protege of Daddy's and when Daddy died, Jim took over in his place. Jim loved his two kids who were nearly grown and away at school when I first met him. His wife was ill and no longer lived in the apartment with him. He was alone. We just sort of understood one another. He gave me something I needed and I gave him whatever I could in return.

Mother had been helpful in the ways she could during this time, but she did not offer me a place to stay. I had to have complete bed rest during the next two weeks and she thought I should have a nurse, but I couldn't afford one so the subject was dropped.

The producers of *Secret Storm* did something that was way beyond anything required of them. They paid me for the ten shows I'd been scheduled to do before my operation. I broke down and wept at their kindness when the check arrived in the mail.

It was a long way back for me. I went to work before I really should have. Gloria, my director, knew that the show was all I had left to hold onto, all I had to look forward to. I found an apartment through the efforts of some friends and my manager who took it upon themselves to do all the work for me while I was in the hospital. I moved into my new building about two weeks after my release from the hospital. Mother was helpful, sending one of the women who worked with her over to my hotel with food and some other essentials as I was unable to go out and do any shopping.

Everyone on the show was wonderful to me upon my return. They treated me with such kindness, such love and such care that I was overwhelmed. I had lost a lot of weight which was immediately obvious the minute they saw me. Clothes had to be hurriedly altered and I had to have somewhere to rest in between scenes. For someone who had been such a workhorse, this was very difficult for me to handle. I felt as though I wasn't properly doing my job. But no one ever made me feel as though I were anything but welcome and loved. Not one person mentioned Mother being on the show.

Months later, I finally got the nerve to ask someone I trusted implicitly what had happened in my absence. The woman looked very uncomfortable and didn't want to say anything. But I told her I realized that Mother had been drunk during the taping and the barriers of silence were broken. What she told me was only a confirmation of what I already knew. It was the same thing I heard later from others, but only when I asked a direct question. No one ever volunteered any comment, they all preferred to behave as though it was best forgotten.

Mother had arrived at the studio with her own entourage, her Pepsi coolers filled with her own vodka and food, every inch the "star"! She also had the California secretary with her who was downright rude to many of the people on the show. They didn't like that secretary at all, about that point everyone agreed. She was doing the show for union scale minimum, which according to her own words quoted in the papers, paid only for her hairdresser and make-up man. She had never worked with three cameras and her difficulties only started there. The scenes had to be taped many times before they got one they could use. Part of the problem was that they were taping on the weekend and only had two days allotted. They couldn't work very late because of union overtime, availability of equipment and because Mother couldn't work past a certain point. Apparently she was drinking the entire time she was at the studio. From what I gathered, it was not a pleasant experience for anyone involved. No one said: "It was great to work with your mother." A few people privately told me they were very sorry about the entire situation. I could see, once again, that old look of pity in their eyes. How I detested that look.

It is very hard to try and behave gratefully when you are really in a state of rage. It is very hard to hold your head up and be proud when all you really feel is shame and humiliation. But that is what I did. There was no use in pretending with the people on the show because they knew the truth. By unspoken mutual agreement, we all went on with our relationships and our show as though nothing had ever happened.

The only thing that changed was what I'd privately predicted. I started doing fewer shows. The producers had to pay my guarantee, but I never did the specified number of segments after my illness. In fact it was only through the efforts of my director and producer that I wasn't phased out *immediately*. The single most important thing a daytime show has is credibility, audience identification with the characters and their problems. Once that is lost, the whole show suffers. There was just no credibility left to my part. When CBS bought out the original producers of *Secret Storm* and took over the show, it was simply a matter of a few months until I was out. I was grateful to Roy Windsor and Tony Converse that they didn't let me go sooner.

CHAPTER 27

Mother was moving into her new apartment. She wanted me to come over and see it immediately, which I did. It was very nice and just as sterile as the last one, but smaller. All the furniture was covered with plastic, which still stuck to you in the summertime. The air-conditioning was kept just as high as before, so everyone except Mother had to wear sweaters. She still wore her cotton shifts and thong sandals, winter or summer. This apartment also had lovely hardwood floors and she'd ordered a beautiful custom designed rug for the living room. I was there the day it was delivered and it was really spectacular, lush and soft. Two weeks later it was rolled up and put into Manhattan Storage. When I asked where the rug had suddenly gone, Mother said it would just get dirty and the bare floors were easier to keep clean. I shook my head and sighed. She'd rather live with bare, cold floors than have a rug get dirty. She'd rather have no rug at all. How it was going to get so dirty was beyond me because no one was allowed to wear their shoes in this apartment either. Finally, when there were no rugs left at all, people could wear their shoes if they really insisted.

Mother gave me some lovely things for my new apartment. Since she was moving into a smaller apartment and already had four floors at Manhattan Storage that were filled with possessions she wasn't able to use, she gave me a few pieces of furniture. It was a shame that she didn't have any use for all the beautiful things she owned. She gave me a couple of much needed chairs, a small glass coffee table and an area rug. She also gave me odds and ends of dishes that were not full sets. I asked her for some of the kitchenware she wasn't using and she gave me that also. Since I didn't have any of these things and what she gave me was beautiful, I was genuinely grateful. Every spare dime I could get my hands on was going to pay off my hospital and medical expenses. The bills had stacked up unrelentingly during my illness and I was having a tough time paying all of them.

After I was well enough to resume some sort of normal activity, she gave me tickets to see shows she'd been invited to attend, she asked me to stand in for her and accept numerous small awards she was given for business and charitable activities she'd lent her name to and then requested that I attend many of the other events she used to attend.

I knew she thought all this exposure would help my career and most of the time I was more than glad to do it. Sometimes she'd ask me at the very last minute, saying she didn't feel well enough and to make her apologies. Sometimes that was embarrassing, but people were glad to have anyone to fill an empty space at the table, so it usually worked out all right. I didn't like giving the little speeches very much, but I thought it was all good training for me.

I became so involved with Mother again that I'd drop whatever I was doing that wasn't directly connected with my own work to be with her whenever she asked or to join her for lunch, cocktails or dinner. I'd break dates and rearrange my own plans, never saying anything to her. I'd cancel whatever I had going and run over to her apartment. She even asked me to do some traveling with her on company business. I went on junkets to Virginia and Pennsylvania on the chartered Lear jets, attended the dinners and went to the bottling plants. There was some company inquiry as to whether I might be useful in a capacity similar to Mother's, for the younger generation since I was not quite thirty years old and she was in her sixties. But every time the subject was tentatively broached by someone connected with the company, she acted as though she hadn't heard it. I never received one cent for the things I did with her on company business.

However, on my thirtieth birthday she gave me a check for $500 and on Christmas she bought me some beautiful clothes which actually fit. I'd finally been very specific with her about what size I wore. I had a talk with her, telling her that I was very grateful for everything, but it was a terrible waste of time and money if the clothes weren't the right size. She finally got the message and everything fit after that. She also gave me a lovely "fun fur" coat for the winter and some attractive jewelry.

The clothes were almost a necessity since I practically had to have two complete wardrobes. One set of clothes I bought for myself and my own private, normal working life. The other set was for those constant occasions when I either stood in for her at some public event or when I was invited to join her and her friends for dinner at one of the expensive restaurants in the city or travel with her on company business. The requirements were quite different, so the clothes were different also.

During this time, her drinking seemed to get worse. It was so serious that sometimes she'd have a new set of bruises in between the time I left her on one afternoon and saw her the following day. She was never totally alone in the apartment, but she was taking bad falls again on the slippery, polished, rugless floors. She hurt herself rather seriously more than once.

One day, a doctor that she liked and trusted was visiting her, partly to check her ankle and partly to just see how she was feeling generally. When he was ready to leave, I had to leave too and I walked him to the elevator. I asked if we could talk and he offered to drive me home in his car.

When I felt it was safe and no one would overhear us, I started telling him how worried I was about Mother's general health and particularly her drinking. I begged him not to tell anyone I'd talked to him, because I knew Mother would be furious if she thought I was going behind her back, even in her own best interest. I told the doctor that something had to be done, someone had to help her, even if it meant substituting something harmless for all the pills she took. I told him that these falls and bruises usually happened in the evening after I'd left, or in the middle of the night after she'd been drinking and then took the sleeping pills.

He listened quietly, keeping his eyes on the traffic ahead of us. I literally begged him to find a way to either talk to her directly about the problem with her drinking or at least to check with her other doctors to see if something couldn't be done about all the pills.

He looked rather sad. I knew Mother trusted him. I knew I couldn't say anything more than I already had, which was precious little. The couple of times I tried to suggest that Mother not have any more to drink, she became angry with me and didn't talk to me for days afterwards. Even when she was briefly in the hospital for plastic surgery and the doctors forbid her to drink, she still had the Pepsi coolers filled with vodka. I tried to have them removed, but again she became angry and told me to mind my own business. Then, afterwards, she'd make a big deal out of having me taste the "glass of water" she was drinking. When I tried to refuse, she insisted . . . even if there were other people in the room. That would last a few days and then the bruises would reappear and the stories about the falls would start.

The problem was no longer an entirely private matter. She'd appeared on several talk shows drunk, blaming it on nerves or her favorite scapegoat: antibiotics. She'd also appeared at public functions drunk, even when she knew she had been invited to sit on the dais and to make a short speech. Several of her close friends in the business who were responsible for these charitable or professional events were really beginning to come down hard on her. They told her in no uncertain terms that if she didn't get her drinking under control, at least in public, that they'd never invite her to another of their events again. They were no longer going to be publicly embarrassed by her behavior.

The two men I know personally who gave her this ultimatum had been friends with Mother for more than forty years. They loved her, admired her as a great lady and were deeply saddened at being forced into the position of confronting her in this way. But their own reputations were now at stake and they were not about to risk their own lifetimes of hard work, nor their own professional standing in the community because of her drinking.

Needless to say, Mother took it very badly. Instead of trying to face the situation or trying to do anything constructive with her problem, she became furious with her friends. She blamed the messengers for the bad news. She became particularly critical of her friends. She said spiteful things about these people who really loved her and were only trying to help her. She used what she considered an unwarranted insult, an unfair attack on her as just another excuse to drink.

Even now she would sometimes go an entire month without leaving the apartment except to go out to an occasional dinner from which she insisted upon returning home by nine o'clock. Most of the world she dealt with would come to her apartment for meetings or social drinks in the afternoon. She rarely, if ever, had anyone over for dinner except me or the people who worked for her.

She never allowed herself to be totally alone. That year when the maid went to visit her daughter for two weeks over Christmas, I stayed with Mother every night. I'd have breakfast in the morning and go back to my own apartment after the secretary arrived. A woman would come in the afternoon just before the secretary left and stay until I arrived in the early evening. The cleaning man who also helped with major packing jobs, came every Saturday and the rest of us cleaned up during the week. Food was ordered by telephone and delivered to the back door. One of the women who normally stayed with her over the weekend did most of the rest of Mother's shopping for her.

I used to try to get Mother interested in going out for a while, even for a drive around Central Park in the car with the windows open just for some fresh air and a change of scenery. I didn't know how she could stand being cooped up in that apartment all the time, looking at the same walls and the same people day in and day out. I even tried to talk her into taking a vacation somewhere quiet and private, but she refused. She said she traveled enough for the company.

There were a number of people around her these days that I didn't like at all. They were what I rather uncharitably and crudely called the "star-fuckers." The people who went mad over celebrities. The people who would go to any lengths to have their own names associated with anyone famous. These people were not just fans, they had professions and usually had something expensive to sell. They had no scruples about what they did if it got them close to a celebrity. Some of them only wanted to be able to name-drop with their own circle of friends. Others more commonly had something they were hustling. It didn't even appear that they were selling something at first. At first they were just fond admirers, fawning over Mother and telling her how wonderful she was. Mother just ate that shit up. She didn't seem to have one bit of common sense when it came to people fawning over her, especially if they did it with a little class. She loved every minute of it, and in fact, I often thought that was really the behavior she preferred. Any person with one shred of intelligence could see where all this pandering was headed, but Mother seemed oblivious. These people would never dare pull their sales deal in front of me, and I tried in vain time after time to tell Mother that all they wanted was a quick sale at outrageous prices. She looked at me as though I'd stabbed her in the heart. She'd explain to me how attentive and loving these people were toward her, how good they'd been to her. Didn't they call her almost every other day, just to see how she was feeling? Didn't they invite her to dinner? Of course, she was usually "too busy" to ever accept any of their kind gestures, but it was the thought that counted. I just knew that the minute I was away for a few days, the minute I turned my back, some new dreadful, ugly painting would arrive or some contribution to a new cause would be made, or she'd lend her name to another activity she'd never participate in, or she'd pay an exorbitant fee for some personal service. Nine times out of ten I was absolutely right. I had to stand by in total helplessness and smile politely while some creep duped her out of something (usually money) just because they said they loved and admired her so tremendously. She repaid them and showed her gratitude for their fawning bullshit most generously. It made me so mad and I felt so helpless to stop it that I gave up talking to her about the entire situation.

I could never get used to the fact that a woman who prided herself on having such strong will power, who was publicly known as such a strong-minded person, whose favorite pastime was giving orders, could so predictably and easily be swayed by these jerks who only had to lay on the sweet talk and wrap her around their fingers. God forbid that you should tell her the truth. She'd fly into a rage and banish you forever. But sweet talk her . . . say "yes" every time she opened her mouth, be at her beck and call, fall all over her with praise and admiration . . . she'd give you the whole goddamned world! I could *never* understand how she could possibly not see through this garbage. The conclusion I came to was that she wanted it just this way.

I couldn't do that, I couldn't be that way. So I had to keep my mouth shut many times rather than tell her a lie, but my silence only emphasized the fact that I didn't agree with her. Now we had a truce about that part of my personality which had given her such a fit all my growing-up years. I tried to be what she wanted as much as I could without compromising my own personal self-respect or sense of dignity. I would not be her servant and I was not a fan. She only trusted and respected me to the extent that I did not allow myself to fall into those two categories, though she never ceased trying to push me into one of them whenever she felt my guard weakening. I would not make the trade-off with her and she knew it by now. If we were to have any relationship at all that had any real meaning, I had to be my own person. Otherwise, I had nothing to bring to that relationship. She had no respect for the people who simply bowed to her wishes, even if that's what she demanded of them. She treated them with contempt and talked to them in a tone of voice I could never bear to hear. The people in the apartment who served her, did so with love and loyalty despite her bad temper and eccentric ways. But I was not one of them and I just couldn't put up with that any more. She understood and accepted our truce in return for a very real friendship.

In March 1969, I gave Mother a party for her sixty-first birthday. It was the first time I'd ever given her a party and I don't even know where I got the idea, except that I thought it would make her happy. Officially, she was sixty-one, unofficially she was closer to sixty-five years old. By either count, I guess that's a long time to wait for your first real family birthday party.

She was absolutely delighted when I suggested the idea of a party to her. I asked her who she'd like me to invite and she made out a list of people. It was going to be quite a feat for my apartment to handle, but I was determined to have it at my home even if some people had to eat dinner in the bedroom! Together, Mother and I decided upon the menu, the hors d'oeuvres and the wine. She insisted on buying the wine through the "21" Club and paying for it as well as half the rest of the food. I tried to talk her out of it, using the argument that she shouldn't have to pay for her own party when I was the one giving it, but she was not to be dissuaded.

It was quite obvious that I couldn't cook for all the guests, so we arranged to have it catered through the establishment that kept her supplied with food at home.

Beginning early in the morning of that particular March 23rd, my doorbell never stopped buzzing. There was a constant stream of deliveries including a case of wine, liquor, flowers, ice, glasses and finally the food. My own maid, Carrie Rose, had agreed to help me through the entire traumatic day and I don't think I could have survived it without her. We cleaned the entire apartment until it sparkled, which is a feat in itself in New York City, then Carrie went home and returned late in the afternoon. I had a bartender also and between the three of us, we managed to keep everything running smoothly in spite of limited work space.

Fortunately, everyone Mother had on her list and wanted to attend the party was able to attend. They were all impeccably punctual, also in her honor. She had specifically told everyone "no gifts" but I'd invited them to celebrate her birthday and no one arrived empty-handed.

At exactly the appointed hour, the guests streamed out of the elevators and down the hall to my apartment. They included Bob and Florence Kriendler from "21", Mr. and Mrs. Bob Kelly from Pepsi, Dr. and Mrs. Anthony Gristina, Jerry and Minette Pickman who had been close friends for many years, Herb Barnett, who was now Chairman of the Board of Pepsi, and my director Gloria Monty with her husband Bob O'Byrne. As a complete surprise for Mother, I'd also invited my sister Cathy and her husband who drove down from Upstate New York.

Everyone was complimentary, outgoing and fully prepared to have a festive time. The party was absolutely perfect from beginning to end. Mother was truly surprised to see Cathy and delighted that they had driven down especially for her party. She was genuinely touched with all the gifts and warm feelings. I couldn't have been happier than I was watching her open her presents just like a little kid on Christmas morning. It had all worked out just as I had hoped. Everyone enjoyed themselves very much.

During the next few months I kept busy going on commercial appointments and working one day a week on the soap. As the weather became warmer, I started going out to Long Island to visit my brother who had just returned from Viet Nam a few months earlier. We'd had a great reunion after what had seemed like the eternity he'd been gone. At first he thought he might stay in the city, but decided he really wanted to live out in the country where he had lots of friends and could get a job outdoors.

I went out several weekends a month through that summer and had a wonderful time. I loved the country, the ocean and the quaint village he'd chosen as his new home. It was a relief from the city's heat and noise and dirt.

The beginning of August, our new producer from CBS called me into his office and told me that I would only be in a couple more shows. He told me that he was very sorry, but the character had lost its usefulness some time ago. I knew there was a general housecleaning going on at all the network daytime shows now and the news honestly didn't surprise me a bit. Indeed I thought it was pretty decent of him to tell me in person. They would pay off the rest of my contract and write me out of the program in just three more segments. It was not an unpleasant meeting, since none of the information came as a shock to me.

I called Mother to tell her the news and to my surprise, she was very upset. She told me that she'd spoken with this man several months before and he assured her that they had no intention of letting me go. All I could reply to her was, "Well, Mother . . . I'm afraid he lied to you."

A month or so later I went out to the Coast for a short visit to explore the possibility of getting work. Everyone was nice enough, but said that in order to be considered seriously for work, I'd have to plan on living in Los Angeles.

I returned to New York and spent the next six months turning over every stone I could find, looking for work. I got close several times but not close enough for anything except some commercials which I welcomed for their residuals.

My brother got married again that fall. Their wedding was simple and the reception held at his new bride's home. It was a beautiful autumn day and a happy occasion.

CHAPTER 28

Finally in June 1970, I mustered up all my courage and decided to give Los Angeles another try. I discussed the plan at some length with Mother and she very generously offered to let me stay in her apartment in West Hollywood until I found out if I would get work. I was overwhelmed. She'd never offered me a place to stay. Of course she paid rent on the apartment year round and almost never used it, but that didn't necessarily make any difference. That alone didn't compel her to offer me the use of it, even temporarily. In addition to the apartment, she offered to call some people for me and see what they could do to help. I sat there looking at her with tears in my eyes. It was also the first time she'd ever offered me any meaningful professional assistance. It was nearly too much for me to handle all in one day. I went to her and put my arms around her, thanking her as I hugged her. She said she'd miss me, but that she knew I was going to do very well.

It took a few weeks to get ready, including finding a friend to look after my own apartment and feed my cats. I said my round of goodbyes and the remaining days went quickly.

On July 4th, Sunday, I flew to Los Angeles. Mother's secretary picked me up at the airport and drove me to the apartment. It was so completely and totally different from my hasty departure four years earlier. I was such a different person, I'd grown and matured considerably in those four years. I felt a sense of hope and confidence now that I hadn't before.

Ever since my operation, my entire attitude toward life had changed. I was so glad to just be alive and able to continue my particular journey that I now dealt with problems and setbacks quite differently than ever before. I had a much more determined and positive attitude toward work, a career, making friends and establishing myself as a successful human being. My good relationship with Mother over these years helped a great deal. I felt as though a heavy burden had been lifted from my shoulders. I really felt she loved me and cared about what happened to me. We had been together almost constantly for a long while now and I believed that we had finally, after all the terrible years, come to a mutual understanding of one another.

I knew she didn't agree with all of my ideas, nor did I always see eye to eye with her, but there was at the very least a mutual truce in those areas of disagreement. At best, we'd had a lot of fun together, she was proud of me and she was showing me in so many little ways that she really cared. In return, I was there for her as a friend, a daughter and when necessary, a companion. She trusted me to tell her the truth as I perceived it and to stand by her when she needed me. Ours was no longer a relationship of emergency, it was no longer a superficial "fix." We'd shared our thoughts and feelings on many levels and were both quite pleased that after all the years, we'd found one another again. I had a much greater appreciation of her professional achievements, having spent years in the business myself. I think that gave us a basis for respect that was an important bond as well. Though I was certainly no "star" yet, I was making steady progress toward being a well-known actress, talented and professional. I knew better than anyone that I still had a long way to go, but I was still young enough and energetic enough to bear the hardships ahead. With her moral support, I was sure I'd have good luck. I knew only too well that the business was difficult and competitive enough without trying to function with her as an active enemy. I'd learned that once before and I didn't have to learn it all over again. I'd had to go outside the establishment for all of my early work in the business and I didn't want to have to be forced to do that again. I really wanted into the mainstream of the business. I wanted to do nighttime television and films. I now had a good deal of experience, a small public following from two years on the soap and a mountain of ambition propelling me onward. If I just didn't have to fight her too, I was sure I could succeed.

At first I felt very uncomfortable in her apartment. I felt weighted with responsibility. I tried to take care of it even better than I would my own home. I didn't have any parties, I tried not to make any noise, I didn't even use two of the rooms. She had a maid who came in to clean whether anyone occupied the apartment or not, so the place was always spotless. I just used the kitchen, dining area and one bedroom.

Just a week after my arrival, my former director Gloria gave me a small part on her new daytime show at NBC. It wasn't anything much, but it was work and I was delighted to be busy so soon. I thought it was probably a good omen.

Every day that I didn't have an appointment, I spent hours on the phone calling the people Mother had referred as well as anyone I knew who might have work. I went out to lunch or dinner almost every day on business. I went to every studio, every independent producer and casting office I could finagle an appointment to see. I hounded the agents until I'm sure they never wanted to hear my name again. I even got an appointment to see Lew Wasserman at Universal Studios. He was very nice to me, asking me about what I'd been doing and why I was in Los Angeles. I told him pointedly that I was here because I wanted to work and I wanted to work at Universal. I'd known Uncle Lew nearly all my life, but mostly when I was just a young girl and he was still Mother's agent at the old MCA. There was no sense trying to hide the past from him, because he knew full well what it was. I simply said that Mother had offered me the use of her apartment until I could get settled. It was rather like trying to tell someone you now have the official stamp of approval. The meeting lasted about fifteen minutes, so I talked as fast as I could without sounding like a magpie. At the end, he leaned forward slightly behind his football-field desk and asked, "Christina, are you happy with your life?" I was quite taken aback with the question. It was so direct. I replied, "Yes, very." It was hardly a profound answer, but it was the best I could muster on such short notice. He nodded his head and wished me good luck. We shook hands and I left.

It had been a very pleasant business meeting with a man who was now very important and almost impossible to get to see. However, I realized as I was going down in the elevator that I had absolutely no idea what the outcome of the meeting was or even if there was an outcome at all!

However, very shortly after that, I was called into the Universal casting office to audition for a small part on Vince Edwards's new series. It turned out to be only one day's work, but I'd said I wanted to work and that's exactly what I meant. I took the job.

~

My rented car was beginning to cost a fortune, so when friends of Mother's told me they were going on vacation for a few weeks and offered me the use of one of their cars I happily accepted. For reasons I never totally understood, Mother was furious with me when I mentioned it to her. I was calling her nearly every day to let her know about my progress and particularly when I actually got work even though the first two jobs were meager. She wanted me to return the car immediately, but I told her I couldn't because her friends wouldn't be home for another week. She told me to return it immediately upon their return and *never* to borrow anything from her friends again! She was really mad at me.

I was very hurt by her outburst. We hadn't had anything like this happen between us in many, many years and I couldn't understand what had set her off about this. The people were very close friends, they were simply being kind to her daughter because of their friendship with her. I didn't understand why that made her so angry. I just tried to rationalize it away by thinking that I'd inadvertently caught her in a bad mood and this was just a momentary thing, she'd forget about tomorrow. But she sounded very cold to me toward the end of our conversation and that tone of voice brought forth all my old insecurities about our relationship. In fact, I was so upset that I called my therapist in New York to ask him for his more objective opinion. He also felt that the outburst was momentary in light of the last four years. We were both wrong.

A few days later, the Los Angeles secretary called me about 7:30 in the morning, waking me up. I thought something was wrong because she never called me this early. Evidently, she'd just spoken to my mother in New York and had called to relay the message. She said that Mother was coming out to do a show, so I'd have to find another place to live. As it turned out, I had exactly two days in which to move. I was barely awake, but I knew something was fishy about the whole thing. Why didn't Mother tell me herself? I'd been talking to her every day. Why did she have the secretary tell me to move? I asked the secretary a couple of questions and then decided to call Mother directly. I couldn't get through to Mother at the apartment. The operator at the Pepsi switchboard said her lines were all busy, so I left a message. But, she didn't call me right back. I didn't talk to her for three days.

Something in my bones told me that this whole situation stunk. I'd only been in Los Angeles six weeks. I'd only been away from Mother six weeks, but something had gone wrong behind my back and I knew it. I just didn't have any idea what it was or exactly where it had come from. Certainly there was no indication of trouble from Mother herself, except just that one minor thing about the borrowed car. She had done nothing but help me the whole time I'd been here. But something about this was wrong or she wouldn't be hiding behind the secretary. It just didn't sit right with my intuition and my intuition was rarely wrong after all these years.

The secretary called me back to say that the maid was coming that morning to change the sheets and clean the apartment and that if I could move out before she finished, she wouldn't have to come back before Mother arrived in Los Angeles two days later. Now I just had today in which to find another place to stay. I called a girlfriend who had an apartment in the Hollywood hills and asked if I could stay with her and then sublet the apartment when she returned to New York. She agreed, so I called another friend with a car and asked him to help me move that afternoon. Mother's secretary arrived a couple hours later and stayed for the rest of the day. I had the distinct feeling that she was watching me to make sure I didn't take anything that didn't belong to me. It was just a feeling. She was the same one who had accused me of taking my own dresser set out of the Brentwood house years before when I left for college, so we had a history of not particularly caring for one another.

It was amazing, but when I finally reached Mother several days later to give her my new telephone number and address, she acted like nothing had happened! The secretary had told me that the locks on the apartment had been changed immediately after my departure and the phone number was also changed a few days later. Yet Mother acted as though everything was normal. It was so strange that if I'd had a brain in my head, I'd have asked Mother what in the hell was going on out here. But, instead, I made the error of opting for continued peace and quiet. I kept it all to myself and didn't say a word.

Needless to say, Mother didn't come out to Los Angeles two days later. Mysteriously enough, after I moved out of her apartment, she changed her plans. In fact she didn't come back to Los Angeles for several months. The whole thing was just a made-up situation, a ploy to get me to move. It was one of those situations I didn't deal with very well at all, even now with all the changing and growing I thought I'd done. So, there the apartment sat, totally unoccupied and locked up for months. In other words, it returned to it's normal state. What was all that upset about, anyway? To this day I do not know because Mother never said another word to me about it. She never voiced her displeasure to me about anything I'd done. She never said a word to me personally.

The next month I did a much larger part on *Medical Center* over at MGM. To my surprise, the show was being directed by one of Mother's former directors and one of my former "uncles." I was delighted to see him and very happy to be working with him.

The show went well and I received some nice publicity out of it. The director wrote Mother a nice note about what a good actress I'd turned out to be and how proud she must be of my talent and professional attitude. Mother wrote back that she was glad he felt that way. Weird.

In October, just three months after my arrival in Los Angeles, I was offered my first guest star part on television. I didn't audition for it, I don't know exactly how it all came about except that I'd been to see a number of the people at Universal and done what amounted to a paid screen test for them in August. My agents called to tell me that I had the guest lead on *Marcus Welby* and that I was to report to the studio immediately for costume fittings. That was Thursday. The show began shooting on Monday morning. I was so excited it's a miracle I didn't have an automobile accident driving the short distance from my apartment to the studio. I had a gate pass waiting for me and drove right up to the wardrobe department. This was the real thing. The producers came to congratulate me while I was being fitted for the clothes and brought me a script. I could hardly wait to get home and read it. I could hardly wait to get home and call my mother with the great news. She was going to be so pleased. My very first guest starring part and I hadn't been here even six months. It was all beginning to pay off.

By the time I returned from the studio it was nearly seven o'clock in the evening. I guess I should have remembered the lessons of the old days a little better and waited until the next morning to call Mother. But it was only 10 o'clock in New York and I didn't think she'd be asleep yet.

I was so filled with joy that my gamble was paying off so quickly that all I could think of was sharing it with her.

I got through on the phone right away. I bubbled over with the good news, telling her that I'd gotten the guest star part on *Marcus Welby*, that I was playing a nun, and that I was in almost every scene throughout the entire episode.

Then I waited for her response and congratulations. But I waited in silence quite a long time. Such a long time, in fact, that I thought we'd been disconnected. "Hello . . . Mother?"

An icy voice replied only, "How did you get the job?" I didn't catch on right away. I was still in my own place of happiness, in spite of the strange welcome I was receiving. "You remember, Mother, I did that one day's work on Vince Edwards's show that they said was like a test, then I met a lot more people, got another show and some good publicity and I guess the meeting with Lew Wasserman certainly didn't hurt."

Her voice never changed. It was cold, icy, chilling. We didn't talk much longer before she hung up on me! I stared at the phone in my hand. Tears welled up in my eyes? What the hell had gone wrong now? How could she turn such good news into this awful feeling I had in my stomach? What in the world was going on? I called to tell her the very best news I've had and she hangs up on me? What the hell is happening to us?

The next evening I had made plans for a small dinner party at the apartment. Just a few close friends were invited, so I decided to turn it into a little celebration of my good fortune. Everyone, of course, asked if Mother wasn't terribly pleased. I lied to all of them, saying that she was delighted.

I could hardly sleep the entire weekend, I was so excited. I worked very hard the following week, but the show went very well judging by the remarks I heard and the compliments I got. Robert Young was really nice, although we didn't have any scenes together. We did have pictures taken together because the studio publicity department had arranged several interviews for me which we did during the lunch hour in the commissary. I was now very careful to say all the right things and never hint at any estrangement between Mother and myself. Except for two occasions of very peculiar behavior on her part, I was still under the impression that everything was generally all right.

I was never more wrong in my life. It was one week after I'd finished shooting the *Marcus Welby* show at Universal that I'd been invited to lunch with the same friend of Mother's who had lent me the family car.

When we met for lunch, he seemed unusually distant. I greeted him as usual, not knowing anything was amiss. After we ordered, he asked me if I'd spoken with Mother lately. I told her I hadn't talked to her in almost two weeks now.

He looked at me carefully but very strangely. I asked him what was wrong. He looked down at his silverware on the table for a long moment as though he was in the midst of a decision he hadn't expected to make.

I was getting very uncomfortable, but I didn't have the vaguest idea what was going on. Then he said that Mother had called him several nights ago. He measured his words carefully as though he were in the midst of a negotiation deal and didn't want to be misunderstood.

He went on to say that Mother was in a terrible rage against *me* when she had called. He said that she went on and on about what a dreadful person I was, how ungrateful I was for all the help she'd given me. The crowning blow was my last phone call. Mother told this man and his wife over the phone that the only reason I'd called to tell her about getting the part on *Marcus Welby* was to *gloat*! She said that I'd just called her to gloat over the fact that I'd gotten a part on the show, when I knew full well that *Marcus Welby* was the one show she'd always wanted to do!!!!

I looked at this man, this longtime friend of Mother's as though he'd struck me with a thunderbolt. I couldn't believe I was hearing this insanity. I actually asked him to repeat the last two sentences he'd said to me, just to make sure I'd heard him correctly. Although it was nearly two weeks since my last conversation with Mother, it was only two *days* since she'd called him on the rampage. My first thought was: if she was so damn steamed up about me, what the hell took her so long to call?

I was totally speechless. I didn't know what to say to him. There was no real reason to defend myself, because I hadn't done anything wrong. But that's not how he felt. His experience with Mother and the phone call were somehow designed to make it look as though I'd done something awful.

"You can't believe that," was all I could say to him. At that moment the waiter brought our order, so I had a moment to collect my thoughts.

"You simply can't believe that," I repeated. "It doesn't make any sense." He didn't say anything. "I mean, for god's sakes, I called to tell her good news . . . I called to share good news, nothing else. As a matter of fact I thought she acted a little strangely that night because she hung up on me. But, I didn't do anything to her."

He looked me squarely in the face. "Christina, she was on a rampage the other night. I don't know how many other people she called, but I don't think we were the first. It was almost 9 o'clock our time when the call came through."

My mind raced to grasp what he was saying to me. That call was made at midnight New York time. God help me. Mother was never up that late unless she was crazy drunk and couldn't sleep even with the pills. What the hell happened? She just got around to calling these friends two days ago and yet I talked to her nearly two weeks ago. Where in God's name did she get these ideas? Who got her so fired up against me? What was going on in that strange mind, in that strange world of hers that she could turn my first real success into such an incredible holocaust? How could she turn it all against me like this?

I looked carefully at the man I'd thought was my friend as well as Mother's friend. And I knew it was going to be just the beginning of the old story all over again. I couldn't leave Mother's sight before she began running into her own insane ideas about me. I didn't know whether she had any help with those ideas or whether she was all alone in the venture, but unless I was personally and physically in her immediate presence, right there in her line of vision, able to defend myself, she seemed to allow her own insanity to run rampant. There was no defense against it because she never said any of this to my face, to me personally and directly. She never told me what was in her strange mind. She told other people after it was all twisted and convoluted by the opinions of the snakes that surrounded her. But by the time it came out, she was dealing with the figments of her own imagination as though it was the absolute truth. She believed all of it, even though she'd made it up herself as though it were rational fact.

I knew there was no use trying to convince this man that the entire thing was Mother's insanity. I knew there was no use trying to tell him that I'd only meant to bring her happiness and proud feelings. I knew it was all useless by the look on his face. I'd seen that look too many times before in my life not to know what it meant.

The truth was so colorless by comparison with his phone call, so harmless that it didn't even seem to fit the situation. I knew I wouldn't be seeing him anymore. Once these vendettas started, people disappeared and the invitations ceased with lightning speed. It was like the rats deserting a sinking ship. No one wanted to be associated with trouble. No one wanted to have their name mentioned in connection with other crazy phone calls Mother might make. After all, if she could call them in the middle of the night ranting and raving against the world in general and her own daughter in particular, there was just no telling who would be next. Who needed that kind of trouble? Business was hard enough, there was no sense in looking for more aggravation.

Indeed, that was the last time I saw this friend of Mother's.

Before that year ended, I did another show at Universal. This time I auditioned three times for the job. It was a good part, a female radical on the show *Ironsides*. I'd gotten myself quite a range of characters in the last few months. I'd played a child psychologist on *Medical Center*, a nun on *Marcus Welby* and now a radical leader on *Ironsides*.

When the agents confirmed that I had the part and would start work again the next week, I took a precaution for my own sake and wrote Mother the good news rather than calling her. I was still very hurt over her reaction to my success, over her phone calls to friends, over the fact that she could not or would not share the good fortune with me. I'd worked so hard just to get this far and I thought she would be so proud. Instead what I got was a slap in the face behind my back and a lot of insults.

I'd only seen Mother once during these last months. When she finally came to Los Angeles, it was to present an award at the Golden Globes. It was a hectic evening, as was customary when Mother had to make a public appearance combined with a speech. She managed to turn everybody upside down and give her own publicity people instant ulcers, but I was so used to it that it didn't bother me much any more.

A few days after the Golden Globe awards dinner, she called to ask if I'd like to join her for lunch at the Bistro restaurant in Beverly Hills with a "man-about-town" friend of hers I'd never met. I just about had time to get dressed and drive to the restaurant if I was going to meet them on time, but I didn't have anything else planned and I was pleased with the invitation. She was supposed to leave town the next day, so it would be another chance to see her before she went back to New York.

I arrived at the Bistro about two minutes late and asked for the gentleman whose name Mother had given me. He was already seated at the table and I noticed Mother had not yet arrived, so I introduced myself to him and sat down. He was a very charming older man and we chatted pleasantly for some time. He ordered us drinks and we continued talking. After about half an hour passed, he started looking at his expensive watch. Both of us were wondering what had happened to my usually punctual mother, but neither of us wanted to initiate the subject of her tardiness. Finally, we had been there waiting for nearly forty-five minutes. He asked me if he should call the apartment. He told me he'd just spoken with her this morning to confirm the appointment which had been made several days in advance, so he was quite sure there couldn't have been any misunderstanding about either the time or the place.

I was beginning to have one of my old intuitive feelings that there was something very fishy about this whole set-up. As casually as I could, I inquired what time it was when he'd spoken to her. He guessed that it was about 10:30 or 11:00 this morning. That was just about the time she'd called me. I was beginning to realize that this was a very embarrassing "set-up" on Mother's part. She never had any intention of meeting this man for lunch. Instead of just telling him she was too busy, or any other polite excuse, she'd maneuvered me into taking the brunt of the social slight for her. I knew she wasn't going to show up now, but I wasn't quite sure how to let this total stranger know that. Finally, I suggested that we order our lunch rather than waiting any longer for her. I simply said that something must have come up and I was sure there was nothing to worry about. So, we ordered and ate a delightful lunch. The man was a very social, very conversant gentleman and I had an interesting time with him. We had ordered some coffee when he was called to the phone.

As he left, I thought . . . poor man, no one deserves this treatment. It was about the rudest thing I'd seen Mother do to a totally innocent person. I guess she figures she can behave any way she damn well pleases and most people will just come back for more. I could *never* understand that.

She'd just stood this man up, plain and simple. She set it all up so that I'd walk into a very rude, very embarrassing situation and have to try and cover up her creation. It wasn't even as though I'd met this man before. He was a total stranger to me!

When he returned to the table, the man looked hurt and puzzled. I'd recognized his name from seeing it a number of times in the social columns and I assumed he wasn't the sort that had very much experience with being stood up! I wanted to just laugh it off and tell him to forget the whole thing, including his bruised ego. I wanted to tell him it was a reflection on her and her bad manners, as insulting as it was. But since I didn't know him well enough, I couldn't say much of anything.

The "story" he repeated to me was so ludicrous and so childish that even he had to see right through it. He just shook his head and sat down. But then he turned to me and said directly to me, "Did you know your mother wasn't going to be here for lunch?" I looked at him with what compassion I could feel for a total stranger and said, "No, I'm sorry I didn't. When I spoke with her, she asked me to join the two of you."

It was so obvious to both of us that we were just pawns in a set-up that it wasn't worth further discussion. He tried to say something polite about my being a charming substitute for my mother and I thanked him for a lovely lunch and it was all a totally meaningless exchange.

We parted company on a cheerful note and drove off in opposite directions.

During the time it took me to drive home, I started thinking back over the other times I'd been sent in at the last minute to make things look good for Mother, to take up the slack for her, under the guise of how good it would be for my career. As I looked back, I tried to separate helpfulness from the times like this one, where she never had any intention of showing up and had planned the whole thing way in advance. In New York, she had set me up with men who could be helpful to her by suggesting they date me. The implication I got from them is that I was supposed to go to bed with them. They were most surprised and pissed off when I refused, as though an agreement had been broken. Perhaps it had, but I was not a party to it.

I tried to call Mother when I returned home to ask her what the hell was going on, but I was told she wasn't feeling well and was resting. I didn't speak to her again before she left. She never returned my phone call.

It so happened that an apartment in my building was going to be vacant around the middle of February 1971. It was a beautiful apartment, high beam ceilings, hardwood floors, stained glass windows and six big rooms with an occasional ghost in residence. I had not seriously thought about moving to California again, but with this apartment available my thoughts turned to making the decision. I liked New York and I'd always done quite well there professionally. I had a good apartment in the Dorcester and my entire family lived in the East. But maybe it was time to make the move. Everything pointed to continued steady progress in Los Angeles. I'd done four shows and a couple of commercials in just six months. Maybe it didn't have to be a bad town for me after all. Maybe it was time to give it another try.

I decided to take the apartment and made the arrangements with the landlord. I even bought a car the woman who was moving had up for sale.

On my way to New York, I stopped in Florida to visit friends and had what amounted to a lovely vacation for ten days.

Once back in the city, it was a hectic stream of phone calls and arrangements. It was the end of February and it was cold. I planned to spend two months in New York and then move back to Los Angeles.

I called Mother upon my return and she was completely cordial. The whole thing was very weird. The first night I was back in the city I attended a dinner party at the home of a very elegant friend of hers. Mother was supposed to be there too, but she never showed up. She never called to cancel either. Her friend was crushed by the social slight. Late in the evening, he called me into another room and asked me point blank if Mother hadn't come to his dinner party which was supposed to have been in her honor, because I was going to be there? I apologized for her not appearing, but I said I didn't think it had anything to do with me. Of course that was a lie. She was punishing her friend for inviting me, but it was too late now. I couldn't do anything to save his dinner party. My god . . . I thought . . . it can't be happening to me all over again . . . it just can't. I haven't done anything wrong! I don't deserve this! Why does she do this to me?

I went to see Mother a number of times. For once, I did ask her about the dinner party and she just brushed it off, saying she wasn't feeling well that night. I couldn't figure her out. To my face she was the same as always, just maybe a little cool, a little distracted. To my face she wished me all good luck and success. It was a very strange time because she never mentioned the phone calls or the other incidents. She never said anything that would indicate there was anything wrong between us. I tried to ask her on several occasions if everything was going all right for her, but she disregarded my questions and went on to other subjects. I gave her the air dates for my last two shows which were scheduled just about a week apart in March. She said she'd watch them.

It was May before I actually got settled in my new home. Moving cross-country is a chore at best and exhausting. My furniture was a week late arriving and the apartment hadn't been completely repainted yet, so everything was a mess.

I thought that my timing was good, though, because the television season was just starting again and I didn't have a doubt in this world that I'd continue to get work.

I spent hours on the phone letting everyone know that I was back in town, living here now. I arranged a couple of small dinner parties in my new apartment and was invited to several parties in return. One such gathering was given by a publicity man who had been at Universal. That evening I saw lots of people I knew and had a wonderful time, even though I'd come to the party alone, as I often did. Toward the end of the evening I sat down to talk with my host who told me a rather strange story.

Evidently, the previous December, when I was scheduled to do the *Iron-sides*, Mother was in negotiation to do another show at the same studio. The publicity department ran a small blurb in the trades to the effect that mother and daughter would be working at the same studio for the first time. Two days later Mother cancelled her appearance on the show. It came as quite a shock to the producers and the studio alike. I do not recall what the official reason was, but she didn't do the show.

"I don't know whether I should be telling you this," he said looking around to see if anyone was standing close enough to overhear. "But the rumor was that she was upset by the bit in the trades and that's why she backed out of the show at the last minute. It left the producers in a hell of a spot with the studio." I had that old sinking feeling again in my stomach, but I cheerfully said that I was sure it was all just coincidence. I thanked him for a lovely evening and left shortly afterwards.

When I got home and had locked the door securely behind me, I sat down and cried. Not again . . . not this same thing all over again. What is the matter with that woman? Why does she go after me behind my back like this? What have I done to her that she thinks is so awful? Is she actually *jealous* of my small amount of success? How can she be that jealous of me when she's had the whole world at her feet? Why in the hell can't she just leave me alone?

I tried not to let anyone see it, but I was depressed for days after that party. It was like voodoo magic. She poked holes in my image behind my back where I couldn't defend myself and I felt the needles of pain in real life. Just getting work was hard enough for anyone in this business, but with her as an enemy it was nearly impossible.

Mother sent me a card and a check for $75 dollars for my birthday that year. I used the money for tennis lessons. I seemed to have a lot of free time on my hands that I just couldn't fill with appointments or lunches or anything. So, like the rest of the town, I took up tennis.

I didn't do one television show during the regular season. I was in my agent's office week after week, trying to get them to tell me why I wasn't getting appointments. I had film, I had good credits from just the previous season, I had good working relationships with every show, the cast and producers I'd worked with. It didn't make any sense. I couldn't even get auditions at the same studios I'd worked just the season before. If it hadn't been for my commercial agent, Mai Cassel, I would have gone totally stir crazy. I also would have starved. The other agents said they didn't know why, they didn't have any explanation. I just didn't seem to be "right" for the parts that came along. I'd been in the business long enough to know that excuse was the most standard and bullshit one of them all. That was the catch-all phrase you couldn't do much about.

It was December, just before Christmas, when I got a call to rush over to Universal right away. There was a brand new show called *Sixth Sense* and they were in a bind finding someone to do a weird part that called for some Kabuki dancing. The casting man was a friend of mine from back in Pittsburgh at Carnegie and he had gone to bat for me. Everyone else with the show liked me and I got the part with two days in which to learn the very complicated dance routine. The studio sent a teacher to my apartment and we went through the dance hour after hour, day after day until I finally got it fairly right.

That was the first television show I'd done in one full year and it was to be the last of my acting career although I didn't know that at the time.

We worked right up until Christmas Eve finishing the show. Everyone was just super and I got the impression we were doing a good job. The show had a strange title which we all joked about, particularly since it was taken from one of my lines. It was called: "I am not a part of the human world."

Bright and early on Christmas morning I called Mother. She'd sent me another black outfit, this time it was a dinner suit that was the wrong size and I was going to return it, but I thanked her anyway. She asked if it fit and I said it didn't but not to worry, because I'd lost some weight. She sounded hurt that I was going to return her gift, but I tried to tell her that I appreciated it very much and *please* not to be upset. Our conversation went downhill from there. It was something I could never get straight. I called her to wish her a Merry Christmas and before the conversation was over, she made me feel terrible. She made me feel as though I'd done something wrong again. She never came right out in the open and said anything you could get a hold on or deal with directly. It was a tone of voice that sounded disapproving, it was an implication that all was not well, it was an innuendo about her health. But the end result was clear as hell: it was total misery. I finally had enough of it and said, "Listen Mother . . . I'm sorry you're not feeling well, but I called to wish you a Merry Christmas. I don't want to argue, I don't want either one of us to feel badly, but I'd appreciate it very much if you didn't speak to me that way." She said, "Merry Christmas, Christina" like a knife coming through the phone and hung up on me!

I slammed that phone down in a fury. Goddammit lady . . . that's going to be the *last* time you're ever going to talk to me like that. That's the last time I'm going to allow myself to be sucked into your goddammed bullshit. That's the last time I'm going to end up feeling like I've done something wrong when all I did was have the consideration to call you and wish you a Merry Christmas. Do you ever call to see how I am? No. Do you ever call to wish me Happy Birthday or Merry Christmas? No. Do you ever try to work anything out between us? No. I'm the one who has to make the relationship work. I'm the one who has to always apologize, even if I know I haven't done anything wrong. I'm the one who has to call and write and try to make it all work, try to keep it all together. And what do I get for my effort? A kick in the teeth as soon as I turn my back. What do I really get? Not one fucking thing but grief. I'm sick to death of every single bit of it. I'm sick of your bullshit and I'm sick of your vicious lies about me, I'm sick of your crazy games, I'm sick of you being jealous of everything I accomplish and I'm sick to death of you treating me like a piece of shit.

I thought back over all the years. The years of worrying about what she would think and how she would react to every small facet of my life, my work, my entire being. I thought of the hundreds of times I'd tried to explain something to her when she wouldn't listen. I thought of what amounted to a life-time of punishment for crimes I never committed. I thought of the humiliation and the shame she'd caused me. The depression and the personal agony of defeat after defeat. I thought about all the times I tried to do something nice for her, something that would please her and make her happy. I lived my whole life reacting to that woman. I lived my entire life scared to death of offending her. And what have I gotten in return? Nothing. I don't have a mother. Yet, I have been tied to this woman all my life. Every decision I've ever made has either been because of her or because of my work. Anything that interfered with those two elements was simply eliminated. I've done everything I could to try and be friends with her. I've done everything I know or could think of to make her happy, to make her proud of me. I may as well resign myself to the fact that, in this lifetime, I may never know why she isn't. But I cannot go on like this. I cannot go on being tied to her in this impossible, unworkable, miserably unhappy condition. If it hasn't worked by now, I better face the fact that no matter what I do, no matter how many years I devote to trying to find the magic formula, it may never work any better than this.

I don't know what I'm going to do and I don't know how I'm going to do it, but I've got to get out of this nightmare. I've got to get out of this lie that has entangled itself throughout my entire life because it's going to strangle me if I don't.

CHAPTER 29

Life was never the same for me afterwards. It took a long time for the seeds planted that day to grow and stand up by themselves. But there was a part of me that was gone forever.

There were more months of frustration. Weeks and weeks of soul searching and painful questions about what I was going to do with my life. I spent most of the time alone, because it was just too painful to be with anyone else. I knew I had to do something about my life before it was too late, before I was so set in the old patterns and the old ways that I couldn't change. I had no idea how to turn it all around. I had no idea in what direction to look for my own salvation.

From the time I was about twelve years old, all I'd ever wanted to do was be an actress. I'd always thought I was one of the lucky ones. My goal was so clear and my destination so straight that I never questioned the future as some of my friends had. I never confronted the "what if's" in the same way, because I thought I knew where I was going. My problem had always been that I didn't know how to get there. I had seen what it was like at the very top, but that wasn't available to me. I had managed to stay alive by starting out at the very bottom, but I never really understood much about the process of the middle. I never seemed to understand how you made one thing turn into the next step in order to continue making progress. I always seemed to be starting all over again. But all that didn't matter anymore, because it was the past and I couldn't change the past. The only thing I could do anything about was the present. I didn't have a clue as to what the future held.

It might have taken me a lot longer to decide to leave show business if it hadn't been for an appointment with an independent producer at Universal. My agents said he was doing a rather strange film, but it might be worth it to go and see him. These were the days of the nudity fad in low budget films and I asked point blank if that's what the film was, because I didn't bother to go on those appointments. The agents said they didn't think so, and I went to the studio.

I was given a script to read in the small outer office. It was not a good picture. In fact, I wanted to just tell the man that I thought it was all a mistake and I wasn't right for the part, in order to save us both the time. But he insisted that I at least read, since I was already here, so I went into the other office with him. I read the scene with him once, but he said that it wasn't exactly what he was looking for and I thoroughly understood. I wished desperately that I wasn't even here in the office. He gave me a creepy feeling when he looked at me and I was very much on my guard in case he made a lunge for me. That was the kind of guy he was . . . just creepy. He wasn't even a regular producer, he was an actor and this was his first production. He was giving me some directions, while I was off in my own thoughts wishing I were somewhere else, so I had to ask him to repeat the directions because I knew I hadn't heard him correctly.

The unfortunate thing was that I had heard him correctly the first time. What he was saying to me with that creepy look on his face . . . what he was asking me to do for him was . . . I couldn't believe it! He was saying that I should be masturbating throughout the last part of the scene. I stared at him blankly. "You're kidding!" I said, feeling my temper begin to show.

"Are you embarrassed?" he asked me.

"No, I'm not embarrassed, I'm disgusted," I said and threw the script on the floor in front of him as I walked toward the door. He jumped up and placed himself between me and the closed door. He actually wanted me to go on with the scene. He wanted me to stay.

"I've been in this business fourteen years and I'm not going to be treated like this by you or anyone else," I said with what pomposity I could manage. "Now you get the hell out of my way and let me out of here!"

He was laughing and he stepped aside, making a gallant gesture as he moved away from me.

I left, slamming the door behind me. I ran all the way to my car, tears streaming down my face.

When I got home, the phone was ringing and the agents told me that the man wanted me to reconsider. The tirade that had been going on in my head was vented on my poor agent. I told him to call that asshole jerk back and tell him to take his masturbating movie and shove it! I told them never to send me out on anything like that again, and then I told them it wouldn't be necessary because I wanted out of my contract with them. He didn't give me any argument.

That night through my tears and my anger, I decided that I didn't want anything more to do with the business. I didn't want to be an actress anymore. I just didn't have the personality that could take this garbage year after year. I loved the actual work, I loved the acting but I absolutely hated all the rest of it. What I finally understood was that "all the rest of it" was the majority and that the work was only a very small part. It was just simply no longer possible for me to put up with the monumental garbage, and if you can't go through that, you can't survive. Talent has precious little to do with it. But I'd never done anything else. I'd never even finished college. What the hell was I going to do?

That is the state I found myself in for three or four months. I was miserable. It was so hard to even think about giving up and walking away from fourteen years of your life. Everything I ever wanted, all my dreams were simply disintegrating before my very eyes. I cried. I pounded my fists in anger. I went into fits of black depression about my wasted life. I turned thirty-three years old that summer. Mother sent me a telegram for my birthday.

My friend Nancy Douglas from New York had moved to San Diego to begin her doctoral work at a private university. She invited me down for a few days to visit and see the school.

During my brief stay, I told her that I admired what she was doing, but just the thought of going back to school myself after nearly twenty years scared me to death. She took me with her to one of the psychology lectures for doctoral students and I was very impressed. We talked for quite a long time about my fears and lack of confidence.

When I returned to Los Angeles, I started really thinking about the possibility seriously. Christ, I'd probably be forty years old before I got through! Looking down the long dark road always brought out the dragons of my own insecurity. I became my own worst obstacle.

I called Nancy back and told her I was going to give it a try. She was wonderful. She was so certain that I'd make it that I felt rather ashamed of myself for being such a coward. I made an appointment to see the dean and sent for my transcript from Carnegie.

By some good fortune, the school accepted me for the fall quarter which was only one month away. Now I'd have to see just how smart I was after all these years.

In April 1973 I transferred to UCLA. There were some monumental changes taking place in my life now. Maybe it was just having the courage to make the first decision in favor of my own life that enabled the rest to come forth, I don't know. I was able to get just enough work in commercials to see me through school. I met a wonderful man with whom I fell deeply in love. Without him, without his love and his belief and his strength to sustain me and give me renewed courage, I don't think I could have made it so smoothly through my transition.

My mother never picked up the phone to call me personally again. We wrote to one another as the result of holidays . . . Christmas, her birthday, Mother's Day and my birthday. There was nothing in between, except once.

The Los Angeles secretary called me unexpectedly one afternoon while I was studying for an exam to ask if I had a particular piece of my mother's jewelry. I had absolutely no idea what she was talking about and I was instantly aggravated that Mother should have her call instead of speaking to me personally about it. I told the secretary that if Mother wanted to speak to me, she had my phone number and I'd be happy to talk to her. I said goodbye and hung up.

The next afternoon, the secretary called back sounding very agitated herself. I almost felt sorry for her, because I could hear how uncomfortable she was. This time I realized that she was only carrying out orders. She tried to repeat the story of the day before, but I interrupted her. "What the hell is this all about?" I asked bluntly. She nervously replied that Mother had received a piece of jewelry from Uncle Charles McCabe many, many years ago and now that he was dead, it was all she had left to remember him by. Perhaps I'd recall it if she described it to me. It was a heart-shaped pin with diamonds and had rubies dripping down it. A heart dripping with rubies? I really didn't recall anything about it and I certainly didn't have it. Then the secretary asked whether I still had it or if I'd sold it! I couldn't believe this entire conversation. This was really insane. I didn't know anything about any dripping heart from

Charles McCabe. I never had it, Mother never gave it to me and I certainly couldn't sell anything I never possessed.

By now I was in a complete rage with the secretary. I told her I didn't know anything about the pin, I never had it and when she spoke with Mother she could tell her never, never to have a secretary call me again about anything she should have the common courtesy to speak to me about personally. If she couldn't find her own jewelry, then she better look to herself to find out where the hell it was because I didn't know one damn thing about it. I told the secretary never again to bother trying to carry out Mother's orders because I'd hang up on her before she got one word out of her mouth. With that I repeated that if Mother wanted to talk to me, she had my phone number and she could damn well use it.

I tried immediately to get Mother on the phone through the Pepsi switchboard which was the only number I now had for her. She didn't take my call that day or any of the other times I tried to reach her.

I was so furious I nearly got on a plane and went to New York in person. I was so damn sick and tired of guilt by association. No one ever bothered to ask "if" . . . they just assumed that whatever that crazy bitch said was the truth. No one asked "if" I knew anything about it, they only asked what I'd done with it. Okay. She wouldn't talk to me. Well, then just as soon as I calmed down enough to think straight, I was going to utilize the only avenue of communication left between us. I was going to write her a long letter.

The following was mailed in early fall 1973.

Dear Mother:

We have some unfinished business, you and I and it is with that understanding on my part that this letter is being written.

For most of my life I have been very angry with you and felt very hurt, wounded by my relationship with you. Even now some of that anger persists. However, some very important changes have taken place that have begun to make me know how far I have traveled from that victimized, worthless, unloved child I felt myself to be. Because of the investment I have in my life, because I truly care about me and not because I hate you, it is necessary for me to express as clearly and fully as possible what my truth is.

First and foremost, I never felt you loved me—I do not understand why you adopted me and certainly not why you then went on to acquire (for that is what happened) three other people. I guess you really wanted to love babies—who unconditionally love in return and are totally dependent and absolutely controllable. Because as soon as each of us began to be people you leveled the full measure of your angry control upon us. I grew up feeling that the thing I'd really done wrong, aside from the never ending stream of things you created, the thing you were really furious with me about—was simply being alive—existing as a human being. All the criteria you set for behavior were really designed to belie humanity, to create machines that could be easily manipulated to give you what you thought you wanted. You traded life experience for discipline, caring for total agreement, love for control and rational discussion for punishment. And systematically pushed away anyone who wouldn't accept your way. I suspect that now you are reaping the rewards of all that and may be very alone. The world, even of your peers, had changed—and people won't accept that anymore. Life is too important to be subjected to your behavior for very long—and the few who remain, you really cannot respect for their weakness and subservience and treat them more miserably than ever.

You don't have any idea who I am, or what I think or how I feel. I can understand how you could think I hate you—because anyone who treated someone the way you've treated me—deserves that reaction. Your image of yourself as the martyred mother, as you well know, is totally false. But perhaps its the only way you can live with what you've done, and is in keeping with the other projections of yourself that you attributed to me. Those qualities I heard so often as a child—selfishness, ingratitude, dishonesty, dirtiness, etc.—those weren't me and it took me a lot of years and a lot of pain to discover that. All those second and last chances—the punishments which lasted six months, the lack of proportion between any act and it's punishment—all that was your problem—your lack of ability or desire to be human and deal with reality as it is and not as one gigantic threat to your shaky house of cards value structure and your image of yourself.

What I think I resent most of all is the time it's taken to restructure my life—the fact that I'm here at all, never mind becoming the person I am, beginning to fulfill my potential, I view as nothing short of a miracle! And certainly no thanks to you. Your dedication to discipline is simply an avoidance of life. Your devotion to independence and being alone a defense against the vulnerability and fulfillment of loving closeness and being human. No doubt you thought you had good reasons in the beginning—but whatever they were, unrevised, they have not served you well in the time I've known you. And I really wanted you to love me. I've tried very hard to achieve, as an adult, a relationship with you. It was important to me and I can say with all honesty that I did everything I knew how to do—the fact that we now do not have that relationship is a loss for both of us. However, I've learned from the experience and I seriously wonder if you have.

The last exchange, face to face, we had serves as an excellent example. You were kind enough to lend me the use of your L.A. apartment for a few weeks—a major step for you. What followed: the whole trip with the locksmith, changing the phone numbers—Betty saying you were coming out—to have me move, etc., and the subsequent vitriol that filtered back about the apartment being dirty, something (an outdoor ashtray as I recall) being broken and then the cessation of your "schedule" being mailed to me was all totally bizarre, unfounded in reality and thoroughly a product of your own mind, though I'm sure you had help.

The important thing is not the stupidity and ludicrous nature of it all—it is that you *chose* to do that—to push me away without ever saying a word to me—and I for my part was wrong in that I didn't call you on it instantly—that I didn't confront you with your unreasonable behavior and in asking the obvious question of "what in the hell is going on here?" force reality and some truth into the situation—for my sake. But I allowed it to slip and slide and I'm not pleased about that—because you and I didn't have the opportunity to see it for what it really was.

Your method of controlling me has always been the threat of taking something away from me—it's run the gamut from Christmas presents and "privileges"—to the attempt on your part to make it impossible for me to earn a living and therefore survive. Through it all your "love" has been put on the basis of an exchange—if I behave (do what you want) and say yes a lot—you'll love me—but even that wasn't a true bargain because I tried it and it didn't work. But, Mother—the time has finally come when there's no more you can take away—I have survived and the shame of being related to you in any way has begun to be solved. Because I have been deeply ashamed of you and everything you represent as well as the person you've become—which has nothing to do with my ability to recognize and admire what you've accomplished which is Herculean and courageous.

I remember the walks by the sea wall in Carmel, Mother—I remember the poetry—I remember moments of genuine caring—that is why, I guess, I tried so hard—because underneath that angry, sadistic, insecure bitch there was a woman who was searching and struggling with her soul's journey and capable of giving and receiving a great deal of love. That is the person I loved, wanted to be loved by and feel close to.

Now—in the light of this reality and the knowledge of the past—with the investment of years of pain and tears and depression—my life, quite separate from you—all of your influence and most of your values, is unfolding with beauty and the joy of being alive. I am in college to finish my bachelor's degree, I am in love with a man who loves me as I never believed possible and within our relationship is a mirror that is so clear it astonishes both of us.

I think there are some real ways in which I have disappointed you, Mother—but since we didn't talk about them I don't know for sure—it's just a feeling. I know you've disappointed me—it's been mutual in many areas. But there comes a time to clean the slate—and for me that time is here and now. For my part in hurting you throughout the years I'm deeply sorry—and hope that in your heart you will forgive me—as I forgive you—in order that I may free myself to be myself. It is sad to say goodbye to all that pain, because it was a connection, however unsatisfactory and twisted. There is a terrible sadness in becoming a sovereign adult—a sense of loss and aloneness. All those feelings are very with me now, even as I write this to you. I can see your face and I know that the tears in my eyes and the lump in my throat are only a small measure of how important you have been to me. How much I needed your love. But I have to go on now, Mother—there's a lot of life out there and I intend to participate very fully in it. That I haven't in the past is not your fault—I wish I could have gotten my shit together sooner—but all that is superfluous.

If ever you want to talk, I am here as an adult capable of being a friend—and though it may not immediately feel that way to you because of this letter—my heart is open. It's important for me to let you hear that—because I am not a dependent child, not a puppet to be controlled, not a servant to do your bidding, not a fan to pay homage.

But, whatever happens, I have done my very best to conclude this portion with honor, openness, honesty and reality—to confront my feelings with tenacity and courage and to take the risks necessary for my freedom, my happiness and my effectiveness as a human being. In short, to take full possession of and responsibility for my life. There is little magnanimity in it—and a lot of pain but that is the real price for growing up. There's still a part of me that feels momentarily like I've over-paid—but in the light of this past year I know that's not true. My whole life has brought me here and that's beautiful. I like me, I enjoy being a woman and am beginning to appreciate the real treasure of life.

With all of my being—I hope you understand.

Christina

I never heard one word from her about my letter. It was mailed and never returned, so I assume she received it. But she never acknowledged my letter in any way. It was as though I had been talking into a vacuum. I might have chalked the whole thing up to another useless venture if it hadn't been for an article published in *McCall's* magazine after her death. The article was written from a series of interviews she did over the phone toward the end of her life. The last question pertained to what she might have done differently with her life. The next to the last paragraph of that article says: "It's hard to explain, but I think I would have been an easier person. Easier on myself, to begin with, not so terribly rigid. I'd have naturally been easier on the people around me, especially the kids. There were times, I'm afraid, when I set standards for Christina and Christopher they couldn't meet. I'm not saying I didn't enjoy life. I did. But there has to be such a thing as working too hard and expecting everyone else to work just as hard."

In August 1974, I had completed three years of undergraduate work at UCLA in a little less than two years by taking twenty units a quarter and going to summer school. I graduated Magna Cum Laude with a degree in communication. September of that same year I began teaching part-time in a small business college and was accepted into the Master's degree program at the new Annenberg School of Communication on the USC campus.

David and I were married on February 14, 1976, in the lovely Palos Verdes home of my longtime friend, Nicki, who had originally befriended me over twenty years ago at Chadwick School. I had not expected Mother to attend. I had written her that we were being married though. Her handwritten letter was sent March 11, 1976.

> *Christina dear—*
> I am so happy that you and David were married on Valentine's Day—It must have been lovely having the ceremony performed in a friend's home in Palos Verdes—and I'm so looking forward to the photographs you are sending—
> My dearest wish is, a glorious life for you and David—
> *Love*
> *Mother*

Perhaps it was the change that comes over you when you are really and truly loved—perhaps it is the change that comes about when you begin to be really proud of yourself and trust in those special qualities that make each of us special—perhaps it was a lot of different things coming together at the same time, but I was no longer such an angry, driven person. I was still determined, I was still stubborn, I was still strong-willed but I was no longer blaming anyone for my life. I had softened and I had humbled and I had matured. I tried to share that with Mother in the letters I wrote to her. I tried to include some information about my life, my husband, the little house we'd bought and were re-doing. I told her about my stepson, about our pets. I tried to give her some idea of what my life had now become. I never asked for anything and she never sent any presents, any money on my marriage or birthday or Christmas. I continued to send birthday and Christmas presents to her as well as cards on other holidays. She thanked me for all of them.

In August 1976 I finished the master's program in Communication Management with a minor in business and a straight 4.0 grade point average. It was the best anyone could do. I was interviewed by several companies and started work August 11, 1976.

Mother's handwritten letter of congratulations was mailed on September 23, 1976.

> Christina dear
>   Many congratulations on your M.A.
>   I'm so happy for you, and delighted you are finding your new job such a joy—
>   *Much love*
>   *Mother*

I had spoken with my sister who lived in Pennsylvania, closest to Mother, on several different occasions and she'd told me that to the best of her knowledge, Mother had stopped drinking completely. I wondered what Mother would be like now. I realized that I'd never really known my mother without her drinking problem since I was a small child. In fact, I believe that her drinking was a major cause of many of our problems all the time I was growing up and even right through the last few years. I thought it would be nice to see Mother again and know something about what she was like sober. Maybe it would be different. Of course I knew that sobriety alone didn't solve all the problems, but maybe it would make enough of a difference that we could talk to one another without all the accusations and imaginings.

I'd also heard that Mother didn't go out much, if at all anymore. She was no longer with Pepsi. She finally had to retire after about sixteen years with the company. That was five times longer than her marriage to Alfred Steele lasted. You had to hand it to her. She'd certainly turned that brief marriage into an entire second career. She was a shrewd and clever woman. By the time she retired in 1975 she was at least sixty-seven years old and probably closer to seventy-one, if Grandmother's memory could be trusted. By either public or private accounting that's a tribute to the woman's sheer determination and tenacity. God only knows what she had to go through during those long years, just to hold onto her position. I know only some of it, only what spilled over at the top of what she was determined to keep inside of her. In the last nineteen years she'd only done seven films, several of them no more than cameo appearances. The last few were horror films that are best forgotten. The real years of glory were far, far behind her, yet still she clung to the great image, the star. Out of that image alone she built another entire career for herself and you have to admire that.

I had made my peace with her now. I could only hope that even silently, she had made her peace with me. I had gone on to build a life that had nothing to do with who she was or the years of past pain. It was not easy walking away from the past. At first I missed it very much. Bad as it was, it was all I had ever known. It was painful giving it up. It was hard to start all over again, but not as hard as going under with the great lie standing on your head like the devil. The past is so seductive, I nearly gave up my struggle several times and went back. But, every time the temptation arose, I sat quietly with myself and thought about the years I'd left behind. Nothing in the world could make me go back there . . . nothing.

David and I had moved into our little house on the half-acre and built a pool. We had a garden and fruit trees. Best of all, it was ours.

January 5, 1977

My dear Christina,

Thank you so much for your Christmas card and the news of you, David and David's son.

Your gift of the Gucci billfold is very beautiful. The simplicity of its design is so elegant. Thank you from my grateful heart. The new pool must be a joy for all of you except perhaps Penelope "The Stalker."

Your job must be very interesting, and I am delighted you are enjoying it. Obviously each day is a challenge to you for accomplishment, which makes for joyous days, instead of the drudgery of going to the office each day.

Happy New Year to the three of you—and much love.

Mother

We got cards for her birthday from the three of us and one for her from all our pets. My husband, David, drew wonderful cartoons of the animals on their card to her with little captions above their heads. We really had a lot of fun and sent them with all our combined love.

The last letter I ever received from my mother was postmarked April 10, 1977, just one month before her death.

Christina dear,

Please forgive this very tardy note to thank you for your two adorable birthday cards. The mail had been extremely heavy this year, and without a secretary in New York, it is very difficult to keep up as I should.

Much love to you and David—and thank you for making my day so special by remembering.

All love

Mother

The weekend before Mother's Day, my husband and I sent flowers to both his mother and mine. I remember it was Friday morning when we ordered the spring bouquets to be delivered, one in Detroit and one in New York. He wrote the card for his mother and I wrote the one for mine. When we finished, we were standing in the kitchen. I was overcome with an incredible feeling of sorrow and loneliness for no apparent reason. Then a thought flashed through my head so strongly that I had to sit down. He asked me if I was sick, I looked so pale. I looked up at him with tears in my eyes. I could hardly get the words out of my mouth, but I knew I had to tell him. We were so very close, David and I, that it would have been wrong not to share my thoughts with him. I said very quietly, "David, I think my mother is going to die very soon." There was nothing to base that feeling on, there was no indication from anyone that she was ill. No one had called to warn me. No one had notified any member of her family that she'd been very ill for months.

But, my mother and I had been bound together for so many years . . . we had been wrapped in the karma of one another's lives for so long . . . we had been through so much pain, so much soul searching agony together that it did not seem in the least bit peculiar to me that I should somehow know through a special channel of communication between us . . . indeed, she was now dying.

That very same day, in New York City, Mother gave away her beloved dog Princess. Mother, too, knew that she was dying.

The Mother's Day flowers arrived one day ahead of time, on Saturday. They were brought into her as she lay in her bed, very ill. She was told that they were from "Tina" and she said, "Oh yes, it must be Mother's Day." Then she requested they be placed on the television set where she could see them, even lying down.

They were the last flowers she ever saw on this earth, they were the last flowers she received in this life. She'd always said, "Send me flowers while I'm alive, they won't do me any good when I'm dead."

Mother died on the morning of May 10, 1977. Almost to the exact hour, it would have been the twenty-second anniversary of her marriage to Alfred N. Steele. By public accounting, she was sixty-nine years old.

IN MEMORIAM

"God has set us free, Mother . . . go in peace." That's what I was thinking as the man from Campbells and I descended the stairs and returned to the small blue room where the rest of my family was gathered.

Everyone except the lawyer was still there when I returned. Since there were no further decisions to be made that day, we left Campbells. It was Wednesday afternoon by this time. David and I had no sleep since Monday night. I was exhausted beyond what a shower and some food would cure. We decided to return to our hotel until it was time to meet everyone later in the afternoon. The two men from Pepsi were going to be at the Drake Hotel around 4 o'clock. David, Chris and I left Cathy, her husband and Cindy at the corner of Madison Avenue. Instead of staying with us, Chris was moving into the extra room reserved at the Drake. We returned to the hotel and he gathered up his things, preferring to make the move during this short, quiet time.

At four that afternoon, we all gathered again at the Drake. The men from Pepsi wanted to discuss some public memorial service with the family. The funeral on Friday was to be very small and private. The secretary was calling only people who were close to Mother and making the other necessary arrangements for that day. There were not supposed to be any flowers, but of course bouquets were already arriving at the funeral home. There wasn't any way to stop them.

The family decided together in a private meeting we had that it was only fitting there be some kind of memorial service for Mother. There were hundreds of people that wanted to pay their respects in some way and at the moment, no such avenue of expression existed. Since we were unable to handle anything of such magnitude as a family, we were all grateful to the company for their extremely considerate gesture.

It was very strange to be called upon to make these kinds of decisions and none of us felt particularly comfortable, but since this particular decision was by consensus, we felt that we'd done the right thing.

The funeral was scheduled for Friday morning. It was not possible to arrange for a memorial service any faster than the following Tuesday, simply because there were too many people being contacted. Many of the Pepsi bottlers had become personal friends with Mother. She had known them, their wives and families for many years. They had corresponded regularly and seen one another on many occasions other than company business.

I did not sleep well Thursday night. It was well after midnight when I finally fell into a light sleep, constantly awakened by the unfamiliar city noises outside our hotel window. When Friday morning dawned, I felt ill. I knew I wasn't really sick, but it would take every bit of will power I had to get up and begin getting ready to leave for the funeral. If my husband hadn't been with me, I don't think I would have had the courage. More than at any other time in my life, all I wanted to do was stay in bed with the sheets over my head until it was all over and I could go home again. I hadn't been able to eat more than a few mouthfuls of food since Tuesday afternoon. Everything just seemed to stick in my throat. I drank some coffee and had a few bites of an English muffin David had been considerate enough to get for us. I took a hot shower, washed my hair and was fully dressed half an hour before the limousine was due to arrive. I had on a simple black suit and white blouse.

It was turning into a warm day for this early in May and I was glad there were no signs of rain. That gray drizzle would have made everything so much more depressing and none of us needed to cope with any more than necessary right now.

Mother's former New York secretary was riding with us in our limousine and she arrived at the hotel exactly on time. It had been many years since I'd seen her, but I'd always liked her very much. She was always absolutely straight and direct. It made you feel as though you could trust her.

After our greetings were over and I'd introduced her to my husband, David, she mentioned the date of the funeral for the first time. I stared at her for a moment. None of us had thought in terms of dates, we'd been dealing only with days when the decisions were being made. All we'd thought of was Friday when the funeral arrangements were planned. No one had stopped to consider that this particular Friday was indeed, Friday, May 13. Unlucky Friday the 13th! My God, I thought, that is very strange. Mother is being buried on Friday the 13th. I never thought about it and maybe nobody else did either. So . . . Mother died on her wedding anniversary and is being buried on Friday the 13th. A strange set of coincidences. A very strange quirk of fate.

We were quite early arriving at the funeral home which was only a few blocks away from our hotel. We were shown into a private room just off the main chapel. There were flowers everywhere. Beautiful roses and other spring floral arrangements that took some of the faint musty odor away from these rooms. I didn't feel quite so shaky now that I'd gotten even a little fresh air. I held onto David's hand almost constantly. He was always right there next to me.

My sisters and Chris arrived just a few minutes later. We went in to look at the chapel by ourselves before the people started arriving. The urn was placed on a pedestal in the front of the chapel, surrounded by flowers. To the left of the urn was a small podium and a lectern where the Christian Science practitioner would read her service.

Now the people were beginning to arrive and we returned to the private waiting room. Some of the guests came in to see the family before the service, but most were being asked to wait until afterwards. It was very difficult to see the many, many faces that had been friends but whom I had not seen in so many years. I was deeply touched at their kindness and the outpouring of sympathy for the family. I looked at the faces of longtime friends I'd known since I was a little girl, the faces of former secretaries and others who had served Mother as hairdressers, manicurists, publicity people. This was intended as a gathering of only the people closest to Mother, but that was not universally the case. Most of the people were from New York, but some had flown in from as far away as Houston and Los Angeles.

It was getting more difficult every minute. My brother came over and stood with me for a while. He knew only a few of the faces, so I introduced him to everyone that came over to see me. Our cousin, Joan, arrived and stood with the rest of the family. Chris knew her and felt more comfortable now that he had someone to talk to. I sat down on one of the little chairs for a minute and David brought me a paper cup with water. He also handed me some extra Kleenex. The next person who came to speak with me was one of the women who had been a companion to Mother for many, many years. She too had begun her friendship and years of service as a fan. She had spent weekends with Mother for years and I'd known her well since I was just one year old. She had been one of the two people left with Mother right up until her death. Her face was slightly swollen with crying over the last few days and she was still very distraught. She clutched my hands and held onto them tightly. I tried to say something to her, but there were no words for either of us. Then she leaned over and said, "Tina . . . Mother *loved* you. You were her first born . . . she always said you were there when she needed you most . . . you brought her great joy. Remember that . . . Tina . . . no matter what happens . . . your mother *loved* you!" She could say no more and had to leave before she was totally overcome with grief.

Whatever faith I had in my turbulent relationship with Mother, whatever disagreements we'd had over the years, the words of this woman struck at the depth of that pain and that love in a way that not even the news of Mother's death had done. I started shaking. Tears streamed down my face. I always knew that Mother loved me . . . that she really loved me . . . that was exactly why the trouble we had with one another was so very difficult to understand. And every time she leveled her guns at me and tried to annihilate me, when the smoke cleared away and the noise died down . . . there I was, standing before her. I may have been wounded . . . I may have been in tatters, but by God . . . I was still standing! We had been joined in a terrible battle, lasting over thirty years.

The funeral service was brief. There is no formal burial service in Christian Science. The woman who had been Mother's last practitioner read from the Bible and then the passages from Mary Baker Eddy. Those passages were so familiar. They reminded me instantly of all those Sundays of my childhood when Mother and I would read the lessons aloud and then call Sorkie in New York. Those things from childhood that you may not think of for twenty years come back instantly like the smell of cookies or a favorite childhood song.

I looked at the woman reading in her clear voice that sounded so peaceful. From her face I looked at the urn sitting on its pedestal, so plain and nondescript. I noticed that lying across the base of the urn, there was one single long-stem red rose that had not been there earlier. It was clearly some very personal gesture of love.

I thought about seeing Mother two days before, lying still with her hands folded, so terribly thin, so old and frail. She was gone now. She would leave an empty space for so many who had been faithful and served her until the very end. It is always painful to say a final goodbye. It is always hard to realize that's the end of a life. But for Mother, I felt a sense of relief. She was at peace now. I felt no guilt, there had been nothing left for me to do. I'd done the best I could.

The organ music began again and the service was over. The family formed a double receiving line in the small private room. The people began streaming through the door, taking our hands and saying what words of condolence they could manage. It was very strange how names I hadn't thought of for several years came back the instant I saw the face again. It was strange how these ghosts of the past, all dressed in black, floated by as just a row of faces that I introduced to my husband. So many people. Each one reminded me of a specific time, a special place, an event in my life. My childhood, the years in New York with Mother, our family trip to Europe with Daddy . . . all the people that had been intertwined through our lives.

We left in the black limousines for the drive to Ferncliff where the urn was to be placed in a family crypt next to Daddy. None of us had even seen where Daddy was buried, so in some strange way, this was almost like a double funeral.

It was a beautiful day. Once we left the decaying streets of East Harlem, everything was green and the sky was clear blue. It was warm, but the cars were air-conditioned. We managed to talk a little with the two secretaries who accompanied us in the lead car. I had a terrible headache which aspirin wasn't going to help, at least not today. I looked out the windows at the lovely countryside and tried not to think about much of anything.

Ferncliff looks just like a beautiful park. There are large trees and green lawns and flowering shrubs everywhere. If you didn't know better, you might think it would be a perfect place for a summer picnic.

Inside it was very cold. The marble floors echoed our footsteps against the marble walls. It was an ancient, hollow sound that accompanied our walk past the other crypts to the final destination. We'd brought one flower arrangement and the urn with us. Again, the Christian Science practitioner read from the Bible. I stared at the marble crypt cover with the names and dates inscribed on it. The urn was placed inside the crypt and looked very small and alone inside the large space. Then this part of the funeral was over too. We all walked slowly back to the entrance and out into the sunlight again.

The family was going back to the Drake Hotel. The lawyer was going to read the will after the funeral.

We ordered some sandwiches and drinks upon our arrival at the hotel. The lawyer arrived a few minutes later and said he'd like to see my brother first and privately. They went to another room. The food arrived from room service but most of us took our drinks first. It was both a strained and a strange time. It was just family. My sister Cathy and her husband, sister Cindy, cousin Joan, Chris, my husband and myself. We'd never been in one room together before. My sisters barely knew their cousin. No one but my brother had met David before.

It wasn't long before Chris reappeared. He looked very much the same as when he'd left. He took his drink off the large room service table. He said that the lawyer wanted to see David and me next, so we departed for the other room. As we walked down the hall, David held my hand as he had consistently done since we'd left Los Angeles four long days ago. We were both tired.

The lawyer asked us to sit down. He was holding a copy of the will in his hand. I sat nearest him. He flipped several pages over and then handed me the copy, with only the last page showing. There at the top of the final page of the will was one short paragraph which read:

"It is my intention to make no provision herein for my son Christopher or my daughter Christina for reasons which are well known to them."

I stared at the words in utter disbelief. I looked up from the page to the lawyer's face. He said only, "I'm very sorry, Tina." I looked across the room at David, then I looked back down at the piece of paper.

With a sense of growing horror I realized that she had not made her peace with me before she died. My first impression was that these words she'd ordered put into her last will and testament were from over twenty years ago. They were the words from the memory of the woman who tried to have my brother left in Switzerland without a passport.

These were the words of the woman who had me locked up in the convent school because of a Christmas card list. These were not the words of the woman who gave me my wedding reception at the "21" Club. These were not the words of the woman who asked me about her son in Viet Nam. These were not the words of the woman who knew about the rebuilding of my entire life over the past five years. They couldn't be. These were the words of the demon lie reaching out of the mists of years gone by and buried with her in her grave. She had made no peace with the world. She had gone out of this life carrying all the years of hatred and cruelty and violent rage with her, clutching at the torment of it as though it were just yesterday.

I was speechless and stunned. Not because of the money. It would have been a nice gesture after all the years of miserable poverty she put me through, but it wasn't the money. It was the insult. It was the lie. The inference that I had committed an unspeakable wrong. It was the humiliating innuendo left to be interpreted publicly. Guilty because she pronounces me so. Wrong because she says I am. Ostracized because she thinks I deserve punishment. And all for what? For just being alive and trying to do the best I can? How could one woman carry so much hatred with her for so many years? I would think that the venom would eat you alive. But then, maybe it did. Maybe it just did. The official cause of death was her heart, but the private conjecture was that she died of cancer. So maybe all that hatred and rage and venom finally did eat her alive and finally kill her.

I flipped the pages of the will back to the beginning and read the entire document silently. It wasn't much. All personal property to Cathy. A miserly trust fund to both Cindy and Cathy. Each of them were given $77,000 spread out over the next *twenty* years. About $70,000 was divided among secretaries and other people who had served her over the years, basically to the people who had said "yes" and done her bidding faithfully. Nothing at all to her only two living blood relatives, her niece and her own aunt who was Grandmother's sister. She'd been sending the aunt a little money each month for years. Now the old woman was left destitute. The rest was split up between various charities. The date of the document was interesting. This will had been written in October 1976, only seven months before her death. I requested a copy.

The lawyer accompanied us back to the suite where the others were waiting. He spoke with my sisters separately.

And then it was all finished. There was nothing more except to attend the formal and more public memorial service next Tuesday. My sisters and I spoke only briefly. They were returning to their respective hometowns in the morning. We finished lunch, then I suggested that Chris might want to accompany David and me to a friend's home a few blocks away. I didn't think my brother really wanted to stay in the room for the rest of the day and he knew Al so it wouldn't be like meeting a stranger. Chris went with us gladly.

We spent the afternoon with Al on his penthouse terrace. Al had shared so much of the rest of my life, that he was the perfect person to be with for the rest of this strange day. He didn't ask any questions and we didn't talk about the funeral or Mother. We talked about everything else though. He was a truly wonderful friend. I didn't know that day, but we wouldn't see Al again after this trip to New York. He died two months later. (When I returned to Los Angeles, I wrote him a long letter, thanking him for his kindness to all of us. I said I knew it sounded silly, but I also wanted him to know how much his twenty years of friendship had meant to me and how much love we sent him. When I heard of his death just a few weeks later, I was eternally grateful that I'd told him what he had meant to me throughout the years.)

Tuesday afternoon the company sent a limousine to pick us up. Again we were accompanied by the two secretaries. There had been some problems getting appropriate people to speak at this memorial. Cesar Romero had topped the list, but he was unavailable. Mitchell Cox was unavailable. A number of other people were also not available. I had nothing to do with these arrangements other than submitting a short list of people I wished to invite. My brother's little girl had become ill so Chris didn't make the trip back in from Long Island. There was no reason for him to attend and go through the pain all over again. He'd paid his last respects privately and conducted himself like a gentleman. He did not deserve any more pain.

The Unitarian church was full when the services began. The people who spoke referred to the long successful career, the dedication and the greatness of the star. Anita Loos spoke first I had always admired her and we had been friends since I was young. She spoke beautifully. Geraldine Brooks went next and spoke of the work they'd done together. Strangely enough, she was also dead within a few months after this memorial service. Pearl Bailey spoke and then sang with a power and electricity that gave me chills. She sang her own mother's favorite hymn: "He'll Understand." Cliff Robertson gave what was closest to a formal eulogy that was brief but well written. The minister then read the *Desiderata* which had been a favorite of Mother's and the service ended. Again, the family had a receiving line and again the ghosts paraded by, offering their condolences. Many of the people at this service were business associates and bottlers that I did not know. Pepsi had handled everything beautifully, tastefully and with fastidious care. The service was dignified, began exactly on time and was orderly throughout.

A number of people wanted interviews with me or to take pictures of me, but as politely as possible, I refused. Whatever was going to be immediately reported about all this would have to be done without any quotes from me. And that's exactly what happened. A lot was written by many columnists during the next few weeks, but it was drawn entirely from their own previous knowledge and hearsay, not from me.

That evening, the paragraph from the will which disinherited my brother and myself was reported on the television news. In fact, to my astonishment, the newscaster read the entire paragraph verbatim. From there it was picked up and reported in newspapers. The stories were mostly the same. They mentioned the trust fund for my sisters, the unspecified sums to charity and then quoted the paragraph ending with "for reasons well known to them."

I suppose that wills were in style now after the fuss over the Howard Hughes and J. Paul Getty documents. I guess there was a momentary fad about reporting wills. I suppose also that a paragraph as suggestive and open to speculation as the one Mother had put in her will about us was too good to pass up on the news. I guess it was almost irresistible. I know too that the entire thing was a public disgrace. Now the lie would continue because it had just been well-fed once again. If she'd simply wanted to disinherit two of her adopted children, if that's all she wanted to do, there are very simple standard ways to do that. There was no need to use the language she chose. There was no need to do what she did, if all she wanted was to make sure we didn't get anything from her estate. But that's not what she did, because that's not all she wanted to accomplish.

As the days passed after the reading of the will, I tried to put the pieces of the puzzle together. What exactly was it that had happened over the years that intervened since last I saw Mother. I'm sure it's not complete, because all the information was secondhand, but the picture that emerged was as follows.

First of all, everyone I spoke with was shocked at what had happened. None of them knew any reasons for it, none of them had any explanation. They all expressed not only their condolences but their empathy.

But, about two years before her death, a number of different incidents coincided to change her life substantially.

Mother had completed her last picture in 1970. It was a terrible film called *Trog* and is best simply forgotten. Her drinking had gotten progressively worse over the years until she was nearly unable to go out in public any longer. It was so serious that the people in the apartment who worked for her put chairs around her bed so she wouldn't hurt herself in the night and stationed other chairs at various places for her to hold onto. Apparently, during one of the rare times when she was left alone in the apartment, she fell, hitting her head on the corner of a table. She was unconscious for as much as several hours before she was discovered with a severe wound to her temple and one eye. Though it was evidently a fairly serious injury and could have resulted in complications from both the length of the black-out and the wound itself, Mother refused any medical attention. She blamed the fall on antibiotics she was supposedly taking, but the conjecture is that she was drunk and slipped on the bare floor. The people who worked for her cleaned up her wound and took care of her as best they could without medical assistance. She categorically refused to see a doctor.

Pepsi had finally retired her. She was well past sixty-five years old but the retirement hurt her feelings. Part of it, I believe, had to do with the fact that she knew there were no more acting offers. She insisted on being the "star" and she just couldn't make the transition that some of the other big stars were somehow able to make. She didn't become the grand dowager or the character woman. She wanted to remain the big star and the world had passed her by. Her fierce tenacity had outlived reality and usefulness. So, with no more "stardom" the only thing she had left was her job. She finally outlived that too, but she couldn't reconcile herself to the fact that those were the natural progressions of life. People who saw her said that she seemed to enjoy private life, but I'm not sure that's totally accurate.

This was one situation she wouldn't be able to will herself out of. She was finally retired and fully a private citizen for the first time since she'd been about sixteen years old. All she had left was the mail and her prolific correspondence. However, with no New York secretary on company salary, even answering the mail was not an easy task.

To the best of anyone's knowledge, the last time Mother saw a doctor was also about two years before her death. I do not know what he told her but she never went back to see him again. I do not know what medication she was given. I do know her health began to decline shortly afterwards. But she refused to allow anyone around her to call for medical care.

After the serious fall and subsequent head injury, Mother is said to have stopped drinking. How she did it no one could tell me. But, it would seem that she stopped drinking also without assistance of any kind. After years of alcoholism, that is quite a feat.

Even during the years I was in New York and saw Mother nearly every day, she had been very conscious of security measures that had to be taken to ensure her safety in the apartment. Unfortunately, she received a crank call from an unknown person, threatening her life. The lawyers and her few friends who knew about the call tried to tell her that it was an accidentally dialed number and that the man who called probably didn't even know the identity of the person answering the phone. But Mother was not convinced of the chance nature of the call. It was reported to the police, but no one was ever charged with any offense. The incident unnerved Mother. She had extra locks put on all the doors. Everyone had to be announced and checked thoroughly before they were allowed on the elevators. She rarely left the apartment to go anywhere except perhaps to the dentist. She also was never alone again. She was really terrified that someone was going to kill her. In fact, for the last two years of her life, I am told that she never left her apartment at all. She continued to have the woman companion buy those shifts for her, but the labels were never even removed. She continued to have the companion buy things for the apartment such as china and other house-wares, though she never entertained. She continued to spend money as though life were going on as usual, but it wasn't.

She made out the last version of her will in October. Until then, she had seen the people she invited to the apartment, including Cathy and her husband. In fact, Cathy's husband had visited her fairly regularly during the previous year since his business brought him into the city often.

However, in December Mother stopped seeing anyone other than the three or four people who worked for her and the Christian Science readers who came regularly. Past December, she never saw any of her old friends, would not allow even Cathy and her husband to visit her. The lawyer told us that the practitioner became concerned about Moth-er's health and she arranged for readers who were also practical nurses. Mother wouldn't let them help her in any way or even touch her. By this time her physical condition was deteriorating rapidly. She'd been losing weight steadily over the past year. Mother was always very proud of her body, but the weight continued to disappear until she was thin and frail. She was no longer strong enough to take care of herself, to bathe, but still she refused to receive help. She refused to allow anyone to notify the family, to call for her doctor or to get medical attention. The only thing anyone says she complained about during those long months was a bad pain in her back which was so severe that she was unable to walk easily or sit for very long. But that is all she would acknowledge: a bad pain in her lower back.

Two months before her death she stopped smoking. By now she was bedridden and had to be attended as best the two women who were left with her could manage. Neither of them were nurses, but they did the best they could to care for her and make her comfortable.

The morning of May 10, 1977, there was only one woman with Mother. She came in the morning to relieve the other woman who had stayed the night. She realized that Mother had a very bad night, but was amazed at the clarity with which she spoke. There were only the two of them in the room when the end finally came. The woman, realizing there was noth-ing more she could do, began praying for Mother. At first the prayers were silent but as she realized how close the end really was, her prayers became audible. She was praying aloud and Mother heard the words. Mother raised her head. The last words from her mouth were: "Dammit . . . don't you *dare* ask God to help me!" A few minutes later she was dead.

They say that death is for each person as they imagine it to be. They say that the journey into the next world is also as each of us imagines it to be. But every religion has something to say about what is waiting in that next world. They say that it depends on what each of us did with this life.

The big memorial service in Los Angeles for the motion picture and television industry was scheduled for June 24, 1977. It was being organized by George Cukor and a committee representing a cross section of the industry. I had nothing to do with that either. I think it was George Cukor's idea.

Jane Ardmore who had written one of Mother's books called to formally invite me to the memorial. I accepted and said I would also bring my husband and stepson. I thought it was important for him to have some understanding of the woman who was so briefly his grandmother. Not including my stepson, Mother had eight grandchildren. The three or four who had met her were not allowed to call her "Grandmother." They had to call her "Aunt Joan." In fact, the only reference to her being a grandmother that I know of was in the obituary and the articles published after her death. I often wondered if that quirk about not wanting to be called grandmother went all the way back some fifty years to her experience with her first mother-in-law, Mary Pickford.

There had been a great deal of publicity about the Los Angeles memorial. Evidently, it was the first time all facets of the industry had cooperated to create a tribute to one of their members. The studios contributed film footage, a number of companies made donations to cover the expenses and numerous people gave of their professional skills to make the event a success. I do not know by what process the committee chose the people who were going to speak at the tribute. The program listed their names and called the event "An Industry-Wide Celebration in Film and Fond Memories."

My husband, stepson and I arrived at the proper time. David spoke with one of the guards at the door and they admitted us through a side entrance. I was not about to stand in the long line that had already formed.

Once inside the Academy of Motion Picture Arts and Sciences building, a man took us to the elevators. Through the partition separating us from the main lobby of the Academy, I could see the crowd. There was a champagne reception in progress before the tribute itself began. There were also television cameras and photographers' flashbulbs going off like strobe lights.

I stood watching the crowd with fascination. Everyone was behaving as though it was a premiere . . . and an opening night of some sort. People were being interviewed and having their pictures taken. It was an "event" and I guess they just didn't know any other appropriate behavior. In fact the entire tribute was being videotaped both for the Academy archives and for future broadcast. So, it was definitely the place to "be seen" that night. And there they all were in the lobby, enjoying the champagne reception and the photographers' flashbulbs, the fans milling around outside the building waiting for a glimpse of their favorite personality and the television cameras inside the lobby.

Special television interviews were going on upstairs on another floor where it was quieter. Up there, former directors and lovers, friends and producers were being interviewed on one subject: Joan Crawford. It was a big event in the careers of the audience tonight. They were definitely "being seen."

The man ushered us upstairs and into a private office that had been turned into a temporary waiting room for the people who were going to speak during the tribute program.

Once we reached the doorway to the office, the man left us without making any introductions. John Wayne was just coming out of the room on his way to one of the pre-taped interviews. I introduced myself and my family and he hurriedly said hello to us, but I'm not sure that he actually heard what I'd said.

Then I led my husband and fourteen-year-old stepson into the office where a sizable group was gathered. I didn't recognize all the people but I knew many of them. George Cukor was seated directly opposite me. Kevin Thomas was standing near him and seated next to Kevin was Robert Young with whom I had worked on *Marcus Welby*. Carmel

Myers was there and Jack Jones was seated on the couch next to Myrna Loy.

I said hello but no one moved or greeted me. There was nearly a total silence which left me standing in the middle of the room with absolutely nowhere to go. George Cukor peered up at me over his glasses, imperiously inquiring, "Who-o-o-o are you?" He sounded just like the Cheshire Cat out of *Alice in Wonderland*! I almost laughed right out loud. Now the room had fallen into total silence as the people waited for this intruder to identify herself.

I let the silence last another brief moment, so there could be no mistake about my introduction. Very clearly and distinctly I replied to George, looking him straight in the eyes as I spoke. "I . . . am . . . Christina Crawford." George Cukor stood up as fast as his elderly years permitted. The rest of the room turned into pandemonium. Several people started talking at once. Myrna Loy got up and left the room! She left her drink, her speech and her mink coat right where they'd been sitting the moment before. Again, I nearly laughed. What a strange night this was and it was just beginning. George took my hand and I introduced him to my husband and stepson. George complimented me on turning into a handsome woman for which I thanked him and sat down next to Jack Jones in the spot Myrna had vacated. We were offered some champagne while various people began trying to pick up the threads of their previous conversations. Jack Jones related a peculiar story to me. It began like the old show *I've Got A Secret* and ended with some tale about how he was Joan Crawford's "Godson." Over the years, that's what she'd called him because she was the first to visit his family after his birth. It had been rather like a standing joke with them, nothing more. And now, he'd been asked to speak at this industry tribute, this memorial, on the basis of that story about being her godson. I was polite.

When the hour finally came for all of us to go downstairs to the theater and we were congregated around the elevators, Myrna came up to me saying she didn't recognize me before. I didn't even smile. Fortunately, the elevators arrived at just that moment. She got into one and I stepped into the other.

My husband, stepson and I were told to sit in any seat of the first two rows. The second row was already full, so we sat alone in the first row. Only three people came up to talk to us.

The program began with an introduction of the speakers. Kathleen Nolan, president of Screen Actors Guild, who had never met Mother, was first. The other speakers were Fay Kanin who had written one of Mother's movies; Robert Young who told about her sending presents on his wedding day and receiving her letters; George Cukor who read his own article on her from the *New York Times*; Leonard Spigelglass recounted some lovely, funny experiences from the old days; Myrna Loy who was there as "Joan's oldest friend" which was simply not true; Steven Spielberg of *Jaws* fame who had made his directorial debut directing Mother in an episode at Universal about seven years before. I remember the incident well. Mother was absolutely furious with the studio for sticking her with a twenty-two-year-old kid who'd never done anything before. They had a miserable time together. I couldn't imagine why he'd agree to be here tonight. But the hype works it's magic in very strange ways. John Wayne was wonderfully candid and got the best laugh of the show. Jack Jones told his "godson" story and sang later to close the program. In between there were film clips from the old movies including a wonderful segment on the early silent films. Naturally, the film broke several times because it was so old.

At the very end John Wayne read off the list of participants, asking each group to stand as their particular affiliation was mentioned. As the people in the theater began standing, I thought back over what we'd just seen. There were several mentions of the letters this woman wrote, several stories about the professional experiences shared years ago, a few silly anecdotes out of nervousness. There was nothing about the woman as a person. There was not one mention about her family. No one ever alluded to the fact that I was seated not three feet away in the first row, right under their noses. In fact no one mentioned that she even had a family and no one offered their condolences to me or the rest of the family. In fact, neither the private funeral nor either of the two public memorials had made one single reference to her family.

At first I had thought that was peculiar, strange behavior. But then I thought about the publicity surrounding the will and I knew that it was all connected. Additionally, most of these people were probably not aware of anyone but themselves and how they looked on public occasions. They may not have even intended to be rude. They were so much a part of the process I'd grown up with all my life that they couldn't separate themselves from it. They couldn't treat me any other way but translated through that same screen. They didn't know any other way professionally and this was certainly a "professional" occasion, anybody could see that. Why, there were television cameras and press photographers and interviews and film being shown and people to be seen with. This was certainly not the time for any of them to start thinking about me.

As John Wayne's voice continued to read off the names of companies and studios and television networks, craft unions, independent producers, actors unions and even the studio cleaners, I realized that I didn't fit into any of those categories. Since there was no category listed for family, I waited until the very end, when the entire rest of the theater was already standing and at last John Wayne added: "Friends and Others."

"Others" was an appropriate enough category, so my husband, stepson and I stood at the very last minute of the memorial tribute to my mother, Joan Crawford, under the category of "Others."

That was it. The show was over. The television cameras were turned off and the full house lights went on. A publicity man and a fan from New York with his family said hello to us on our way out of the theater. We spoke with no one else.

As we walked out into the cool night air, I held onto my husband's hand and thought . . . at last it is over.

But . . . is it?

". . . for reasons which are well known to them."

RECOLLECTIONS FROM DEANNE TILTON
AND MICHAEL DURFEE

I first met Christina Crawford in 1978, soon after *Mommie Dearest* had become a best seller and front page story. For some, the story was about an underside of Hollywood and a glamorous star. In reality, it was vindication, inspiration and hope for countless child abuse victims and survivors around the world. It turned the heads and hearts of millions. What the 1962 release of the landmark publication "The Battered Child

Syndrome" had done to enlighten the professional world, *Mommie Dearest* did for the rest of the world sixteen years later.

As Director of Los Angeles County's Inter-Agency Council on Child Abuse and Neglect, I was understandably anxious about meeting this brave and talented person who had taken my cause to new heights. This anxiety was at once dissolved by her warm and unassuming personality. It was difficult to imagine that she realized the impact of *Mommie Dearest*. It was impossible for me to appreciate the price she was continuing to pay for doing so.

Christina was quiet and careful. I had no idea that, while she was becoming our heroine, she was also withstanding cruel treatment by a relentless cadre of angry disbelievers.

I soon began to wonder how one whose life had been so unpredictable, so tumultuous and controversial could be so serene. I was to learn a great deal about resiliency, and about the true challenges of facing life as a celebrity, a survivor of childhood abuse, public disdain, physical disability, personal loss.

We became best friends. I found in Christina a selfless and giving person who, to this day, is hard pressed to acknowledge the difference she has made in this world. She also, for whatever reason, has been able to maintain a unique and delightful sense of humor. I'll never forget the day Michael and I visited her after her paralyzing stroke in 1981. With unparalleled determination, Christina had regained most of her mobility and speech. However, there were lapses. She told us of the phone calls she would receive and, when she could not articulate a simple answer, she would "just hang up." Then she broke into delightful laughter. Many would have cried.

Michael, a child psychiatrist specializing in child abuse prevention, met Christina one afternoon at an ICAN Neighborhood Family Center. Her speech was rapid and strained. Michael was compelled to touch her arm. She paused, took a breath and explained that the day before, she had filmed a scene for a documentary in front of a prison. The prisoners rioted and she could hear their yells and the clanking of bars in the background. Being locked up was a ghost of her past; memories rekindled by this experience.

Over the years it has been our privilege to know and share experiences, including our wedding celebration, with this woman who has brought so much to so many. We do not know or understand how often and how fiercely she must fight the scars of confusion, mistrust and feeling alone. We can only guess. We do know that such battles have been a major part of her life. We are in awe of her fierce drive to keep her life in order and continue to serve others.

Christina was President of ICAN Associates, Commissioner of Children's Services, a keynote speaker at countless conferences and conventions. She published books, appeared on talk shows and documentaries. She was, and is, a national phenomenon. But she has never lost track of reality or her friends.

She founded the first national support group for survivors of child abuse and other assaults. She noted her intentions to do so in a national magazine, opened a post office box and received mail, and more mail. Sacks of mail. All to be answered. No one to be left out in a project that was more massive and more understaffed than anyone, including Christina, could have known. She always answered letters from prisoners first. As she began to receive their responses, the abusive childhoods and terrible ghosts of these people emerged from behind bars and walls.

Christina has entered and affected our lives personally and professionally. An image of her sits somewhere in that part of the brain reserved for people whom you can call up to speak with inside your head. A friend who let child abuse and neglect out of the closet twenty years ago and has carried a banner for children and survivors ever since. A unique human being who has survived the scars of her childhood and given hope to others. Armed with a powerful sense of humor and grinding intent to make the world better, she is a true success story.

Twenty years later, *Mommie Dearest* is a classic. Happy Anniversary, Christina, and Thank You.

Deanne Tilton Durfee
Executive Director, Los Angeles County Inter-Agency
Council on Child Abuse and Neglect
Past Chairperson, U.S. Advisory Board on Child Abuse and Neglect

Michael Durfee, M.D,
Medical Director, Child Abuse Prevention Program
Department of Health Services

ABOUT THE AUTHOR

Christina Crawford is the #1 *New York Times*–bestselling author of the memoirs *Mommie Dearest* and *Survivor*, as well as the women's history book *Daughters of the Inquisition*. Crawford graduated magna cum laude from the University of California, Los Angeles, after spending nearly fourteen years as an actress in television, theater, and film. She received her master's degree in communication management from the Annenberg School at the University of Southern California.

Since then, Crawford has worked in corporate public relations, was a partner in a winery, owned and operated a country inn, and spent eight years booking concert entertainment for a North Idaho casino. One of the first people appointed to the Los Angeles County Commission for Children's Services, she also served one term as county commissioner in Idaho. Her regional TV show *Northwest Entertainment* has won three Telly Awards for excellence.

Crawford has been a lifelong advocate of issues for social justice, from the early days of child abuse prevention and family violence intervention to issues of the rights of women across the world. She lives in Idaho, where she continues to write and pursue creative projects.

Follow Christina on her Facebook fan page: https://www.facebook.com/ChristinaCrawfordAuthor.

Mommie Dearest, *1978 original cover (Tom Bert).*

Survivor, *front cover 1988 (Tom Bert).*

No Safe Place, *back cover 1994*
(Bonnie Colodzin).

Sedona, Arizona, vortex, 1989
(Kiki Borlenghi).

Sedona, Arizona, 1989 (Kiki Borlenghi).

Daughters of the Inquisition, *2004 (Jim Swoboda, ILF Media).*

Entertainment Northwest TV, 2007 (Robert Breckenridge RTN 24 TV Spokane, Washington).

With brother Chris, pre–Viet Nam, 1967.

CHRISTINA CRAWFORD

FROM OPEN ROAD MEDIA

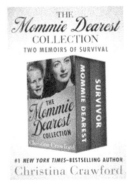

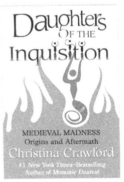

OPEN  ROAD

INTEGRATED MEDIA

INTEGRATED MEDIA

CPSIA information can be obtained
at www.ICGtesting.com
Printed in the USA
BVHW031515140220
572003BV00001B/1

9 781504 057714